Ancient Hebrew Torah

Ancient Hebrew Torah

~~~~~~~~~~~~~~~~~~~~~~~~~~~~~~~~~~~~

By Jeff A. Benner
~~~~~~~~~~~~~~~~~~~~~~~~~~~~~~~~~~~~

Cover design by Jeff A. Benner.

"Ancient Hebrew Torah," by Jeff A. Benner. ISBN 978-1-60264-594-3.

Published 2010 by Virtualbookworm.com Publishing Inc., P.O. Box 9949, College Station, TX 77842, US. ©2010, Jeff A. Benner. All rights reserved. No part of this publication may be reproduced, stored in a retrieval system, or transmitted in any form or by any means, electronic, mechanical, recording or otherwise, without the prior written permission of Jeff A. Benner.

Manufactured in the United States of America.

Table of Contents

About the Ancient Hebrew Torah

The Waw and Yud

Until 1947, the oldest manuscript of the Hebrew Bible was the Codex Leningrad which is dated to around 1,000 A.D. With the discovery of the Dead Sea Scrolls in 1947 we now have manuscripts that are 1000 years older than the Codex Leningrad. While the Hebrew texts from the Dead Sea Scrolls (2000 years old) and the Hebrew text from the Codex Leningrad (1000 years old) are very similar, there are differences. One of the largest differences is the vowels used for the text. Throughout the Codex Leningrad vowel sounds are represented by dots and dashes placed above and below the letters. For instance, the Hebrew word for 'no', as it appears in the codex, is לֹא (*lo*). The dot above the letter *aleph* is called a *hholam* and represents the vowel sound 'o'. These dots and dashes (called *nikkudot, nikkud* in the singular) were created by the Masorites during the time the codex Leningrad was written. The Dead Sea Scrolls, written long before the Masorites, used the letter ו (*waw, vav* in Modern Hebrew) for the consonant 'w,' but also the vowel sound 'o'. Throughout the Dead Sea Scrolls this word appears as לוא. In the Masoretic text the name David is written as דָוִד (*dawid*). The dot, called the *hhireq*, below the ו represents the 'i' sound. However, in the

Dead Sea Scrolls the name David is written as דויד where the letter י (*yud*) is used for the 'i' sound.

From the vast amount of manuscripts unearthed in the Dead Sea Caves it has been discovered that the letters *waw* and *yud* (and to a lesser extent the letters *hey* and *aleph*) were widely used as vowels. When and why they were removed from the text and replaced with the *nikkudot* appears to be a mystery. In the *Ancient Hebrew Torah* all of the *hholam* and *hhireq nikkudot* have been replaced with the letter *waw* and *yud* respectively in order to attempt to restore the text to its pre-Masoretic state. The reinsertions of these vowels will also aid in the pronunciation of the text.

The Shin, Sin and Samehh

In the Modern Hebrew alphabet the letter *shin* (ש) represents two different sounds, a "sh" and an "s". To differentiate between these two sounds, a dot is placed above the *shin* in different locations. For the "sh" sound, the dot is placed on the right (שׁ) and is called a *shin* and for the "s" sound it is placed on the left (שׂ) and called a *sin*.

In most cases, words spelled with the *sin* (שׂ) are more closely related in meaning with words spelled with the *samehh* (ס). In addition, Hebrew words in the Masoretic text spelled with the *sin* (שׂ) in some places, are also written with a *samehh* in other places. For these reasons, Hebrew words that are spelled with a *sin* (שׂ) in the Masoretic text, will be written with a *samehh* (𐤎) in the *Ancient Hebrew Torah*. As an example, in the Masoretic text you will find the name ישׂראל (*yisra'el*/Israel), but in the *Ancient Hebrew Torah* it will be written as 𐤉𐤎𐤓𐤀𐤋.

The Pictographic Script

Because the original manuscripts of the Bible are long gone there is no way to know which Hebrew script was used. We can make an educated guess that most of them were written with the middle Hebrew script (also called Paleo-Hebrew) while the older books may have been written in the early (or pictographic) Hebrew script. The *Ancient Hebrew Torah* employs the early Hebrew script for the sole reason that this script is the foundation to all later scripts. In addition, each pictographic letter represents an object of action and provides the concrete foundation to the words of the text.

Book Names

The *Ancient Hebrew Torah* uses the Hebrew names for each of the books. 𐤁𐤓𐤀𐤔𐤉𐤕 (*bereshiyt*) is Genesis; 𐤔𐤌𐤅𐤕 (*shemot*) is Exodus; 𐤅𐤉𐤒𐤓𐤀 (*wayiqra*) is

Leviticus; 𐤁𐤌𐤃𐤁𐤓 (*bemidbar*) is Numbers and 𐤃𐤁𐤓𐤉𐤌 (*devariym*) is Deuteronomy.

Chapter and Verse Numbers

The original texts did not include a numbering system for the chapters (𐤐𐤓𐤒 *paraq*) or verses; these were added later for ease of finding a particular passage within the text. The *Ancient Hebrew Torah* includes the traditional Hebrew Bible numbering system for the same reason.

The Ancient Hebrew Alphabet

Early	Modern	Name	Picture	Meaning
𐤀	א	Aleph	Ox head	Strong, Power, Leader
𐤁	ב	Beyt	Tent floorplan	Family, House, In
𐤂	ג	Gimal	Foot	Gather, Walk
𐤃	ד	Dalet	Door	Move, Hang, Entrance
𐤄	ה	Hey	Man with arms raised	Look, Reveal, Breath
𐤅	ו	Vav	Tent peg	Add, Secure, Hook
𐤆	ז	Zayin	Mattock	Food, Cut, Nourish
𐤇	ח	Chet	Tent wall	Outside, Divide, Half

	ט	Tet	Basket	Surround, Contain, Mud
	י	Yud	Arm and closed hand	Work, Throw, Worship
	כ	Kaph	Open palm	Bend, Open, Allow, Tame
	ל	Lamed	Shepherd Staff	Teach, Yoke, To, Bind
	מ	Mem	Water	Chaos, Mighty, Blood
	נ	Nun	Seed	Continue, Heir, Son
	ס	Samech	Thorn	Grab, Hate, Protect
	ע	Ayin	Eye	Watch, Know, Shade
	פ	Pey	Mouth	Blow, Scatter, Edge
	צ	Tsade	Man on his side	Wait, Chase, Snare, Hunt
	ק	Quph	Sun on the horizon	Condense, Circle, Time
	ר	Resh	Head of a man	First, Top, Beginning
	ש	Shin	Two front teeth	Sharp, Press, Eat, Two
	ת	Tav	Crossed sticks	Mark, Sign, Signal, Monument

Bereshiyt / Genesis

1

1
2
3
4
5
6
7
8
9
10
11
12
13
14

אלוהים יהי מאורות ברקיע השמיים
להבדיל בין היום ובין הלילה והיו לאותות
ולמועדים ולימים ושנים 15 והיו
לימאורות ברקיע השמיים להאיר על
הארץ ויהי כן 16 ויעס אלוהים את שני
המאורות הגדולים את המאור הגדול לממשלת
היום ואת המאור הקטון לממשלת הלילה ואת
הכוכבים 17 ויתן אותם אלוהים ברקיע
השמיים להאיר על הארץ 18 ולימשול ביום
ובלילה ולהבדיל בין האור ובין החושך וירא
אלוהים כי טו 19 ויהי ערב ויהי בוקר יום
רביעי 20 ויאמר אלוהים ישרצו המיים
שרץ נפש חיה ועוף יעופף על הארץ על
פני רקיע השמיים 21 ויברא אלוהים את
התנינים הגדולים ואת כל נפש החיה
הרומסת אשר שרצו המיים למינהם ואת כל
עוף כנף למינהו וירא אלוהים כי טו
22 ויברך אותם אלוהים לאמור פרו ורבו ומילאו
את המיים בימים והעוף ירב בארץ
23 ויהי ערב ויהי בוקר יום חמישי
24 ויאמר אלוהים תוצא הארץ נפש חיה
למינה בהמה ורמס וחיתו ארץ למינה ויהי
כן 25 ויעס אלוהים את חית הארץ למינה ואת
הבהמה למינה ואת כל רמס האדמה למינהו
וירא אלוהים כי טו 26 ויאמר אלוהים נעסה
אדם בצלמנו כידמותנו ויירדו בידגת הים
ובעוף השמיים ובבהמה ובכל הארץ ובכל הרמס
הרומס על הארץ 27 ויברא אלוהים את האדם
בצלמו בצלם אלוהים ברא אותו זכר ונקבה ברא
אותם 28 ויברך אותם אלוהים ויאמר להם
אלוהים פרו ורבו ומילאו את הארץ וכיבשוה
ורדו בידגת הים ובעוף השמיים ובכל חיה
הרומסת על הארץ 29 ויאמר אלוהים הינה
נתתי לכם את כל עסב זורע זרע אשר על פני
כל הארץ ואת כל העץ אשר בו פרי עץ זורע זרע
לכם יהיה לאכלה 30 ולכל חית הארץ ולכל עוף
השמיים ולכול רומס על הארץ אשר בו נפש
חיה את כל ירק עסב לאכלה ויהי כן 31 וירא
אלוהים את כל אשר עסה והינה טוב מאד ויהי
ערב ויהי בוקר יום השישי

בראשית פרק 2

1 ויכלו השמים והארץ וכל צבאם 2 ויכל
אלהים ביום השביעי מלאכתו אשר עשה
וישבת ביום השביעי מכל מלאכתו אשר
עשה 3 ויברך אלהים את יום השביעי ויקדש
אתו כי בו שבת מכל מלאכתו אשר ברא אלהים
לעשות 4 אלה תולדות השמים והארץ בהבראם
ביום עשות יהוה אלהים ארץ ושמים 5 וכל
שיח השדה טרם יהיה בארץ וכל עשב השדה טרם
יצמח כי לא המטיר יהוה אלהים על
הארץ ואדם אין לעבד את האדמה 6 ואד יעלה
מן הארץ והשקה את כל פני האדמה
7 וייצר יהוה אלהים את האדם עפר מן
האדמה ויפח באפיו נשמת חיים ויהי
האדם לנפש חיה 8 ויטע יהוה אלהים גן
בעדן מקדם וישם שם את האדם אשר
יצר 9 ויצמח יהוה אלהים מן האדמה כל עץ
נחמד למראה וטוב למאכל ועץ החיים בתוך הגן
ועץ הדעת טוב ורע 10 ונהר יצא מעדן להשקות
את הגן ומשם יפרד והיה לארבעה ראשים
11 שם האחד פישון הוא הסבב את כל ארץ
החוילה אשר שם הזהב 12 וזהב הארץ ההוא טוב
שם הבדלח ואבן השהם 13 ושם הנהר השני
גיחון הוא הסובב את כל ארץ כוש 14 ושם הנהר
השלישי חדקל הוא ההלך קדמת אשור והנהר
הרביעי הוא פרת 15 ויקח יהוה אלהים את
האדם וינחהו בגן עדן לעבדה ולשמרה
16 ויצו יהוה אלהים על האדם לאמר מכל
עץ הגן אכל תאכל 17 ומעץ הדעת טוב ורע
לא תאכל ממנו כי ביום אכלך ממנו מות
תמות 18 ויאמר יהוה אלהים לא טוב היות
האדם לבדו אעשה לו עזר כנגדו 19 ויצר יהוה
אלהים מן האדמה כל חית השדה ואת כל עוף
השמים ויבא אל האדם לראות מה יקרא לו
וכל אשר יקרא לו האדם נפש חיה הוא שמו
20 ויקרא האדם שמות לכל הבהמה ולעוף
השמים ולכל חית השדה ולאדם לא מצא עזר
כנגדו 21 ויפל יהוה אלהים תרדמה על האדם
ויישן ויקח אחת מצלעתיו ויסגר בשר
תחתנה 22 ויבן יהוה אלהים את הצלע אשר

לקח מין האדם לאישה ויביאה אל האדם
23 ויואמר האדם זואת הפעם עצם מעצמי
ובסר מיבסרי לזואת יקרא אישה כי מאיש
לוקחה זואת 24 על כן יעזב איש את אביו ואת
אימו ודבק באישתו והיו לבסר אחד 25 ויהיו
שניהם ערומים האדם ואישתו ולוא
יתבוששו

בראשית פרק 3

1 והנחש היה ערום מיכול חית הסדה אשר עסה
יהוה אלוהים ויואמר אל האישה אף כי אמר
אלוהים לוא תואכלו מיכול עץ הגן 2 ותואמר
האישה אל הנחש מיפרי עץ הגן נואכל
3 ומיפרי העץ אשר בתוך הגן אמר אלוהים
לוא תואכלו מימנו ולוא תיגעו בו פן תמותון
4 ויואמר הנחש אל האישה לוא מות תמותון
5 כי יודע אלוהים כי ביום אכלכם מימנו
וניפקחו עיניכם ויהייתם כאלוהים
יודעי טוב ורע 6 ותרא האישה כי טוב העץ
למאכל וכי תאוה הוא לעיניים ונחמד העץ
להסכיל ותיקח מיפריו ותואכל ותיתן גם
לאישה עימה ויואכל 7 ותיפקחנה עיני
שניהם וידעו כי עירומים הם ויתפרו
עלה תאנה ויעסו להם חגורות 8 וישמעו את קול
יהוה אלוהים מיתהלך בגן לרוח היום ויתחבא
האדם ואישתו מיפני יהוה אלוהים בתוך עץ
הגן 9 ויקרא יהוה אלוהים אל האדם ויואמר לו
איכה 10 ויואמר את קולכה שמעתי בגן ואירא
כי עירום אנוכי ואחבא 11 ויואמר מי
היגיד לכה כי עירום אתה המין העץ אשר
ציויתיכה לבילתי אכל מימנו אכלת
12 ויואמר האדם האישה אשר נתתה עימדי
היוא נתנה לי מין העץ ואוכל 13 ויואמר
יהוה אלוהים לאישה מה זואת עסית ותואמר
האישה הנחש הישיאני ואוכל 14 ויואמר
יהוה אלוהים אל הנחש כי עסית זואת ארור
אתה מיכל הבהמה ומיכול חית הסדה על גחונכה
תלך ועפר תואכל כל ימי חייכה 15 ואיבה
אשית בינכה ובין האישה ובין זרעכה
ובין זרעה הוא ישופכה רואש ואתה תשופנו

13
14
15
16
17
18
19
20
21
22
23
24
25
26

5

1
2
3
4
5
6
7

8
9
10
11
12
13
14
15
16
17
18
19
20
21
22
23
24
25
26
27
28
29
30
31

שנה וימות 32 ויהי נוח בן חמש מאות שנה
ויולד נוח את שם את חם ואת יפת

בראשית פרק 6

1 ויהי כי החל האדם לרוב על פני האדמה
ובנות יולדו להם 2 ויראו בני האלוהים את
בנות האדם כי טובות הנה ויקחו להם נשים
מיכול אשר בחרו 3 ויואמר יהוה לוא ידון רוחי
באדם לעולם בשגם הוא בסר והיו ימיו מאה
ועסרים שנה 4 הנפילים היו בארץ
בימים ההם וגם אחרי כן אשר יבואו בני
האלוהים אל בנות האדם וילדו להם המה
הגיבורים אשר מעולם אנשי השם 5 וירא
יהוה כי רבה רעת האדם בארץ וכל יצר מחשבות
ליבו רק רע כל היום 6 וינחם יהוה כי עסה את
האדם בארץ ויתעצב אל ליבו 7 ויואמר יהוה
אמחה את האדם אשר בראתי מעל פני האדמה
מאדם עד בהמה עד רמס ועד עוף השמיים כי
ניחמתי כי עסיתים 8 ונוח מצא חן
בעיני יהוה 9 אלה תולדות נוח נוח איש צדיק
תמים היה בדורותיו את האלוהים היתהלך נוח
10 ויולד נוח שלושה בנים את שם את חם ואת
יפת 11 ותישחת הארץ לפני האלוהים
ותמלא הארץ חם 12 וירא אלוהים את הארץ
והינה נישחתה כי השחית כל בסר את דרכו
על הארץ 13 ויואמר אלוהים לנוח קץ כל בסר בא
לפני כי מלאה הארץ חמס מיפניהם
והינני משחיתם את הארץ 14 עסה לכה תבת
עצי גופר קינים תעסה את התבה וכפרת אותה
מיביית ומיחוץ בכופר 15 וזה אשר תעסה
אותה שלוש מאות אמה אורך התבה חמישים
אמה רחבה ושלושים אמה קומתה 16 צוהר תעסה
לתבה ואל אמה תכלנה מילמעלה ופתח התבה
בצידה תסים תחתים שנים ושלישים תעסה
17 ואני הינני מביא את המבול מיים על
הארץ לשחת כל בסר אשר בו רוח חיים מיתחת
השמיים כול אשר בארץ יגוע 18 והקימותי
את בריתי איתך ובאת אל התבה אתה ובניכה
ואשתכה ונשי בניכה איתך 19 ומיכל החי
מיכל בסר שנים מיכול תביא אל התבה

להחיות איתך זכר ונקבה יהיו 20 מהעוף
למינהו ומין הבהמה למינה מיכול רמס
האדמה למינהו שניים מיכול יבואו אליכה
להחיות 21 ואתה קח לכה מיכל מאכל אשר יאכל
ואספת אליכה והיה לכה ולהם לאכלה 22 ויעס
נוח ככול אשר ציוה אותו אלוהים כן עסה

בראשית פרק 7

1 ויואמר יהוה לנוח בוא אתה וכל ביתכה אל
התבה כי אותכה ראיתי צדיק לפני בדור הזה
2 מיכול הבהמה הטהורה תיקח לכה שיבעה
שיבעה איש ואישתו ומין הבהמה אשר לוא
טהורה היוא שניים איש ואישתו 3 גם
מעוף השמיים שיבעה שיבעה זכר ונקבה
לחיות זרע על פני כל הארץ 4 כי לימים עוד
שיבעה אנוכי ממטיר על הארץ ארבעים
יום וארבעים לילה ומחיתי את כל היקום
אשר עסיתי מעל פני האדמה 5 ויעס נוח
ככול אשר ציוהו יהוה 6 ונוח בן שש מאות שנה
והמבול היה מיים על הארץ 7 ויבוא נוח
ובניו ואישתו ונשי בניו איתו אל התבה
מיפני מי המבול 8 מין הבהמה הטהורה
ומין הבהמה אשר איננה טהורה ומין העוף
וכול אשר רומס על האדמה 9 שניים שניים
באו אל נוח אל התבה זכר ונקבה כאשר ציוה
אלוהים את נוח 10 ויהי לשיבעת הימים
ומי המבול היו על הארץ 11 בישנת שש מאות
שנה לחיי נוח בחודש השני בשיבעה עסר
יום לחודש ביום הזה ניבקעו כל מעינות
תהום רבה וארבות השמיים ניפתחו 12 ויהי
הגשם על הארץ ארבעים יום וארבעים לילה
13 בעצם היום הזה בא נוח ושם וחם ויפת בני
נוח ואשת נוח ושלושת נשי בניו איתם אל
התבה 14 המה וכל החיה למינה וכל הבהמה
למינה וכל הרמס הרומס על הארץ למינהו וכל
העוף למינהו כול ציפור כל כנ 15 ויבואו אל
נוח אל התבה שניים שניים מיכל הבסר
אשר בו רוח חיים 16 והבאים זכר ונקבה מיכל
בסר באו כאשר ציוה אותו אלוהים ויסגור יהוה
בעדו 17 ויהי המבול ארבעים יום על הארץ

𐤅𐤉𐤓𐤁𐤅 𐤄𐤌𐤉𐤌 𐤅𐤉𐤎𐤀𐤅 𐤀𐤕 𐤄𐤕𐤁𐤄 𐤅𐤕𐤓𐤌 𐤌𐤏𐤋 𐤄𐤀𐤓𐤑
18 𐤅𐤉𐤂𐤁𐤓𐤅 𐤄𐤌𐤉𐤌 𐤅𐤉𐤓𐤁𐤅 𐤌𐤀𐤅𐤃 𐤏𐤋 𐤄𐤀𐤓𐤑 𐤅𐤕𐤋𐤊
𐤄𐤕𐤁𐤄 𐤏𐤋 𐤐𐤍𐤉 𐤄𐤌𐤉𐤌 19 𐤅𐤄𐤌𐤉𐤌 𐤂𐤁𐤓𐤅 𐤌𐤀𐤅𐤃
𐤌𐤀𐤅𐤃 𐤏𐤋 𐤄𐤀𐤓𐤑 𐤅𐤉𐤊𐤅𐤎𐤅 𐤊𐤋 𐤄𐤄𐤓𐤉𐤌 𐤄𐤂𐤁𐤅𐤄𐤉𐤌 𐤀𐤔𐤓
𐤕𐤇𐤕 𐤊𐤋 𐤄𐤔𐤌𐤉𐤌 20 𐤇𐤌𐤔 𐤏𐤎𐤓𐤄 𐤀𐤌𐤄
𐤌𐤋𐤌𐤏𐤋𐤄 𐤂𐤁𐤓𐤅 𐤄𐤌𐤉𐤌 𐤅𐤉𐤊𐤅𐤎𐤅 𐤄𐤄𐤓𐤉𐤌
21 𐤅𐤉𐤂𐤅𐤏 𐤊𐤋 𐤁𐤎𐤓 𐤄𐤓𐤅𐤌𐤎 𐤏𐤋 𐤄𐤀𐤓𐤑 𐤁𐤏𐤅𐤐 𐤅𐤁𐤁𐤄𐤌𐤄
𐤅𐤁𐤇𐤉𐤄 𐤅𐤁𐤊𐤋 𐤄𐤔𐤓𐤑 𐤄𐤔𐤅𐤓𐤑 𐤏𐤋 𐤄𐤀𐤓𐤑 𐤅𐤊𐤅𐤋 𐤄𐤀𐤃𐤌
22 𐤊𐤅𐤋 𐤀𐤔𐤓 𐤍𐤉𐤔𐤌𐤕 𐤓𐤅𐤇 𐤇𐤉𐤉𐤌 𐤁𐤀𐤐𐤉𐤅 𐤌𐤊𐤅𐤋
𐤀𐤔𐤓 𐤁𐤇𐤓𐤁𐤄 𐤌𐤕𐤅 23 𐤅𐤉𐤌𐤇 𐤀𐤕 𐤊𐤋 𐤄𐤉𐤒𐤅𐤌 𐤀𐤔𐤓 𐤏𐤋
𐤐𐤍𐤉 𐤄𐤀𐤃𐤌𐤄 𐤌𐤀𐤃𐤌 𐤏𐤃 𐤁𐤄𐤌𐤄 𐤏𐤃 𐤓𐤌𐤎 𐤅𐤏𐤃 𐤏𐤅𐤐
𐤄𐤔𐤌𐤉𐤌 𐤅𐤉𐤌𐤇𐤅 𐤌𐤉𐤍 𐤄𐤀𐤓𐤑 𐤅𐤉𐤔𐤀𐤓 𐤀𐤊 𐤍𐤅𐤇
𐤅𐤀𐤔𐤓 𐤀𐤉𐤕𐤅 𐤁𐤕𐤁𐤄 24 𐤅𐤉𐤂𐤁𐤓𐤅 𐤄𐤌𐤉𐤌 𐤏𐤋 𐤄𐤀𐤓𐤑
𐤇𐤌𐤉𐤔𐤉𐤌 𐤅𐤌𐤀𐤕 𐤉𐤅𐤌

𐤁𐤓𐤀𐤔𐤉𐤕 𐤐𐤓𐤒 8

1 𐤅𐤉𐤆𐤊𐤅𐤓 𐤀𐤋𐤅𐤄𐤉𐤌 𐤀𐤕 𐤍𐤅𐤇 𐤅𐤀𐤕 𐤊𐤋 𐤄𐤇𐤉𐤄 𐤅𐤀𐤕 𐤊𐤋
𐤄𐤁𐤄𐤌𐤄 𐤀𐤔𐤓 𐤀𐤉𐤕𐤅 𐤁𐤕𐤁𐤄 𐤅𐤉𐤏𐤁𐤓 𐤀𐤋𐤅𐤄𐤉𐤌 𐤓𐤅𐤇 𐤏𐤋
𐤄𐤀𐤓𐤑 𐤅𐤉𐤔𐤅𐤊𐤅 𐤄𐤌𐤉𐤌 2 𐤅𐤉𐤎𐤊𐤓𐤅 𐤌𐤏𐤉𐤍𐤅𐤕 𐤕𐤄𐤅𐤌
𐤅𐤀𐤓𐤁𐤅𐤕 𐤄𐤔𐤌𐤉𐤌 𐤅𐤉𐤊𐤋𐤀 𐤄𐤂𐤔𐤌 𐤌𐤉𐤍
𐤄𐤔𐤌𐤉𐤌 3 𐤅𐤉𐤔𐤅𐤁𐤅 𐤄𐤌𐤉𐤌 𐤌𐤏𐤋 𐤄𐤀𐤓𐤑 𐤄𐤋𐤅𐤊
𐤅𐤔𐤅𐤁 𐤅𐤉𐤇𐤎𐤓𐤅 𐤄𐤌𐤉𐤌 𐤌𐤉𐤒𐤑𐤄 𐤇𐤌𐤉𐤔𐤉𐤌 𐤅𐤌𐤀𐤕
𐤉𐤅𐤌 4 𐤅𐤕𐤍𐤇 𐤄𐤕𐤁𐤄 𐤁𐤇𐤅𐤃𐤔 𐤄𐤔𐤁𐤉𐤏𐤉 𐤁𐤔𐤉𐤁𐤏𐤄 𐤏𐤎𐤓
𐤉𐤅𐤌 𐤋𐤇𐤅𐤃𐤔 𐤏𐤋 𐤄𐤓𐤉 𐤀𐤓𐤓𐤈 5 𐤅𐤄𐤌𐤉𐤌 𐤄𐤉𐤅 𐤄𐤋𐤅𐤊
𐤅𐤇𐤎𐤅𐤓 𐤏𐤃 𐤄𐤇𐤅𐤃𐤔 𐤄𐤏𐤎𐤉𐤓𐤉 𐤁𐤏𐤎𐤉𐤓𐤉 𐤁𐤀𐤇𐤃 𐤋𐤇𐤅𐤃𐤔
𐤍𐤓𐤀𐤅 𐤓𐤀𐤔𐤉 𐤄𐤄𐤓𐤉𐤌 6 𐤅𐤉𐤄𐤉 𐤌𐤉𐤒𐤑 𐤀𐤓𐤁𐤏𐤉𐤌
𐤉𐤅𐤌 𐤅𐤉𐤐𐤕𐤇 𐤍𐤅𐤇 𐤀𐤕 𐤇𐤋𐤅𐤍 𐤄𐤕𐤁𐤄 𐤀𐤔𐤓 𐤏𐤎𐤄
7 𐤅𐤉𐤔𐤋𐤇 𐤀𐤕 𐤄𐤏𐤅𐤓𐤁 𐤅𐤉𐤑𐤀 𐤉𐤑𐤅𐤀 𐤅𐤔𐤅𐤁 𐤏𐤃 𐤉𐤁𐤅𐤔𐤕
𐤄𐤌𐤉𐤌 𐤌𐤏𐤋 𐤄𐤀𐤓𐤑 8 𐤅𐤉𐤔𐤋𐤇 𐤀𐤕 𐤄𐤉𐤅𐤍𐤄
𐤌𐤀𐤉𐤕𐤅 𐤋𐤓𐤀𐤅𐤕 𐤄𐤒𐤋𐤅 𐤄𐤌𐤉𐤌 𐤌𐤏𐤋 𐤐𐤍𐤉
𐤄𐤀𐤃𐤌𐤄 9 𐤅𐤋𐤅𐤀 𐤌𐤑𐤀𐤄 𐤄𐤉𐤅𐤍𐤄 𐤌𐤍𐤅𐤇 𐤋𐤊𐤐 𐤓𐤂𐤋𐤄
𐤅𐤕𐤔𐤁 𐤀𐤋𐤉𐤅 𐤀𐤋 𐤄𐤕𐤁𐤄 𐤊𐤉 𐤌𐤉𐤌 𐤏𐤋 𐤐𐤍𐤉 𐤊𐤋
𐤄𐤀𐤓𐤑 𐤅𐤉𐤔𐤋𐤇 𐤉𐤃𐤅 𐤅𐤉𐤒𐤇𐤄 𐤅𐤉𐤁𐤀 𐤀𐤕𐤄 𐤀𐤋𐤉𐤅 𐤀𐤋
𐤄𐤕𐤁𐤄 10 𐤅𐤉𐤇𐤋 𐤏𐤅𐤃 𐤔𐤉𐤁𐤏𐤕 𐤉𐤌𐤉𐤌 𐤀𐤇𐤓𐤉𐤌
𐤅𐤉𐤅𐤎𐤐 𐤔𐤋𐤇 𐤀𐤕 𐤄𐤉𐤅𐤍𐤄 𐤌𐤉𐤍 𐤄𐤕𐤁𐤄 11 𐤅𐤕𐤁𐤅𐤀 𐤀𐤋𐤉𐤅
𐤄𐤉𐤅𐤍𐤄 𐤋𐤏𐤕 𐤏𐤓𐤁 𐤅𐤄𐤉𐤍𐤄 𐤏𐤋𐤄 𐤆𐤉𐤕 𐤈𐤓𐤐
𐤁𐤐𐤉𐤄 𐤅𐤉𐤃𐤏 𐤍𐤅𐤇 𐤊𐤉 𐤒𐤋𐤅 𐤄𐤌𐤉𐤌 𐤌𐤏𐤋 𐤄𐤀𐤓𐤑
12 𐤅𐤉𐤉𐤇𐤋 𐤏𐤅𐤃 𐤔𐤉𐤁𐤏𐤕 𐤉𐤌𐤉𐤌 𐤀𐤇𐤓𐤉𐤌 𐤅𐤉𐤔𐤋𐤇
𐤀𐤕 𐤄𐤉𐤅𐤍𐤄 𐤅𐤋𐤅𐤀 𐤉𐤎𐤐𐤄 𐤔𐤅𐤁 𐤀𐤋𐤉𐤅 𐤏𐤅𐤃 13 𐤅𐤉𐤄𐤉
𐤁𐤀𐤇𐤕 𐤅𐤔𐤔 𐤌𐤀𐤅𐤕 𐤔𐤍𐤄 𐤁𐤓𐤀𐤔𐤅𐤍 𐤁𐤀𐤇𐤃 𐤋𐤇𐤅𐤃𐤔 𐤇𐤓𐤁𐤅

המים מעל הארץ ויסר נח את מכסה התבה
וירא והנה חרבו פני האדמה 14 ובחדש
השני בשבעה ועשרים יום לחדש יבשה
הארץ 15 וידבר אלהים אל נח לאמר 16 צא
מן התבה אתה ואשתך ובניך ונשי
בניך אתך 17 כל החיה אשר אתך מכל
בשר בעוף ובבהמה ובכל הרמש הרמש על הארץ
הוצא ק= היצא אתך ושרצו בארץ ופרו ורבו על
הארץ 18 ויצא נח ובניו ואשתו ונשי בניו
אתו 19 כל החיה כל הרמש וכל העוף כל רומש על
הארץ למשפחתיהם יצאו מן התבה
20 ויבן נח מזבח ליהוה ויקח מכל הבהמה
הטהרה ומכל העוף הטהר ויעל עלת
במזבח 21 וירח יהוה את ריח הניחח ויאמר
יהוה אל לבו לא אסף לקלל עוד את האדמה
בעבור האדם כי יצר לב האדם רע מנעריו
ולא אסף עוד להכות את כל חי כאשר עשיתי
22 עד כל ימי הארץ זרע וקציר וקר וחם
וקיץ וחרף ויום ולילה לא ישבתו

בראשית פרק 9

1 ויברך אלהים את נח ואת בניו ויאמר להם
פרו ורבו ומלאו את הארץ 2 ומוראכם וחתכם
יהיה על כל חית הארץ ועל כל עוף השמים
בכל אשר תרמש האדמה ובכל דגי הים בידכם
נתנו 3 כל רמש אשר הוא חי לכם יהיה לאכלה
כירק עשב נתתי לכם את כל 4 אך בשר בנפשו
דמו לא תאכלו 5 ואך את דמכם לנפשתיכם
אדרש מיד כל חיה אדרשנו ומיד האדם מיד
איש אחיו אדרש את נפש האדם 6 שפך דם
האדם באדם דמו ישפך כי בצלם אלהים עשה
את האדם 7 ואתם פרו ורבו שרצו בארץ ורבו בה
8 ויאמר אלהים אל נח ואל בניו אתו
לאמר 9 ואני הנני מקים את בריתי
אתכם ואת זרעכם אחריכם 10 ואת כל נפש
החיה אשר אתכם בעוף בבהמה ובכל חית הארץ
אתכם מכל יצאי התבה לכל חית הארץ
11 והקמתי את בריתי אתכם ולא יכרת כל
בשר עוד ממי המבול ולא יהיה עוד מבול
לשחת הארץ 12 ויאמר אלהים זאת אות

הברית אשר אני נתן ביני וביניכם
ובין כל נפש חיה אשר אתכם לדורות עולם
13 את קשתי נתתי בענן והיתה לאות ברית
ביני ובין הארץ 14 והיה בענני ענן על
הארץ ונראתה הקשת בענן 15 וזכרתי את
בריתי אשר ביני וביניכם ובין כל נפש
חיה בכל בשר ולא יהיה עוד המים למבול
לשחת כל בשר 16 והיתה הקשת בענן וראיתיה
לזכר ברית עולם בין אלהים ובין כל
נפש חיה בכל בשר אשר על הארץ 17 ויאמר
אלהים אל נח זאת אות הברית אשר הקמתי
ביני ובין כל בשר אשר על הארץ 18 ויהיו
בני נח היצאים מן התבה שם וחם ויפת
וחם הוא אבי כנען 19 שלשה אלה בני נח
ומאלה נפצה כל הארץ 20 ויחל נח איש האדמה
ויטע כרם 21 וישת מן היין וישכר
ויתגל בתוך אהלה 22 וירא חם אבי כנען את
ערות אביו ויגד לשני אחיו בחוץ 23 ויקח שם
ויפת את השמלה וישימו על שכם שניהם
וילכו אחרנית ויכסו את ערות אביהם
ופניהם אחרנית וערות אביהם לא ראו
24 וייקץ נח מיינו וידע את אשר עשה לו
בנו הקטן 25 ויאמר ארור כנען עבד עבדים יהיה
לאחיו 26 ויאמר ברוך יהוה אלהי שם ויהי
כנען עבד למו 27 יפת אלהים ליפת
וישכן באהלי שם ויהי כנען עבד למו
28 ויחי נח אחר המבול שלש מאות שנה
וחמשים שנה 29 ויהיו כל ימי נח תשע
מאות שנה וחמשים שנה וימת

בראשית פרק 10

1 ואלה תולדות בני נח שם חם ויפת ויולדו
להם בנים אחר המבול 2 בני יפת גמר ומגוג
ומדי ויון ותבל ומשך ותירס 3 ובני גמר
אשכנז וריפת ותגרמה 4 ובני יון אלישה
ותרשיש כתים ודדנים 5 מאלה נפרדו איי
הגוים בארצתם איש ללשנו למשפחתם
בגויהם 6 ובני חם כוש ומצרים ופוט
וכנען 7 ובני כוש סבא וחוילה וסבתה
ורעמה וסבתכא ובני רעמה שבא ודדן

ודדן 8 וכוש ילד את נימרוד הוא החל ליהיות
גיבור בארץ 9 הוא היה גיבור צייד ליפני
יהוה על כן יאמר כנימרוד גיבור צייד
ליפני יהוה 10 ותהי ראשית ממלכתו בבל
וארך ואכד וכלנה בארץ שינער 11 מין הארץ
ההיוא יצא אשור ויבן את נינוה ואת רחובות
עיר ואת כלח 12 ואת רסן בין נינוה ובין כלח
היוא העיר הגדולה 13 ומיצריים ילד את
לודים ואת ענמים ואת להבים ואת נפתוחים
14 ואת פתרוסים ואת כסלוחים אשר יצאו
מישם פלישתים ואת כפתורים 15 וכנען
ילד את צידון בכורו ואת חת 16 ואת היבוסי ואת
האמורי ואת הגירגשי 17 ואת החיוי ואת
הערקי ואת הסיני 18 ואת הארודי ואת הצמרי
ואת החמתי ואחר נפוצו מישפחות הכנעני
19 ויהי גבול הכנעני מיצידון בואכה גררה
עד עזה בואכה סדומה ועמורה ואדמה וצבויים
עד לשע 20 אלה בני חם למישפחותם
לילשונותם בארצותם בגויהם 21 ולשם יולד
גם הוא אבי כל בני עבר אחי יפת הגדול
22 בני שם עילם ואשור וארפכשד ולוד וארם
23 ובני ארם עוץ וחול וגתר ומש 24 וארפכשד
ילד את שלח ושלח ילד את עבר 25 ולעבר יולד
שני בנים שם האחד פלג כי בימיו
ניפלגה הארץ ושם אחיו יקטן 26 ויקטן ילד
את אלמודד ואת שלף ואת חצרמות ואת ירח 27 ואת
הדורם ואת אוזל ואת דיקלה 28 ואת עובל ואת
אבימאל ואת שבא 29 ואת אופיר ואת חוילה ואת
יובב כל אלה בני יקטן 30 ויהי מושבם
ממשא בואכה ספרה הר הקדם 31 אלה בני שם
למישפחותם לילשונותם בארצותם לגויהם
32 אלה מישפחות בני נוח לתולדותם בגויהם
ומאלה ניפרדו הגויים בארץ אחר המבול

בראשית פרק 11

1 ויהי כל הארץ ספה אחת ודברים אחדים
2 ויהי בנסעם מיקדם וימצאו ביקעה בארץ
שינער וישבו שם 3 ויאמרו איש אל רעהו
הבה נילבנה לבנים וניסרפה ליסרפה
ותהי להם הלבנה לאבן והחמר היה להם לחומר

4 ויואמרו הבה ניבנה לנו עיר ומיגדל
ורואשו בשמיים ונעסה לנו שם פן נפוץ על
פני כל הארץ 5 וירד יהוה ליראות את העיר
ואת המיגדל אשר בנו בני האדם 6 ויואמר
יהוה הן עם אחד וספה אחת לכולם וזה החילם
לעסות ועתה לוא יבצר מהם כול אשר יזמו לעסות
7 הבה נרדה ונבלה שם ספתם אשר לוא ישמעו
איש ספת רעהו 8 ויפץ יהוה אותם מישם על
פני כל הארץ ויחדלו ליבנות העיר 9 על כן
קרא שמה בבל כי שם בלל יהוה ספת כל הארץ
ומישם היפיצם יהוה על פני כל הארץ
10 אלה תולדות שם שם בן מאת שנה ויולד את
ארפכשד שנתיים אחר המבול 11 ויחי שם
אחרי הולידו את ארפכשד חמש מאות שנה
ויולד בנים ובנות 12 וארפכשד חי חמש
ושלושים שנה ויולד את שלח 13 ויחי ארפכשד
אחרי הולידו את שלח שלוש שנים וארבע מאות
שנה ויולד בנים ובנות 14 ושלח חי שלושים
שנה ויולד את עבר 15 ויחי שלח אחרי הולידו
את עבר שלוש שנים וארבע מאות שנה ויולד
בנים ובנות 16 ויחי עבר ארבע ושלושים
שנה ויולד את פלג 17 ויחי עבר אחרי הולידו
את פלג שלושים שנה וארבע מאות שנה ויולד
בנים ובנות 18 ויחי פלג שלושים שנה
ויולד את רעו 19 ויחי פלג אחרי הולידו את רעו
תשע שנים ומאתיים שנה ויולד בנים
ובנות 20 ויחי רעו שתיים ושלושים שנה
ויולד את סרוג 21 ויחי רעו אחרי הולידו את סרוג
שבע שנים ומאתיים שנה ויולד בנים
ובנות 22 ויחי סרוג שלושים שנה ויולד את
נחור 23 ויחי סרוג אחרי הולידו את נחור
מאתיים שנה ויולד בנים ובנות 24 ויחי
נחור תשע ועסרים שנה ויולד את תרח 25 ויחי
נחור אחרי הולידו את תרח תשע עסרה שנה ומאת
שנה ויולד בנים ובנות 26 ויחי תרח
שיבעים שנה ויולד את אברם את נחור ואת
הרן 27 ואלה תולדות תרח תרח הוליד את אברם את
נחור ואת הרן והרן הוליד את לוט 28 וימת הרן
על פני תרח אביו בארץ מולדתו באור כסדים
29 ויקח אברם ונחור להם נשים שם אשת אברם

סרי ושם אשת נחור מילכה בת הרן אבי מילכה
ואבי יסכה 30 ותהי סרי עקרה אין לה ולד
31 ויקח תרח את אברם בנו ואת לוט בן הרן בן בנו
ואת סרי כלתו אשת אברם בנו ויצאו איתם מאור
כסדים ללכת ארצה כנען ויבואו עד חרן וישבו
שם 32 ויהיו ימי תרח חמש שנים
ומאתיים שנה וימת תרח בחרן

בראשית פרק 12

1 ויואמר יהוה אל אברם לך לכה מארצכה
וממולדתכה ומיבית אביכה אל הארץ אשר
אראכה 2 ואעסכה לגוי גדול ואברככה ואגדלה
שמכה והיה ברכה 3 ואברכה מברכיכה ומקללכה
אאור וניברכו בכה כול מישפחות האדמה 4 וילך
אברם כאשר דיבר אליו יהוה וילך איתו לוט
ואברם בן חמש שנים ושיבעים שנה בצאתו
מחרן 5 ויקח אברם את סרי אישתו ואת לוט בן
אחיו ואת כל רכושם אשר רכשו ואת הנפש אשר
עסו בחרן ויצאו ללכת ארצה כנען ויבואו ארצה
כנען 6 ויעבור אברם בארץ עד מקום שכם עד
אלון מורה והכנעני אז בארץ 7 וירא יהוה אל
אברם ויואמר לזרעכה אתן את הארץ הזואת
ויבן שם מיזבח ליהוה הנראה אליו
8 ויעתק מישם ההרה מיקדם לבית אל ויט
אהלוה בית אל מים והעי מיקדם ויבן שם
מיזבח ליהוה ויקרא בשם יהוה 9 ויסע אברם
הלוך ונסוע הנגבה 10 ויהי רעב בארץ וירד
אברם מיצרימה לגור שם כי כבד הרעב בארץ
11 ויהי כאשר היקריב לבוא מיצרימה
ויואמר אל סרי אישתו הינה נא ידעתי כי
אישה יפת מראה את 12 והיה כי יראו אותך
המיצרים ואמרו אישתו זואת והרגו אותי
13 ואותך יחיו אימרי נא אחותי את למען
ייטב לי בעבורך וחיתה נפשי ביגללך
14 ויהי כבוא אברם מיצרימה ויראו
המיצרים את האישה כי יפה היוא מאוד
15 ויראו אותה סרי פרעוה ויהללו אותה אל
פרעוה ותוקח האישה בית פרעוה 16 ולאברם
היטיב בעבורה ויהי לו צואן ובקר וחמורים
ועבדים ושפחת ואתונות וגמלים 17 וינגע

𐤉𐤄𐤅𐤄 𐤀𐤕 𐤐𐤓𐤏𐤅𐤄 𐤍𐤂𐤏𐤉𐤌 𐤂𐤃𐤅𐤋𐤉𐤌 𐤅𐤀𐤕 𐤁𐤉𐤕𐤅 𐤏𐤋
𐤃𐤁𐤓 𐤎𐤓𐤉 𐤀𐤔𐤕 𐤀𐤁𐤓𐤌 18 𐤅𐤉𐤒𐤓𐤀 𐤐𐤓𐤏𐤅𐤄 𐤋𐤀𐤁𐤓𐤌
𐤅𐤉𐤅𐤀𐤌𐤓 𐤌𐤄 𐤆𐤅𐤀𐤕 𐤏𐤎𐤉𐤕 𐤋𐤉 𐤋𐤌𐤄 𐤋𐤅𐤀 𐤄𐤉𐤂𐤃𐤕 𐤋𐤉
𐤊𐤉 𐤀𐤉𐤔𐤕𐤊𐤄 𐤄𐤉𐤅𐤀 19 𐤋𐤌𐤄 𐤀𐤌𐤓𐤕 𐤀𐤇𐤅𐤕𐤉 𐤄𐤉𐤅𐤀
𐤅𐤀𐤒𐤇 𐤀𐤅𐤕𐤄 𐤋𐤉 𐤋𐤀𐤉𐤔𐤄 𐤅𐤏𐤕𐤄 𐤄𐤉𐤍𐤄 𐤀𐤉𐤔𐤕𐤊𐤄 𐤒𐤇
𐤅𐤋𐤊 20 𐤅𐤉𐤑𐤅 𐤏𐤋𐤉𐤅 𐤐𐤓𐤏𐤅𐤄 𐤀𐤍𐤔𐤉𐤌 𐤅𐤉𐤔𐤋𐤇𐤅 𐤀𐤅𐤕𐤅
𐤅𐤀𐤕 𐤀𐤉𐤔𐤕𐤅 𐤅𐤀𐤕 𐤊𐤋 𐤀𐤔𐤓 𐤋𐤅

𐤁𐤓𐤀𐤔𐤉𐤕 𐤐𐤓𐤒 13

1 𐤅𐤉𐤏𐤋 𐤀𐤁𐤓𐤌 𐤌𐤉𐤌𐤉𐤑𐤓𐤉𐤉𐤌 𐤄𐤅𐤀 𐤅𐤀𐤉𐤔𐤕𐤅 𐤅𐤊𐤋
𐤀𐤔𐤓 𐤋𐤅 𐤅𐤋𐤅𐤈 𐤏𐤉𐤌𐤅 𐤄𐤍𐤂𐤁𐤄 2 𐤅𐤀𐤁𐤓𐤌 𐤊𐤁𐤃 𐤌𐤀𐤅𐤃
𐤁𐤌𐤉𐤒𐤍𐤄 𐤁𐤊𐤎𐤐 𐤅𐤁𐤆𐤄 3 𐤅𐤉𐤋𐤊 𐤋𐤌𐤎𐤏𐤉𐤅 𐤌𐤉𐤍𐤂𐤁
𐤅𐤏𐤃 𐤁𐤉𐤕 𐤀𐤋 𐤏𐤃 𐤄𐤌𐤒𐤅𐤌 𐤀𐤔𐤓 𐤄𐤉𐤄 𐤔𐤌 𐤀𐤄𐤋𐤅𐤄
𐤁𐤕𐤇𐤉𐤋𐤄 𐤁𐤉𐤍 𐤁𐤉𐤕 𐤀𐤋 𐤅𐤁𐤉𐤍 𐤄𐤏𐤉 4 𐤀𐤋 𐤌𐤒𐤅𐤌
𐤄𐤌𐤉𐤆𐤁𐤇 𐤀𐤔𐤓 𐤏𐤎𐤄 𐤔𐤌 𐤁𐤓𐤉𐤀𐤔𐤅𐤍𐤄 𐤅𐤉𐤒𐤓𐤀 𐤔𐤌
𐤀𐤁𐤓𐤌 𐤁𐤔𐤌 𐤉𐤄𐤅𐤄 5 𐤅𐤂𐤌 𐤋𐤋𐤅𐤈 𐤄𐤄𐤅𐤋𐤊 𐤀𐤕 𐤀𐤁𐤓𐤌
𐤄𐤉𐤄 𐤑𐤅𐤀𐤍 𐤅𐤁𐤒𐤓 𐤅𐤀𐤅𐤄𐤋𐤉𐤌 6 𐤅𐤋𐤅𐤀 𐤍𐤎𐤀 𐤀𐤅𐤕𐤌 𐤄𐤀𐤓𐤑
𐤋𐤔𐤁𐤕 𐤉𐤇𐤃𐤅 𐤊𐤉 𐤄𐤉𐤄 𐤓𐤊𐤅𐤔𐤌 𐤓𐤁 𐤅𐤋𐤅𐤀 𐤉𐤊𐤋𐤅 𐤋𐤔𐤁𐤕
𐤉𐤇𐤃𐤅 7 𐤅𐤉𐤄𐤉 𐤓𐤉𐤁 𐤁𐤉𐤍 𐤓𐤅𐤏𐤉 𐤌𐤉𐤒𐤍𐤄 𐤀𐤁𐤓𐤌
𐤅𐤁𐤉𐤍 𐤓𐤅𐤏𐤉 𐤌𐤉𐤒𐤍𐤄 𐤋𐤅𐤈 𐤅𐤄𐤊𐤍𐤏𐤍𐤉 𐤅𐤄𐤐𐤓𐤉𐤆𐤉
𐤀𐤆 𐤉𐤅𐤔𐤁 𐤁𐤀𐤓𐤑 8 𐤅𐤉𐤅𐤀𐤌𐤓 𐤀𐤁𐤓𐤌 𐤀𐤋 𐤋𐤅𐤈 𐤀𐤋 𐤍𐤀
𐤕𐤄𐤉 𐤌𐤓𐤉𐤁𐤄 𐤁𐤉𐤍𐤉 𐤅𐤁𐤉𐤍𐤉𐤊𐤄 𐤅𐤁𐤉𐤍 𐤓𐤅𐤏𐤉
𐤅𐤁𐤉𐤍 𐤓𐤅𐤏𐤉𐤊𐤄 𐤊𐤉 𐤀𐤍𐤔𐤉𐤌 𐤀𐤇𐤉𐤌 𐤀𐤍𐤇𐤍𐤅
9 𐤄𐤋𐤅𐤀 𐤊𐤋 𐤄𐤀𐤓𐤑 𐤋𐤐𐤍𐤉𐤊𐤄 𐤄𐤉𐤐𐤓𐤃 𐤍𐤀 𐤌𐤏𐤋𐤉
𐤀𐤉𐤌 𐤄𐤎𐤌𐤅𐤀𐤋 𐤅𐤀𐤉𐤌𐤉𐤍𐤄 𐤅𐤀𐤉𐤌 𐤄𐤉𐤌𐤉𐤍
𐤅𐤀𐤎𐤌𐤀𐤉𐤋𐤄 10 𐤅𐤉𐤎𐤀 𐤋𐤅𐤈 𐤀𐤕 𐤏𐤉𐤍𐤉𐤅 𐤅𐤉𐤓𐤀 𐤀𐤕 𐤊𐤋
𐤊𐤊𐤓 𐤄𐤉𐤓𐤃𐤍 𐤊𐤉 𐤊𐤅𐤋𐤄 𐤌𐤔𐤒𐤄 𐤋𐤐𐤍𐤉 𐤔𐤇𐤕
𐤉𐤄𐤅𐤄 𐤀𐤕 𐤎𐤅𐤃𐤌 𐤅𐤀𐤕 𐤏𐤌𐤅𐤓𐤄 𐤊𐤂𐤍 𐤉𐤄𐤅𐤄 𐤊𐤀𐤓𐤑
𐤌𐤉𐤑𐤓𐤉𐤉𐤌 𐤁𐤅𐤀𐤊𐤄 𐤑𐤅𐤏𐤓 11 𐤅𐤉𐤁𐤇𐤓 𐤋𐤅 𐤋𐤅𐤈 𐤀𐤕 𐤊𐤋
𐤊𐤊𐤓 𐤄𐤉𐤓𐤃𐤍 𐤅𐤉𐤎𐤏 𐤋𐤅𐤈 𐤌𐤉𐤒𐤃𐤌 𐤅𐤉𐤐𐤓𐤃𐤅 𐤀𐤉𐤔
𐤌𐤏𐤋 𐤀𐤇𐤉𐤅 12 𐤀𐤁𐤓𐤌 𐤉𐤔𐤁 𐤁𐤀𐤓𐤑 𐤊𐤍𐤏𐤍 𐤅𐤋𐤅𐤈 𐤉𐤔𐤁
𐤁𐤏𐤓𐤉 𐤄𐤊𐤉𐤊𐤓 𐤅𐤉𐤀𐤄𐤋 𐤏𐤃 𐤎𐤅𐤃𐤌 13 𐤅𐤀𐤍𐤔𐤉 𐤎𐤅𐤃𐤌
𐤓𐤏𐤉𐤌 𐤅𐤇𐤈𐤀𐤉𐤌 𐤋𐤉𐤄𐤅𐤄 𐤌𐤀𐤅𐤃 14 𐤅𐤉𐤄𐤅𐤄 𐤀𐤌𐤓 𐤀𐤋
𐤀𐤁𐤓𐤌 𐤀𐤇𐤓𐤉 𐤄𐤉𐤐𐤓𐤃 𐤋𐤅𐤈 𐤌𐤏𐤉𐤌𐤅 𐤎𐤀 𐤍𐤀
𐤏𐤉𐤍𐤉𐤊𐤄 𐤅𐤓𐤀𐤄 𐤌𐤉𐤍 𐤄𐤌𐤒𐤅𐤌 𐤀𐤔𐤓 𐤀𐤕𐤄 𐤔𐤌
𐤑𐤐𐤅𐤍𐤄 𐤅𐤍𐤂𐤁𐤄 𐤅𐤒𐤃𐤌𐤄 𐤅𐤉𐤌𐤄 15 𐤊𐤉 𐤀𐤕 𐤊𐤋 𐤄𐤀𐤓𐤑
𐤀𐤔𐤓 𐤀𐤕𐤄 𐤓𐤅𐤀𐤄 𐤋𐤊𐤄 𐤀𐤕𐤍𐤍𐤄 𐤅𐤋𐤆𐤓𐤏𐤊𐤄 𐤏𐤃 𐤏𐤅𐤋𐤌
16 𐤅𐤎𐤌𐤕𐤉 𐤀𐤕 𐤆𐤓𐤏𐤊𐤄 𐤊𐤏𐤐𐤓 𐤄𐤀𐤓𐤑 𐤀𐤔𐤓 𐤀𐤉𐤌
𐤉𐤅𐤊𐤋 𐤀𐤉𐤔 𐤋𐤌𐤍𐤅𐤕 𐤀𐤕 𐤏𐤐𐤓 𐤄𐤀𐤓𐤑 𐤂𐤌 𐤆𐤓𐤏𐤊𐤄
𐤉𐤌𐤍𐤄 17 𐤒𐤅𐤌 𐤄𐤉𐤕𐤄𐤋𐤊 𐤁𐤀𐤓𐤑 𐤋𐤀𐤓𐤊𐤄 𐤅𐤋𐤓𐤇𐤁𐤄 𐤊𐤉

לכה אתננה 18 ויאהל אברם ויבוא וישב
באלוני ממרא אשר בחברון ויבן שם מיזבח
ליהוה

בראשית פרק 14

1 ויהי בימי אמרפל מלך שינער אריוך
מלך אלסר כדרלעומר מלך עילם ותידעל מלך
גויים 2 עסו מילחמה את ברע מלך סדום ואת
בירשע מלך עמורה שינאב מלך אדמה ושמאבר
מלך צבויים ומלך בלע היא צוער 3 כל אלה חברו
אל עמק הסידים הוא ים המלח 4 שתים עסרה
שנה עבדו את כדרלעומר ושלוש עסרה שנה מרדו
5 ובארבע עסרה שנה בא כדרלעומר והמלכים
אשר איתו ויכו את רפאים בעשתרות
קרנים ואת הזוזים בהם ואת האימים
בשוה קיריתיים 6 ואת החורי בהררם סעיר
עד איל פארן אשר על המידבר 7 וישובו
ויבואו אל עין מישפט היוא קדש ויכו את כל
סדה העמלקי וגם את האמורי היושב בחצצון
תמר 8 ויצא מלך סדום ומלך עמורה ומלך אדמה
ומלך צבויים ומלך בלע היוא צוער ויערכו
אתם מילחמה בעמק הסידים 9 את כדרלעומר
מלך עילם ותידעל מלך גויים ואמרפל מלך
שינער ואריוך מלך אלסר ארבעה מלכים את
החמישה 10 ועמק הסידים בארות בארות חמר
וינוסו מלך סדום ועמורה ויפלו שמה
והנישארים הרה נסו 11 ויקחו את כל רכוש סדום
ועמורה ואת כל אכלם וילכו 12 ויקחו את לוט ואת
רכושו בן אחי אברם וילכו והוא יושב ביסדום
13 ויבוא הפליט ויגד לאברם העיברי והוא
שוכן באלוני ממרא האמורי אחי אשכול ואחי
ענר והם בעלי ברית אברם 14 וישמע אברם
כי נישבה אחיו וירק את חניכיו ילידי
ביתו שמונה עסר ושלוש מאות וירדוף עד דן
15 ויחלק עליהם לילה הוא ועבדיו ויכם
וירדפם עד חובה אשר מיסמואל לדמסק 16 וישב
את כל הרכוש וגם את לוט אחיו ורכושו השיב וגם
את הנשים ואת העם 17 ויצא מלך סדום
ליקראתו אחרי שובו מהכות את כדר לעומר ואת
המלכים אשר איתו אל עמק שוה הוא עמק המלך
18 ומלכי צדק מלך שלם הוציא לחם ויין

והוא כוהן לאל עליון 19 ויברכהו ויואמר ברוך
אברם לאל עליון קונה שמיים וארץ 20 וברוך
אל עליון אשר מיגן צריכה בידכה ויתן לו
מעסר מיכול 21 ויואמר מלך סדום אל אברם תן
לי הנפש והרכוש קח לך 22 ויואמר אברם אל
מלך סדום הרימותי ידי אל יהוה אל עליון
קונה שמיים וארץ 23 אים מיחוט ועד סרוך
נעל ואים אקח מיכל אשר לך ולוא תואמר אני
העשרתי את אברם 24 בילעדי רק אשר אכלו
הנערים וחלק האנשים אשר הלכו איתי ענר
אשכול וממרא הם יקחו חלקם

בראשית פרק 15

1 אחר הדברים האלה היה דבר יהוה אל אברם
במחזה לאמור אל תירא אברם אנוכי מגן לך
סכרכה הרבה מאוד 2 ויואמר אברם אדוני יהוה
מה תיתן לי ואנוכי הולך ערירי ובן משק
ביתי הוא דמסק אליעזר 3 ויואמר אברם הן
לי לוא נתתה זרע והינה בן ביתי יורש אותי
4 והינה דבר יהוה אליו לאמור לוא יירשכה
זה כי אים אשר יצא מימעיכה הוא
יירשכה 5 ויוצא אותו החוצה ויואמר הבט נא
השמימה וספור הכוכבים אים תוכל ליספור
אותם ויואמר לו כוה יהיה זרעכה 6 והאמין
ביהוה ויחשבה לו צדקה 7 ויואמר אליו אני
יהוה אשר הוצאתיכה מאור כסדים לתת לכה את
הארץ הזואת לרישתה 8 ויואמר אדוני יהוה
במה אדע כי אירשנה 9 ויואמר אליו קחה לי
עגלה משולשת ועז משולשת ואייל משולש
ותור וגוזל 10 ויקח לו את כל אלה ויבתר אותם בתוך
ויתן איש בתרו ליקראת רעהו ואת הציפור
לוא בתר 11 וירד העייט על הפגרים וישב
אותם אברם 12 ויהי השמש לבוא ותרדמה נפלה
על אברם והינה אימה חשכה גדולה נופלת
עליו 13 ויואמר לאברם ידוע תדע כי גר יהיה
זרעכה בארץ לוא להם ועבדום ועינו אותם ארבע
מאות שנה 14 וגם את הגוי אשר יעבודו דן
אנוכי ואחרי כן יצאו ברכוש גדול 15 ואתה
תבוא אל אבותיכה בשלום תיקבר בסיבה טובה
16 ודור רביעי ישובו הנה כי לוא שלם עון

האמורי עד הנה 17 ויהי השמש באה ועלטה
היה והינה תנור עשן ולפיד אש אשר עבר
בין הגזרים האלה 18 ביום ההוא כרת יהוה את
אברם ברית לאמור לזרעכה נתתי את הארץ
הזואת מינהר מיצריים עד הנהר הגדול
נהר פרת 19 את הקיני ואת הקניזי ואת
הקדמוני 20 ואת החיתי ואת הפריזי ואת
הרפאים 21 ואת האמורי ואת הכנעני ואת
הגירגשי ואת היבוסי

בראשית פרק 16

1 וסרי אשת אברם לוא ילדה לו ולה שיפחה
מיצרית ושמה הגר 2 ותואמר סרי אל אברם
הינה נא עצרני יהוה מילדת בוא נא אל
שיפחתי אולי איבנה מימנה וישמע
אברם לקול סרי 3 ותיקח סרי אשת אברם את הגר
המיצרית שיפחתה מיקץ עסר שנים לשבת
אברם בארץ כנען ותיתן אותה לאברם אישה לו
לאישה 4 ויבוא אל הגר ותהר ותרא כי הרתה ותקל
גבירתה בעיניה 5 ותואמר סרי אל אברם
חמסי עליכה אנוכי נתתי שיפחתי בחיקכה
ותרא כי הרתה ואקל בעיניה ישפוט יהוה
ביני וביניכה 6 ויואמר אברם אל סרי
הינה שיפחתך בידך עסי לה הטוב בעינייך
ותענה סרי ותיברח מיפניה 7 וימצאה
מלאך יהוה על עין המיים במידבר על
העיין בדרך שור 8 ויואמר הגר שיפחת סרי
אי מיזה באת ואנה תלכי ותואמר מיפני
סרי גבירתי אנוכי בורחת 9 ויואמר לה מלאך
יהוה שובי אל גבירתך והיתעני תחת ידיה
10 ויואמר לה מלאך יהוה הרבה ארבה את זרעך
ולוא יספר מרו 11 ויואמר לה מלאך יהוה הינך
הרה וילדת בן וקראת שמו ישמעאל כי שמע
יהוה אל עניך 12 והוא יהיה פרא אדם ידו
בכול ויד כול בו ועל פני כל אחיו ישכון
13 ותיקרא שם יהוה הדובר אליה אתה אל ראי
כי אמרה הגם הלום ראיתי אחרי רואי 14 על
כן קרא לבאר באר לחי רואי הינה בין קדש
ובין ברד 15 ותלד הגר לאברם בן ויקרא אברם
שם בנו אשר ילדה הגר ישמעאל 16 ואברם בן

[illegible]
[illegible]

17 [illegible]

[illegible] 1
[illegible]
[illegible] 2 [illegible]
[illegible]
[illegible] 3 [illegible]
[illegible] 4 [illegible]
[illegible] 5 [illegible]
[illegible]
[illegible] 6 [illegible]
[illegible]
[illegible] 7 [illegible]
[illegible]
[illegible]
[illegible] 8
[illegible]
[illegible] 9 [illegible]
[illegible]
[illegible] 10
[illegible]
[illegible] 11 [illegible]
[illegible] 12 [illegible]
[illegible]
[illegible]
[illegible] 13 [illegible]
[illegible]
[illegible] 14 [illegible]
[illegible]
[illegible] 15 [illegible]
[illegible]
[illegible] 16 [illegible]
[illegible]
[illegible] 17 [illegible]
[illegible]
[illegible] 18 [illegible]
[illegible]
[illegible] 19 [illegible]
[illegible]

[illegible]
[illegible] 20
[illegible]
[illegible]
[illegible] 21 [illegible]
[illegible] 22 [illegible]
[illegible] 23 [illegible]
[illegible]
[illegible]
[illegible]
[illegible] 24 [illegible]
[illegible] 25 [illegible]
[illegible]
[illegible] 26
[illegible] 27 [illegible]
[illegible]

18 [illegible]

[illegible] 1
[illegible] 2 [illegible]
[illegible]
[illegible]
[illegible] 3
[illegible] 4 [illegible]
[illegible]
[illegible] 5
[illegible]
[illegible] 6 [illegible]
[illegible]
[illegible] 7
[illegible] 8 [illegible]
[illegible]
[illegible] 9 [illegible]
[illegible] 10 [illegible]
[illegible]
[illegible]
[illegible] 11
[illegible] 12 [illegible]
[illegible]
[illegible] 13 [illegible]

14

15

16

17

18

19

20

21

22

23

24

25

26

27

28

29

30

31

32

33

𐤉𐤄𐤅𐤄 𐤊𐤀𐤔𐤓 𐤊𐤉𐤋𐤄 𐤋𐤃𐤁𐤓 𐤀𐤋 𐤀𐤁𐤓𐤄𐤌 𐤅𐤀𐤁𐤓𐤄𐤌 𐤔𐤁
𐤋𐤉𐤌𐤒𐤅𐤌𐤅

𐤁𐤓𐤀𐤔𐤉𐤕 𐤐𐤓𐤒 19

1 𐤅𐤉𐤁𐤅𐤀𐤅 𐤔𐤍𐤉 𐤄𐤌𐤋𐤀𐤊𐤉𐤌 𐤎𐤃𐤅𐤌𐤄 𐤁𐤏𐤓𐤁 𐤅𐤋𐤅𐤈
𐤉𐤅𐤔𐤁 𐤁𐤔𐤏𐤓 𐤎𐤃𐤅𐤌 𐤅𐤉𐤓𐤀 𐤋𐤅𐤈 𐤅𐤉𐤒𐤌 𐤋𐤉𐤒𐤓𐤀𐤕𐤌
𐤅𐤉𐤔𐤕𐤇𐤅 𐤀𐤐𐤉𐤌 𐤀𐤓𐤑𐤄 2 𐤅𐤉𐤅𐤀𐤌𐤓 𐤄𐤉𐤍𐤄 𐤍𐤀
𐤀𐤃𐤅𐤍𐤉 𐤎𐤅𐤓𐤅 𐤍𐤀 𐤀𐤋 𐤁𐤉𐤕 𐤏𐤁𐤃𐤊𐤌 𐤅𐤋𐤉𐤍𐤅 𐤅𐤓𐤇𐤑𐤅
𐤓𐤂𐤋𐤉𐤊𐤌 𐤅𐤄𐤉𐤔𐤊𐤌𐤕𐤌 𐤅𐤄𐤋𐤊𐤕𐤌 𐤋𐤃𐤓𐤊𐤊𐤌 𐤅𐤉𐤅𐤀𐤌𐤓𐤅
𐤋𐤅𐤀 𐤊𐤉 𐤁𐤓𐤇𐤅𐤁 𐤍𐤋𐤉𐤍 3 𐤅𐤉𐤐𐤑𐤓 𐤁𐤌 𐤌𐤀𐤅𐤃 𐤅𐤉𐤎𐤅𐤓𐤅
𐤀𐤋𐤉𐤅 𐤅𐤉𐤁𐤅𐤀𐤅 𐤀𐤋 𐤁𐤉𐤕𐤅 𐤅𐤉𐤏𐤎 𐤋𐤄𐤌 𐤌𐤉𐤔𐤕𐤄 𐤅𐤌𐤑𐤅𐤕
𐤀𐤐𐤄 𐤅𐤉𐤅𐤀𐤊𐤋𐤅 4 𐤈𐤓𐤌 𐤉𐤔𐤊𐤁𐤅 𐤅𐤀𐤍𐤔𐤉 𐤄𐤏𐤉𐤓
𐤀𐤍𐤔𐤉 𐤎𐤃𐤅𐤌 𐤍𐤎𐤁𐤅 𐤏𐤋 𐤄𐤁𐤉𐤕 𐤌𐤍𐤏𐤓 𐤅𐤏𐤃 𐤆𐤒𐤍
𐤊𐤋 𐤄𐤏𐤌 𐤌𐤉𐤒𐤑𐤄 5 𐤅𐤉𐤒𐤓𐤀𐤅 𐤀𐤋 𐤋𐤅𐤈 𐤅𐤉𐤅𐤀𐤌𐤓𐤅 𐤋𐤅
𐤀𐤉𐤄 𐤄𐤀𐤍𐤔𐤉𐤌 𐤀𐤔𐤓 𐤁𐤀𐤅 𐤀𐤋𐤉𐤊𐤄 𐤄𐤋𐤉𐤋𐤄
𐤄𐤅𐤑𐤉𐤀𐤌 𐤀𐤋𐤉𐤍𐤅 𐤅𐤍𐤃𐤏𐤄 𐤀𐤅𐤕𐤌 6 𐤅𐤉𐤑𐤀 𐤀𐤋𐤄𐤌 𐤋𐤅𐤈
𐤄𐤐𐤕𐤇𐤄 𐤅𐤄𐤃𐤋𐤕 𐤎𐤂𐤓 𐤀𐤇𐤓𐤉𐤅 7 𐤅𐤉𐤅𐤀𐤌𐤓 𐤀𐤋 𐤍𐤀 𐤀𐤇𐤉
𐤕𐤓𐤏𐤅 8 𐤄𐤉𐤍𐤄 𐤍𐤀 𐤋𐤉 𐤔𐤕𐤉 𐤁𐤍𐤅𐤕 𐤀𐤔𐤓 𐤋𐤅𐤀 𐤉𐤃𐤏𐤅
𐤀𐤉𐤔 𐤀𐤅𐤑𐤉𐤀𐤄 𐤍𐤀 𐤀𐤕𐤄𐤍 𐤀𐤋𐤉𐤊𐤌 𐤅𐤏𐤎𐤅 𐤋𐤄𐤍 𐤊𐤈𐤅𐤁
𐤁𐤏𐤉𐤍𐤉𐤊𐤌 𐤓𐤒 𐤋𐤀𐤍𐤔𐤉𐤌 𐤄𐤀𐤋 𐤀𐤋 𐤕𐤏𐤎𐤅 𐤃𐤁𐤓 𐤊𐤉 𐤏𐤋
𐤊𐤍 𐤁𐤀𐤅 𐤁𐤑𐤋 𐤒𐤅𐤓𐤕𐤉 9 𐤅𐤉𐤅𐤀𐤌𐤓𐤅 𐤂𐤔 𐤄𐤋𐤀𐤄 𐤅𐤉𐤅𐤀𐤌𐤓𐤅
𐤄𐤀𐤇𐤃 𐤁𐤀 𐤋𐤂𐤅𐤓 𐤅𐤉𐤔𐤐𐤅𐤈 𐤔𐤐𐤅𐤈 𐤏𐤕𐤄 𐤍𐤓𐤏 𐤋𐤊𐤄 𐤌𐤄𐤌
𐤅𐤉𐤐𐤑𐤓𐤅 𐤁𐤀𐤉𐤔 𐤁𐤋𐤅𐤈 𐤌𐤀𐤅𐤃 𐤅𐤉𐤂𐤔𐤅 𐤋𐤉𐤔𐤁𐤅𐤓 𐤄𐤃𐤋𐤕
10 𐤅𐤉𐤔𐤋𐤇𐤅 𐤄𐤀𐤍𐤔𐤉𐤌 𐤀𐤕 𐤉𐤃𐤌 𐤅𐤉𐤁𐤉𐤀𐤅 𐤀𐤕 𐤋𐤅𐤈
𐤀𐤋𐤉𐤄𐤌 𐤄𐤁𐤉𐤕𐤄 𐤅𐤀𐤕 𐤄𐤃𐤋𐤕 𐤎𐤂𐤓𐤅 11 𐤅𐤀𐤕 𐤄𐤀𐤍𐤔𐤉𐤌
𐤀𐤔𐤓 𐤐𐤕𐤇 𐤄𐤁𐤉𐤕 𐤄𐤉𐤊𐤅 𐤁𐤎𐤍𐤅𐤓𐤉𐤌 𐤌𐤉𐤒𐤈𐤅𐤍 𐤅𐤏𐤃
𐤂𐤃𐤅𐤋 𐤅𐤉𐤋𐤀𐤅 𐤋𐤉𐤌𐤑𐤅𐤀 𐤄𐤐𐤕𐤇 12 𐤅𐤉𐤅𐤀𐤌𐤓𐤅
𐤄𐤀𐤍𐤔𐤉𐤌 𐤀𐤋 𐤋𐤅𐤈 𐤏𐤅𐤃 𐤌𐤉 𐤋𐤊𐤄 𐤐𐤅𐤄 𐤇𐤕𐤍 𐤅𐤁𐤍𐤉𐤊𐤄
𐤅𐤁𐤍𐤅𐤕𐤉𐤊𐤄 𐤅𐤊𐤅𐤋 𐤀𐤔𐤓 𐤋𐤊𐤄 𐤁𐤏𐤉𐤓 𐤄𐤅𐤑𐤀 𐤌𐤉𐤍
𐤄𐤌𐤒𐤅𐤌 13 𐤊𐤉 𐤌𐤔𐤇𐤉𐤕𐤉𐤌 𐤀𐤍𐤇𐤍𐤅 𐤀𐤕 𐤄𐤌𐤒𐤅𐤌 𐤄𐤆𐤄
𐤊𐤉 𐤂𐤃𐤋𐤄 𐤑𐤏𐤒𐤕𐤌 𐤀𐤕 𐤐𐤍𐤉 𐤉𐤄𐤅𐤄 𐤅𐤉𐤔𐤋𐤇𐤍𐤅 𐤉𐤄𐤅𐤄
𐤋𐤔𐤇𐤕𐤄 14 𐤅𐤉𐤑𐤀 𐤋𐤅𐤈 𐤅𐤉𐤃𐤁𐤓 𐤀𐤋 𐤇𐤕𐤍𐤉𐤅 𐤋𐤅𐤒𐤇𐤉
𐤁𐤍𐤅𐤕𐤉𐤅 𐤅𐤉𐤅𐤀𐤌𐤓 𐤒𐤅𐤌𐤅 𐤑𐤀𐤅 𐤌𐤉𐤍 𐤄𐤌𐤒𐤅𐤌 𐤄𐤆𐤄 𐤊𐤉
𐤌𐤔𐤇𐤉𐤕 𐤉𐤄𐤅𐤄 𐤀𐤕 𐤄𐤏𐤉𐤓 𐤅𐤉𐤄𐤉 𐤊𐤉𐤌𐤑𐤇𐤒
𐤁𐤏𐤉𐤍𐤉 𐤇𐤕𐤍𐤉𐤅 15 𐤅𐤊𐤌𐤅 𐤄𐤔𐤇𐤓 𐤏𐤋𐤄 𐤅𐤉𐤀𐤉𐤑𐤅
𐤄𐤌𐤋𐤀𐤊𐤉𐤌 𐤁𐤋𐤅𐤈 𐤋𐤀𐤌𐤅𐤓 𐤒𐤅𐤌 𐤒𐤇 𐤀𐤕 𐤀𐤉𐤔𐤕𐤊𐤄 𐤅𐤀𐤕
𐤔𐤕𐤉 𐤁𐤍𐤅𐤕𐤉𐤊𐤄 𐤄𐤍𐤉𐤌𐤑𐤀𐤅𐤕 𐤐𐤍 𐤕𐤉𐤎𐤐𐤄 𐤁𐤏𐤅𐤍
𐤄𐤏𐤉𐤓 16 𐤅𐤉𐤕𐤌𐤄𐤌𐤄 𐤅𐤉𐤇𐤆𐤉𐤒𐤅 𐤄𐤀𐤍𐤔𐤉𐤌 𐤁𐤉𐤃𐤅
𐤅𐤁𐤉𐤃 𐤀𐤉𐤔𐤕𐤅 𐤅𐤁𐤉𐤃 𐤔𐤕𐤉 𐤁𐤍𐤅𐤕𐤉𐤅 𐤁𐤇𐤌𐤋𐤕 𐤉𐤄𐤅𐤄
𐤏𐤋𐤉𐤅 𐤅𐤉𐤅𐤑𐤉𐤀𐤅𐤄𐤅 𐤅𐤉𐤍𐤇𐤅𐤄𐤅 𐤌𐤇𐤅𐤑 𐤋𐤏𐤉𐤓
17 𐤅𐤉𐤄𐤉 𐤊𐤄𐤅𐤑𐤉𐤀𐤌 𐤀𐤅𐤕𐤌 𐤄𐤇𐤅𐤑𐤄 𐤅𐤉𐤅𐤀𐤌𐤓

הימלט על נפשכה אל תביט אחריכה ואל
תעמוד בכל הכיכר ההרה הימלט פן תיספה
18 ויואמר לוט אלהם אל נא אדוני 19 הינה נא
מצא עבדכה חן בעיניכה ותגדל חסדכה אשר
עסית עימדי להחיות את נפשי ואנוכי לוא
אוכל להימלט ההרה פן תידבקני הרעה ומתי
20 הינה נא העיר הזואת קרובה לנוס שמה
והיא מיצער אמלטה נא שמה הלוא מיצער
היוא ותחי נפשי 21 ויואמר אליו הינה
נסאתי פניכה גם לדבר הזה לבילתי הפכי
את העיר אשר דיברת 22 מהר הימלט שמה כי
לוא אוכל לעסות דבר עד בואכה שמה על כן קרא שם
העיר צוער 23 השמש יצא על הארץ ולוט בא
צוערה 24 ויהוה הימטיר על סדום ועל עמורה
גפרית ואש מאת יהוה מין השמיים
25 ויהפוך את הערים האל ואת כל הכיכר ואת כל
יושבי הערים וצמח האדמה 26 ותבט אישתו
מאחריו ותהי נציב מלח 27 וישכם אברהם
בבוקר אל המקום אשר עמד שם את פני יהוה
28 וישקף על פני סדום ועמורה ועל כל פני
ארץ הכיכר וירא והינה עלה קיטור הארץ
כקיטור הכיבשן 29 ויהי בשחת אלוהים את
ערי הכיכר ויזכור אלוהים את אברהם וישלח
את לוט מיתוך ההפכה בהפוך את הערים אשר
ישב בהן 30 ויעל לוט מיצוער וישב בהר
ושתי בנותיו עימו כי ירא לשבת בצוער
וישב במערה הוא ושתי בנותיו 31 ותואמר
הבכירה אל הצעירה אבינו זקן ואיש אין
בארץ לבוא עלינו כדרך כל הארץ 32 לכה נשקה את
אבינו יין ונשכבה עימו ונחיה מאבינו
זרע 33 ותשקין את אביהן יין בלילה הוא
ותבוא הבכירה ותישכב את אביה ולוא ידע
בשיכבה ובקומה 34 ויהי מימחרת ותואמר
הבכירה אל הצעירה הן שכבתי אמש את אבי
נשקנו יין גם הלילה ובואי שיכבי עימו
ונחיה מאבינו זרע 35 ותשקין גם בלילה
ההוא את אביהן יין ותקם הצעירה ותישכב
עימו ולוא ידע בשיכבה ובקומה 36 ותהרין
שתי בנות לוט מאביהן 37 ותלד הבכירה בן
ותיקרא שמו מואב הוא אבי מואב עד היום

38 𐤅𐤄𐤑𐤏𐤉𐤓𐤄 𐤂𐤌 𐤄𐤉𐤅𐤀 𐤉𐤋𐤃𐤄 𐤁𐤍 𐤅𐤕𐤉𐤒𐤓𐤀 𐤔𐤌𐤅 𐤁𐤍
𐤏𐤌𐤉 𐤄𐤅𐤀 𐤀𐤁𐤉 𐤁𐤍𐤉 𐤏𐤌𐤅𐤍 𐤏𐤃 𐤄𐤉𐤅𐤌

𐤁𐤓𐤀𐤔𐤉𐤕 𐤐𐤓𐤒 20

1 𐤅𐤉𐤎𐤏 𐤌𐤉𐤔𐤌 𐤀𐤁𐤓𐤄𐤌 𐤀𐤓𐤑𐤄 𐤄𐤍𐤂𐤁 𐤅𐤉𐤔𐤁 𐤁𐤉𐤍
𐤒𐤃𐤔 𐤅𐤁𐤉𐤍 𐤔𐤅𐤓 𐤅𐤉𐤂𐤓 𐤁𐤉𐤂𐤓𐤓 2 𐤅𐤉𐤅𐤀𐤌𐤓 𐤀𐤁𐤓𐤄𐤌
𐤀𐤋 𐤎𐤓𐤄 𐤀𐤉𐤔𐤕𐤅 𐤀𐤇𐤅𐤕𐤉 𐤄𐤉𐤅𐤀 𐤅𐤉𐤔𐤋𐤇 𐤀𐤁𐤉𐤌𐤋𐤊
𐤌𐤋𐤊 𐤂𐤓𐤓 𐤅𐤉𐤒𐤇 𐤀𐤕 𐤎𐤓𐤄 3 𐤅𐤉𐤁𐤅𐤀 𐤀𐤋𐤅𐤄𐤉𐤌 𐤀𐤋
𐤀𐤁𐤉𐤌𐤋𐤊 𐤁𐤇𐤋𐤅𐤌 𐤄𐤋𐤉𐤋𐤄 𐤅𐤉𐤅𐤀𐤌𐤓 𐤋𐤅 𐤄𐤉𐤍𐤊𐤄 𐤌𐤕
𐤏𐤋 𐤄𐤀𐤉𐤔𐤄 𐤀𐤔𐤓 𐤋𐤒𐤇𐤕 𐤅𐤄𐤉𐤅𐤀 𐤁𐤏𐤅𐤋𐤕 𐤁𐤏𐤋
4 𐤅𐤀𐤁𐤉𐤌𐤋𐤊 𐤋𐤅𐤀 𐤒𐤓𐤁 𐤀𐤋𐤉𐤄 𐤅𐤉𐤅𐤀𐤌𐤓 𐤀𐤃𐤅𐤍𐤉 𐤄𐤂𐤅𐤉
𐤂𐤌 𐤑𐤃𐤉𐤒 𐤕𐤄𐤓𐤅𐤂 5 𐤄𐤋𐤅𐤀 𐤄𐤅𐤀 𐤀𐤌𐤓 𐤋𐤉 𐤀𐤇𐤅𐤕𐤉 𐤄𐤉𐤅𐤀
𐤅𐤄𐤉𐤀 𐤂𐤌 𐤄𐤉𐤅𐤀 𐤀𐤌𐤓𐤄 𐤀𐤇𐤉 𐤄𐤅𐤀 𐤁𐤕𐤌 𐤋𐤁𐤁𐤉
𐤅𐤁𐤍𐤉𐤒𐤉𐤅𐤍 𐤊𐤐𐤉 𐤏𐤎𐤉𐤕𐤉 𐤆𐤅𐤀𐤕 6 𐤅𐤉𐤅𐤀𐤌𐤓 𐤀𐤋𐤉𐤅
𐤄𐤀𐤋𐤅𐤄𐤉𐤌 𐤁𐤇𐤋𐤅𐤌 𐤂𐤌 𐤀𐤍𐤅𐤊𐤉 𐤉𐤃𐤏𐤕𐤉 𐤊𐤉 𐤁𐤕𐤌
𐤋𐤁𐤁𐤊𐤄 𐤏𐤎𐤉𐤕 𐤆𐤅𐤀𐤕 𐤅𐤀𐤇𐤎𐤅𐤊 𐤂𐤌 𐤀𐤍𐤅𐤊𐤉 𐤀𐤅𐤕𐤊𐤄 𐤌𐤇𐤈𐤅
𐤋𐤉 𐤏𐤋 𐤊𐤍 𐤋𐤅𐤀 𐤍𐤕𐤕𐤉𐤊𐤄 𐤋𐤉𐤍𐤂𐤅𐤏 𐤀𐤋𐤉𐤄 7 𐤅𐤏𐤕𐤄
𐤄𐤔𐤁 𐤀𐤔𐤕 𐤄𐤀𐤉𐤔 𐤊𐤉 𐤍𐤁𐤉𐤀 𐤄𐤅𐤀 𐤅𐤉𐤕𐤐𐤋𐤋
𐤁𐤏𐤃𐤊𐤄 𐤅𐤇𐤉𐤄 𐤅𐤀𐤉𐤌 𐤀𐤉𐤍𐤊𐤄 𐤌𐤔𐤉𐤁 𐤃𐤏 𐤊𐤉 𐤌𐤅𐤕
𐤕𐤌𐤅𐤕 𐤀𐤕𐤄 𐤅𐤊𐤋 𐤀𐤔𐤓 𐤋𐤊 8 𐤅𐤉𐤔𐤊𐤌 𐤀𐤁𐤉𐤌𐤋𐤊 𐤁𐤁𐤅𐤒𐤓
𐤅𐤉𐤒𐤓𐤀 𐤋𐤊𐤋 𐤏𐤁𐤃𐤉𐤅 𐤅𐤉𐤃𐤁𐤓 𐤀𐤕 𐤊𐤋 𐤄𐤃𐤁𐤓𐤉𐤌 𐤄𐤀𐤋𐤄
𐤁𐤀𐤆𐤍𐤉𐤄𐤌 𐤅𐤉𐤉𐤓𐤀𐤅 𐤄𐤀𐤍𐤔𐤉𐤌 𐤌𐤀𐤅𐤃 9 𐤅𐤉𐤒𐤓𐤀
𐤀𐤁𐤉𐤌𐤋𐤊 𐤋𐤀𐤁𐤓𐤄𐤌 𐤅𐤉𐤅𐤀𐤌𐤓 𐤋𐤅 𐤌𐤄 𐤏𐤎𐤉𐤕 𐤋𐤍𐤅 𐤅𐤌𐤄
𐤇𐤈𐤀𐤕𐤉 𐤋𐤊 𐤊𐤉 𐤄𐤁𐤀𐤕 𐤏𐤋𐤉 𐤅𐤏𐤋 𐤌𐤌𐤋𐤊𐤕𐤉 𐤇𐤈𐤀𐤄
𐤂𐤃𐤅𐤋𐤄 𐤌𐤏𐤎𐤉𐤌 𐤀𐤔𐤓 𐤋𐤅𐤀 𐤉𐤏𐤎𐤅 𐤏𐤎𐤉𐤕 𐤏𐤉𐤌𐤃𐤉
10 𐤅𐤉𐤅𐤀𐤌𐤓 𐤀𐤁𐤉𐤌𐤋𐤊 𐤀𐤋 𐤀𐤁𐤓𐤄𐤌 𐤌𐤄 𐤓𐤀𐤉𐤕 𐤊𐤉
𐤏𐤎𐤉𐤕 𐤀𐤕 𐤄𐤃𐤁𐤓 𐤄𐤆𐤄 11 𐤅𐤉𐤅𐤀𐤌𐤓 𐤀𐤁𐤓𐤄𐤌 𐤊𐤉
𐤀𐤌𐤓𐤕𐤉 𐤓𐤒 𐤀𐤉𐤍 𐤉𐤓𐤀𐤕 𐤀𐤋𐤅𐤄𐤉𐤌 𐤁𐤌𐤒𐤅𐤌 𐤄𐤆𐤄
𐤅𐤄𐤓𐤂𐤅𐤍𐤉 𐤏𐤋 𐤃𐤁𐤓 𐤀𐤉𐤔𐤕𐤉 12 𐤅𐤂𐤌 𐤀𐤌𐤍𐤄 𐤀𐤇𐤅𐤕𐤉
𐤁𐤕 𐤀𐤁𐤉 𐤄𐤉𐤅𐤀 𐤀𐤊 𐤋𐤅𐤀 𐤁𐤕 𐤀𐤉𐤌𐤉 𐤅𐤕𐤄𐤉 𐤋𐤉
𐤋𐤀𐤉𐤔𐤄 13 𐤅𐤉𐤄𐤉 𐤊𐤀𐤔𐤓 𐤄𐤉𐤕𐤏𐤅 𐤀𐤅𐤕𐤉 𐤀𐤋𐤅𐤄𐤉𐤌
𐤌𐤉𐤁𐤉𐤕 𐤀𐤁𐤉 𐤅𐤀𐤅𐤌𐤓 𐤋𐤄 𐤆𐤄 𐤇𐤎𐤃𐤊 𐤀𐤔𐤓 𐤕𐤏𐤎𐤉
𐤏𐤉𐤌𐤃𐤉 𐤀𐤋 𐤊𐤋 𐤄𐤌𐤒𐤅𐤌 𐤀𐤔𐤓 𐤍𐤁𐤅𐤀 𐤔𐤌𐤄 𐤀𐤉𐤌𐤓𐤉
𐤋𐤉 𐤀𐤇𐤉 𐤄𐤅𐤀 14 𐤅𐤉𐤒𐤇 𐤀𐤁𐤉𐤌𐤋𐤊 𐤑𐤅𐤀𐤍 𐤅𐤁𐤒𐤓
𐤅𐤏𐤁𐤃𐤉𐤌 𐤅𐤔𐤐𐤇𐤅𐤕 𐤅𐤉𐤕𐤍 𐤋𐤀𐤁𐤓𐤄𐤌 𐤅𐤉𐤔𐤁 𐤋𐤅 𐤀𐤕 𐤎𐤓𐤄
𐤀𐤉𐤔𐤕𐤅 15 𐤅𐤉𐤅𐤀𐤌𐤓 𐤀𐤁𐤉𐤌𐤋𐤊 𐤄𐤉𐤍𐤄 𐤀𐤓𐤑𐤉
𐤋𐤐𐤍𐤉𐤊𐤄 𐤁𐤈𐤅𐤁 𐤁𐤏𐤉𐤍𐤉𐤊𐤄 𐤔 16 𐤅𐤋𐤎𐤓𐤄 𐤀𐤌𐤓
𐤄𐤉𐤍𐤄 𐤍𐤕𐤕𐤉 𐤀𐤋𐤐 𐤊𐤎𐤐 𐤋𐤀𐤇𐤉𐤊 𐤄𐤉𐤍𐤄 𐤄𐤅𐤀 𐤋𐤊
𐤊𐤎𐤅𐤕 𐤏𐤉𐤍𐤉𐤉𐤌 𐤋𐤊𐤅𐤋 𐤀𐤔𐤓 𐤀𐤉𐤕𐤊 𐤅𐤀𐤕 𐤊𐤅𐤋 𐤅𐤍𐤅𐤊𐤇𐤕
17 𐤅𐤉𐤕𐤐𐤋𐤋 𐤀𐤁𐤓𐤄𐤌 𐤀𐤋 𐤄𐤀𐤋𐤅𐤄𐤉𐤌 𐤅𐤉𐤓𐤐𐤀
𐤀𐤋𐤅𐤄𐤉𐤌 𐤀𐤕 𐤀𐤁𐤉𐤌𐤋𐤊 𐤅𐤀𐤕 𐤀𐤉𐤔𐤕𐤅 𐤅𐤀𐤌𐤄𐤅𐤕𐤉𐤅

וילדו 18 כי עצור עצר יהוה בעד כל רחם לבית
אבימלך על דבר שרה אשת אברהם

בראשית פרק 21

1 ויהוה פקד את שרה כאשר אמר ויעש יהוה לשרה
כאשר דיבר 2 ותהר ותלד שרה לאברהם בן
ליזקוניו למועד אשר דיבר אותו אלוהים
3 ויקרא אברהם את שם בנו הנולד לו אשר ילדה
לו שרה יצחק 4 וימל אברהם את יצחק בנו בן
שמונת ימים כאשר ציוה אותו אלוהים
5 ואברהם בן מאת שנה בהיולד לו את יצחק בנו
6 ותואמר שרה צחוק עשה לי אלוהים כל השומע
יצחק לי 7 ותואמר מי מילל לאברהם
היניקה בנים שרה כי ילדתי בן ליזקוניו
8 ויגדל הילד ויגמל ויעש אברהם מישתה
גדול ביום היגמל את יצחק 9 ותרא שרה את בן
הגר המיצרית אשר ילדה לאברהם מצחק
10 ותואמר לאברהם גרש האמה הזואת ואת בנה
כי לוא יירש בן האמה הזואת עים בני
עים יצחק 11 וירע הדבר מאוד בעיני אברהם
על אודות בנו 12 ויאמר אלוהים אל אברהם אל
ירע בעיניכה על הנער ועל אמתכה כול אשר
תואמר אליכה שרה שמע בקולה כי בייצחק
יקרא לכה זרע 13 וגם את בן האמה לגוי
אשימנו כי זרעכה הוא 14 וישכם אברהם בבוקר
ויקח לחם וחמת מיים ויתן אל הגר שם על
שיכמה ואת הילד וישלחה ותלך ותתע במידבר
באר שבע 15 ויכלו המיים מין החמת ותשלך
את הילד תחת אחד השיחים 16 ותלך ותשב לה
מינגד הרחק כמטחוי קשת כי אמרה אל אראה
במות הילד ותשב מינגד ותישא את קולה ותבך
17 וישמע אלוהים את קול הנער ויקרא מלאך
אלוהים אל הגר מין השמיים ויואמר לה
מה לך הגר אל תיראי כי שמע אלוהים אל קול
הנער באשר הוא שם 18 קומי שאי את הנער
והחזיקי את ידך בו כי לגוי גדול אשימנו
19 ויפקח אלוהים את עיניה ותרא באר
מיים ותלך ותמלא את החמת מיים ותשק את
הנער 20 ויהי אלוהים את הנער ויגדל וישב
במידבר ויהי רובה קשת 21 וישב במידבר

פארן ותיקח לו אימו אישה מארץ
מיצריים 22 ויהי בעת ההיוא ויואמר
אבימלך ופיכול סר צבאו אל אברהם לאמור
אלוהים עימכה בכול אשר אתה עוסה 23 ועתה
הישבעה לי באלוהים הנה אים תישקור לי
ולניני ולנכדי כחסד אשר עסיתי עימכה
תעסה עימדי ועים הארץ אשר גרתה בה
24 ויואמר אברהם אנוכי אישבע 25 והוכיח
אברהם את אבימלך על אודות באר המיים אשר
גזלו עבדי אבימלך 26 ויואמר אבימלך לוא
ידעתי מי עסה את הדבר הזה וגם אתה לוא
היגדת לי וגם אנוכי לוא שמעתי בילתי
היום 27 ויקח אברהם צואן ובקר ויתן
לאבימלך ויכרתו שניהם ברית 28 ויצב
אברהם את שבע כיבסות הצואן לבדהן
29 ויואמר אבימלך אל אברהם מה הנה שבע
כבסות האלה אשר היצבת לבדנה 30 ויואמר כי
את שבע כבסות תיקח מידי בעבור תיהיה לי
לעדה כי חפרתי את הבאר הזואת 31 על כן קרא
למקום ההוא באר שבע כי שם נישבעו שניהם
32 ויכרתו ברית ביבאר שבע ויקם אבימלך
ופיכול סר צבאו וישובו אל ארץ פלישתים
33 ויטע אשל ביבאר שבע ויקרא שם בשם יהוה
אל עולם 34 ויגר אברהם בארץ פלישתים
ימים רבים

בראשית פרק 22

1 ויהי אחר הדברים האלה והאלוהים ניסה את
אברהם ויואמר אליו אברהם ויואמר הינני
2 ויואמר קח נא את בינכה את יחידכה אשר
אהבת את יצחק ולך לכה אל ארץ המוריה והעלהו
שם לעולה על אחד ההרים אשר אומר אליכה
3 וישכם אברהם בבוקר ויחבוש את חמורו ויקח את
שני נעריו איתו ואת יצחק בנו ויבקע עצי
עולה ויקם וילך אל המקום אשר אמר לו
האלוהים 4 ביום השלישי ויסא אברהם את
עיניו וירא את המקום מרחוק 5 ויואמר
אברהם אל נעריו שבו לכם פוה עים החמור
ואני והנער נלכה עד כוה ונישתחוה ונשובה
אליכם 6 ויקח אברהם את עצי העולה ויסם על
יצחק בנו ויקח בידו את האש ואת המאכלת וילכו

שניהם יחדו 7 ויאמר יצחק אל אברהם אביו
ויאמר אבי ויאמר הנני בני ויאמר
הנה האש והעצים ואיה השה לעלה
8 ויאמר אברהם אלהים יראה לו השה לעלה
בני וילכו שניהם יחדו 9 ויבאו אל המקום
אשר אמר לו האלהים ויבן שם אברהם את
המזבח ויערך את העצים ויעקד את יצחק
בנו וישם אתו על המזבח ממעל לעצים
10 וישלח אברהם את ידו ויקח את המאכלת
לשחט את בנו 11 ויקרא אליו מלאך יהוה
מן השמים ויאמר אברהם אברהם
ויאמר הנני 12 ויאמר אל תשלח ידך
אל הנער ואל תעש לו מאומה כי עתה ידעתי כי
ירא אלהים אתה ולא חשכת את בנך את
יחידך ממני 13 וישא אברהם את עיניו
וירא והנה איל אחר נאחז בסבך בקרניו
וילך אברהם ויקח את האיל ויעלהו לעלה תחת
בנו 14 ויקרא אברהם שם המקום ההוא יהוה
יראה אשר יאמר היום בהר יהוה
יראה 15 ויקרא מלאך יהוה אל אברהם שנית מן
השמים 16 ויאמר בי נשבעתי נאם יהוה
כי יען אשר עשית את הדבר הזה ולא
חשכת את בנך את יחידך 17 כי ברך אברכך
והרבה ארבה את זרעך ככוכבי השמים וכחול
אשר על שפת הים וירש זרעך את שער
איביו 18 והתברכו בזרעך כל גויי הארץ עקב
אשר שמעת בקלי 19 וישב אברהם אל
נעריו ויקמו וילכו יחדו אל באר שבע
וישב אברהם בבאר שבע 20 ויהי אחרי הדברים
האלה ויגד לאברהם לאמר הנה ילדה מלכה
גם הוא בנים לנחור אחיך 21 את
עוץ בכרו ואת בוז אחיו ואת קמואל אבי ארם
22 ואת כשד ואת חזו ואת פלדש ואת ידלף ואת
בתואל 23 ובתואל ילד את רבקה שמנה אלה
ילדה מלכה לנחור אחי אברהם 24 ופילגשו
ושמה ראומה ותלד גם הוא את טבח ואת גחם ואת
תחש ואת מעכה

𐤁𐤓𐤀𐤔𐤉𐤕 𐤐𐤓𐤒 23

1 𐤅𐤉𐤄𐤉𐤅 𐤇𐤉𐤉 𐤎𐤓𐤄 𐤌𐤀𐤄 𐤔𐤍𐤄 𐤅𐤏𐤎𐤓𐤉𐤌 𐤔𐤍𐤄
𐤅𐤔𐤁𐤏 𐤔𐤍𐤉𐤌 𐤔𐤍𐤉 𐤇𐤉𐤉 𐤎𐤓𐤄 2 𐤅𐤕𐤌𐤕 𐤎𐤓𐤄
𐤁𐤒𐤉𐤓𐤉𐤕 𐤀𐤓𐤁𐤏 𐤄𐤉𐤅𐤀 𐤇𐤁𐤓𐤅𐤍 𐤁𐤀𐤓𐤑 𐤊𐤍𐤏𐤍 𐤅𐤉𐤁𐤅𐤀
𐤀𐤁𐤓𐤄𐤌 𐤋𐤉𐤎𐤐𐤅𐤃 𐤋𐤎𐤓𐤄 𐤅𐤋𐤉𐤁𐤊𐤅𐤕𐤄 3 𐤅𐤉𐤒𐤌 𐤀𐤁𐤓𐤄𐤌
𐤌𐤏𐤋 𐤐𐤍𐤉 𐤌𐤕𐤅 𐤅𐤉𐤃𐤁𐤓 𐤀𐤋 𐤁𐤍𐤉 𐤇𐤕 𐤋𐤀𐤌𐤅𐤓 4 𐤂𐤓
𐤅𐤕𐤅𐤔𐤁 𐤀𐤍𐤅𐤊𐤉 𐤏𐤉𐤌𐤊𐤌 𐤕𐤍𐤅 𐤋𐤉 𐤀𐤇𐤅𐤆𐤕 𐤒𐤁𐤓
𐤏𐤉𐤌𐤊𐤌 𐤅𐤀𐤒𐤁𐤓𐤄 𐤌𐤕𐤉 𐤌𐤉𐤋𐤐𐤍𐤉 5 𐤅𐤉𐤏𐤍𐤅 𐤁𐤍𐤉
𐤇𐤕 𐤀𐤕 𐤀𐤁𐤓𐤄𐤌 𐤋𐤀𐤌𐤅𐤓 𐤋𐤅 6 𐤔𐤌𐤏𐤍𐤅 𐤀𐤃𐤅𐤍𐤉 𐤍𐤎𐤉𐤀
𐤀𐤋𐤅𐤄𐤉𐤌 𐤀𐤕𐤄 𐤁𐤕𐤅𐤊𐤍𐤅 𐤁𐤌𐤉𐤁𐤇𐤓 𐤒𐤁𐤓𐤉𐤍𐤅 𐤒𐤁𐤅𐤓 𐤀𐤕
𐤌𐤕𐤊𐤄 𐤀𐤉𐤔 𐤌𐤉𐤌𐤍𐤅 𐤀𐤕 𐤒𐤉𐤁𐤓𐤅 𐤋𐤅𐤀 𐤉𐤊𐤋𐤄
𐤌𐤉𐤌𐤊𐤄 𐤌𐤉𐤒𐤁𐤅𐤓 𐤌𐤕𐤊𐤄 7 𐤅𐤉𐤒𐤌 𐤀𐤁𐤓𐤄𐤌 𐤅𐤉𐤔𐤕𐤇𐤅
𐤋𐤏𐤌 𐤄𐤀𐤓𐤑 𐤋𐤉𐤁𐤍𐤉 𐤇𐤕 8 𐤅𐤉𐤃𐤁𐤓 𐤀𐤉𐤕𐤌 𐤋𐤀𐤌𐤅𐤓
𐤀𐤉𐤌 𐤉𐤔 𐤀𐤕 𐤍𐤐𐤔𐤊𐤌 𐤋𐤉𐤒𐤁𐤅𐤓 𐤀𐤕 𐤌𐤕𐤉
𐤌𐤉𐤋𐤐𐤍𐤉 𐤔𐤌𐤏𐤅𐤍𐤉 𐤅𐤐𐤉𐤂𐤏𐤅 𐤋𐤉 𐤁𐤏𐤐𐤓𐤅𐤍 𐤁𐤍
𐤑𐤅𐤇𐤓 9 𐤅𐤉𐤕𐤍 𐤋𐤉 𐤀𐤕 𐤌𐤏𐤓𐤕 𐤄𐤌𐤊𐤐𐤋𐤄 𐤀𐤔𐤓 𐤋𐤅
𐤀𐤔𐤓 𐤁𐤉𐤒𐤑𐤄 𐤎𐤃𐤄𐤅 𐤁𐤊𐤎𐤐 𐤌𐤋𐤀 𐤉𐤕𐤍𐤍𐤄 𐤋𐤉𐤁𐤕𐤅𐤊𐤊𐤌
𐤋𐤀𐤇𐤅𐤆𐤕 𐤒𐤁𐤓 10 𐤅𐤏𐤐𐤓𐤅𐤍 𐤉𐤅𐤔𐤁 𐤁𐤕𐤅𐤊 𐤁𐤍𐤉 𐤇𐤕 𐤅𐤉𐤏𐤍
𐤏𐤐𐤓𐤅𐤍 𐤄𐤇𐤉𐤕𐤉 𐤀𐤕 𐤀𐤁𐤓𐤄𐤌 𐤁𐤀𐤆𐤍𐤉 𐤁𐤍𐤉 𐤇𐤕 𐤋𐤊𐤅𐤋
𐤁𐤀𐤉 𐤔𐤏𐤓 𐤏𐤉𐤓𐤅 𐤋𐤀𐤌𐤅𐤓 11 𐤋𐤅𐤀 𐤀𐤃𐤅𐤍𐤉 𐤔𐤌𐤏𐤍𐤉
𐤄𐤎𐤃𐤄 𐤍𐤕𐤕𐤉 𐤋𐤊 𐤅𐤄𐤌𐤏𐤓𐤄 𐤀𐤔𐤓 𐤁𐤅 𐤋𐤊𐤄 𐤍𐤕𐤕𐤉𐤄
𐤋𐤏𐤉𐤍𐤉 𐤁𐤍𐤉 𐤏𐤌𐤉 𐤍𐤕𐤕𐤉𐤄 𐤋𐤊 𐤒𐤁𐤅𐤓 𐤌𐤕𐤊𐤄
12 𐤅𐤉𐤔𐤕𐤇𐤅 𐤀𐤁𐤓𐤄𐤌 𐤋𐤉𐤐𐤍𐤉 𐤏𐤌 𐤄𐤀𐤓𐤑 13 𐤅𐤉𐤃𐤁𐤓
𐤀𐤋 𐤏𐤐𐤓𐤅𐤍 𐤁𐤀𐤆𐤍𐤉 𐤏𐤌 𐤄𐤀𐤓𐤑 𐤋𐤀𐤌𐤅𐤓 𐤀𐤊 𐤀𐤉𐤌
𐤀𐤕𐤄 𐤋𐤅 𐤔𐤌𐤏𐤍𐤉 𐤍𐤕𐤕𐤉 𐤊𐤎𐤐 𐤄𐤎𐤃𐤄 𐤒𐤇 𐤌𐤉𐤌𐤍𐤉
𐤅𐤀𐤒𐤁𐤓𐤄 𐤀𐤕 𐤌𐤕𐤉 𐤔𐤌𐤄 14 𐤅𐤉𐤏𐤍 𐤏𐤐𐤓𐤅𐤍 𐤀𐤕
𐤀𐤁𐤓𐤄𐤌 𐤋𐤀𐤌𐤅𐤓 𐤋𐤅 15 𐤀𐤃𐤅𐤍𐤉 𐤔𐤌𐤏𐤍𐤉 𐤀𐤓𐤑 𐤀𐤓𐤁𐤏
𐤌𐤀𐤅𐤕 𐤔𐤒𐤋 𐤊𐤎𐤐 𐤁𐤉𐤍𐤉 𐤅𐤁𐤉𐤍𐤊𐤄 𐤌𐤄 𐤄𐤉𐤅𐤀 𐤅𐤀𐤕
𐤌𐤕𐤊𐤄 𐤒𐤁𐤅𐤓 16 𐤅𐤉𐤔𐤌𐤏 𐤀𐤁𐤓𐤄𐤌 𐤀𐤋 𐤏𐤐𐤓𐤅𐤍 𐤅𐤉𐤔𐤒𐤅𐤋
𐤀𐤁𐤓𐤄𐤌 𐤋𐤏𐤐𐤓𐤅𐤍 𐤀𐤕 𐤄𐤊𐤎𐤐 𐤀𐤔𐤓 𐤃𐤉𐤁𐤓 𐤁𐤀𐤆𐤍𐤉
𐤁𐤍𐤉 𐤇𐤕 𐤀𐤓𐤁𐤏 𐤌𐤀𐤅𐤕 𐤔𐤒𐤋 𐤊𐤎𐤐 𐤏𐤅𐤁𐤓 𐤋𐤎𐤅𐤇𐤓 17 𐤅𐤉𐤒𐤌
𐤎𐤃𐤄 𐤏𐤐𐤓𐤅𐤍 𐤀𐤔𐤓 𐤁𐤌𐤊𐤐𐤋𐤄 𐤀𐤔𐤓 𐤋𐤉𐤐𐤍𐤉 𐤌𐤌𐤓𐤀
𐤄𐤎𐤃𐤄 𐤅𐤄𐤌𐤏𐤓𐤄 𐤀𐤔𐤓 𐤁𐤅 𐤅𐤊𐤋 𐤄𐤏𐤑 𐤀𐤔𐤓 𐤁𐤎𐤃𐤄 𐤀𐤔𐤓 𐤁𐤊𐤋
𐤂𐤁𐤅𐤋𐤅 𐤎𐤁𐤉 18 𐤋𐤀𐤁𐤓𐤄𐤌 𐤋𐤌𐤒𐤍𐤄 𐤋𐤏𐤉𐤍𐤉 𐤁𐤍𐤉 𐤇𐤕
𐤁𐤊𐤅𐤋 𐤁𐤀𐤉 𐤔𐤏𐤓 𐤏𐤉𐤓𐤅 19 𐤅𐤀𐤇𐤓𐤉 𐤊𐤍 𐤒𐤁𐤓 𐤀𐤁𐤓𐤄𐤌 𐤀𐤕
𐤎𐤓𐤄 𐤀𐤉𐤔𐤕𐤅 𐤀𐤋 𐤌𐤏𐤓𐤕 𐤎𐤃𐤄 𐤄𐤌𐤊𐤐𐤋𐤄 𐤏𐤋 𐤐𐤍𐤉
𐤌𐤌𐤓𐤀 𐤄𐤉𐤅𐤀 𐤇𐤁𐤓𐤅𐤍 𐤁𐤀𐤓𐤑 𐤊𐤍𐤏𐤍 20 𐤅𐤉𐤒𐤌 𐤄𐤎𐤃𐤄
𐤅𐤄𐤌𐤏𐤓𐤄 𐤀𐤔𐤓 𐤁𐤅 𐤋𐤀𐤁𐤓𐤄𐤌 𐤋𐤀𐤇𐤅𐤆𐤕 𐤒𐤁𐤓 𐤌𐤀𐤕 𐤁𐤍𐤉
𐤇𐤕

בראשית פרק 24

1 ואברהם זקן בא בימים ויהוה ברך את אברהם
בכול 2 ויואמר אברהם אל עבדו זקן ביתו המושל
בכל אשר לו סים נא ידכה תחת ירכי
3 ואשביעכה ביהוה אלוהי השמיים ואלוהי
הארץ אשר לוא תיקח אישה ליבני מיבנות
הכנעני אשר אנוכי יושב בקירבו 4 כי אל
ארצי ואל מולדתי תלך ולקחת אישה ליבני
לייצחק 5 ויואמר אליו העבד אולי לוא תואבה
האישה ללכת אחרי אל הארץ הזואת ההשב
אשיב את בינכה אל הארץ אשר יצאת מישם
6 ויואמר אליו אברהם הישמר לכה פן תשיב
את בני שמה 7 יהוה אלוהי השמיים אשר
לקחני מיבית אבי ומארץ מולדתי ואשר
דיבר לי ואשר נישבע לי לאמור לזרעכה אתן
את הארץ הזואת הוא ישלח מלאכו לפניכה
ולקחת אישה ליבני מישם 8 ואם לוא
תואבה האישה ללכת אחריכה וניקית מישבועתי
זואת רק את בני לוא תשב שמה 9 ויסם העבד את
ידו תחת ירך אברהם אדוניו ויישבע לו על
הדבר הזה 10 ויקח העבד עסרה גמלים מיגמלי
אדוניו וילך וכל טוב אדוניו בידו ויקם וילך אל
ארם נהריים אל עיר נחור 11 ויברך
הגמלים מיחוץ לעיר אל באר המיים לעת
ערב לעת צאת השואבות 12 ויואמר יהוה אלוהי
אדוני אברהם הקרה נא לפני היום ועסה חסד
עים אדוני אברהם 13 הינה אנוכי ניצב על
עין המיים ובנות אנשי העיר יוצאות
לישאוב מיים 14 והיה הנער אשר אומר
אליה הטי נא כדך ואשתה ואמרה שתה וגם
גמליכה אשקה אותה הוכחת לעבדכה לייצחק ובה
אדע כי עסית חסד עים אדוני 15 ויהי הוא
טרם כילה לדבר והנה ריבקה יוצאת אשר
יולדה ליבתואל בן מילכה אשת נחור אחי
אברהם וכדה על שיכמה 16 והנערה טובת מראה
מאוד בתולה ואיש לוא ידעה ותרד העינה
ותמלא כדה ותעל 17 וירץ העבד ליקראתה
ויואמר הגמיאיני נא מעט מיים מיכדך
18 ותואמר שתה אדוני ותמהר ותורד כדה על ידה
19 ותשקהו ותכל להשקותו ותואמר גם ליגמליכה

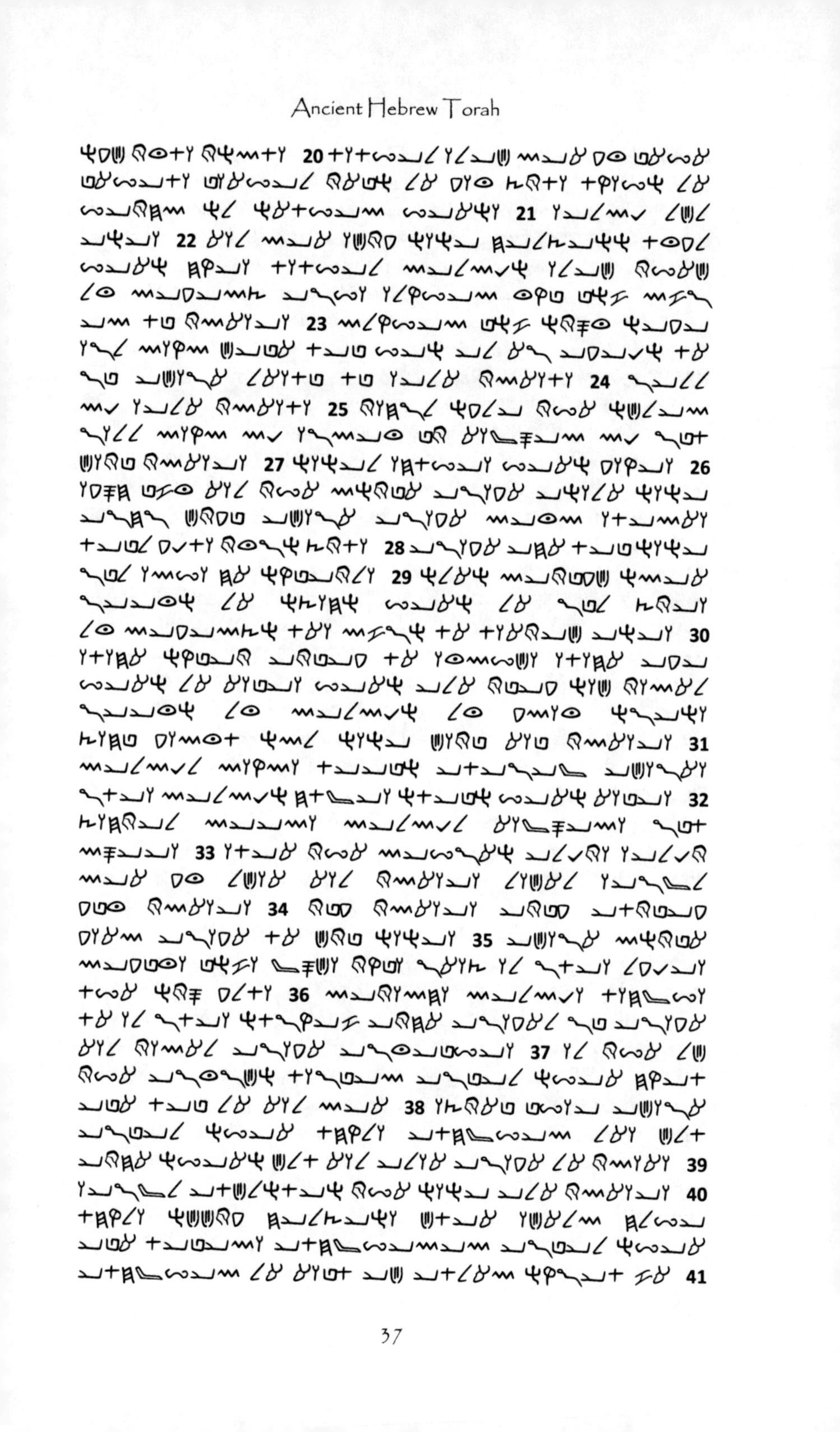

20

21

22

23

24

25

27 26

28

29

30

31

32

33

34

35

36

37

38

39

40

41

[illegible]
[illegible] 42
[illegible]
[illegible] 43 [illegible]
[illegible]
[illegible]
[illegible] 44 [illegible]
[illegible]
[illegible] 45 [illegible]
[illegible]
[illegible]
[illegible] 46 [illegible]
[illegible]
[illegible] 47
[illegible]
[illegible] 48 [illegible]
[illegible]
[illegible]
[illegible] 49 [illegible]
[illegible]
[illegible] 50 [illegible]
[illegible]
[illegible] 51 [illegible]
[illegible]
[illegible] 52 [illegible]
[illegible] 53 [illegible]
[illegible]
[illegible] 54 [illegible]
[illegible]
[illegible]
[illegible] 55
[illegible] 56 [illegible]
[illegible]
[illegible] 57 [illegible]
[illegible] 58 [illegible]
[illegible]
[illegible] 59
[illegible] 60 [illegible]
[illegible]
[illegible] 61 [illegible]
[illegible]

אחרי האיש ויקח העבד את ריבקה וילך
62 וייצחק בא מיבוא באר לחי רואי והוא יושב
בארץ הנג 63 ויצא יצחק לסוח בסדה ליפנות
ערב ויסא עיניו וירא והינה גמלים באים
64 ותיסא ריבקה את עיניה ותרא את יצחק
ותיפול מעל הגמל 65 ותואמר אל העבד מי
האיש הלזה ההולך בסדה ליקראתנו ויואמר
העבד הוא אדוני ותיקח הצעיף ותיתכ
66 ויספר העבד לייצחק את כל הדברים אשר
עסה 67 ויביאה יצחק האוהלה סרה אימו ויקח
את ריבקה ותהי לו לאישה ויאהבה וינחם
יצחק אחרי אימו

בראשית פרק 25

1 ויוסף אברהם ויקח אישה ושמה קטורה 2 ותלד
לו את זימרן ואת יקשן ואת מדן ואת מידין
ואת ישבק ואת שוח 3 ויקשן ילד את שבא ואת
דדן ובני דדן היו אשורים ולטושים
ולאומים 4 ובני מידין עיפה ועפר וחנוך
ואבידע ואלדעה כל אלה בני קטורה 5 ויתן
אברהם את כל אשר לו לייצחק 6 וליבני
הפילגשים אשר לאברהם נתן אברהם מתנות
וישלחם מעל יצחק בנו בעודנו חי קדמה אל ארץ
קדם 7 ואלה ימי שני חיי אברהם אשר חי
מאת שנה ושבעים שנה וחמש שנים
8 ויגוע וימת אברהם בסיבה טובה זקן וסבע
ויאסף אל עמיו 9 ויקברו אותו יצחק
ויישמעאל בניו אל מערת המכפלה אל סדה
עפרון בן צחר החתי אשר על פני ממרא
10 הסדה אשר קנה אברהם מאתבני חת שמה קובר
אברהם וסרה אשתו 11 ויהי אחרי מות אברהם
ויברך אלוהים את יצחק בנו וישב יצחק עים
באר לחי רואי 12 ואלה תולדות ישמעאל בן
אברהם אשר ילדה הגר המיצרית שיפחת סרה
לאברהם 13 ואלה שמות בני ישמעאל
בישמותם לתולדותם בכור ישמעאל נביות וקדר
ואדבאל ומיבסם 14 ומישמע ודומה ומסא 15 חדד
ותימא יטור נפיש וקדמה 16 אלה הם בני
ישמעאל ואלה שמותם בחצריהם ובטירותם
שנים עסר נסיאים לאומותם 17 ואלה שני

חיי ישמעאל מאת שנה ושלושים שנה
ושבע שנים ויגוע וימת ויאסף אל עמיו
18 וישכנו מחוילה עד שור אשר על פני
מיצרים בואכה אשורה על פני כל אחיו
נפל 19 ואלה תולדות יצחק בן אברהם אברהם
הוליד את יצחק 20 ויהי יצחק בן ארבעים
שנה בקחתו את ריבקה בת בתואל הארמי מיפדן
ארם אחות לבן הארמי לו לאישה 21 ויעתר
יצחק ליהוה לנוכח אישתו כי עקרה היוא
ויעתר לו יהוה ותהר ריבקה אישתו
22 ויתרוצצו הבנים בקירבה ותואמר אים כן
למה זה אנוכי ותלך לידרוש את יהוה
23 ויואמר יהוה לה שני גויים בביטנך
ושני לאומים מימעיך יפרדו ולאום
מילאום יאמץ ורב יעבוד צעיר 24 וימלאו
ימיה ללדת והינה תומים בביטנה 25 ויצא
הריאשון אדמוני כולו כאדרת סער ויקראו שמו
עסו 26 ואחרי כן יצא אחיו וידו אוחזת בעקב עסו
ויקרא שמו יעקוב ויצחק בן שישים שנה
בלדת אותם 27 ויגדלו הנערים ויהי עסו איש
יודע ציד איש סדה ויעקב איש תם יושב
אוהלים 28 ויאהב יצחק את עסו כי ציד
בפיו וריבקה אוהבת את יעקו 29 ויזד יעקוב
נזיד ויבוא עסו מין הסדה והוא עי 30 ויואמר
עסו אל יעקוב הלעיטני נא מין האדום
האדום הזה כי עיף אנוכי על כן קרא שמו
אדום 31 ויואמר יעקוב מיכרה כיום את
בכורתכה לי 32 ויואמר עסו הינה אנוכי הולך
למות ולמה זה לי בכורה 33 ויואמר יעקוב
הישבעה לי כיום וישבע לו וימכור את בכורתו
ליעקו 34 ויעקוב נתן לעסו לחם ונזיד
עדשים ויואכל וישת ויקם וילך ויבז עסו את
הבכורה

בראשית פרק 26

1 ויהי רעב בארץ מילבד הרעב הריאשון אשר
היה בימי אברהם וילך יצחק אל אבימלך מלך
פלישתים גררה 2 וירא אליו יהוה ויואמר
אל תרד מיצרימה שכון בארץ אשר אומר
אליכה 3 גור בארץ הזואת ואהיה עימכה

𐤅𐤀𐤁𐤓𐤊𐤊𐤄 𐤊𐤉 𐤋𐤊𐤄 𐤅𐤋𐤆𐤓𐤏𐤊𐤄 𐤀𐤕𐤍 𐤀𐤕 𐤊𐤋 𐤄𐤀𐤓𐤑𐤅𐤕 𐤄𐤀𐤋
𐤅𐤄𐤒𐤉𐤌𐤅𐤕𐤉 𐤀𐤕 𐤄𐤔𐤁𐤅𐤏𐤄 𐤀𐤔𐤓 𐤍𐤉𐤔𐤁𐤏𐤕𐤉
𐤋𐤀𐤁𐤓𐤄𐤌 𐤀𐤁𐤉𐤊𐤄 4 𐤅𐤄𐤉𐤓𐤁𐤉𐤕𐤉 𐤀𐤕 𐤆𐤓𐤏𐤊𐤄 𐤊𐤊𐤅𐤊𐤁𐤉
𐤄𐤔𐤌𐤉𐤉𐤌 𐤅𐤍𐤕𐤕𐤉 𐤋𐤆𐤓𐤏𐤊𐤄 𐤀𐤕 𐤊𐤋 𐤄𐤀𐤓𐤑𐤅𐤕 𐤄𐤀𐤋
𐤅𐤄𐤉𐤕𐤁𐤓𐤊𐤅 𐤁𐤆𐤓𐤏𐤊𐤄 𐤊𐤅𐤋 𐤂𐤅𐤉𐤉 𐤄𐤀𐤓𐤑 5 𐤏𐤒𐤁 𐤀𐤔𐤓
𐤔𐤌𐤏 𐤀𐤁𐤓𐤄𐤌 𐤁𐤒𐤅𐤋𐤉 𐤅𐤉𐤔𐤌𐤅𐤓 𐤌𐤉𐤔𐤌𐤓𐤕𐤉
𐤌𐤉𐤑𐤅𐤕𐤉 𐤇𐤅𐤒𐤅𐤕𐤉 𐤅𐤕𐤅𐤓𐤅𐤕𐤉 6 𐤅𐤉𐤔𐤁 𐤉𐤑𐤇𐤒 𐤁𐤉𐤂𐤓𐤓
𐤅𐤉𐤔𐤀𐤋𐤅 𐤀𐤍𐤔𐤉 𐤄𐤌𐤒𐤅𐤌 𐤋𐤀𐤉𐤔𐤕𐤅 𐤅𐤉𐤅𐤀𐤌𐤓 7
𐤀𐤇𐤅𐤕𐤉 𐤄𐤉𐤅𐤀 𐤊𐤉 𐤉𐤓𐤀 𐤋𐤀𐤌𐤅𐤓 𐤀𐤉𐤔𐤕𐤉 𐤐𐤍
𐤉𐤄𐤓𐤂𐤅𐤍𐤉 𐤀𐤍𐤔𐤉 𐤄𐤌𐤒𐤅𐤌 𐤏𐤋 𐤓𐤉𐤁𐤒𐤄 𐤊𐤉 𐤈𐤅𐤁𐤕
𐤌𐤓𐤀𐤄 𐤄𐤉𐤀 8 𐤅𐤉𐤄𐤉 𐤊𐤉 𐤀𐤓𐤊𐤅 𐤋𐤅 𐤔𐤌 𐤄𐤉𐤌𐤉𐤌
𐤅𐤉𐤔𐤒𐤐 𐤀𐤁𐤉𐤌𐤋𐤊 𐤌𐤋𐤊 𐤐𐤋𐤉𐤔𐤕𐤉𐤌 𐤁𐤏𐤃 𐤄𐤇𐤋𐤅𐤍
𐤅𐤉𐤓𐤀 𐤅𐤄𐤍𐤄 𐤉𐤑𐤇𐤒 𐤌𐤑𐤇𐤒 𐤀𐤕 𐤓𐤉𐤁𐤒𐤄 𐤀𐤉𐤔𐤕𐤅
9 𐤅𐤉𐤒𐤓𐤀 𐤀𐤁𐤉𐤌𐤋𐤊 𐤋𐤉𐤑𐤇𐤒 𐤅𐤉𐤅𐤀𐤌𐤓 𐤀𐤊 𐤄𐤉𐤍𐤄
𐤀𐤉𐤔𐤕𐤊𐤄 𐤄𐤉𐤅𐤀 𐤅𐤀𐤉𐤊 𐤀𐤌𐤓𐤕 𐤀𐤇𐤅𐤕𐤉 𐤄𐤉𐤅𐤀
𐤅𐤉𐤅𐤀𐤌𐤓 𐤀𐤋𐤉𐤅 𐤉𐤑𐤇𐤒 𐤊𐤉 𐤀𐤌𐤓𐤕𐤉 𐤐𐤍 𐤀𐤌𐤅𐤕
𐤏𐤋𐤉𐤄 10 𐤅𐤉𐤅𐤀𐤌𐤓 𐤀𐤁𐤉𐤌𐤋𐤊 𐤌𐤄 𐤆𐤅𐤀𐤕 𐤏𐤎𐤉𐤕 𐤋𐤍𐤅
𐤊𐤉𐤌𐤏𐤈 𐤔𐤊𐤁 𐤀𐤇𐤃 𐤄𐤏𐤌 𐤀𐤕 𐤀𐤉𐤔𐤕𐤊𐤄 𐤅𐤄𐤁𐤀𐤕
𐤏𐤋𐤉𐤍𐤅 𐤀𐤔𐤌 11 𐤅𐤉𐤑𐤅 𐤀𐤁𐤉𐤌𐤋𐤊 𐤀𐤕 𐤊𐤋 𐤄𐤏𐤌
𐤋𐤀𐤌𐤅𐤓 𐤄𐤍𐤅𐤂𐤏 𐤁𐤀𐤉𐤔 𐤄𐤆𐤄 𐤅𐤁𐤀𐤉𐤔𐤕𐤅 𐤌𐤅𐤕 𐤉𐤅𐤌𐤕
12 𐤅𐤉𐤆𐤓𐤏 𐤉𐤑𐤇𐤒 𐤁𐤀𐤓𐤑 𐤄𐤄𐤉𐤅𐤀 𐤅𐤉𐤌𐤑𐤀 𐤁𐤔𐤍𐤄
𐤄𐤄𐤉𐤅𐤀 𐤌𐤀𐤄 𐤔𐤏𐤓𐤉𐤌 𐤅𐤉𐤁𐤓𐤊𐤄𐤅 𐤉𐤄𐤅𐤄 13 𐤅𐤉𐤂𐤃𐤋
𐤄𐤀𐤉𐤔 𐤅𐤉𐤋𐤊 𐤄𐤋𐤅𐤊 𐤅𐤂𐤃𐤋 𐤏𐤃 𐤊𐤉 𐤂𐤃𐤋 𐤌𐤀𐤅𐤃 14 𐤅𐤉𐤄𐤉
𐤋𐤅 𐤌𐤉𐤒𐤍𐤄 𐤑𐤅𐤀𐤍 𐤅𐤌𐤉𐤒𐤍𐤄 𐤁𐤒𐤓 𐤅𐤏𐤁𐤅𐤃𐤄 𐤓𐤁𐤄
𐤅𐤉𐤒𐤍𐤀𐤅 𐤀𐤅𐤕𐤅 𐤐𐤋𐤉𐤔𐤕𐤉𐤌 15 𐤅𐤊𐤋 𐤄𐤁𐤀𐤓𐤅𐤕 𐤀𐤔𐤓
𐤇𐤐𐤓𐤅 𐤏𐤁𐤃𐤉 𐤀𐤁𐤉𐤅 𐤁𐤉𐤌𐤉 𐤀𐤁𐤓𐤄𐤌 𐤀𐤁𐤉𐤅 𐤎𐤉𐤕𐤌𐤅𐤌
𐤐𐤋𐤉𐤔𐤕𐤉𐤌 𐤅𐤉𐤌𐤋𐤀𐤅𐤌 𐤏𐤐𐤓 16 𐤅𐤉𐤅𐤀𐤌𐤓
𐤀𐤁𐤉𐤌𐤋𐤊 𐤀𐤋 𐤉𐤑𐤇𐤒 𐤋𐤊 𐤌𐤏𐤉𐤌𐤍𐤅 𐤊𐤉 𐤏𐤑𐤌𐤕
𐤌𐤉𐤌𐤍𐤅 𐤌𐤀𐤅𐤃 17 𐤅𐤉𐤋𐤊 𐤌𐤉𐤔𐤌 𐤉𐤑𐤇𐤒 𐤅𐤉𐤇𐤍 𐤁𐤍𐤇𐤋
𐤂𐤓𐤓 𐤅𐤉𐤔𐤁 𐤔𐤌 18 𐤅𐤉𐤔𐤁 𐤉𐤑𐤇𐤒 𐤅𐤉𐤇𐤐𐤅𐤓 𐤀𐤕 𐤁𐤀𐤓𐤅𐤕
𐤄𐤌𐤉𐤌 𐤀𐤔𐤓 𐤇𐤐𐤓𐤅 𐤁𐤉𐤌𐤉 𐤀𐤁𐤓𐤄𐤌 𐤀𐤁𐤉𐤅
𐤅𐤉𐤎𐤕𐤌𐤅𐤌 𐤐𐤋𐤉𐤔𐤕𐤉𐤌 𐤀𐤇𐤓𐤉 𐤌𐤅𐤕 𐤀𐤁𐤓𐤄𐤌 𐤅𐤉𐤒𐤓𐤀
𐤋𐤄𐤍 𐤔𐤌𐤅𐤕 𐤊𐤔𐤌𐤅𐤕 𐤀𐤔𐤓 𐤒𐤓𐤀 𐤋𐤄𐤍 𐤀𐤁𐤉𐤅
19 𐤅𐤉𐤇𐤐𐤓𐤅 𐤏𐤁𐤃𐤉 𐤉𐤑𐤇𐤒 𐤁𐤍𐤇𐤋 𐤅𐤉𐤌𐤑𐤀𐤅 𐤔𐤌 𐤁𐤀𐤓
𐤌𐤉𐤌 𐤇𐤉𐤉𐤌 20 𐤅𐤉𐤓𐤉𐤁𐤅 𐤓𐤅𐤏𐤉 𐤂𐤓𐤓 𐤏𐤉𐤌
𐤓𐤅𐤏𐤉 𐤉𐤑𐤇𐤒 𐤋𐤀𐤌𐤅𐤓 𐤋𐤍𐤅 𐤄𐤌𐤉𐤌 𐤅𐤉𐤒𐤓𐤀 𐤔𐤌
𐤄𐤁𐤀𐤓 𐤏𐤎𐤒 𐤊𐤉 𐤄𐤉𐤕𐤏𐤎𐤒𐤅 𐤏𐤉𐤌𐤅 21 𐤅𐤉𐤇𐤐𐤓𐤅 𐤁𐤀𐤓
𐤀𐤇𐤓𐤕 𐤅𐤉𐤓𐤉𐤁𐤅 𐤂𐤌 𐤏𐤋𐤉𐤄 𐤅𐤉𐤒𐤓𐤀 𐤔𐤌𐤄 𐤎𐤉𐤈𐤍𐤄
22 𐤅𐤉𐤏𐤕𐤒 𐤌𐤉𐤔𐤌 𐤅𐤉𐤇𐤐𐤅𐤓 𐤁𐤀𐤓 𐤀𐤇𐤓𐤕 𐤅𐤋𐤅𐤀 𐤓𐤁𐤅
𐤏𐤋𐤉𐤄 𐤅𐤉𐤒𐤓𐤀 𐤔𐤌𐤄 𐤓𐤇𐤅𐤁𐤅𐤕 𐤅𐤉𐤅𐤀𐤌𐤓 𐤊𐤉 𐤏𐤕𐤄
𐤄𐤉𐤓𐤇𐤉𐤁 𐤉𐤄𐤅𐤄 𐤋𐤍𐤅 𐤅𐤐𐤓𐤉𐤍𐤅 𐤁𐤀𐤓𐤑 23 𐤅𐤉𐤏𐤋

𐤌𐤉𐤔𐤌 𐤁𐤀𐤓 𐤔𐤁𐤏 24 𐤅𐤉𐤓𐤀 𐤀𐤋𐤉𐤅 𐤉𐤄𐤅𐤄 𐤁𐤋𐤉𐤋𐤄
𐤄𐤄𐤅𐤀 𐤅𐤉𐤅𐤀𐤌𐤓 𐤀𐤍𐤅𐤊𐤉 𐤀𐤋𐤅𐤄𐤉 𐤀𐤁𐤓𐤄𐤌 𐤀𐤁𐤉𐤊𐤄 𐤀𐤋
𐤕𐤉𐤓𐤀 𐤊𐤉 𐤀𐤉𐤕𐤊𐤄 𐤀𐤍𐤅𐤊𐤉 𐤅𐤁𐤓𐤊𐤕𐤉𐤊𐤄 𐤅𐤄𐤉𐤓𐤁𐤉𐤕𐤉
𐤀𐤕 𐤆𐤓𐤏𐤊𐤄 𐤁𐤏𐤁𐤅𐤓 𐤀𐤁𐤓𐤄𐤌 𐤏𐤁𐤃𐤉 25 𐤅𐤉𐤁𐤍 𐤔𐤌
𐤌𐤉𐤆𐤁𐤇 𐤅𐤉𐤒𐤓𐤀 𐤁𐤔𐤌 𐤉𐤄𐤅𐤄 𐤅𐤉𐤈 𐤔𐤌 𐤀𐤄𐤋𐤅 𐤅𐤉𐤊𐤓𐤅
𐤔𐤌 𐤏𐤁𐤃𐤉 𐤉𐤑𐤇𐤒 𐤁𐤀𐤓 26 𐤅𐤀𐤁𐤉𐤌𐤋𐤊 𐤄𐤋𐤊 𐤀𐤋𐤉𐤅
𐤌𐤉𐤂𐤓𐤓 𐤅𐤀𐤇𐤅𐤆𐤕 𐤌𐤓𐤏𐤄𐤅 𐤅𐤐𐤉𐤊𐤅𐤋 𐤎𐤓 𐤑𐤁𐤀𐤅
27 𐤅𐤉𐤅𐤀𐤌𐤓 𐤀𐤋𐤄𐤌 𐤉𐤑𐤇𐤒 𐤌𐤃𐤅𐤏 𐤁𐤀𐤕𐤌 𐤀𐤋𐤉 𐤅𐤀𐤕𐤌
𐤎𐤍𐤀𐤕𐤌 𐤀𐤅𐤕𐤉 𐤅𐤕𐤔𐤋𐤇𐤅𐤍𐤉 𐤌𐤀𐤉𐤕𐤊𐤌 28 𐤅𐤉𐤅𐤀𐤌𐤓𐤅
𐤓𐤀𐤅 𐤓𐤀𐤉𐤍𐤅 𐤊𐤉 𐤄𐤉𐤄 𐤉𐤄𐤅𐤄 𐤏𐤉𐤌𐤊 𐤅𐤍𐤅𐤀𐤌𐤓 𐤕𐤄𐤉
𐤍𐤀 𐤀𐤋𐤄 𐤁𐤉𐤍𐤅𐤕𐤉𐤍𐤅 𐤁𐤉𐤍𐤉𐤍𐤅 𐤅𐤁𐤉𐤍𐤊𐤄
𐤅𐤍𐤉𐤊𐤓𐤕𐤄 𐤁𐤓𐤉𐤕 𐤏𐤉𐤌𐤊 29 𐤀𐤉𐤌 𐤕𐤏𐤎𐤄 𐤏𐤉𐤌𐤍𐤅
𐤓𐤏𐤄 𐤊𐤀𐤔𐤓 𐤋𐤅𐤀𐤍𐤂𐤏𐤍𐤅𐤊𐤄 𐤅𐤊𐤀𐤔𐤓 𐤏𐤎𐤉𐤍𐤅 𐤏𐤉𐤌𐤊𐤄
𐤓𐤒 𐤈𐤅𐤁 𐤅𐤍𐤔𐤋𐤇𐤊𐤄 𐤁𐤔𐤋𐤅𐤌 𐤀𐤕𐤄 𐤏𐤕𐤄 𐤁𐤓𐤅𐤊 𐤉𐤄𐤅𐤄
30 𐤅𐤉𐤏𐤎 𐤋𐤄𐤌 𐤌𐤉𐤔𐤕𐤄 𐤅𐤉𐤅𐤀𐤊𐤋𐤅 𐤅𐤉𐤔𐤕𐤅
31 𐤅𐤉𐤔𐤊𐤉𐤌𐤅 𐤁𐤁𐤅𐤒𐤓 𐤅𐤉𐤔𐤁𐤏𐤅 𐤀𐤉𐤔 𐤋𐤀𐤇𐤉𐤅
𐤅𐤉𐤔𐤋𐤇𐤌 𐤉𐤑𐤇𐤒 𐤅𐤉𐤋𐤊𐤅 𐤌𐤀𐤉𐤕𐤅 𐤁𐤔𐤋𐤅𐤌 32 𐤅𐤉𐤄𐤉
𐤁𐤉𐤅𐤌 𐤄𐤄𐤅𐤀 𐤅𐤉𐤁𐤅𐤀𐤅 𐤏𐤁𐤃𐤉 𐤉𐤑𐤇𐤒 𐤅𐤉𐤂𐤉𐤃𐤅 𐤋𐤅 𐤏𐤋
𐤀𐤅𐤃𐤅𐤕 𐤄𐤁𐤀𐤓 𐤀𐤔𐤓 𐤇𐤐𐤓𐤅 𐤅𐤉𐤅𐤀𐤌𐤓𐤅 𐤋𐤅 𐤌𐤑𐤀𐤍𐤅
𐤌𐤉𐤌 33 𐤅𐤉𐤒𐤓𐤀 𐤀𐤅𐤕𐤄 𐤔𐤉𐤁𐤏𐤄 𐤏𐤋 𐤊𐤍 𐤔𐤌
𐤄𐤏𐤉𐤓 𐤁𐤀𐤓 𐤔𐤁𐤏 𐤏𐤃 𐤄𐤉𐤅𐤌 𐤄𐤆𐤄 34 𐤅𐤉𐤄𐤉 𐤏𐤎𐤅 𐤁𐤍
𐤀𐤓𐤁𐤏𐤉𐤌 𐤔𐤍𐤄 𐤅𐤉𐤒𐤇 𐤀𐤉𐤔𐤄 𐤀𐤕 𐤉𐤄𐤅𐤃𐤉𐤕 𐤁𐤕
𐤁𐤀𐤓𐤉 𐤄𐤇𐤉𐤕𐤉 𐤅𐤀𐤕 𐤁𐤎𐤌𐤕 𐤁𐤕 𐤀𐤉𐤋𐤅𐤍 𐤄𐤇𐤉𐤕𐤉
35 𐤅𐤕𐤉𐤄𐤉𐤉𐤍 𐤌𐤅𐤓𐤕 𐤓𐤅𐤇 𐤋𐤉𐤉𐤑𐤇𐤒 𐤅𐤋𐤓𐤉𐤁𐤒𐤄

𐤁𐤓𐤀𐤔𐤉𐤕 𐤐𐤓𐤒 27

1 𐤅𐤉𐤄𐤉 𐤊𐤉 𐤆𐤒𐤍 𐤉𐤑𐤇𐤒 𐤅𐤕𐤉𐤊𐤄𐤉𐤍 𐤏𐤉𐤍𐤉𐤅
𐤌𐤓𐤀𐤅𐤕 𐤅𐤉𐤒𐤓𐤀 𐤀𐤕 𐤏𐤎𐤅 𐤁𐤍𐤅 𐤄𐤂𐤃𐤅𐤋 𐤅𐤉𐤅𐤀𐤌𐤓 𐤀𐤋𐤉𐤅
𐤁𐤍𐤉 𐤅𐤉𐤅𐤀𐤌𐤓 𐤀𐤋𐤉𐤅 𐤄𐤉𐤍𐤍𐤉 2 𐤅𐤉𐤅𐤀𐤌𐤓 𐤄𐤉𐤍𐤄
𐤍𐤀 𐤆𐤒𐤍𐤕𐤉 𐤋𐤅𐤀 𐤉𐤃𐤏𐤕𐤉 𐤉𐤅𐤌 𐤌𐤅𐤕𐤉 3 𐤅𐤏𐤕𐤄 𐤎𐤀
𐤍𐤀 𐤊𐤋𐤉𐤊𐤄 𐤕𐤋𐤉𐤊𐤄 𐤅𐤒𐤔𐤕𐤊𐤄 𐤅𐤑𐤀 𐤄𐤎𐤃𐤄 𐤅𐤑𐤅𐤃𐤄 𐤋𐤉
𐤑𐤉𐤃𐤄 4 𐤅𐤏𐤎𐤄 𐤋𐤉 𐤌𐤈𐤏𐤌𐤉𐤌 𐤊𐤀𐤔𐤓 𐤀𐤄𐤁𐤕𐤉
𐤅𐤄𐤁𐤉𐤀𐤄 𐤋𐤉 𐤅𐤀𐤅𐤊𐤋𐤄 𐤁𐤏𐤁𐤅𐤓 𐤕𐤁𐤓𐤊𐤊𐤄 𐤍𐤐𐤔𐤉 𐤁𐤈𐤓𐤌
𐤀𐤌𐤅𐤕 5 𐤅𐤓𐤉𐤁𐤒𐤄 𐤔𐤅𐤌𐤏𐤕 𐤁𐤃𐤁𐤓 𐤉𐤑𐤇𐤒 𐤀𐤋 𐤏𐤎𐤅 𐤁𐤍𐤅
𐤅𐤉𐤋𐤊 𐤏𐤎𐤅 𐤄𐤎𐤃𐤄 𐤋𐤑𐤅𐤃 𐤑𐤉𐤉𐤃 𐤋𐤄𐤁𐤉𐤀 6 𐤅𐤓𐤉𐤁𐤒𐤄
𐤀𐤌𐤓𐤄 𐤀𐤋 𐤉𐤏𐤒𐤅𐤁 𐤁𐤍𐤄 𐤋𐤀𐤌𐤓 𐤄𐤉𐤍𐤄 𐤔𐤌𐤏𐤕𐤉 𐤀𐤕
𐤀𐤁𐤉𐤊𐤄 𐤌𐤃𐤁𐤓 𐤀𐤋 𐤏𐤎𐤅 𐤀𐤇𐤉𐤊𐤄 𐤋𐤀𐤌𐤅𐤓 7 𐤄𐤁𐤉𐤀𐤄 𐤋𐤉
𐤑𐤉𐤉𐤃 𐤅𐤏𐤎𐤄 𐤋𐤉 𐤌𐤈𐤏𐤌𐤉𐤌 𐤅𐤀𐤅𐤊𐤋𐤄 𐤅𐤀𐤁𐤓𐤊𐤊𐤄
𐤋𐤐𐤍𐤉 𐤉𐤄𐤅𐤄 𐤋𐤐𐤍𐤉 𐤌𐤅𐤕𐤉 8 𐤅𐤏𐤕𐤄 𐤁𐤍𐤉
𐤔𐤌𐤏 𐤁𐤒𐤅𐤋𐤉 𐤋𐤀𐤔𐤓 𐤀𐤍𐤉 𐤌𐤑𐤅𐤄 𐤀𐤅𐤕𐤊 9 𐤋𐤊 𐤍𐤀 𐤀𐤋

[illegible]
[illegible]
[illegible] 10 [illegible]
[illegible] 11 [illegible]
[illegible]
[illegible] 12 [illegible]
[illegible]
[illegible] 13
[illegible] 14 [illegible]
[illegible] 15 [illegible]
[illegible]
[illegible] 16 [illegible]
[illegible]
[illegible] 17 [illegible]
[illegible] 18 [illegible]
[illegible]
[illegible] 19 [illegible]
[illegible]
[illegible]
[illegible] 20
[illegible]
[illegible] 21
[illegible] 22 [illegible]
[illegible]
[illegible] 23 [illegible]
[illegible]
[illegible] 24
[illegible] 25
[illegible]
[illegible] 26 [illegible]
[illegible] 27 [illegible]
[illegible]
[illegible] 28 [illegible]
[illegible]
[illegible] 29 [illegible]
[illegible]
[illegible]
[illegible]
[illegible] 30
[illegible]
[illegible] 31 [illegible]
[illegible]

אבי ויואכל מיציד בנו בעבור תברכני
נפשכה 32 ויואמר לו יצחק אביו מי אתה
ויואמר אני בינכה בכורכה עשו 33 ויחרד יצחק
חרדה גדולה עד מאוד ויואמר מי אפוא הוא הצד
צייד ויבא לי ואוכל מיכול בטרם תבוא ואברכהו
גם ברוך יהיה 34 כישמוע עשו את דיברי אביו
ויצעק צעקה גדולה ומרה עד מאוד ויואמר
לאביו ברכני גם אני אבי 35 ויואמר בא
אחיכה במירמה ויקח בירכתכה 36 ויואמר
הכי קרא שמו יעקוב ויעקבני זה פעמיים
את בכורתי לקח והינה עתה לקח בירכתי
ויואמר הלוא אצלת לי ברכה 37 ויען יצחק
ויואמר לעשו הן גביר שמתיו לך ואת כל אחיו
נתתי לו לעבדים ודגן ותירוש סמכתיו ולכה
אפוא מה אעשה בני 38 ויואמר עשו אל אביו
הברכה אחת היוא לכה אבי ברכני גם אני אבי
וישא עשו קולו ויבך 39 ויען יצחק אביו ויואמר
אליו הינה מישמני הארץ יהיה מושבכה
ומיטל השמיים מעל 40 ועל חרבכה תיחיה
ואת אחיכה תעבוד והיה כאשר תריד ופרקת עולו
מעל צוארכה 41 וישטום עשו את יעקוב על הברכה
אשר ברכו אביו ויואמר עשו בליבו יקרבו ימי
אבל אבי ואהרגה את יעקוב אחי 42 ויוגד
לריבקה את דיברי עשו בנה הגדול ותישלח
ותיקרא ליעקוב בנה הקטן ותאומר אליו הינה
עשו אחיכה מיתנחם לכה להרגכה 43 ועתה בני
שמע בקולי וקום ברח לכה אל לבן אחי חרנה
44 וישבת עימו ימים אחדים עד אשר תשוב
חמת אחיכה 45 עד שוב אף אחיכה מימכה ושכח
את אשר עשית לו ושלחתי ולקחתיכה מישם
למה אשכל גם שניכם יום אחד 46 ותאומר
ריבקה אל יצחק קצתי בחיי מיפני בנות חת
אים לוקח יעקוב אישה מיבנות חת כאלה
מיבנות הארץ למה לי חיים

בראשית פרק 28

1 ויקרא יצחק אל יעקוב ויברך אותו ויצוהו
ויואמר לו לוא תיקח אישה מיבנות כנען
2 קום לך פדנה ארם ביתה בתואל אבי אימכה
וקח לכה מישם אישה מיבנות לבן אחי
אימכה 3 ואל שדי יברך אותכה ויפרכה

וירבכה והיית ליקהל עמים 4 וייתן לכה
את בירכת אברהם לכה ולזרעכה איתך לרישתכה
את ארץ מגוריכה אשר נתן אלוהים לאברהם
5 וישלח יצחק את יעקוב וילך פדנה ארם אל
לבן בן בתואל הארמי אחי ריבקה אם יעקוב
ועסו 6 וירא עסו כי ברך יצחק את יעקוב ושילח
אותו פדנה ארם לקחת לו מישם אישה בברכו
אותו ויצו עליו לאמור לוא תיקח אישה
מיבנות כנען 7 וישמע יעקוב אל אביו ואל
אמו וילך פדנה ארם 8 וירא עסו כי רעות
בנות כנען בעיני יצחק אביו 9 וילך עסו אל
ישמעאל ויקח את מחלת בת ישמעאל בן
אברהם אחות נביות על נשיו לו לאישה
10 ויצא יעקוב מיבאר שבע וילך חרנה
11 ויפגע במקום וילן שם כי בא השמש ויקח
מאבני המקום ויסם מראשותיו וישכב במקום
ההוא 12 ויחלום והינה סולם מוצב ארצה וראושו
מגיע השמימה והינה מלאכי אלוהים
עולים ויורדים בו 13 והינה יהוה ניצב
עליו ויאמר אנכי יהוה אלוהי אברהם אביכה
ואלוהי יצחק הארץ אשר אתה שוכב עליה לכה
אתננה ולזרעכה 14 והיה זרעכה כעפר הארץ
ופרצת ימה וקדמה וצפנה ונגבה וניברכו בכה
כל מישפחות האדמה ובזרעכה 15 והינה
אנוכי עימך ושמרתיכה בכול אשר תלך
והשיבותיכה אל האדמה הזואת כי לוא אעזבכה
עד אשר אם עסיתי את אשר דיברתי לך
16 וייקץ יעקוב מישנתו ויאמר אכן יש
יהוה במקום הזה ואנוכי לוא ידעתי
17 ויירא ויאמר מה נורא המקום הזה אין
זה כי אם בית אלוהים וזה שער השמיים
18 וישכם יעקוב בבוקר ויקח את האבן אשר סם
מראשותיו ויסם אותה מצבה ויצוק שמן על
ראשה 19 ויקרא את שם המקום ההוא בית אל
ואולם לוז שם העיר לראשונה 20 וידר יעקוב
נדר לאמור אם יהיה אלוהים עימדי
ושמרני בדרך הזה אשר אנוכי הולך ונתן לי
לחם לאכול ובגד לילבוש 21 ושבתי בשלום אל
בית אבי והיה יהוה לי לאלוהים 22 והאבן
הזואת אשר סמתי מצבה יהיה בית אלוהים
וכול אשר תיתן לי עסר אעסרנו לך

29

1
2
3
4
5
6
7
8
9
10
11 12
13
14
15
16
17
18
19
20
21
22

משתה 23 ויהי בערב ויקח את לאה בתו ויבא
אותה אליו ויבוא אליה 24 ויתן לבן לה את
זלפה שפחתו ללאה בתו שפחה 25 ויהי
בבוקר והנה הוא לאה ויאמר אל לבן מה זאת
עשית לי הלוא ברחל עבדתי עמך ולמה
רמיתני 26 ויאמר לבן לוא יעשה כן
במקומנו לתת הצעירה לפני הבכירה
27 מלא שבוע זאת ונתנה לך גם את זאת
בעבודה אשר תעבוד עמדי עוד שבוע שנים
אחרות 28 ויעש יעקב כן וימלא שבוע זאת
ויתן לו את רחל בתו לו לאשה 29 ויתן לבן
לרחל בתו את בלהה שפחתו לה לשפחה
30 ויבוא גם אל רחל ויאהב גם את רחל מלאה
ויעבוד עמו עוד שבע שנים אחרות 31 וירא
יהוה כי שנואה לאה ויפתח את רחמה ורחל עקרה
32 ותהר לאה ותלד בן ותקרא שמו ראובן כי
אמרה כי ראה יהוה בעניי כי עתה יאהבני
אישי 33 ותהר עוד ותלד בן ותאמר כי שמע
יהוה כי שנואה אנכי ויתן לי גם את זה
ותקרא שמו שמעון 34 ותהר עוד ותלד בן
ותאמר עתה הפעם ילוה אישי אלי כי
ילדתי לו שלשה בנים על כן קרא שמו לוי
35 ותהר עוד ותלד בן ותאמר הפעם אודה את
יהוה על כן קראה שמו יהודה ותעמוד מלדת

בראשית פרק 30

1 ותרא רחל כי לוא ילדה ליעקב ותקנא רחל
באחותה ותאמר אל יעקב הבה לי בנים ואם
אין מתה אנכי 2 ויחר אף יעקב ברחל
ויאמר התחת אלהים אנכי אשר מנע
ממך פרי בטן 3 ותאמר הנה אמתי
בלהה בוא אליה ותלד על ברכי ואבנה גם
אנכי ממנה 4 ותתן לו את בלהה
שפחתה לאשה ויבוא אליה יעקב 5 ותהר
בלהה ותלד ליעקב בן 6 ותאמר רחל דנני
אלהים וגם שמע בקולי ויתן לי בן על כן
קראה שמו דן 7 ותהר עוד ותלד בלהה שפחת
רחל בן שני ליעקב 8 ותאמר רחל נפתולי
אלהים נפתלתי עם אחותי גם יכולתי
ותקרא שמו נפתלי 9 ותרא לאה כי עמדה

10
11
12
13
14
15
16
17
18
19
20
21
22
23
24
25
26
27
28
29
30
31
32

בעיזים והיה שכרי 33 וענתה בי צידקתי
ביום מחר כי תבוא על שכרי לפניכה כול אשר
איננו נקוד וטלוא בעיזים וחום בכשבים גנוב
הוא איתי 34 ויואמר לבן הן לו יהי כידברכה
35 ויסר ביום ההוא את התישים העקודים
והטלואים ואת כל העיזים הנקודות והטלואות
כול אשר לבן בו וכל חום בכשבים ויתן ביד בניו
36 וישם דרך שלושת ימים בינו ובין יעקוב
ויעקוב רועה את צואן לבן הנותרות 37 ויקח לו
יעקוב מקל ליבנה לח ולוז וערמון ויפצל בהן
פצלות לבנות מחשוף הלבן אשר על המקלות
38 ויצג את המקלות אשר פיצל ברהטים
בשיקתות המיים אשר תבואן הצואן לישתות
לנוכח הצואן ויחמנה בבואן לישתות 39 ויחמו
הצואן אל המקלות ותלדן הצואן עקודים
נקודים וטלואים 40 והכשבים הפריד יעקוב
ויתן פני הצואן אל עקוד וכל חום בצואן לבן
וישת לו עדרים לבדו ולוא שתם על צואן לבן
41 והיה בכל יחם הצואן המקושרות ושם יעקוב
את המקלות לעיני הצואן ברהטים ליחמנה
במקלות 42 ובהעטיף הצואן לוא ישים והיה
העטופים ללבן והקשורים ליעקו 43 ויפרוץ
האיש מאוד מאוד ויהי לו צואן רבות ושפחות
ועבדים וגמלים וחמורים

בראשית פרק 31

1 וישמע את דברי בני לבן לאמור לקח
יעקוב את כל אשר לאבינו ומאשר לאבינו עשה
את כל הכבוד הזה 2 וירא יעקוב את פני לבן
והינה איננו עימו כיתמול שילשום
3 ויואמר יהוה אל יעקוב שוב אל ארץ אבותיכה
ולמולדתכה ואהיה עימך 4 וישלח יעקוב
ויקרא לרחל וללאה השדה אל צואנו 5 ויואמר להן
רואה אנוכי את פני אביכן כי איננו אלי
כיתמול שילשום ואלוהי אבי היה עימדי
6 ואתנה ידעתן כי בכל כוחי עבדתי את אביכן
7 ואביכן התל בי והחליף את משכורתי עשרת
מונים ולוא נתנו אלוהים להרע עימדי
8 אם כוה יואמר נקודים יהיה שכרכה וילדו
כל הצואן נקודים ואם כוה יואמר עקודים

𐤉𐤄𐤉𐤄 𐤎𐤊𐤓𐤊𐤄 𐤅𐤉𐤋𐤃𐤅 𐤊𐤋 𐤄𐤑𐤅𐤀𐤍 𐤏𐤒𐤅𐤃𐤉𐤌 9 𐤅𐤉𐤑𐤋
𐤀𐤋𐤅𐤄𐤉𐤌 𐤀𐤕 𐤌𐤉𐤒𐤍𐤄 𐤀𐤁𐤉𐤊𐤌 𐤅𐤉𐤕𐤍 𐤋𐤉 10 𐤅𐤉𐤄𐤉
𐤁𐤏𐤕 𐤉𐤇𐤌 𐤄𐤑𐤅𐤀𐤍 𐤅𐤀𐤎𐤀 𐤏𐤉𐤍𐤉 𐤅𐤀𐤓𐤀 𐤁𐤇𐤋𐤅𐤌
𐤅𐤄𐤉𐤍𐤄 𐤄𐤏𐤕𐤅𐤃𐤉𐤌 𐤄𐤏𐤅𐤋𐤉𐤌 𐤏𐤋 𐤄𐤑𐤅𐤀𐤍 𐤏𐤒𐤅𐤃𐤉𐤌
𐤍𐤒𐤅𐤃𐤉𐤌 𐤅𐤁𐤓𐤅𐤃𐤉𐤌 11 𐤅𐤉𐤀𐤌𐤓 𐤀𐤋𐤉 𐤌𐤋𐤀𐤊
𐤄𐤀𐤋𐤅𐤄𐤉𐤌 𐤁𐤇𐤋𐤅𐤌 𐤉𐤏𐤒𐤅𐤁 𐤅𐤀𐤅𐤌𐤓 𐤄𐤉𐤍𐤍𐤉
12 𐤅𐤉𐤀𐤌𐤓 𐤎𐤀 𐤍𐤀 𐤏𐤉𐤍𐤉𐤊𐤄 𐤅𐤓𐤀𐤄 𐤊𐤋 𐤄𐤏𐤕𐤅𐤃𐤉𐤌
𐤄𐤏𐤅𐤋𐤉𐤌 𐤏𐤋 𐤄𐤑𐤅𐤀𐤍 𐤏𐤒𐤅𐤃𐤉𐤌 𐤍𐤒𐤅𐤃𐤉𐤌 𐤅𐤁𐤓𐤅𐤃𐤉𐤌
𐤊𐤉 𐤓𐤀𐤉𐤕𐤉 𐤀𐤕 𐤊𐤋 𐤀𐤔𐤓 𐤋𐤁𐤍 𐤏𐤅𐤎𐤄 𐤋𐤊 13 𐤀𐤍𐤅𐤊𐤉
𐤄𐤀𐤋 𐤁𐤉𐤕 𐤀𐤋 𐤀𐤔𐤓 𐤌𐤔𐤇𐤕 𐤔𐤌 𐤌𐤑𐤁𐤄 𐤀𐤔𐤓 𐤍𐤃𐤓𐤕 𐤋𐤉
𐤔𐤌 𐤍𐤃𐤓 𐤏𐤕𐤄 𐤒𐤅𐤌 𐤑𐤀 𐤌𐤉𐤍 𐤄𐤀𐤓𐤑 𐤄𐤆𐤅𐤀𐤕 𐤅𐤔𐤅𐤁 𐤀𐤋
𐤀𐤓𐤑 𐤌𐤅𐤋𐤃𐤕𐤊𐤄 14 𐤅𐤕𐤏𐤍 𐤓𐤇𐤋 𐤅𐤋𐤀𐤄 𐤅𐤕𐤅𐤀𐤌𐤓𐤍𐤄 𐤋𐤅
𐤄𐤏𐤅𐤃 𐤋𐤍𐤅 𐤇𐤋𐤒 𐤅𐤍𐤇𐤋𐤄 𐤁𐤁𐤉𐤕 𐤀𐤁𐤉𐤍𐤅 15 𐤄𐤋𐤅𐤀
𐤍𐤊𐤓𐤉𐤅𐤕 𐤍𐤇𐤔𐤁𐤍𐤅 𐤋𐤅 𐤊𐤉 𐤌𐤊𐤓𐤍𐤅 𐤅𐤉𐤅𐤀𐤊𐤋 𐤂𐤌 𐤀𐤊𐤅𐤋
𐤀𐤕 𐤊𐤎𐤐𐤍𐤅 16 𐤊𐤉 𐤊𐤋 𐤄𐤏𐤅𐤔𐤓 𐤀𐤔𐤓 𐤄𐤉𐤑𐤉𐤋
𐤀𐤋𐤅𐤄𐤉𐤌 𐤌𐤀𐤁𐤉𐤍𐤅 𐤋𐤍𐤅 𐤄𐤅𐤀 𐤅𐤋𐤁𐤍𐤉𐤍𐤅 𐤅𐤏𐤕𐤄 𐤊𐤅𐤋
𐤀𐤔𐤓 𐤀𐤌𐤓 𐤀𐤋𐤅𐤄𐤉𐤌 𐤀𐤋𐤉𐤊𐤄 𐤏𐤎𐤄 17 𐤅𐤉𐤒𐤌 𐤉𐤏𐤒𐤅𐤁
𐤅𐤉𐤎𐤀 𐤀𐤕 𐤁𐤍𐤉𐤅 𐤅𐤀𐤕 𐤍𐤔𐤉𐤅 𐤏𐤋 𐤄𐤂𐤌𐤋𐤉𐤌
18 𐤅𐤉𐤍𐤄𐤂 𐤀𐤕 𐤊𐤋 𐤌𐤉𐤒𐤍𐤄𐤅 𐤅𐤀𐤕 𐤊𐤋 𐤓𐤊𐤅𐤔𐤅 𐤀𐤔𐤓 𐤓𐤊𐤔
𐤌𐤉𐤒𐤍𐤄 𐤒𐤉𐤍𐤉𐤍𐤅 𐤀𐤔𐤓 𐤓𐤊𐤔 𐤁𐤐𐤃𐤍 𐤀𐤓𐤌 𐤋𐤁𐤅𐤀 𐤀𐤋
𐤉𐤑𐤇𐤒 𐤀𐤁𐤉𐤅 𐤀𐤓𐤑𐤄 𐤊𐤍𐤏𐤍 19 𐤅𐤋𐤁𐤍 𐤄𐤋𐤊 𐤋𐤉𐤂𐤆𐤅𐤆 𐤀𐤕
𐤑𐤅𐤀𐤍𐤅 𐤅𐤕𐤉𐤂𐤍𐤅𐤁 𐤓𐤇𐤋 𐤀𐤕 𐤄𐤕𐤓𐤐𐤉𐤌 𐤀𐤔𐤓 𐤋𐤀𐤁𐤉𐤄
20 𐤅𐤉𐤂𐤍𐤅𐤁 𐤉𐤏𐤒𐤅𐤁 𐤀𐤕 𐤋𐤁 𐤋𐤁𐤍 𐤄𐤀𐤓𐤌𐤉 𐤏𐤋 𐤁𐤋𐤉
𐤄𐤉𐤂𐤉𐤃 𐤋𐤅 𐤊𐤉 𐤁𐤅𐤓𐤇 𐤄𐤅𐤀 21 𐤅𐤉𐤁𐤓𐤇 𐤄𐤅𐤀 𐤅𐤊𐤋 𐤀𐤔𐤓 𐤋𐤅
𐤅𐤉𐤒𐤌 𐤅𐤉𐤏𐤁𐤅𐤓 𐤀𐤕 𐤄𐤍𐤄𐤓 𐤅𐤉𐤎𐤌 𐤀𐤕 𐤐𐤍𐤉𐤅 𐤄𐤓
𐤄𐤂𐤉𐤋𐤏𐤃 22 𐤅𐤉𐤅𐤂𐤃 𐤋𐤋𐤁𐤍 𐤁𐤉𐤅𐤌 𐤄𐤔𐤋𐤉𐤔𐤉 𐤊𐤉 𐤁𐤓𐤇
𐤉𐤏𐤒𐤅𐤁 23 𐤅𐤉𐤒𐤇 𐤀𐤕 𐤀𐤇𐤉𐤅 𐤏𐤌𐤅 𐤅𐤉𐤓𐤃𐤅𐤐 𐤀𐤇𐤓𐤉𐤅 𐤃𐤓𐤊
𐤔𐤁𐤏𐤕 𐤉𐤌𐤉𐤌 𐤅𐤉𐤃𐤁𐤒 𐤀𐤅𐤕𐤅 𐤁𐤄𐤓 𐤄𐤂𐤉𐤋𐤏𐤃
24 𐤅𐤉𐤁𐤅𐤀 𐤀𐤋𐤅𐤄𐤉𐤌 𐤀𐤋 𐤋𐤁𐤍 𐤄𐤀𐤓𐤌𐤉 𐤁𐤇𐤋𐤅𐤌 𐤄𐤋𐤉𐤋𐤄
𐤅𐤉𐤅𐤀𐤌𐤓 𐤋𐤅 𐤄𐤔𐤌𐤓 𐤋𐤊𐤄 𐤐𐤍 𐤕𐤃𐤁𐤓 𐤏𐤌 𐤉𐤏𐤒𐤅𐤁
𐤌𐤉𐤈𐤅𐤁 𐤏𐤃 𐤓𐤏 25 𐤅𐤉𐤎𐤂 𐤋𐤁𐤍 𐤀𐤕 𐤉𐤏𐤒𐤅𐤁 𐤅𐤉𐤏𐤒𐤅𐤁 𐤕𐤒𐤏
𐤀𐤕 𐤀𐤄𐤋𐤅 𐤁𐤄𐤓 𐤅𐤋𐤁𐤍 𐤕𐤒𐤏 𐤀𐤕 𐤀𐤇𐤉𐤅 𐤁𐤄𐤓 𐤄𐤂𐤉𐤋𐤏𐤃
26 𐤅𐤉𐤅𐤀𐤌𐤓 𐤋𐤁𐤍 𐤋𐤉𐤏𐤒𐤅𐤁 𐤌𐤄 𐤏𐤎𐤉𐤕 𐤅𐤕𐤉𐤂𐤍𐤅𐤁 𐤀𐤕
𐤋𐤁𐤁𐤉 𐤅𐤕𐤍𐤄𐤂 𐤀𐤕 𐤁𐤍𐤅𐤕𐤉 𐤊𐤉𐤔𐤁𐤅𐤉𐤅𐤕 𐤇𐤓 27 𐤋𐤌𐤄
𐤍𐤇𐤁𐤀𐤕 𐤋𐤉𐤁𐤅𐤓𐤇 𐤅𐤕𐤉𐤂𐤍𐤅𐤁 𐤀𐤅𐤕𐤉 𐤅𐤋𐤅𐤀 𐤄𐤉𐤂𐤃𐤕 𐤋𐤉
𐤅𐤀𐤔𐤋𐤇𐤊𐤄 𐤁𐤎𐤉𐤌𐤇𐤄 𐤅𐤁𐤔𐤉𐤓𐤉𐤌 𐤁𐤕𐤅𐤐 𐤅𐤁𐤊𐤉𐤍𐤅𐤓
28 𐤅𐤋𐤅𐤀 𐤍𐤈𐤔𐤕𐤍𐤉 𐤋𐤍𐤔𐤒 𐤋𐤁𐤍𐤉 𐤅𐤋𐤁𐤍𐤅𐤕𐤉 𐤏𐤕𐤄
𐤄𐤉𐤎𐤊𐤋𐤕 𐤏𐤎𐤅 29 𐤉𐤔 𐤋𐤀𐤋 𐤉𐤃𐤉 𐤋𐤏𐤎𐤅𐤕 𐤏𐤉𐤌𐤊𐤌 𐤓𐤏
𐤅𐤀𐤋𐤅𐤄𐤉 𐤀𐤁𐤉𐤊𐤌 𐤀𐤌𐤔 𐤀𐤌𐤓 𐤀𐤋𐤉 𐤋𐤀𐤌𐤅𐤓 𐤄𐤉𐤔𐤌𐤓
𐤋𐤊𐤄 𐤌𐤉𐤃𐤁𐤓 𐤏𐤉𐤌 𐤉𐤏𐤒𐤅𐤁 𐤌𐤉𐤈𐤅𐤁 𐤏𐤃 𐤓𐤏 30 𐤅𐤏𐤕𐤄
𐤄𐤋𐤅𐤊 𐤄𐤋𐤊𐤕 𐤊𐤉 𐤍𐤉𐤊𐤎𐤅𐤐 𐤍𐤉𐤊𐤎𐤐𐤕𐤄 𐤋𐤁𐤉𐤕 𐤀𐤁𐤉𐤊𐤄

למה גנבת את אלוהי 31 ויען יעקוב ויואמר
ללבן כי יראתי כי אמרתי פן תיגזול את
בנותיכה מעימי 32 עים אשר תימצא את
אלוהיכה לוא יחיה נגד אחינו הכר לכה מה
עימדי וקח לך ולוא ידע יעקוב כי רחל גנבתם
33 ויבוא לבן באוהל יעקוב ובאוהל לאה ובאוהל
שתי האמהות ולוא מצא ויצא מאוהל לאה ויבוא
באוהל רחל 34 ורחל לקחה את התרפים ותסימם
בכר הגמל ותשב עליהם וימשש לבן את כל
האוהל ולוא מצא 35 ותואמר אל אביה אל יחר
בעיני אדוני כי לוא אוכל לקום מיפניכה
כי דרך נשים לי ויחפס ולוא מצא את
התרפים 36 ויחר ליעקוב וירב בלבן ויען
יעקוב ויואמר ללבן מה פשעי מה חטאתי
כי דלקת אחרי 37 כי מששת את כל כלי מה
מצאת מיכול כלי ביתיכה סים כוה נגד אחי
ואחיכה ויוכיחו בין שנינו 38 זה עסרים
שנה אנוכי עימך רחליכה ועיזיכה לוא
שיכלו ואילי צואנך לוא אכלתי 39 טרפה לוא
הבאתי אליכה אנוכי אחטנה מידי תבקשנה
גנובתי יום וגנובתי לילה 40 הייתי ביום
אכלני חורב וקרח בלילה ותידד שנתי מעיני
41 זה לי עסרים שנה בביתכה עבדתיכה ארבע
עסרה שנה בישתי בנותיכה ושש שנים
בצואנכה ותחלף את מסכורתי עסרת מונים
42 לולי אלוהי אבי אלוהי אברהם ופחד יצחק
היה לי כי עתה ריקם שילחתני את עניי
ואת יגיע כפי ראה אלוהים ויוכח אמש
43 ויען לבן ויואמר אל יעקוב הבנות בנותי
והבנים בני והצואן צואני וכול אשר אתה
רואה לי הוא וליבנותי מה אעסה לאלה היום או
ליבניהן אשר ילדו 44 ועתה לכה ניכרתה
ברית אני ואתה והיה לעד ביני ובינכה
45 ויקח יעקוב אבן וירימה מצבה 46 ויואמר
יעקוב לאחיו לקטו אבנים ויקחו אבנים
ויעסו גל ויאכלו שם על הגל 47 ויקרא לו לבן
יגר סהדותא ויעקוב קרא לו גלעד 48 ויואמר לבן
הגל הזה עד ביני ובינכה היום על כן קרא
שמו גלעד 49 והמיצפה אשר אמר יצף יהוה
ביני ובינכה כי ניסתר איש מרעהו
50 אים תענה את בנותי ואים תיקח נשים

על בנותי אין איש עימנו ראה אלוהים עד
ביני ובינכה 51 ויואמר לבן ליעקוב הינה
הגל הזה והינה המצבה אשר יריתי ביני
ובינכה 52 עד הגל הזה ועדה המצבה אים אני
לוא אעבור אליכה את הגל הזה ואים אתה לוא
תעבור אלי את הגל הזה ואת המצבה הזואת לרעה
53 אלוהי אברהם ואלוהי נחור ישפטו
בינינו אלוהי אביהם וישבע יעקוב בפחד
אביו יצחק 54 ויזבח יעקוב זבח בהר ויקרא
לאחיו לאכל לחם ויואכלו לחם וילינו בהר

בראשית פרק 32

1 וישכם לבן בבוקר וינשק לבניו ולבנותיו
ויברך אתהם וילך וישב לבן למקומו
2 ויעקוב הלך לדרכו ויפגעו בו מלאכי אלוהים
3 ויואמר יעקוב כאשר ראם מחנה אלוהים זה
ויקרא שם המקום ההוא מחניים 4 וישלח
יעקוב מלאכים לפניו אל עשו אחיו ארצה
שעיר שדה אדום 5 ויצו אותם לאמור כוה
תואמרון לאדוני לעשו כוה אמר עבדך יעקוב
עים לבן גרתי ואחר עד עתה 6 ויהי לי שור
וחמור צואן ועבד ושפחה ואשלחה להגיד
לאדוני לימצוא חן בעיניכה 7 וישובו
המלאכים אל יעקוב לאמור באנו אל אחיכה אל
עשו וגם הולך ליקראתכה וארבע מאות איש
עימו 8 ויירא יעקוב מאוד ויצר לו ויחץ את
העם אשר איתו ואת הצואן ואת הבקר והגמלים
לישני מחנות 9 ויואמר אים יבוא עשו אל
המחנה האחת והיכהו והיה המחנה הנישאר
לפליטה 10 ויואמר יעקוב אלוהי אבי
אברהם ואלוהי אבי יצחק יהוה האומר אלי שוב
לארצכה ולמולדתכה ואיטיבה עימך 11 קטונתי
מיכול החסדים ומיכל האמת אשר עשית את
עבדכה כי במקלי עברתי את הירדן הזה ועתה
הייתי לישני מחנות 12 הצילני נא מיד
אחי מיד עשו כי ירא אנוכי אותו פן יבוא
והיכני אם על בנים 13 ואתה אמרת היטב
איטיב עימך ושמתי את זרעכה כחול הים אשר
לוא יספר מרו 14 וילן שם בלילה ההוא ויקח
מין הבא בידו מנחה לעשו אחיו 15 עיזים
מאתיים ותישים עשרים רחלים

𐤌𐤀𐤕𐤉𐤌 𐤅𐤀𐤉𐤋𐤉𐤌 𐤏𐤎𐤓𐤉𐤌 16 𐤂𐤌𐤋𐤉𐤌
𐤌𐤉𐤍𐤉𐤒𐤅𐤕 𐤅𐤁𐤍𐤉𐤄𐤌 𐤔𐤋𐤅𐤔𐤉𐤌 𐤐𐤓𐤅𐤕 𐤀𐤓𐤁𐤏𐤉𐤌
𐤅𐤐𐤓𐤉𐤌 𐤏𐤎𐤓𐤄 𐤀𐤕𐤅𐤍𐤅𐤕 𐤏𐤎𐤓𐤉𐤌 𐤅𐤏𐤉𐤓𐤉𐤌 𐤏𐤎𐤓𐤄
17 𐤅𐤉𐤕𐤍 𐤁𐤉𐤃 𐤏𐤁𐤃𐤉𐤅 𐤏𐤃𐤓 𐤏𐤃𐤓 𐤋𐤁𐤃𐤅 𐤅𐤉𐤅𐤀𐤌𐤓 𐤀𐤋
𐤏𐤁𐤃𐤉𐤅 𐤏𐤉𐤁𐤓𐤅 𐤋𐤐𐤍𐤉 𐤅𐤓𐤅𐤇 𐤕𐤎𐤉𐤌𐤅 𐤁𐤉𐤍 𐤏𐤃𐤓
𐤅𐤁𐤉𐤍 𐤏𐤃𐤓 18 𐤅𐤉𐤑𐤅 𐤀𐤕 𐤄𐤓𐤉𐤀𐤔𐤅𐤍 𐤋𐤀𐤌𐤅𐤓 𐤊𐤉
𐤉𐤐𐤂𐤔𐤊𐤄 𐤏𐤎𐤅 𐤀𐤇𐤉 𐤅𐤉𐤔𐤀𐤋𐤊𐤄 𐤋𐤀𐤌𐤅𐤓 𐤋𐤌𐤉 𐤀𐤕𐤄
𐤅𐤀𐤍𐤄 𐤕𐤋𐤊 𐤅𐤋𐤌𐤉 𐤀𐤋𐤄 𐤋𐤐𐤍𐤉𐤊𐤄 19 𐤅𐤀𐤌𐤓𐤕 𐤋𐤏𐤁𐤃𐤊𐤄
𐤋𐤉𐤏𐤒𐤅𐤁 𐤌𐤉𐤍𐤇𐤄 𐤄𐤉𐤅𐤀 𐤔𐤋𐤅𐤇𐤄 𐤋𐤀𐤃𐤅𐤍𐤉 𐤋𐤏𐤎𐤅
𐤅𐤄𐤉𐤍𐤄 𐤂𐤌 𐤄𐤅𐤀 𐤀𐤇𐤓𐤉𐤍𐤅 20 𐤅𐤉𐤑𐤅 𐤂𐤌 𐤀𐤕 𐤄𐤔𐤍𐤉
𐤂𐤌 𐤀𐤕 𐤄𐤔𐤋𐤉𐤔𐤉 𐤂𐤌 𐤀𐤕 𐤊𐤋 𐤄𐤄𐤅𐤋𐤊𐤉𐤌 𐤀𐤇𐤓𐤉
𐤄𐤏𐤃𐤓𐤉𐤌 𐤋𐤀𐤌𐤅𐤓 𐤊𐤃𐤁𐤓 𐤄𐤆𐤄 𐤕𐤃𐤁𐤓𐤅𐤍 𐤀𐤋 𐤏𐤎𐤅
𐤁𐤌𐤅𐤑𐤀𐤊𐤌 𐤀𐤅𐤕𐤅 21 𐤅𐤀𐤌𐤓𐤕𐤌 𐤂𐤌 𐤄𐤉𐤍𐤄 𐤏𐤁𐤃𐤊𐤄
𐤉𐤏𐤒𐤅𐤁 𐤀𐤇𐤓𐤉𐤍𐤅 𐤊𐤉 𐤀𐤌𐤓 𐤀𐤊𐤐𐤓𐤄 𐤐𐤍𐤉𐤅
𐤁𐤌𐤉𐤍𐤇𐤄 𐤄𐤄𐤅𐤋𐤊𐤕 𐤋𐤐𐤍𐤉 𐤅𐤀𐤇𐤓𐤉 𐤊𐤍 𐤀𐤓𐤀𐤄 𐤐𐤍𐤉𐤅
𐤀𐤅𐤋𐤉 𐤉𐤎𐤀 𐤐𐤍𐤉 22 𐤅𐤕𐤏𐤁𐤅𐤓 𐤄𐤌𐤉𐤍𐤇𐤄 𐤏𐤋 𐤐𐤍𐤉𐤅
𐤅𐤄𐤅𐤀 𐤋𐤍 𐤁𐤋𐤉𐤋𐤄 𐤄𐤄𐤅𐤀 𐤁𐤌𐤇𐤍𐤄 23 𐤅𐤉𐤒𐤌 𐤁𐤋𐤉𐤋𐤄 𐤄𐤅𐤀
𐤅𐤉𐤒𐤇 𐤀𐤕 𐤔𐤕𐤉 𐤍𐤔𐤉𐤅 𐤅𐤀𐤕 𐤔𐤕𐤉 𐤔𐤉𐤐𐤇𐤕𐤉𐤅 𐤅𐤀𐤕
𐤀𐤇𐤃 𐤏𐤎𐤓 𐤉𐤋𐤃𐤉𐤅 𐤅𐤉𐤏𐤁𐤅𐤓 𐤀𐤕 𐤌𐤏𐤁𐤓 𐤉𐤁𐤅𐤒 24 𐤅𐤉𐤒𐤇𐤌
𐤅𐤉𐤏𐤁𐤓𐤌 𐤀𐤕 𐤄𐤍𐤇𐤋 𐤅𐤉𐤏𐤁𐤓 𐤀𐤕 𐤀𐤔𐤓 𐤋𐤅 25 𐤅𐤉𐤅𐤕𐤓
𐤉𐤏𐤒𐤅𐤁 𐤋𐤁𐤃𐤅 𐤅𐤉𐤀𐤁𐤒 𐤀𐤉𐤔 𐤏𐤉𐤌𐤅 𐤏𐤃 𐤏𐤋𐤅𐤕 𐤄𐤔𐤇𐤓
26 𐤅𐤉𐤓𐤀 𐤊𐤉 𐤋𐤅𐤀 𐤉𐤊𐤅𐤋 𐤋𐤅 𐤅𐤉𐤂𐤏 𐤁𐤊𐤐 𐤉𐤓𐤊𐤅 𐤅𐤕𐤒𐤏
𐤊𐤐 𐤉𐤓𐤊 𐤉𐤏𐤒𐤅𐤁 𐤁𐤄𐤀𐤁𐤒𐤅 𐤏𐤉𐤌𐤅 27 𐤅𐤉𐤅𐤀𐤌𐤓
𐤔𐤋𐤇𐤍𐤉 𐤊𐤉 𐤏𐤋𐤄 𐤄𐤔𐤇𐤓 𐤅𐤉𐤅𐤀𐤌𐤓 𐤋𐤅𐤀 𐤀𐤔𐤋𐤇𐤊𐤄 𐤊𐤉
𐤀𐤉𐤌 𐤁𐤓𐤊𐤕𐤍𐤉 28 𐤅𐤉𐤅𐤀𐤌𐤓 𐤀𐤋𐤉𐤅 𐤌𐤄 𐤔𐤌𐤊𐤄
𐤅𐤉𐤅𐤀𐤌𐤓 𐤉𐤏𐤒𐤅 29 𐤅𐤉𐤅𐤀𐤌𐤓 𐤋𐤅𐤀 𐤉𐤏𐤒𐤅𐤁 𐤉𐤀𐤌𐤓 𐤏𐤅𐤃
𐤔𐤉𐤌𐤊𐤄 𐤊𐤉 𐤀𐤉𐤌 𐤉𐤎𐤓𐤀𐤋 𐤊𐤉 𐤎𐤓𐤉𐤕 𐤏𐤉𐤌
𐤀𐤋𐤅𐤄𐤉𐤌 𐤅𐤏𐤉𐤌 𐤀𐤍𐤔𐤉𐤌 𐤅𐤕𐤅𐤊𐤋 30 𐤅𐤉𐤔𐤀𐤋 𐤉𐤏𐤒𐤅𐤁
𐤅𐤉𐤅𐤀𐤌𐤓 𐤄𐤂𐤉𐤃𐤄 𐤍𐤀 𐤔𐤌𐤊𐤄 𐤅𐤉𐤅𐤀𐤌𐤓 𐤋𐤌𐤄 𐤆𐤄
𐤕𐤉𐤔𐤀𐤋 𐤋𐤉𐤔𐤌𐤉 𐤅𐤉𐤁𐤓𐤊 𐤀𐤅𐤕𐤅 𐤔𐤌 31 𐤅𐤉𐤒𐤓𐤀
𐤉𐤏𐤒𐤅𐤁 𐤔𐤌 𐤄𐤌𐤒𐤅𐤌 𐤐𐤍𐤉𐤀𐤋 𐤊𐤉 𐤓𐤀𐤉𐤕𐤉
𐤀𐤋𐤅𐤄𐤉𐤌 𐤐𐤍𐤉𐤌 𐤀𐤋 𐤐𐤍𐤉𐤌 𐤅𐤕𐤉𐤍𐤑𐤋 𐤍𐤐𐤔𐤉
32 𐤅𐤉𐤆𐤓𐤇 𐤋𐤅 𐤄𐤔𐤌𐤔 𐤊𐤀𐤔𐤓 𐤏𐤁𐤓 𐤀𐤕 𐤐𐤍𐤅𐤀𐤋 𐤅𐤄𐤅𐤀
𐤑𐤅𐤋𐤏 𐤏𐤋 𐤉𐤓𐤊𐤅 33 𐤏𐤋 𐤊𐤍 𐤋𐤅𐤀 𐤉𐤅𐤀𐤊𐤋𐤅 𐤁𐤍𐤉 𐤉𐤎𐤓𐤀𐤋
𐤀𐤕 𐤂𐤉𐤃 𐤄𐤍𐤔𐤄 𐤀𐤔𐤓 𐤏𐤋 𐤊𐤐 𐤄𐤉𐤓𐤊 𐤏𐤃 𐤄𐤉𐤅𐤌 𐤄𐤆𐤄
𐤊𐤉 𐤍𐤂𐤏 𐤁𐤊𐤐 𐤉𐤓𐤊 𐤉𐤏𐤒𐤅𐤁 𐤁𐤂𐤉𐤃 𐤄𐤍𐤔𐤄

𐤁𐤓𐤀𐤔𐤉𐤕 𐤐𐤓𐤒 33

1 𐤅𐤉𐤎𐤀 𐤉𐤏𐤒𐤅𐤁 𐤏𐤉𐤍𐤉𐤅 𐤅𐤉𐤓𐤀 𐤅𐤄𐤉𐤍𐤄 𐤏𐤎𐤅 𐤁𐤀
𐤅𐤏𐤉𐤌𐤅 𐤀𐤓𐤁𐤏 𐤌𐤀𐤅𐤕 𐤀𐤉𐤔 𐤅𐤉𐤇𐤑 𐤀𐤕 𐤄𐤉𐤋𐤃𐤉𐤌 𐤏𐤋

לאה ועל רחל ועל שתי השפחות 2 ויסם את
השפחות ואת ילדיהן ריאשונה ואת לאה
וילדיה אחרונים ואת רחל ואת יוסף אחרונים
3 והוא עבר ליפניהם וישתחו ארצה שבע
פעמים עד גישתו עד אחיו 4 וירץ עסו
ליקראתו ויחבקהו ויפול על צוארו וישקהו
ויבכו 5 ויסא את עיניו וירא את הנשים ואת
הילדים ויואמר מי אלה לך ויואמר הילדים
אשר חנן אלוהים את עבדכה 6 ותיגשן
השפחות הנה וילדיהן ותישתחוין 7 ותיגש
גם לאה וילדיה וישתחוו ואחר ניגש יוסף
ורחל וישתחוו 8 ויואמר מי לכה כל המחנה הזה
אשר פגשתי ויואמר לימצוא חן בעיני
אדוני 9 ויואמר עסו יש לי רב אחי יהי לכה
אשר לך 10 ויואמר יעקוב אל נא אים נא
מצאתי חן בעיניכה ולקחת מינחתי מידי
כי על כן ראיתי פניכה כיראות פני
אלוהים ותירצני 11 קח נא את בירכתי אשר
הובאת לך כי חנני אלוהים וכי יש לי כול
ויפצר בו ויקח 12 ויואמר ניסעה ונלכה ואלכה
לנגדכה 13 ויואמר אליו אדוני יודע כי
הילדים רכים והצואן והבקר עלות עלי
ודפקום יום אחד ומתו כל הצואן 14 יעבר נא
אדוני ליפני עבדו ואני אתנהלה לאיטי
לרגל המלאכה אשר לפני ולרגל הילדים עד
אשר אבוא אל אדוני סעירה 15 ויואמר עסו
אציגה נא עימכה מין העם אשר איתי
ויואמר למה זה אמצא חן בעיני אדוני
16 וישב ביום ההוא עסו לדרכו סעירה 17 ויעקוב
נסע סוכותה ויבן לו ביית ולמיקנהו עסה סוכות
על כן קרא שם המקום סוכות 18 ויבוא יעקוב
שלם עיר שכם אשר בארץ כנען בבואו מיפדן
ארם ויחן את פני העיר 19 ויקן את חלקת
השדה אשר נטה שם אהלו מיד בני חמור אבי
שכם במאה קסיטה 20 ויצב שם מיזבח ויקרא לו
אל אלוהי יסראל

בראשית פרק 34

1 ותצא דינה בת לאה אשר ילדה ליעקוב ליראות
בבנות הארץ 2 וירא אותה שכם בן חמור

החוי נסיא הארץ ויקח אותה וישכב אותה
ויענה 3 ותדבק נפשו בדינה בת יעקוב
ויאהב את הנער וידבר על לב הנער 4 ויאמר
שכם אל חמור אביו לאמור קח לי את הילדה
הזואת לאישה 5 ויעקוב שמע כי טימא את
דינה ביתו ובניו היו את מיקנהו בסדה
והחריש יעקוב עדבואם 6 ויצא חמור אבי שכם
אל יעקוב לדבר איתו 7 ובני יעקוב באו מין
הסדה כשמעם ויתעצבו האנשים ויחר להם
מאוד כינבלה עסה ביסראל לישכב אתבת יעקוב
וכן לוא יעסה 8 וידבר חמור איתם לאמור שכם
בני חשקה נפשו בביתכם תנו נא אותה לו
לאישה 9 והיתחתנו אותנו בנותיכם תיתנו
לנו ואת בנותינו תיקחו לכם 10 ואיתנו תשבו
והארץ תיהיה ליפניכם שבו וסחרוה והאחזו
בה 11 ויואמר שכם אל אביה ואל אחיה אמצאחן
בעיניכם ואשר תואמרו אלי אתן 12 הרבו עלי
מאוד מוהר ומתן ואתנה כאשר תואמרו אלי ותנו
לי את הנער לאישה 13 ויענו בני יעקוב את
שכם ואת חמור אביו במירמה וידברו אשר
טימא את דינה אחותם 14 ויואמרו אליהם לוא
נוכל לעסות הדבר הזה לתת את אחותנו לאיש אשר
לו ערלה כי חרפה היוא לנו 15 אך בזואת נאות
לכם אים תהיו כמונו להימול לכם כל זכר
16 ונתנו את בנותינו לכם ואת בנותיכם ניקח
לנו וישבנו איתכם והיינו לעם אחד 17 ואים
לוא תישמעו אלינו להימול ולקחנו את ביתנו
והלכנו 18 וייטבו דבריהם בעיני חמור
ובעיני שכם בן חמור 19 ולוא אחר הנער לעסות
הדבר כי חפץ בבת יעקוב והוא נכבד מיכול
בית אביו 20 ויבוא חמור ושכם בנו אל שער
עירם וידברו אל אנשי עירם לאמור
21 האנשים האלה שלמים הם איתנו וישבו
בארץ וייסחרו אותה והארץ הינה רחבת
ידיים ליפניהם את בנותם ניקח לנו
לנשים ואת בנותינו ניתן להם 22 אכבזואת
יאותו לנו האנשים לשבת איתנו ליהיות
לעם אחד בהימול לנו כל זכר כאשר הם
נימולים 23 מיקנהם וקינינם וכלבהמתם
הלוא לנו הם אך נאותה להם וישבו איתנו
24 וישמעו אל חמור ואל שכם בנו כל יוצאי

[illegible]
[illegible] 25
[illegible]
[illegible]
[illegible] 26 [illegible]
[illegible] 27 [illegible]
[illegible]
[illegible] 28 [illegible]
[illegible]
[illegible] 29
[illegible] 30 [illegible]
[illegible]
[illegible]
[illegible]
[illegible] 31 [illegible]
[illegible]

35 [illegible]

[illegible] 1
[illegible]
[illegible] 2 [illegible]
[illegible]
[illegible]
[illegible] 3 [illegible]
[illegible]
[illegible] 4 [illegible]
[illegible]
[illegible]
[illegible] 5 [illegible]
[illegible]
[illegible] 6 [illegible]
[illegible]
[illegible] 7 [illegible]
[illegible]
[illegible] 8 [illegible]
[illegible]
[illegible] 9 [illegible]
[illegible] 10 [illegible]
[illegible]
[illegible]
[illegible] 11 [illegible]

פרה ורבה גוי וקהל גויים יהיה מימכה
ומלכים מחלציכה יצאו 12 ואת הארץ אשר
נתתי לאברהם ולייצחק לכה אתננה ולזרעכה
אחריכה אתן את הארץ 13 ויעל מעליו אלוהים
במקום אשר דיבר איתו 14 ויצב יעקוב מצבה
במקום אשר דיבר איתו מצבת אבן ויסך עליה
נסך ויצוק עליה שמן 15 ויקרא יעקוב את שם
המקום אשר דיבר איתו שם אלוהים בית אל
16 ויסעו מבית אל ויהי עוד כיברת הארץ
לבוא אפרתה ותלד רחל ותקש בלידתה 17 ויהי
בהקשותה בלידתה ותואמר לה המילדת אל
תיראי כי גם זה לך בן 18 ויהי בצאת נפשה
כי מתה ותיקרא שמו בן אוני ואביו קרא לו
בנימין 19 ותמת רחל ותיקבר בדרך אפרתה
הוא בית לחם 20 ויצב יעקוב מצבה על קבורתה
הוא מצבת קבורת רחל עד היום 21 ויסע יסראל
ויט אהלוה מהלאה למגידל עדר 22 ויהי
בישכון יסראל בארץ ההיוא וילך ראובן
וישכב את בילהה פילגש אביו וישמע
יסראל ויהיו בני יעקוב שנים עסר 23 בני
לאה בכור יעקוב ראובן ושימעון ולוי ויהודה
וייסשכר וזבולון 24 בני רחל יוסף
ובנימין 25 ובני בילהה שיפחת רחל דן
ונפתלי 26 ובני זילפה שיפחת לאה גד
ואשר אלה בני יעקוב אשר יולד לו בפדן ארם
27 ויבוא יעקוב אל יצחק אביו ממרא קירית
הארבע הוא חברון אשר גר שם אברהם וייצחק
28 ויהיו ימי יצחק מאת שנה ושמונים
שנה 29 ויגוע יצחק וימת ויאסף אל עמיו
זקן וסבע ימים ויקברו אותו עסו ויעקוב בניו

בראשית פרק 36

1 ואלה תולדות עסו הוא אדום 2 עסו לקח את נשיו
מיבנות כנען את עדה בת אילון החיתי ואת
אהליבמה בת ענה בת ציבעון החיוי 3 ואת
בסמת בת ישמעאל אחות נביות 4 ותלד עדה לעסו
את אליפז ובסמת ילדה את רעואל 5 ואהליבמה
ילדה את יעיש ואת יעלם ואת קורח אלה בני
עסו אשר יולדו לו בארץ כנען 6 ויקח עסו את
נשיו ואת בניו ואת בנותיו ואת כל נפשות

יסראל 32 וימלוך באדום בלע בן בעור ושם עירו
דינהבה 33 וימת בלע וימלוך תחתיו יובב בן
זרח מיבצרה 34 וימת יובב וימלוך תחתיו
חושם מארץ התימני 35 וימת חושם וימלוך
תחתיו הדד בן בדד המכה את מידין ביסדה מואב
ושם עירו עוית 36 וימת הדד וימלוך תחתיו
סמלה מימסרקה 37 וימת סמלה וימלוך תחתיו
שאול מרחובות הנהר 38 וימת שאול וימלוך
תחתיו בעל חנן בן עכבור 39 וימת בעל חנן בן
עכבור וימלוך תחתיו הדר ושם עירו פעו ושם
אישתו מהיטבאל בת מטרד בת מי זה 40 ואלה
שמות אלופי עסו למשפחותם לימקומותם
בישמותם אלוף תימנע אלוף עלוה אלוף
יתת 41 אלוף אהליבמה אלוף אלה אלוף
פינן 42 אלוף קנז אלוף תימן אלוף
מיבצר 43 אלוף מגדיאל אלוף עירם אלוף
אלופי אדום למושבותם בארץ אחוזתם הוא עסו
אבי אדום

בראשית פרק 37

1 וישב יעקוב בארץ מגורי אביו בארץ כנען
2 אלה תולדות יעקוב יוסף בן שבע עסרה שנה
היה רועה את אחיו בצואן והוא נער את בני
בילהה ואת בני זילפה נשי אביו ויבא
יוסף את דיבתם רעה אל אביהם 3 וישראל אהב
את יוסף מיכל בניו כי בן זקונים הוא לו
ועסה לו כתונת פסים 4 ויראו אחיו כי אותו אהב
אביהם מיכל אחיו ויסנאו אותו ולוא יכלו דברו
לשלום 5 ויחלום יוסף חלום ויגד לאחיו
ויוסיפו עוד סנוא אותו 6 ויואמר אליהם
שימעו נא החלום הזה אשר חלמתי 7 והינה
אנחנו מאלמים אלומים בתוך הסדה והינה
קמה אלומתי וגם ניצבה והינה תסובינה
אלומותיכם ותישתחוינה לאלומתי 8 ויואמרו
לו אחיו המלוך תימלוך עלינו אים משול
תימשול בנו ויוסיפו עוד סנוא אותו על
חלומותיו ועל דבריו 9 ויחלום עוד חלום אחר
ויספר אותו לאחיו ויואמר הינה חלמתי חלום
עוד והינה השמש והירח ואחד עסר כוכבים
מישתחוים לי 10 ויספר אל אביו ואל אחיו

11
12
13
14
15
16
17
18
19
20
21
22
23
24
25
26
27
28
29
30
31

סעיר עיזים ויטבלו את הכותונת בדם
32 וישלחו את כתונת הפסים ויביאו אל
אביהם ויואמרו זואת מצאנו הכר נא הכתונת
בינכה היוא אים לוא 33 ויכירה ויואמר
כתונת בני חיה רעה אכלתהו טרוף טורף יוס
34 ויקרע יעקוב סימלותיו ויסם סק במתניו
ויתאבל על בנו ימים רבים 35 ויקומו כל
בניו וכל בנותיו לנחמו וימאן להיתנחם
ויואמר כי ארד אל בני אבל שאולה ויבך אותו
אביו 36 והמדנים מכרו אותו אל מיצריים
לפוטיפר סריס פרעוה סר הטבחים

בראשית פרק 38

1 ויהי בעת ההיוא וירד יהודה מאת אחיו ויט
עד איש עדולמי ושמו חירה 2 וירא שם יהודה
בת איש כנעני ושמו שוע ויקחה ויבוא אליה
3 ותהר ותלד בן ויקרא את שמו ער 4 ותהר עוד ותלד
בן ותיקרא את שמו אונן 5 ותוסף עוד ותלד בן
ותיקרא את שמו שלה והיה ביכזיב בלידתה
אותו 6 ויקח יהודה אישה לער בכורו ושמה תמר
7 ויהי ער בכור יהודה רע בעיני יהוה
וימיתהו יהוה 8 ויואמר יהודה לאונן בוא אל
אשת אחיכה ויבם אותה והקם זרע לאחיכה
9 וידע אונן כי לוא לו יהיה הזרע והיה אים
בא אל אשת אחיו ושיחת ארצה לבילתי נתן
זרע לאחיו 10 וירע בעיני יהוה אשר עסה
וימת גם אותו 11 ויואמר יהודה לתמר כלתו
שבי אלמנה בית אביך עד יגדל שלה בני כי
אמר פן ימות גם הוא כאחיו ותלך תמר ותשב
בית אביה 12 וירבו הימים ותמת בת שוע אשת
יהודה וינחם יהודה ויעל על גוזזי צואנו
הוא וחירה רעהו העדולמי תימנתה 13 ויגד
לתמר לאמור הינה חמיך עלה תימנתה לגוז
צואנו 14 ותסר ביגדי אלמנותה מעליה ותכס
בצעיף ותיתעלף ותשב בפתח עיניים אשר
על דרך תימנתה כי ראתה כי גדל שלה והיוא
לוא ניתנה לו לאישה 15 ויראה יהודה
ויחשבה לזונה כי כיסתה פניה 16 ויט אליה
אל הדרך ויואמר הבה נא אבוא אלייך כי לוא
ידע כי כלתו היוא ותואמר מה תיתן לי כי

17
18
19
20
21
22
23
24
25
26
27
28
29
30

39

1
2
3
4
5

[illegible]
[illegible] 6 [illegible]
[illegible]
7 [illegible]
[illegible]
8 [illegible]
[illegible] 9 [illegible]
[illegible]
[illegible] 10 [illegible]
[illegible]
[illegible] 11 [illegible]
[illegible]
[illegible] 12 [illegible]
[illegible]
[illegible] 13 [illegible]
[illegible] 14 [illegible]
[illegible]
[illegible] 15 [illegible]
[illegible]
16 [illegible]
17 [illegible]
[illegible] 18 [illegible]
[illegible]
[illegible] 19 [illegible]
[illegible]
[illegible] 20 [illegible]
[illegible]
[illegible] 21 [illegible]
[illegible] 22 [illegible]
[illegible]
[illegible] 23 [illegible]
[illegible]

בראשית פרק 40

1 ויהי אחר הדברים האלה חטאו משקה מלך
מיצריים והאופה לאדוניהם למלך
מיצריים 2 ויקצוף פרעוה על שני
סריסיו על סר המשקים ועל סר האופים
3 ויתן אותם במישמר בית סר הטבחים אל
בית הסוהר מקום אשר יוסף אסור שם 4 ויפקוד
סר הטבחים את יוסף איתם וישרת אותם
ויהיו ימים במישמר 5 ויחלמו חלום
שניהם איש חלומו בלילה אחד איש
כפיתרון חלומו המשקה והאופה אשר למלך
מיצריים אשר אסורים בבית הסוהר 6 ויבוא
אליהם יוסף בבוקר וירא אותם והינם
זועפים 7 וישאל את סריסי פרעוה אשר
איתו במישמר בית אדוניו לאמור מדוע
פניכם רעים היום 8 ויואמרו אליו חלום
חלמנו ופותר אין אותו ויואמר אלהם יוסף
הלוא לאלוהים פיתרונים ספרו נא לי
9 ויספר סר המשקים את חלומו ליוסף ויואמר
לו בחלומי והינה גפן לפני 10 ובגפן
שלושה סריגים והיא כפורחת עלתה ניצה
הבשילו אשכלותיה ענבים 11 וכוס פרעוה
בידי ואקח את הענבים ואסחט אותם אל כוס
פרעוה ואתן את הכוס על כף פרעוה 12 ויואמר
לו יוסף זה פיתרונו שלושת הסריגים
שלושת ימים הם 13 בעוד שלושת ימים יסא
פרעוה את רואשכה והשיבכה על כנכה ונתת כוס
פרעוה בידו כמישפט הריאשון אשר היית
משקהו 14 כי אים זכרתני איתכה כאשר
ייטב לך ועסית נא עימדי חסד והיזכרתני
אל פרעוה והוצאתני מין הביית הזה 15 כי
גונב גונבתי מארץ העיברים וגם פוה לוא
עסיתי מאומה כי סמו אותי בבור 16 וירא סר
האופים כי טוב פתר ויואמר אל יוסף אף
אני בחלומי והינה שלושה סלי חורי על
רואשי 17 ובסל העליון מיכול מאכל פרעוה
מעסה אופה והעוף אוכל אותם מין הסל מעל
רואשי 18 ויען יוסף ויואמר זה פיתרונו
שלושת הסלים שלושת ימים הם 19 בעוד
שלושת ימים יסא פרעוה את רואשכה

מעליכה ותלה אותכה על עץ ואכל העוף את בסרכה
מעליכה 20 ויהי ביום השלישי יום הולדת
את פרעוה ויעס מישתה לכל עבדיו ויסא את
רואש סר המשקים ואת רואש סר האופים בתוך
עבדיו 21 וישב את סר המשקים על משקהו
ויתן הכוס על כף פרעוה 22 ואת סר האופים
תלה כאשר פתר להם יוס 23 ולוא זכר סר
המשקים את יוסף וישכחהו

בראשית פרק 41

1 ויהי מיקץ שנתיים ימים ופרעוה
חולם והינה עומד על היאור 2 והינה מין
היאור עולות שבע פרות יפות מראה ובריאות
בסר ותירעינה באחו 3 והינה שבע פרות אחרות
עולות אחריהן מין היאור רעות מראה ודקות
בסר ותעמודנה אצל הפרות על ספת היאור
4 ותאכלנה הפרות רעות המראה ודקות הבסר את
שבע הפרות יפות המראה והבריאות וייקץ
פרעוה 5 ויישן ויחלום שנית והינה שבע
שיבלים עולות בקנה אחד בריאות וטובות
6 והינה שבע שיבלים דקות ושדופות קדים
צומחות אחריהן 7 ותבלענה השיבלים הדקות
את שבע השיבלים הבריאות והמלאות וייקץ
פרעוה והינה חלום 8 ויהי בבוקר ותיפעם
רוחו ויישלח ויקרא את כל חרטומי מיצריים
ואת כל חכמיה ויספר פרעוה להם את חלומו
ואין פותר אותם לפרעוה 9 וידבר סר
המשקים את פרעוה לאמור את חטאי אני
מזכיר היום 10 פרעוה קצף על עבדיו ויתן
אותי במישמר בית סר הטבחים אותי ואת סר
האופים 11 ונחלמה חלום בלילה אחד אני והוא
איש כפיתרון חלומו חלמנו 12 ושם איתנו
נער עיברי עבד לסר הטבחים ונספר לו ויפתר
לנו את חלומותינו איש כחלומו פתר 13 ויהי
כאשר פתר לנו כן היה אותי השיב על כני
ואותו תלה 14 ויישלח פרעוה ויקרא את יוסף
ויריצוהו מין הבור ויגלח ויחלף סימלותיו
ויבוא אל פרעוה 15 ויואמר פרעוה אל יוסף
חלום חלמתי ופותר אין אותו ואני שמעתי
עליכה לאמור תישמע חלום ליפתור אותו

16 ויען יוסף את פרעוה לאמור בילעדי
אלוהים יענה את שלום פרעוה 17 וידבר
פרעוה אל יוסף בחלומי הינני עומד על
ספת היאור 18 והינה מין היאור עולות שבע
פרות בריאות בסר ויפות תואר ותירעינה באחו
19 והינה שבע פרות אחרות עולות אחריהן דלות
ורעות תואר מאוד ורקות בסר לוא ראיתי כהנה בכל
ארץ מיצריים לרוע 20 ותואכלנה הפרות
הרקות והרעות את שבע הפרות הריאשונות
הבריאות 21 ותבואנה אל קירבנה ולוא נודע כי
באו אל קירבנה ומראיהן רע כאשר בתחילה
ואיקץ 22 וארא בחלומי והינה שבע שיבלים
עולות בקנה אחד מלאות וטובות 23 והינה שבע
שיבלים צנומות דקות שדופות קדים צומחות
אחריהם 24 ותיבלען השיבלים הדקות את שבע
השיבלים הטובות ואומר אל החרטומים ואין
מגיד לי 25 ויואמר יוסף אל פרעוה חלום
פרעוה אחד הוא את אשר האלוהים עוסה היגיד
לפרעוה 26 שבע פרות הטובות שבע שנים הנה
ושבע השיבלים הטובות שבע שנים הנה חלום
אחד הוא 27 ושבע הפרות הרקות והרעות העולות
אחריהן שבע שנים הנה ושבע השיבלים
הרקות שדופות הקדים יהיו שבע שני רע
28 הוא הדבר אשר דיברתי אל פרעוה אשר
האלוהים עוסה הראה את פרעוה 29 הינה שבע
שנים באות סבע גדול בכל ארץ מיצריים
30 וקמו שבע שני רעב אחריהן ונישכח כל
הסבע בארץ מיצריים וכילה הרעב את הארץ
31 ולוא יודע הסבע בארץ מיפני הרעב ההוא
אחרי כן כי כבד הוא מאוד 32 ועל הישנות
החלום אל פרעוה פעמיים כי נכון הדבר
מעים האלוהים וממהר האלוהים לעסותו
33 ועתה ירא פרעוה איש נבון וחכם וישיתהו
על ארץ מיצריים 34 יעסה פרעוה ויפקד
פקידים על הארץ וחימש את ארץ
מיצריים בשבע שני הסבע 35 וייקבצו את
כל אוכל השנים הטובות הבאות האלה וייצברו בר
תחת יד פרעוה אוכל בערים ושמרו 36 והיה
האוכל לפיקדון לארץ לשבע שני הרעב אשר
תיהיין בארץ מיצריים ולוא תיכרת הארץ
ברעב 37 וייטב הדבר בעיני פרעוה ובעיני

כל עבדיו 38 ויואמר פרעוה אל עבדיו
הנימצא כזה איש אשר רוח אלוהים בו
39 ויואמר פרעוה אל יוסף אחרי הודיע
אלוהים אותכה את כל זואת אין נבון וחכם
כמוכה 40 אתה תיהיה על ביתי ועל פיכה
ישק כל עמי רק הכיסא אגדל מימכה
41 ויואמר פרעוה אל יוסף ראה נתתי אותכה
על כל ארץ מיצריים 42 ויסר פרעוה את
טבעתו מעל ידו ויתן אתה על יד יוסף וילבש
אותו ביגדי שש ויסם רביד הזהב על צוארו
43 וירכב אותו במירכבת המישנה אשר לו
ויקראו לפניו אברך ונתון אותו על כל ארץ
מיצריים 44 ויואמר פרעוה אל יוסף אני
פרעוה ובילעדיכה לוא ירים איש את ידו
ואת רגלו בכל ארץ מיצריים 45 ויקרא פרעוה
שם יוסף צפנת פענח ויתן לו את אסנת בת
פוטי פרע כוהן און לאישה ויצא יוסף על
ארץ מיצריים 46 ויוסף בן שלושים שנה
בעמדו ליפני פרעוה מלך מיצריים ויצא
יוסף מיליפני פרעוה ויעבור בכל ארץ
מיצריים 47 ותעס הארץ בשבע שני הסבע
ליקמצים 48 ויקבוץ את כל אוכל שבע שנים
אשר היו בארץ מיצריים ויתן אוכל בערים
אוכל סדה העיר אשר סביבותיה נתן בתוכה
49 ויצבור יוסף בר כחול הים הרבה מאוד עד כי
חדל ליספור כי אין מיספר 50 וליוסף יולד
שני בנים בטרם תבוא שנת הרעב אשר ילדהלו
אסנת בת פוטי פרע כוהן און 51 ויקרא יוסף
את שם הבכור מנשה כי נשני אלוהים את כל
עמלי ואת כל בית אבי 52 ואת שם השני קרא
אפריים כי היפרני אלוהים בארץ
עניי 53 ותיכלינה שבע שני הסבע אשר
היה בארץ מיצריים 54 ותחילינה שבע
שני הרעב לבוא כאשר אמר יוסף ויהי רעב
בכל הארצות ובכל ארץ מיצריים היה לחם
55 ותירעב כל ארץ מיצריים ויצעק העם אל
פרעוה ללחם ויואמר פרעוה לכל מיצריים
לכו אל יוסף אשר יואמר לכם תעסו 56 והרעב
היה על כל פני הארץ ויפתח יוסף את כל
אשר בהם וישבור למיצריים ויחזק הרעב

[illegible] 57 [illegible]
[illegible]

42 [illegible]

[illegible] 1
[illegible] 2 [illegible]
[illegible]
[illegible]
[illegible] 3
[illegible] 4 [illegible]
[illegible]
[illegible] 5 [illegible]
[illegible] 6 [illegible]
[illegible]
[illegible]
[illegible] 7
[illegible]
[illegible]
[illegible] 8 [illegible]
[illegible] 9
[illegible]
[illegible] 10 [illegible]
[illegible] 11 [illegible]
[illegible]
[illegible] 12 [illegible]
[illegible] 13 [illegible]
[illegible]
[illegible]
[illegible] 14
[illegible] 15 [illegible]
[illegible]
[illegible] 16 [illegible]
[illegible]
[illegible]
[illegible] 17
[illegible] 18
[illegible] 19 [illegible]
[illegible]
[illegible]
[illegible] 20

דיבריכם ולוא תמותו ויעסו כן 21 ויואמרו
איש אל אחיו אבל אשמים אנחנו על אחינו
אשר ראינו צרת נפשו בהיתחננו אלינו ולוא
שמענו על כן באה אלינו הצרה הזואת
22 ויען ראובן אותם לאמור הלוא אמרתי
אליכם לאמור אל תחטאו בילד ולוא שמעתם וגם
דמו הינה נידרש 23 והם לוא ידעו כי שומע
יוסף כי המליץ בינותם 24 ויסוב מעליהם
ויבך וישב אלהם וידבר אלהם ויקח מאיתם את
שמעון ויאסור אותו לעיניהם 25 ויצו
יוסף וימלאו את כליהם בר ולהשיב כספיהם
איש אל סקו ולתת להם צדה לדרך ויעס להם כן
26 ויסאו את שיברם על חמוריהם וילכו
מישם 27 ויפתח האחד את סקו לתת מיספוא
לחמורו במלון וירא את כספו והינה הוא בפי
אמתחתו 28 ויואמר אל אחיו הושב כספי וגם
הינה באמתחתי ויצא לבם ויחרדו איש אל
אחיו לאמור מה זואת עסה אלוהים לנו
29 ויבואו אל יעקב אביהם ארצה כנען
ויגידו לו את כל הקורות אותם לאמור 30 דיבר
האיש אדוני הארץ איתנו קשות ויתן אותנו
כימרגלים את הארץ 31 ונואמר אליו כנים
אנחנו לוא היינו מרגלים 32 שנים עסר
אנחנו אחים בני אבינו האחד איננו והקטון
היום את אבינו בארץ כנען 33 ויואמר אלינו
האיש אדוני הארץ בזואת אדע כי כנים אתם
אחיכם האחד הניחו איתי ואת רעבון בתיכם
קחו ולכו 34 והביאו את אחיכם הקטון אלי ואדעה
כי לוא מרגלים אתם כי כנים אתם את
אחיכם אתן לכם ואת הארץ תיסחרו 35 ויהי הם
מריקים סקיהם והינה איש צרור כספו בסקו
ויראו את צרורות כספיהם המה ואביהם
וייראו 36 ויואמר אלהם יעקב אביהם אותי
שיכלתם יוסף איננו ושמעון איננו ואת
בינימין תיקחו עלי היו כולנה 37 ויואמר
ראובן אל אביו לאמור את שני בני תמית
אים לוא אביאנו אליכה תנה אותו על ידי
ואני אשיבנו אליכה 38 ויואמר לוא ירד בני
עימכם כי אחיו מת והוא לבדו נישאר וקראהו
אסון בדרך אשר תלכו בה והורדתם את סיבתי
ביגון שאולה

43 [illegible]

[illegible] 2 [illegible] 1
[illegible]
[illegible]
[illegible] 3
[illegible]
[illegible] 4 [illegible]
[illegible] 5 [illegible]
[illegible]
[illegible] 6 [illegible]
[illegible]
[illegible] 7 [illegible]
[illegible]
[illegible]
[illegible] 8 [illegible]
[illegible]
[illegible]
[illegible] 9 [illegible]
[illegible]
[illegible] 10 [illegible]
[illegible]
[illegible] 11
[illegible]
[illegible]
[illegible] 12 [illegible]
[illegible]
[illegible] 13 [illegible]
[illegible] 14 [illegible]
[illegible]
[illegible]
[illegible] 15 [illegible]
[illegible]
[illegible]
[illegible] 16 [illegible]
[illegible]
[illegible]
[illegible] 17 [illegible]
[illegible]
[illegible] 18 [illegible]
[illegible]
[illegible]

ולהיתנפל עלינו ולקחת אותנו לעבדים ואת
חמורינו 19 ויגשו אל האיש אשר על בית
יוסף וידברו אליו פתח הביית 20 ויואמרו בי
אדוני ירוד ירדנו בתחילה לישבר אוכל
21 ויהי כי באנו אל המלון וניפתחה את
אמתחותינו והינה כסף איש בפי אמתחתו
כספנו במישקלו ונשב אותו בידנו 22 וכסף אחר
הורדנו בידנו לישבר אוכל לוא ידענו מי שם
כספנו באמתחותינו 23 ויואמר שלום לכם אל
תיראו אלוהיכם ואלוהי אביכם נתן לכם
מטמון באמתחותיכם כספכם בא אלי ויוצא
אלהם את שימעון 24 ויבא האיש את
האנשים ביתה יוסף ויתן מים וירחצו
רגליהם ויתן מספוא לחמוריהם
25 ויכינו את המינחה עד בוא יוסף
בצהריים כי שמעו כי שם יואכלו לחם
26 ויבוא יוסף הביתה ויביאו לו את המינחה
אשר בידם הביתה וישתחוו לו ארצה 27 וישאל
להם לשלום ויואמר השלום אביכם הזקן אשר
אמרתם העודנו חי 28 ויואמרו שלום לעבדכה
לאבינו עודנו חי ויקדו וישתחוו 29 וישא
עיניו וירא את בינימין אחיו בן אימו
ויואמר הזה אחיכם הקטון אשר אמרתם אלי
ויואמר אלהים יחנכה בני 30 וימהר יוסף
כי ניכמרו רחמיו אל אחיו ויבקש לבכות
ויבוא החדרה ויבך שמה 31 וירחץ פניו ויצא
ויתאפק ויואמר שימו לחם 32 וישימו לו לבדו
ולהם לבדם ולמיצרים האוכלים איתו לבדם
כי לוא יוכלון המיצרים לאכול את
העיברים לחם כי תועבה היוא למיצריים
33 וישבו לפניו הבכור כיבכורתו והצעיר
כיצעירתו ויתמהו האנשים איש אל רעהו
34 וישא משאות מאת פניו אלהם ותרב משאת
בינימין מימשאות כולם חמש ידות וישתו
וישכרו עימו

בראשית פרק 44

1 ויצו את אשר על ביתו לאמור מלא את אמתחות
האנשים אוכל כאשר יוכלון שאת ושים כסף
איש בפי אמתחתו 2 ואת גביעי גביע הכסף
תשים בפי אמתחת הקטון ואת כסף שיברו ויעש

כידבר יוסף אשר דיבר 3 הבוקר אור והאנשים
שולחו המה וחמוריהם 4 הם יצאו את העיר לוא
הירחיקו ויוסף אמר לאשר על ביתו קום רדוף
אחרי האנשים והיסגתם ואמרת אלהם למה
שילמתם רעה תחת טובה 5 הלוא זה אשר ישתה
אדוני בו והוא נחש ינחש בו הרעותם אשר
עסיתם 6 ויסיגם וידבר אלהם את הדברים
האלה 7 ויואמרו אליו למה ידבר אדוני
כדברים האלה חלילה לעבדיכה מעסות כדבר הזה
8 הן כסף אשר מצאנו בפי אמתחותינו
השיבונו אליכה מארץ כנען ואיך ניגנוב
מיבית אדוניכה כסף או זה 9 אשר ימצא
איתו מעבדיכה ומת וגם אנחנו ניהיה
לאדוני לעבדים 10 ויואמר גם עתה
כדיבריכם כן הוא אשר ימצא איתו יהיה לי
עבד ואתם תיהיו נקים 11 וימהרו ויורידו
איש את אמתחתו ארצה ויפתחו איש אמתחתו
12 ויחפס בגדול החל ובקטון כילה וימצא
הגביע באמתחת בינימין 13 ויקרעו
סימלותם ויעמוס איש על חמורו וישובו
העירה 14 ויבוא יהודה ואחיו ביתה יוסף והוא
עודנו שם ויפלו לפניו ארצה 15 ויואמר להם
יוסף מה המעסה הזה אשר עסיתם הלוא
ידעתם כי נחש ינחש איש אשר כמוני
16 ויואמר יהודה מה נואמר לאדוני מה נדבר
ומה ניצטדק האלוהים מצא את עון עבדיכה
היננו עבדים לאדוני גם אנחנו גם אשר
נימצא הגביע בידו 17 ויואמר חלילה לי
מעסות זואת האיש אשר נימצא הגביע בידו
הוא יהיה לי עבד ואתם עלו לשלום אל אביכם
18 ויגש אליו יהודה ויואמר בי אדוני ידבר
נא עבדכה דבר באזני אדוני ואל יחר אפכה
בעבדכה כי כמוכה כפרעוה 19 אדוני שאל את
עבדיו לאמור היש לכם אב או אח 20 ונואמר אל
אדוני יש לנו אב זקן וילד זקונים קטן
ואחיו מת ויותר הוא לבדו לאימו ואביו אהבו
21 ותואמר אל עבדיכה הורידוהו אלי ואסימה
עיני עליו 22 ונואמר אל אדוני לוא יוכל
הנער לעזוב את אביו ועזב את אביו ומת
23 ותואמר אל עבדיכה אים לוא ירד אחיכם
הקטון איתכם לוא תוסיפון ליראות פני

[illegible] 3
[illegible] 4 [illegible]
[illegible]
[illegible]
[illegible] 5 [illegible]
[illegible]
[illegible]
[illegible] 6 [illegible]
[illegible]
[illegible] 7 [illegible]
[illegible]
[illegible]
[illegible] 8
[illegible] 9
[illegible]
[illegible] 10
[illegible]
[illegible] 11
[illegible]
[illegible] 12 [illegible]
[illegible] 13 [illegible]
[illegible]
[illegible]
[illegible] 14 [illegible]
[illegible]
[illegible]
[illegible] 15
[illegible]
[illegible]
[illegible] 16
[illegible]
[illegible]
[illegible] 17
[illegible]
[illegible]
[illegible] 18 [illegible]
[illegible]
[illegible] 19
[illegible]
[illegible]
[illegible] 20 [illegible]

יברך ישראל לאמור ישמכה אלוהים
כאפרים וכימנשה וישם את אפרים
ליפני מנשה 21 ויאמר ישראל אל יוסף
הנה אנוכי מת והיה אלוהים עימכם
והשיב אתכם אל ארץ אבותיכם 22 ואני נתתי
לכה שכם אחד על אחיכה אשר לקחתי מיד
האמורי בחרבי ובקשתי

בראשית פרק 49

1 ויקרא יעקוב אל בניו ויאמר האספו
ואגידה לכם את אשר יקרא אתכם באחרית
הימים 2 היקבצו ושימעו בני יעקוב
ושימעו אל ישראל אביכם 3 ראובן בכורי אתה
כוחי וראשית אוני יתר שאת ויתר עז 4 פחז
כמים אל תותר כי עלית מישכבי אביכה
אז חיללת יצועי עלה 5 שימעון ולוי אחים
כלי חמס מכרותיהם 6 בסודם אל תבוא נפשי
בקהלם אל תחד כבודי כי באפם הרגו איש
ובירצונם עיקרו שור 7 ארור אפם כי עז
ועברתם כי קשתה אחלקם ביעקוב ואפיצם
בישראל 8 יהודה אתה יודוכה אחיכה ידכה
בעורף אויביכה ישתחוו לכה בני אביכה 9 גור
אריה יהודה מיטרף בני עלית כרע רבץ
כאריה וכלביא מי יקימנו 10 לוא יסור שבט
מיהודה ומחוקק מבין רגליו עד כי יבוא
שילה ולו יקהת עמים 11 אוסרי לגפן
עירה ולשורקה בני אתונו כיבס ביין לבושו
ובדם ענבים סותה 12 חכלילי עינים
מיין ולבן שינים מחלב 13 זבולון לחוף
ימים ישכון והוא לחוף אוניות וירכתו על
צידון 14 יששכר חמור גרם רובץ בין
המישפתים 15 וירא מנוחה כי טוב ואת
הארץ כי נעמה ויט שכמו ליסבול ויהי למס
עובד 16 דן ידין עמו כאחד שבטי ישראל
17 יהי דן נחש עלי דרך שפיפון עלי אורח
הנושך עיקבי סוס ויפול רוכבו אחור
18 לישועתכה קיויתי יהוה 19 גד גדוד יגודנו
והוא יגוד עקב 20 מאשר שמנה לחמו והוא יתן
מעדני מלך 21 נפתלי אילה שלוחה הנותן
אמרי שפר 22 בן פורת יוסף בן פורת עלי

עין בנות צעדה עלי שור 23 וימררוהו ורובו
ויסטמוהו בעלי חיצים 24 ותשב באיתן קשתו
ויפוזו זרועי ידיו מידי אביר יעקוב
מישם רועה אבן יסראל 25 מאל אביכה
ויעזרכה ואת שדי ויברככה בירכות שמים
מעל בירכות תהום רובצת תחת בירכות שדים
ורחם 26 בירכות אביכה גברו על בירכות הורי עד
תאות גיבעות עולם תיהיין לרואש יוסף
ולקדקוד נזיר אחיו 27 בינימין זאב יטרף
בבוקר יואכל עד ולערב יחלק שלל 28 כל אלה
שיבטי יסראל שנים עסר וזואת אשר דיבר
להם אביהם ויברך אותם איש אשר כבירכתו
ברך אותם 29 ויצו אותם ויואמר אלהם אני
נאסף אל עמי קיברו אותי אל אבותי אל
המערה אשר ביסדה עפרון החיתי 30 במערה
אשר ביסדה המכפלה אשר על פני ממרא
בארץ כנען אשר קנה אברהם את הסדה מאת
עפרון החיתי לאחוזת קבר 31 שמה קוברו את
אברהם ואת סרה אשתו שמה קוברו את יצחק ואת
ריבקה אשתו ושמה קברתי את לאה 32 מיקנה
הסדה והמערה אשר בו מאת בני חת 33 ויכל
יעקוב לצות את בניו ויאסוף רגליו אל המיטה
ויגוע ויאסף אל עמיו

בראשית פרק 50

1 ויפול יוסף על פני אביו ויבך עליו
וישק לו 2 ויצו יוסף את עבדיו את הרופאים
לחנוט את אביו ויחנטו הרופאים את יסראל
3 וימלאו לו ארבעים יום כי כן ימלאו ימי
החנוטים ויבכו אותו מיצרים שיבעים
יום 4 ויעברו ימי בכיתו וידבר יוסף אל
בית פרעוה לאמור אים נא מצאתי חן
בעיניכם דברו נא באזני פרעוה לאמור
5 אבי השביעני לאמור הינה אנוכי מת
בקברי אשר כריתי לי בארץ כנען שמה
תקברני ועתה אעלה נא ואקברה את אבי
ואשובה 6 ויאמר פרעוה עלה וקבור את אביכה
כאשר השביעכה 7 ויעל יוסף ליקבור את
אביו ויעלו אתו כל עבדי פרעוה זקני
ביתו וכול זקני ארץ מיצרים 8 וכול בית
יוסף ואחיו ובית אביו רק טפם וצואנם ובקרם

עזבו בארץ גושן 9 ויעל עימו גם רכב גם
פרשים ויהי המחנה כבד מאוד 10 ויבואו עד
גורן האטד אשר בעבר הירדן ויספדו שם
מיספד גדול וכבד מאוד ויעס לאביו אבל שיבעת
ימים 11 וירא יושב הארץ הכנעני את האבל
בגורן האטד ויואמרו אבל כבד זה למיצריים
על כן קרא שמה אבל מיצריים אשר בעבר
הירדן 12 ויעסו בניו לו כן כאשר ציום
13 ויסאו אותו בניו ארצה כנען ויקברו אותו
בימערת סדה המכפלה אשר קנה אברהם את הסדה
לאחוזת קבר מאת עפרון החיתי על פני
ממרא 14 וישב יוסף מיצריימה הוא ואחיו וכל
העולים איתו ליקבור את אביו אחרי קברו את
אביו 15 ויראו אחי יוסף כי מת אביהם
ויואמרו לו יסטמנו יוסף והשב ישיב לנו את
כל הרעה אשר גמלנו אותו 16 ויצוו אל
יוסף לאמור אביכה ציוה ליפני מותו לאמור 17 כוה
תואמרו ליוסף אנא סא נא פשע אחיכה
וחטאתם כי רעה גמלוכה ועתה סא נא לפשע
עבדי אלהי אביכה ויבך יוסף בדברם אליו
18 וילכו גם אחיו ויפלו ליפניו ויואמרו
היננו לכה לעבדים 19 ויואמר אלהם יוסף אל
תיראו כי התחת אלהים אני 20 ואתם חשבתם
עלי רעה אלהים חשבה לטובה למען עסוה
כיום הזה להחיות עם ר 21 ועתה אל תיראו
אנוכי אכלכל אתכם ואת טפכם וינחם אותם
וידבר על ליבם 22 וישב יוסף במיצריים
הוא ובית אביו ויחי יוסף מאה ועסר שנים
23 וירא יוסף לאפריים בני שילשים גם
בני מכיר בן מנשה יולדו על בירכי יוס
24 ויואמר יוסף אל אחיו אנוכי מת ואלהים
פוקד יפוקד אתכם והעלה אתכם מין הארץ
הזואת אל הארץ אשר נישבע לאברהם לייצחק
וליעקב 25 וישבע יוסף את בני יסראל לאמור
פוקד יפוקד אלהים אתכם והעליתם את
עצמותי מיזה 26 וימת יוסף בן מאה ועסר
שנים ויחנטו אותו וייסם בארון
במיצריים

שמות

shemot / Exodus

שמות פרק 1

1 ואלה שמות בני יסראל הבאים מיצרימה
את יעקוב איש וביתו באו 2 ראובן שימעון
לוי ויהודה 3 יסשכר זבולון ובינימין 4 דן
ונפתלי גד ואשר 5 ויהי כל נפש יוצאי
ירך יעקוב שיבעים נפש ויוסף היה
במיצריים 6 וימת יוסף וכל אחיו וכול הדור
ההוא 7 ובני יסראל פרו וישרצו וירבו
ויעצמו בימאוד מאוד ותימלא הארץ אותם
8 ויקם מלך חדש על מיצריים אשר לוא ידע
את יוס 9 ויואמר אל עמו הינה עם בני
יסראל רב ועצום מימנו 10 הבה ניתחכמה לו
פן ירבה והיה כי תיקראנה מילחמה ונוסף
גם הוא על סונאינו ונילחם בנו ועלה מין
הארץ 11 ויסימו עליו סרי מיסים למען
ענותו בסיבלותם ויבן ערי מיסכנות לפרעוה
את פיתום ואת רעמס 12 וכאשר יענו אותו כן
ירבה וכן יפרוץ ויקוצו מיפני בני
יסראל 13 ויעבידו מיצריים את בני
יסראל בפרך 14 וימררו את חייהם בעבודה קשה
בחומר ובילבנים ובכל עבודה בסדה את כל עבודתם
אשר עבדו בהם בפרך 15 ויואמר מלך
מיצריים למילדות העבריות אשר שם
האחת שיפרה ושם השנית פועה 16 ויואמר
בילדכן את העבריות וראיתן על האבניים
אים בן הוא והמיתן אותו ואים בת היא וחיה

[illegible] 17
[illegible]
[illegible] 18 [illegible]
[illegible]
[illegible] 19 [illegible]
[illegible]
[illegible]
[illegible] 20 [illegible]
[illegible] 21 [illegible]
[illegible]
[illegible] 22
[illegible]

2 [illegible]

[illegible] 1
[illegible] 2
[illegible] 3 [illegible]
[illegible]
[illegible]
[illegible] 4 [illegible]
[illegible] 5
[illegible]
[illegible] 6 [illegible]
[illegible]
[illegible] 7 [illegible]
[illegible]
[illegible] 8 [illegible]
[illegible]
[illegible] 9
[illegible]
[illegible] 10 [illegible]
[illegible]
[illegible]
[illegible] 11
[illegible]
[illegible] 12 [illegible]
[illegible]
[illegible] 13
[illegible]
[illegible] 14 [illegible]

[illegible]
[illegible]
[illegible] 15 [illegible]
[illegible]
[illegible] 16 [illegible]
[illegible]
[illegible] 17 [illegible]
[illegible]
[illegible] 18 [illegible]
[illegible] 19 [illegible]
[illegible]
[illegible] 20 [illegible]
[illegible]
[illegible] 21 [illegible]
[illegible] 22 [illegible]
[illegible]
[illegible] 23 [illegible]
[illegible]
[illegible]
[illegible] 24 [illegible]
[illegible]
[illegible] 25 [illegible]
[illegible]

3 [illegible]

[illegible] 1
[illegible]
[illegible] 2 [illegible]
[illegible]
[illegible] 3 [illegible]
[illegible]
[illegible] 4 [illegible]
[illegible]
[illegible] 5 [illegible]
[illegible]
[illegible] 6 [illegible]
[illegible]
[illegible]
[illegible] 7 [illegible]
[illegible]
[illegible]

את מכאוביו 8 וארד להצילו מיד מיצריים
ולהעלותו מין הארץ ההיוא אל ארץ טובה ורחבה
אל ארץ זבת חלב ודבש אל מקום הכנעני
והחיתי והאמורי והפריזי והחיוי
והיבוסי 9 ועתה הינה צעקת בני יסראל באה
אלי וגם ראיתי את הלחץ אשר מיצריים
לוחצים אותם 10 ועתה לכה ואשלחכה אל פרעוה
והוצא את עמי בני יסראל מימיצריים
11 ויואמר מושה אל האלוהים מי אנוכי כי
אלך אל פרעוה וכי אוציא את בני יסראל
מימיצריים 12 ויואמר כי אהיה עימך
וזה לכה האות כי אנוכי שלחתיכה בהוציאכה
את העם מימיצריים תעבדון את האלוהים
על ההר הזה 13 ויואמר מושה אל האלוהים
הינה אנוכי בא אל בני יסראל ואמרתי להם
אלוהי אבותיכם שלחני אליכם ואמרו לי מה
שמו מה אומר אלהם 14 ויואמר אלוהים אל
מושה אהיה אשר אהיה ויואמר כוה תואמר
ליבני יסראל אהיה שלחני אליכם
15 ויואמר עוד אלוהים אל מושה כוה תואמר אל
בני יסראל יהוה אלוהי אבותיכם אלוהי
אברהם אלוהי יצחק ואלוהי יעקב שלחני
אליכם זה שמי לעולם וזה זיכרי לדור דור
16 לך ואספת את זיקני יסראל ואמרת אלהם
יהוה אלוהי אבותיכם ניראה אלי אלוהי
אברהם יצחק ויעקוב לאמור פקוד פקדתי אתכם
ואת העסוי לכם במיצריים 17 ואומר אעלה
אתכם מעני מיצריים אל ארץ הכנעני
והחיתי והאמורי והפריזי והחיוי
והיבוסי אל ארץ זבת חלב ודבש 18 ושמעו לקולכה
ובאת אתה וזיקני יסראל אל מלך מיצריים
ואמרתם אליו יהוה אלוהי העיבריים
ניקרה עלינו ועתה נלכה נא דרך שלושת
ימים במידבר וניזבחה ליהוה אלוהינו
19 ואני ידעתי כי לוא יתן אתכם מלך
מיצריים להלוך ולוא ביד חזקה 20 ושלחתי את
ידי והיכיתי את מיצריים בכול
ניפלאותי אשר אעסה בקירבו ואחרי כן
ישלח אתכם 21 ונתתי את חן העם הזה בעיני
מיצריים והיה כי תלכון לוא תלכו ריקם
22 ושאלה אישה מישכנתה ומיגרת ביתה

[illegible]
[illegible]

4 [illegible]

[illegible] 1
[illegible]
[illegible] 2 [illegible]
[illegible] 3 [illegible]
[illegible]
[illegible] 4 [illegible]
[illegible]
[illegible] 5 [illegible]
[illegible]
[illegible] 6 [illegible]
[illegible]
[illegible] 7 [illegible]
[illegible]
[illegible] 8 [illegible]
[illegible]
[illegible] 9 [illegible]
[illegible]
[illegible]
[illegible]
[illegible] 10 [illegible]
[illegible]
[illegible]
[illegible] 11 [illegible]
[illegible]
[illegible] 12 [illegible]
[illegible]
[illegible] 13 [illegible]
[illegible] 14
[illegible]
[illegible]
[illegible] 15
[illegible]
[illegible] 16 [illegible]
[illegible]
[illegible] 17 [illegible]
[illegible] 18 [illegible]
[illegible]

𐤀𐤋 𐤀𐤇𐤉 𐤀𐤔𐤓 𐤁𐤌𐤉𐤑𐤓𐤉𐤉𐤌 𐤅𐤀𐤓𐤀𐤄 𐤄𐤏𐤅𐤃𐤌 𐤇𐤉𐤉𐤌
𐤅𐤉𐤅𐤀𐤌𐤓 𐤉𐤕𐤓𐤅 𐤋𐤌𐤅𐤔𐤄 𐤋𐤊 𐤋𐤔𐤋𐤅𐤌 19 𐤅𐤉𐤅𐤀𐤌𐤓
𐤉𐤄𐤅𐤄 𐤀𐤋 𐤌𐤅𐤔𐤄 𐤁𐤌𐤉𐤃𐤉𐤍 𐤋𐤊 𐤔𐤅𐤁 𐤌𐤉𐤑𐤓𐤉𐤉𐤌
𐤊𐤉 𐤌𐤕𐤅 𐤊𐤋 𐤄𐤀𐤍𐤔𐤉𐤌 𐤄𐤌𐤁𐤒𐤔𐤉𐤌 𐤀𐤕 𐤍𐤐𐤔𐤊𐤄
20 𐤅𐤉𐤒𐤇 𐤌𐤅𐤔𐤄 𐤀𐤕 𐤀𐤉𐤔𐤕𐤅 𐤅𐤀𐤕 𐤁𐤍𐤉𐤅 𐤅𐤉𐤓𐤊𐤉𐤁𐤌
𐤏𐤋 𐤄𐤇𐤌𐤅𐤓 𐤅𐤉𐤔𐤁 𐤀𐤓𐤑𐤄 𐤌𐤉𐤑𐤓𐤉𐤉𐤌 𐤅𐤉𐤒𐤇 𐤌𐤅𐤔𐤄
𐤀𐤕 𐤌𐤈𐤄 𐤄𐤀𐤋𐤅𐤄𐤉𐤌 𐤁𐤉𐤃𐤅 21 𐤅𐤉𐤅𐤀𐤌𐤓 𐤉𐤄𐤅𐤄 𐤀𐤋
𐤌𐤅𐤔𐤄 𐤁𐤋𐤊𐤕𐤊𐤄 𐤋𐤔𐤅𐤁 𐤌𐤉𐤑𐤓𐤉𐤌𐤄 𐤓𐤀𐤄 𐤊𐤋
𐤄𐤌𐤅𐤐𐤕𐤉𐤌 𐤀𐤔𐤓 𐤔𐤌𐤕𐤉 𐤁𐤉𐤃𐤊𐤄 𐤅𐤏𐤎𐤉𐤕𐤌
𐤋𐤉𐤐𐤍𐤉 𐤐𐤓𐤏𐤅𐤄 𐤅𐤀𐤍𐤉 𐤀𐤇𐤆𐤒 𐤀𐤕 𐤋𐤉𐤁𐤅 𐤅𐤋𐤅𐤀
𐤉𐤔𐤋𐤇 𐤀𐤕 𐤄𐤏𐤌 22 𐤅𐤀𐤌𐤓𐤕 𐤀𐤋 𐤐𐤓𐤏𐤅𐤄 𐤊𐤅𐤄 𐤀𐤌𐤓
𐤉𐤄𐤅𐤄 𐤁𐤍𐤉 𐤁𐤊𐤅𐤓𐤉 𐤉𐤎𐤓𐤀𐤋 23 𐤅𐤀𐤅𐤌𐤓 𐤀𐤋𐤉𐤊𐤄 𐤔𐤋𐤇
𐤀𐤕 𐤁𐤍𐤉 𐤅𐤉𐤏𐤁𐤃𐤍𐤉 𐤅𐤕𐤌𐤀𐤍 𐤋𐤔𐤋𐤇𐤅 𐤄𐤉𐤍𐤄 𐤀𐤍𐤅𐤊𐤉
𐤄𐤅𐤓𐤂 𐤀𐤕 𐤁𐤉𐤍𐤊𐤄 𐤁𐤊𐤅𐤓𐤊𐤄 24 𐤅𐤉𐤄𐤉 𐤁𐤃𐤓𐤊 𐤁𐤌𐤋𐤅𐤍
𐤅𐤉𐤐𐤂𐤔𐤄𐤅 𐤉𐤄𐤅𐤄 𐤅𐤉𐤁𐤒𐤔 𐤄𐤌𐤉𐤕𐤅 25 𐤅𐤕𐤒𐤇
𐤑𐤉𐤐𐤅𐤓𐤄 𐤑𐤅𐤓 𐤅𐤕𐤉𐤊𐤓𐤅𐤕 𐤀𐤕 𐤏𐤓𐤋𐤕 𐤁𐤍𐤄 𐤅𐤕𐤂𐤏
𐤋𐤓𐤂𐤋𐤉𐤅 𐤅𐤕𐤅𐤀𐤌𐤓 𐤊𐤉 𐤇𐤕𐤍 𐤃𐤌𐤉𐤌 𐤀𐤕𐤄 𐤋𐤉
26 𐤅𐤉𐤓𐤐 𐤌𐤉𐤌𐤍𐤅 𐤀𐤆 𐤀𐤌𐤓𐤄 𐤇𐤕𐤍 𐤃𐤌𐤉𐤌 𐤋𐤌𐤅𐤋𐤅𐤕
27 𐤅𐤉𐤅𐤀𐤌𐤓 𐤉𐤄𐤅𐤄 𐤀𐤋 𐤀𐤄𐤓𐤅𐤍 𐤋𐤊 𐤋𐤉𐤒𐤓𐤀𐤕 𐤌𐤅𐤔𐤄
𐤄𐤌𐤉𐤃𐤁𐤓𐤄 𐤅𐤉𐤋𐤊 𐤅𐤉𐤐𐤂𐤔𐤄𐤅 𐤁𐤄𐤓 𐤄𐤀𐤋𐤅𐤄𐤉𐤌 𐤅𐤉𐤔𐤒
𐤋𐤅 28 𐤅𐤉𐤂𐤃 𐤌𐤅𐤔𐤄 𐤋𐤀𐤄𐤓𐤅𐤍 𐤀𐤕 𐤊𐤋 𐤃𐤉𐤁𐤓𐤉 𐤉𐤄𐤅𐤄
𐤀𐤔𐤓 𐤔𐤋𐤇𐤅 𐤅𐤀𐤕 𐤊𐤋 𐤄𐤀𐤅𐤕𐤅𐤕 𐤀𐤔𐤓 𐤑𐤉𐤅𐤄𐤅 29 𐤅𐤉𐤋𐤊
𐤌𐤅𐤔𐤄 𐤅𐤀𐤄𐤓𐤅𐤍 𐤅𐤉𐤀𐤎𐤐𐤅 𐤀𐤕 𐤊𐤋 𐤆𐤉𐤒𐤍𐤉 𐤁𐤍𐤉
𐤉𐤎𐤓𐤀𐤋 30 𐤅𐤉𐤃𐤁𐤓 𐤀𐤄𐤓𐤅𐤍 𐤀𐤕 𐤊𐤋 𐤄𐤃𐤁𐤓𐤉𐤌 𐤀𐤔𐤓
𐤃𐤉𐤁𐤓 𐤉𐤄𐤅𐤄 𐤀𐤋 𐤌𐤅𐤔𐤄 𐤅𐤉𐤏𐤎 𐤄𐤀𐤅𐤕𐤅𐤕 𐤋𐤏𐤉𐤍𐤉
𐤄𐤏𐤌 31 𐤅𐤉𐤀𐤌𐤍 𐤄𐤏𐤌 𐤅𐤉𐤔𐤌𐤏𐤅 𐤊𐤉 𐤐𐤒𐤃 𐤉𐤄𐤅𐤄 𐤀𐤕
𐤁𐤍𐤉 𐤉𐤎𐤓𐤀𐤋 𐤅𐤊𐤉 𐤓𐤀𐤄 𐤀𐤕 𐤏𐤍𐤉𐤌 𐤅𐤉𐤒𐤃𐤅 𐤅𐤉𐤔𐤕𐤇𐤅𐤅

𐤔𐤌𐤅𐤕 𐤐𐤓𐤒 5

1 𐤅𐤀𐤇𐤓 𐤁𐤀𐤅 𐤌𐤅𐤔𐤄 𐤅𐤀𐤄𐤓𐤅𐤍 𐤅𐤉𐤅𐤀𐤌𐤓𐤅 𐤀𐤋 𐤐𐤓𐤏𐤅𐤄 𐤊𐤅𐤄
𐤀𐤌𐤓 𐤉𐤄𐤅𐤄 𐤀𐤋𐤅𐤄𐤉 𐤉𐤎𐤓𐤀𐤋 𐤔𐤋𐤇 𐤀𐤕 𐤏𐤌𐤉 𐤅𐤉𐤇𐤅𐤂𐤅
𐤋𐤉 𐤁𐤌𐤉𐤃𐤁𐤓 2 𐤅𐤉𐤅𐤀𐤌𐤓 𐤐𐤓𐤏𐤅𐤄 𐤌𐤉 𐤉𐤄𐤅𐤄 𐤀𐤔𐤓
𐤀𐤔𐤌𐤏 𐤁𐤒𐤅𐤋𐤅 𐤋𐤔𐤋𐤇 𐤀𐤕 𐤉𐤎𐤓𐤀𐤋 𐤋𐤅𐤀 𐤉𐤃𐤏𐤕𐤉 𐤀𐤕
𐤉𐤄𐤅𐤄 𐤅𐤂𐤌 𐤀𐤕 𐤉𐤎𐤓𐤀𐤋 𐤋𐤅𐤀 𐤀𐤔𐤋𐤇 3 𐤅𐤉𐤅𐤀𐤌𐤓𐤅
𐤀𐤋𐤅𐤄𐤉 𐤄𐤏𐤉𐤁𐤓𐤉𐤌 𐤍𐤉𐤒𐤓𐤀 𐤏𐤋𐤉𐤍𐤅 𐤍𐤋𐤊𐤄 𐤍𐤀 𐤃𐤓𐤊
𐤔𐤋𐤅𐤔𐤕 𐤉𐤌𐤉𐤌 𐤁𐤌𐤉𐤃𐤁𐤓 𐤅𐤍𐤉𐤆𐤁𐤇𐤄 𐤋𐤉𐤄𐤅𐤄
𐤀𐤋𐤅𐤄𐤉𐤍𐤅 𐤐𐤍 𐤉𐤐𐤂𐤏𐤍𐤅 𐤁𐤃𐤁𐤓 𐤀𐤅 𐤁𐤇𐤓 4 𐤅𐤉𐤅𐤀𐤌𐤓
𐤀𐤋𐤄𐤌 𐤌𐤋𐤊 𐤌𐤉𐤑𐤓𐤉𐤉𐤌 𐤋𐤌𐤄 𐤌𐤅𐤔𐤄 𐤅𐤀𐤄𐤓𐤅𐤍
𐤕𐤐𐤓𐤉𐤏𐤅 𐤀𐤕 𐤄𐤏𐤌 𐤌𐤉𐤌𐤏𐤎𐤉𐤅 𐤋𐤊𐤅 𐤋𐤎𐤉𐤁𐤋𐤅𐤕𐤉𐤊𐤌
5 𐤅𐤉𐤅𐤀𐤌𐤓 𐤐𐤓𐤏𐤅𐤄 𐤄𐤍 𐤓𐤁𐤉𐤌 𐤏𐤕𐤄 𐤏𐤌 𐤄𐤀𐤓𐤑
𐤅𐤄𐤉𐤔𐤁𐤕𐤌 𐤀𐤅𐤕𐤌 𐤌𐤉𐤎𐤉𐤁𐤋𐤅𐤕𐤌 6 𐤅𐤉𐤑𐤅 𐤐𐤓𐤏𐤅𐤄

ביום ההוא את הנוגשים בעם ואת שוטריו
לאמור 7 לוא תואסיפון לתת תבן לעם לילבון
הלבנים כיתמול שילשום הם ילכו וקוששו
להם תבן 8 ואת מתכונת הלבנים אשר הם
עושים תמול שילשום תשימו עליהם לוא
תיגרעו מימנו כי נירפים הם על כן הם
צועקים לאמור נלכה ניזבחה לאלוהינו
9 תיכבד העבודה על האנשים ויעשו בה ואל
ישעו בדיברי שקר 10 ויצאו נוגשי העם
ושוטריו ויואמרו אל העם לאמור כוה אמר
פרעוה אינני נותן לכם תבן 11 אתם לכו קחו
לכם תבן מאשר תימצאו כי אין ניגרע
מעבודתכם דבר 12 ויפץ העם בכל ארץ
מיצריים לקושש קש לתבן 13 והנוגשים
אצים לאמור כלו מעשיכם דבר יום ביומו
כאשר ביהיות התבן 14 ויכו שוטרי בני
ישראל אשר שמו עלהם נוגשי פרעוה לאמור
מדוע לוא כיליתם חקכם לילבון כיתמול
שילשום גם תמול גם היום 15 ויבואו שוטרי
בני ישראל ויצעקו אל פרעוה לאמור למה
תעשה כוה לעבדיכה 16 תבן אין ניתן
לעבדיכה ולבנים אומרים לנו עשו והינה
עבדיכה מוכים וחטאת עמכה 17 ויואמר
נירפים אתם נירפים על כן אתם
אומרים נלכה ניזבחה ליהוה 18 ועתה לכו
עבדו ותבן לוא ינתן לכם ותוכן לבנים
תיתנו 19 ויראו שוטרי בני ישראל אותם ברע
לאמור לוא תיגרעו מילבניכם דבר יום
ביומו 20 ויפגעו את מושה ואת אהרון
ניצבים ליקראתם בצאתם מאת פרעוה
21 ויואמרו אלהם ירא יהוה עליכם
וישפוט אשר היבאשתם את ריחנו בעיני
פרעוה ובעיני עבדיו לתת חרב בידם להרגנו
22 וישב מושה אל יהוה ויואמר אדוני למה
הרעותה לעם הזה למה זה שלחתני 23 ומאז
באתי אל פרעוה לדבר בישמכה הרע לעם הזה
והצל לוא היצלת את עמכה

שמות פרק 6

1 ויואמר יהוה אל מושה עתה תיראה אשר
אעשה לפרעוה כי ביד חזקה ישלחם וביד חזקה

יגרשם מארצו 2 וידבר אלוהים אל מושה
ויואמר אליו אני יהוה 3 וארא אל אברהם אל
יצחק ואל יעקב באל שדי ושמי יהוה לוא
נודעתי להם 4 וגם הקימותי את בריתי
איתם לתת להם את ארץ כנען את ארץ
מגוריהם אשר גרו בה 5 וגם אני שמעתי את
נאקת בני ישראל אשר מיצריים
מעבידים אותם ואזכור את בריתי 6 לכן אמור
לבני ישראל אני יהוה והוצאתי אתכם
מיתחת סיבלות מיצריים והיצלתי אתכם
מעבודתם וגאלתי אתכם בזרוע נטויה
ובישפטים גדולים 7 ולקחתי אתכם לי לעם
והייתי לכם לאלוהים וידעתם כי אני
יהוה אלוהיכם המוציא אתכם מיתחת סיבלות
מיצריים 8 והבאתי אתכם אל הארץ אשר
נשאתי את ידי לתת אותה לאברהם לייצחק
וליעקוב ונתתי אותה לכם מורשה אני יהוה
9 וידבר מושה כן אל בני ישראל ולוא שמעו אל
מושה מיקוצר רוח ומעבודה קשה 10 וידבר יהוה
אל מושה לאמור 11 בוא דבר אל פרעוה מלך
מיצריים וישלח את בני ישראל מארצו
12 וידבר מושה לפני יהוה לאמור הן בני
ישראל לוא שמעו אלי ואיך ישמעני פרעוה
ואני ערל שפתים 13 וידבר יהוה אל מושה
ואל אהרון ויצום אל בני ישראל ואל פרעוה
מלך מיצריים להוציא את בני ישראל
מארץ מיצריים 14 אלה ראשי בית אבותם
בני ראובן בכור ישראל חנוך ופלוא חצרון
וכרמי אלה משפחות ראובן 15 ובני
שימעון ימואל וימין ואוהד ויכין וצוחר
ושאול בן הכנענית אלה משפחות שימעון
16 ואלה שמות בני לוי לתולדותם גרשון וקהת
ומררי ושני חיי לוי שבע ושלושים ומאת
שנה 17 בני גרשון לבני ושימעי
למשפחותם 18 ובני קהת עמרם וייצהר
וחברון ועוזיאל ושני חיי קהת שלוש
ושלושים ומאת שנה 19 ובני מררי מחלי
ומושי אלה משפחות הלוי לתולדותם 20 ויקח
עמרם את יוכבד דודתו לו לאישה ותלד לו את
אהרון ואת מושה ושני חיי עמרם שבע
ושלושים ומאת שנה 21 ובני יצהר קורח ונפג

וזיכרי 22 ובני עוזיאל מישאל ואלצפן
וסיתרי 23 ויקח אהרון את אלישבע בת
עמינדב אחות נחשון לו לאישה ותלד לו את נדב
ואת אביהוא את אלעזר ואת איתמר 24 ובני קורח
אסיר ואלקנה ואביאסף אלה משפחות הקרחי
25 ואלעזר בן אהרון לקח לו מיבנות פוטיאל לו
לאישה ותלד לו את פינחס אלה ראשי אבות
הלוים למשפחותם 26 הוא אהרון ומושה אשר
אמר יהוה להם הוציאו את בני יסראל מארץ
מיצריים על ציבאותם 27 הם המדברים אל
פרעוה מלך מיצריים להוציא את בני
יסראל מימיצריים הוא מושה ואהרון
28 ויהי ביום דיבר יהוה אל מושה בארץ
מיצריים 29 וידבר יהוה אל מושה לאמור
אני יהוה דבר אל פרעוה מלך מיצריים את
כל אשר אני דובר אליכה 30 ויואמר מושה
ליפני יהוה הן אני ערל ספתיים ואיך
ישמע אלי פרעוה

שמות פרק 7

1 ויואמר יהוה אל מושה ראה נתתיכה אלוהים
לפרעוה ואהרון אחיכה יהיה נביאכה 2 אתה
תדבר את כל אשר אצוכה ואהרון אחיכה ידבר אל
פרעוה ושילח את בני יסראל מארצו 3 ואני
אקשה את לב פרעוה והירביתי את אותותי ואת
מופתי בארץ מיצריים 4 ולוא ישמע אלכם
פרעוה ונתתי את ידי במיצריים והוצאתי
את ציבאותי את עמי בני יסראל מארץ
מיצריים בישפטים גדולים 5 וידעו
מיצריים כי אני יהוה בינטותי את ידי
על מיצריים והוצאתי את בני יסראל
מיתוכם 6 ויעס מושה ואהרון כאשר ציוה
יהוה אותם כן עסו 7 ומושה בן שמונים שנה
ואהרון בן שלוש ושמונים שנה בדברם אל
פרעוה 8 ויואמר יהוה אל מושה ואל אהרון
לאמור 9 כי ידבר אלכם פרעוה לאמור תנו לכם
מופת ואמרת אל אהרון קח את מטכה והשלך
ליפני פרעוה יהי לתנין 10 ויבוא מושה
ואהרון אל פרעוה ויעסו כן כאשר ציוה יהוה
וישלך אהרון את מטהו ליפני פרעוה

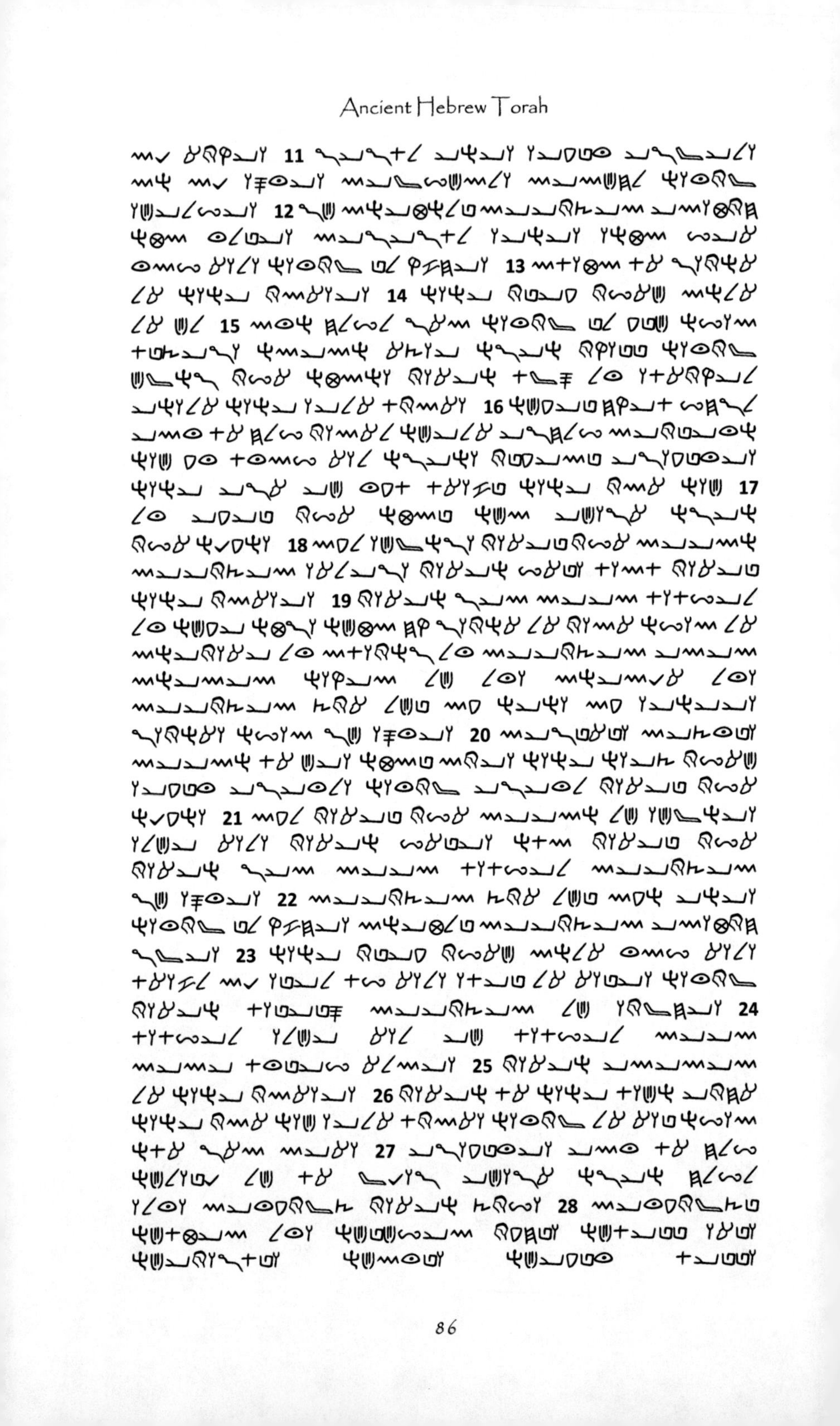

11
12
13
14
15
16
17
18
19
20
21
22
23
24
25
26
27
28

ובמישארותיכה 29 ובכה ובעמכה ובכל עבדיכה
יעלו הצפרדעיים

שמות פרק 8

1 ויואמר יהוה אל מושה אמור אל אהרון נטה
את ידכה במטכה על הנהרות על היאוריים ועל
האגמים והעל את הצפרדעיים על ארץ
מיצריים 2 ויט אהרון את ידו על מיימי
מיצריים ותעל הצפרדע ותכס את ארץ
מיצריים 3 ויעסו כן החרטומיים בלטיהם
ויעלו את הצפרדעיים על ארץ מיצריים
4 ויקרא פרעוה למושה ולאהרון ויואמר
העתירו אל יהוה ויסר הצפרדעיים מימני
ומעמי ואשלחה את העם ויזבחו ליהוה
5 ויואמר מושה לפרעוה היתפאר עלי למתי
אעתיר לכה ולעבדיכה ולעמכה להכרית
הצפרדעיים מימכה ומיבתיכה רק ביאור
תישארנה 6 ויואמר למחר ויואמר כידברכה
למען תדע כי אין כיהוה אלוהינו 7 וסרו
הצפרדעיים מימכה ומיבתיכה ומעבדיכה
ומעמכה רק ביאור תישארנה 8 ויצא מושה
ואהרון מעם פרעוה ויצעק מושה אל יהוה
על דבר הצפרדעיים אשר סם לפרעוה 9 ויעס
יהוה כידבר מושה וימותו הצפרדעיים מין
הבתים מין החצרות ומין הסדות 10 ויצברו
אותם חמרים חמרים ותיבאש הארץ 11 וירא
פרעוה כי היתה הרוחה והכבד את ליבו ולוא שמע
אלהם כאשר דיבר יהוה 12 ויואמר יהוה אל
מושה אמור אל אהרון נטה את מטכה והכ את עפר
הארץ והיה לכיניים בכל ארץ מיצריים
13 ויעסו כן ויט אהרון את ידו במטהו ויכ את
עפר הארץ ותהי הכינם באדם ובבהמה כל עפר
הארץ היה כיניים בכל ארץ מיצריים
14 ויעסו כן החרטומיים בלטיהם להוציא את
הכיניים ולוא יכולו ותהי הכינם באדם
ובבהמה 15 ויואמרו החרטומיים אל פרעוה אצבע
אלוהים היוא ויחזק לב פרעוה ולוא שמע
אלהם כאשר דיבר יהוה 16 ויואמר יהוה אל
מושה השכם בבוקר והיתיצב ליפני פרעוה
הינה יוצא המימה ואמרת אליו כוה אמר
יהוה שלח עמי ויעבדיני 17 כי אים אינכה

משלח את עמי הנני משליח בך ובעבדיך
ובעמך ובבתיך את הערב ומלאו בתי
מצרים את הערב וגם האדמה אשר הם
עליה 18 והפליתי ביום ההוא את ארץ גשן
אשר עמי עמד עליה לבלתי היות שם ערב
למען תדע כי אני יהוה בקרב הארץ 19 ושמתי
פדת בין עמי ובין עמך למחר יהיה האות
הזה 20 ויעש יהוה כן ויבא ערב כבד ביתה
פרעה ובית עבדיו ובכל ארץ מצרים
תשחת הארץ מפני הערב 21 ויקרא פרעה
אל משה ולאהרן ויאמר לכו זבחו לאלהיכם
בארץ 22 ויאמר משה לא נכון לעשות כן כי
תועבת מצרים נזבח ליהוה אלהינו הן
נזבח את תועבת מצרים לעיניהם ולא
יסקלנו 23 דרך שלשת ימים נלך במדבר
וזבחנו ליהוה אלהינו כאשר יאמר אלינו
24 ויאמר פרעה אנכי אשלח אתכם וזבחתם
ליהוה אלהיכם במדבר רק הרחק לא תרחיקו
ללכת העתירו בעדי 25 ויאמר משה הנה
אנכי יוצא מעמך והעתרתי אל יהוה וסר
הערב מפרעה מעבדיו ומעמו מחר רק אל
יסף פרעה התל לבלתי שלח את העם
לזבח ליהוה 26 ויצא משה מעם פרעה
ויעתר אל יהוה 27 ויעש יהוה כדבר משה
ויסר הערב מפרעה מעבדיו ומעמו לא
נשאר אחד 28 ויכבד פרעה את לבו גם
בפעם הזאת ולא שלח את העם

שמות פרק 9

1 ויאמר יהוה אל משה בא אל פרעה ודברת
אליו כה אמר יהוה אלהי העברים שלח את
עמי ויעבדני 2 כי אם מאן אתה לשלח
ועודך מחזיק בם 3 הנה יד יהוה הויה
במקנך אשר בשדה בסוסים בחמרים
בגמלים בבקר ובצאן דבר כבד מאד 4 והפלה
יהוה בין מקנה ישראל ובין מקנה
מצרים ולא ימות מכל לבני ישראל
דבר 5 וישם יהוה מועד לאמר מחר יעשה יהוה
הדבר הזה בארץ 6 ויעש יהוה את הדבר הזה
ממחרת וימת כל מקנה מצרים
וממקנה בני ישראל לא מת אחד 7 וישלח

[illegible]
[illegible]
[illegible] 8
[illegible]
[illegible] 9 [illegible]
[illegible]
[illegible]
[illegible] 10
[illegible]
[illegible] 11 [illegible]
[illegible]
[illegible]
[illegible] 12 [illegible]
[illegible]
[illegible] 13
[illegible]
[illegible]
[illegible] 14 [illegible]
[illegible]
[illegible] 15 [illegible]
[illegible]
[illegible] 16 [illegible]
[illegible]
[illegible] 17 [illegible]
[illegible] 18 [illegible]
[illegible]
[illegible] 19 [illegible]
[illegible]
[illegible]
[illegible] 20 [illegible]
[illegible]
[illegible] 21 [illegible]
[illegible] 22 [illegible]
[illegible]
[illegible]
[illegible]
[illegible] 23
[illegible]
[illegible] 24 [illegible]
[illegible]
[illegible]

25 𐤅𐤉𐤊 𐤄𐤁𐤓𐤃 𐤁𐤊𐤋 𐤀𐤓𐤑 𐤌𐤉𐤑𐤓𐤉𐤉𐤌 𐤀𐤕 𐤊𐤋 𐤀𐤔𐤓
𐤁𐤎𐤃𐤄 𐤌𐤀𐤃𐤌 𐤅𐤏𐤃 𐤁𐤄𐤌𐤄 𐤅𐤀𐤕 𐤊𐤋 𐤏𐤎𐤁 𐤄𐤎𐤃𐤄 𐤄𐤉𐤊𐤄
𐤄𐤁𐤓𐤃 𐤅𐤀𐤕 𐤊𐤋 𐤏𐤑 𐤄𐤎𐤃𐤄 𐤔𐤉𐤁𐤓 26 𐤓𐤒 𐤁𐤀𐤓𐤑 𐤂𐤅𐤔𐤍
𐤀𐤔𐤓 𐤔𐤌 𐤁𐤍𐤉 𐤉𐤎𐤓𐤀𐤋 𐤋𐤅𐤀 𐤄𐤉𐤄 𐤁𐤓𐤃 27 𐤅𐤉𐤔𐤋𐤇
𐤐𐤓𐤏𐤅𐤄 𐤅𐤉𐤒𐤓𐤀 𐤋𐤌𐤅𐤔𐤄 𐤅𐤋𐤀𐤄𐤓𐤅𐤍 𐤅𐤉𐤅𐤀𐤌𐤓 𐤀𐤋𐤄𐤌
𐤇𐤈𐤀𐤕𐤉 𐤄𐤐𐤏𐤌 𐤉𐤄𐤅𐤄 𐤄𐤑𐤃𐤉𐤒 𐤅𐤀𐤍𐤉 𐤅𐤏𐤌𐤉
𐤄𐤓𐤔𐤏𐤉𐤌 28 𐤄𐤏𐤕𐤉𐤓𐤅 𐤀𐤋 𐤉𐤄𐤅𐤄 𐤅𐤓𐤁 𐤌𐤉𐤄𐤉𐤅𐤕
𐤒𐤅𐤋𐤅𐤕 𐤀𐤋𐤅𐤄𐤉𐤌 𐤅𐤁𐤓𐤃 𐤅𐤀𐤔𐤋𐤇𐤄 𐤀𐤕𐤊𐤌 𐤅𐤋𐤅𐤀 𐤕𐤅𐤎𐤉𐤐𐤅𐤍
𐤋𐤏𐤌𐤅𐤃 29 𐤅𐤉𐤅𐤀𐤌𐤓 𐤀𐤋𐤉𐤅 𐤌𐤅𐤔𐤄 𐤊𐤑𐤀𐤕𐤉 𐤀𐤕 𐤄𐤏𐤉𐤓
𐤀𐤐𐤓𐤅𐤎 𐤀𐤕 𐤊𐤐𐤉 𐤀𐤋 𐤉𐤄𐤅𐤄 𐤄𐤒𐤅𐤋𐤅𐤕 𐤉𐤇𐤃𐤋𐤅𐤍 𐤅𐤄𐤁𐤓𐤃
𐤋𐤅𐤀 𐤉𐤄𐤉𐤄 𐤏𐤅𐤃 𐤋𐤌𐤏𐤍 𐤕𐤃𐤏 𐤊𐤉 𐤋𐤉𐤄𐤅𐤄 𐤄𐤀𐤓𐤑
30 𐤅𐤀𐤕𐤄 𐤅𐤏𐤁𐤃𐤉𐤊𐤄 𐤉𐤃𐤏𐤕𐤉 𐤊𐤉 𐤈𐤓𐤌 𐤕𐤉𐤓𐤀𐤅𐤍
𐤌𐤉𐤐𐤍𐤉 𐤉𐤄𐤅𐤄 𐤀𐤋𐤅𐤄𐤉𐤌 31 𐤅𐤄𐤐𐤉𐤔𐤕𐤄 𐤅𐤄𐤎𐤏𐤅𐤓𐤄
𐤍𐤅𐤊𐤕𐤄 𐤊𐤉 𐤄𐤎𐤏𐤅𐤓𐤄 𐤀𐤁𐤉𐤁 𐤅𐤄𐤐𐤉𐤔𐤕𐤄 𐤂𐤉𐤁𐤏𐤅𐤋
32 𐤅𐤄𐤇𐤉𐤈𐤄 𐤅𐤄𐤊𐤅𐤎𐤌𐤕 𐤋𐤅𐤀 𐤍𐤅𐤊𐤅 𐤊𐤉 𐤀𐤐𐤉𐤋𐤅𐤕 𐤄𐤍𐤄
33 𐤅𐤉𐤑𐤀 𐤌𐤅𐤔𐤄 𐤌𐤏𐤉𐤌 𐤐𐤓𐤏𐤅𐤄 𐤀𐤕 𐤄𐤏𐤉𐤓
𐤅𐤉𐤐𐤓𐤅𐤎 𐤊𐤐𐤉𐤅 𐤀𐤋 𐤉𐤄𐤅𐤄 𐤅𐤉𐤇𐤃𐤋𐤅 𐤄𐤒𐤅𐤋𐤅𐤕 𐤅𐤄𐤁𐤓𐤃
𐤅𐤌𐤈𐤓 𐤋𐤅𐤀 𐤍𐤉𐤕𐤊 𐤀𐤓𐤑𐤄 34 𐤅𐤉𐤓𐤀 𐤐𐤓𐤏𐤅𐤄 𐤊𐤉 𐤇𐤃𐤋
𐤄𐤌𐤈𐤓 𐤅𐤄𐤁𐤓𐤃 𐤅𐤄𐤒𐤅𐤋𐤅𐤕 𐤅𐤉𐤅𐤎𐤐 𐤋𐤇𐤈𐤅𐤀 𐤅𐤉𐤊𐤁𐤃 𐤋𐤉𐤁𐤅 𐤄𐤅𐤀
𐤅𐤏𐤁𐤃𐤉𐤅 35 𐤅𐤉𐤇𐤆𐤒 𐤋𐤁 𐤐𐤓𐤏𐤅𐤄 𐤅𐤋𐤅𐤀 𐤔𐤉𐤋𐤇 𐤀𐤕 𐤁𐤍𐤉
𐤉𐤎𐤓𐤀𐤋 𐤊𐤀𐤔𐤓 𐤃𐤉𐤁𐤓 𐤉𐤄𐤅𐤄 𐤁𐤉𐤃 𐤌𐤅𐤔𐤄

𐤔𐤌𐤅𐤕 𐤐𐤓𐤒 10

1 𐤅𐤉𐤅𐤀𐤌𐤓 𐤉𐤄𐤅𐤄 𐤀𐤋 𐤌𐤅𐤔𐤄 𐤁𐤅𐤀 𐤀𐤋 𐤐𐤓𐤏𐤅𐤄 𐤊𐤉
𐤀𐤍𐤉 𐤄𐤉𐤊𐤁𐤃𐤕𐤉 𐤀𐤕 𐤋𐤉𐤁𐤅 𐤅𐤀𐤕 𐤋𐤁 𐤏𐤁𐤃𐤉𐤅 𐤋𐤌𐤏𐤍
𐤔𐤉𐤕𐤉 𐤀𐤅𐤕𐤅𐤕𐤉 𐤀𐤋𐤄 𐤁𐤒𐤉𐤓𐤁𐤅 2 𐤅𐤋𐤌𐤏𐤍 𐤕𐤎𐤐𐤓
𐤁𐤀𐤆𐤍𐤉 𐤁𐤉𐤍𐤊𐤄 𐤅𐤁𐤍 𐤁𐤉𐤍𐤊𐤄 𐤀𐤕 𐤀𐤔𐤓
𐤄𐤉𐤕𐤏𐤋𐤋𐤕𐤉 𐤁𐤌𐤉𐤑𐤓𐤉𐤉𐤌 𐤅𐤀𐤕 𐤀𐤅𐤕𐤅𐤕𐤉 𐤀𐤔𐤓
𐤎𐤌𐤕𐤉 𐤁𐤌 𐤅𐤉𐤃𐤏𐤕𐤌 𐤊𐤉 𐤀𐤍𐤉 𐤉𐤄𐤅𐤄 3 𐤅𐤉𐤁𐤅𐤀
𐤌𐤅𐤔𐤄 𐤅𐤀𐤄𐤓𐤅𐤍 𐤀𐤋 𐤐𐤓𐤏𐤅𐤄 𐤅𐤉𐤅𐤀𐤌𐤓𐤅 𐤀𐤋𐤉𐤅 𐤊𐤅𐤄 𐤀𐤌𐤓
𐤉𐤄𐤅𐤄 𐤀𐤋𐤅𐤄𐤉 𐤄𐤏𐤉𐤁𐤓𐤉𐤌 𐤏𐤃 𐤌𐤕𐤉 𐤌𐤀𐤍𐤕 𐤋𐤏𐤍𐤅𐤕
𐤌𐤉𐤐𐤍𐤉 𐤔𐤋𐤇 𐤏𐤌𐤉 𐤅𐤉𐤏𐤁𐤃𐤅𐤍𐤉 4 𐤊𐤉 𐤀𐤉𐤌
𐤌𐤀𐤍 𐤀𐤕𐤄 𐤋𐤔𐤋𐤇 𐤀𐤕 𐤏𐤌𐤉 𐤄𐤉𐤍𐤍𐤉 𐤌𐤁𐤉𐤀 𐤌𐤇𐤓
𐤀𐤓𐤁𐤄 𐤁𐤉𐤂𐤁𐤅𐤋𐤊𐤄 5 𐤅𐤊𐤉𐤎𐤄 𐤀𐤕 𐤏𐤉𐤍 𐤄𐤀𐤓𐤑 𐤅𐤋𐤅𐤀
𐤉𐤅𐤊𐤋 𐤋𐤉𐤓𐤀𐤅𐤕 𐤀𐤕 𐤄𐤀𐤓𐤑 𐤅𐤀𐤊𐤋 𐤀𐤕 𐤉𐤕𐤓 𐤄𐤐𐤋𐤈𐤄
𐤄𐤍𐤉𐤔𐤀𐤓𐤕 𐤋𐤊𐤌 𐤌𐤉𐤍 𐤄𐤁𐤓𐤃 𐤅𐤀𐤊𐤋 𐤀𐤕 𐤊𐤋 𐤄𐤏𐤑
𐤄𐤑𐤅𐤌𐤇 𐤋𐤊𐤌 𐤌𐤉𐤍 𐤄𐤎𐤃𐤄 6 𐤅𐤌𐤋𐤀𐤅 𐤁𐤕𐤉𐤊𐤄 𐤅𐤁𐤕𐤉 𐤊𐤋
𐤏𐤁𐤃𐤉𐤊𐤄 𐤅𐤁𐤕𐤉 𐤊𐤋 𐤌𐤉𐤑𐤓𐤉𐤉𐤌 𐤀𐤔𐤓 𐤋𐤅𐤀 𐤓𐤀𐤅
𐤀𐤁𐤅𐤕𐤉𐤊𐤄 𐤅𐤀𐤁𐤅𐤕 𐤀𐤁𐤅𐤕𐤉𐤊𐤄 𐤌𐤉𐤅𐤌 𐤄𐤉𐤅𐤕𐤌 𐤏𐤋
𐤄𐤀𐤃𐤌𐤄 𐤏𐤃 𐤄𐤉𐤅𐤌 𐤄𐤆𐤄 𐤅𐤉𐤐𐤍 𐤅𐤉𐤑𐤀 𐤌𐤏𐤉𐤌
𐤐𐤓𐤏𐤅𐤄 7 𐤅𐤉𐤅𐤀𐤌𐤓𐤅 𐤏𐤁𐤃𐤉 𐤐𐤓𐤏𐤅𐤄 𐤀𐤋𐤉𐤅 𐤏𐤃 𐤌𐤕𐤉

[illegible]
[illegible]
[illegible] 8 [illegible]
[illegible]
[illegible] 9 [illegible]
[illegible]
[illegible]
[illegible] 10 [illegible]
[illegible]
[illegible] 11 [illegible]
[illegible]
[illegible] 12 [illegible]
[illegible]
[illegible]
[illegible] 13 [illegible]
[illegible]
[illegible]
[illegible] 14 [illegible]
[illegible]
[illegible]
[illegible] 15 [illegible]
[illegible]
[illegible]
[illegible] 16 [illegible]
[illegible]
[illegible] 17 [illegible]
[illegible]
[illegible] 18 [illegible]
[illegible] 19 [illegible]
[illegible]
[illegible] 20 [illegible]
[illegible] 21 [illegible]
[illegible]
[illegible] 22 [illegible]
[illegible]
[illegible] 23 [illegible]
[illegible]
[illegible]
[illegible] 24
[illegible]
[illegible] 25 [illegible]

זבחים ועולות ועסינו ליהוה אלוהינו 26 וגם
מיקננו ילך עימנו לוא תישאר פרסה כי
מימנו ניקח לעבוד את יהוה אלוהינו ואנחנו
לוא נדע מה נעבוד את יהוה עד בואנו שמה
27 ויחזק יהוה את לב פרעוה ולוא אבה לשלחם
28 ויואמר לו פרעוה לך מעלי הישמר לכה אל
תוסף ראות פני כי ביום ראותכה פני תמות
29 ויואמר מושה כן דיברת לוא אוסיף עוד ראות
פניכה

שמות פרק 11

1 ויואמר יהוה אל מושה עוד נגע אחד אביא על
פרעוה ועל מיצריים אחרי כן ישלח אתכם
מיזה כשלחו כלה גרש יגרש אתכם מיזה 2 דבר
נא באזני העם ויישאלו איש מאת רעהו
ואשה מאת רעותה כלי כסף וכלי זהב 3 ויתן
יהוה את חן העם בעיני מיצריים גם
האיש מושה גדול מאוד בארץ מיצריים
בעיני עבדי פרעוה ובעיני העם 4 ויואמר
מושה כוה אמר יהוה כחצות הלילה אני יוצא
בתוך מיצריים 5 ומת כל בכור בארץ
מיצריים מיבכור פרעוה היושב על כיסאו
עד בכור השיפחה אשר אחר הרחיים וכול בכור
בהמה 6 והיתה צעקה גדולה בכל ארץ
מיצריים אשר כמוהו לוא ניהיתה וכמוהו
לוא תוסיף 7 ולכול בני יסראל לוא יחרץ כלב
לשונו למאיש ועד בהמה למען תדעון אשר
יפלה יהוה בין מיצריים ובין יסראל
8 וירדו כל עבדיכה אלה אלי והשתחוו לי
לאמור צא אתה וכל העם אשר ברגליכה ואחרי כן
אצא ויצא מעם פרעוה בחרי אף 9 ויואמר
יהוה אל מושה לוא ישמע אליכם פרעוה
למען רבות מופתי בארץ מיצריים
10 ומושה ואהרון עסו את כל המופתים האלה
לפני פרעוה ויחזק יהוה את לב פרעוה ולוא
שלח את בני יסראל מארצו

שמות פרק 12

1 ויואמר יהוה אל מושה ואל אהרון בארץ
מיצריים לאמור 2 החודש הזה לכם ראש

חדשים ריאשון הוא לכם לחדשי השנה 3 דברו
אל כל עדת ישראל לאמור בעשור לחודש הזה
ויקחו להם איש שה לבית אבות שה לבית
4 ואים יימעט הבית מיהיות מישה ולקח
הוא ושכנו הקרוב אל ביתו במיכסת נפשות איש
לפי אכלו תכוסו על השה 5 שה תמים זכר בן
שנה יהיה לכם מין הכבשים ומין
העיזים תיקחו 6 והיה לכם למישמרת עד
ארבעה עשר יום לחודש הזה ושחטו אותו כול קהל
עדת ישראל בין הערבים 7 ולקחו מין הדם
ונתנו על שתי המזוזות ועל המשקוף על
הבתים אשר יואכלו אותו בהם 8 ואכלו את הבשר
בלילה הזה צלי אש ומצות על מרורים
יואכלוהו 9 אל תואכלו מימנו נא ובשל מבושל
במים כי אם צלי אש רואשו על כרעיו ועל
קירבו 10 ולוא תותירו מימנו עד בוקר והנותר
מימנו עד בוקר באש תישרופו 11 וככה תואכלו
אותו מתניכם חגורים נעליכם ברגליכם
ומקלכם בידכם ואכלתם אותו בחיפזון פסח הוא
ליהוה 12 ועברתי בארץ מיצרים בלילה
הזה והיכיתי כל בכור בארץ מיצרים מאדם
ועד בהמה ובכל אלהי מיצרים אעשה
שפטים אני יהוה 13 והיה הדם לכם לאות על
הבתים אשר אתם שם וראיתי את הדם ופסחתי
עלכם ולוא יהיה בכם נגף למשחית בהכותי
בארץ מיצרים 14 והיה היום הזה לכם
לזיכרון וחגותם אותו חג ליהוה לדורותיכם חוקת
עולם תחוגוהו 15 שיבעת ימים מצות תואכלו אך
ביום הריאשון תשביתו שאור מבתיכם כי
כל אוכל חמץ וניכרתה הנפש ההיוא מישראל
מיום הריאשון עד יום השיביעי 16 וביום
הריאשון מיקרא קודש וביום השיביעי
מיקרא קודש יהיה לכם כל מלאכה לוא יעשה
בהם אך אשר יאכל לכל נפש הוא לבדו יעשה לכם
17 ושמרתם את המצות כי בעצם היום הזה
הוצאתי את צבאותיכם מארץ מיצרים
ושמרתם את היום הזה לדורותיכם חוקת עולם
18 בריאשון בארבעה עשר יום לחודש בערב
תואכלו מצות עד יום האחד ועשרים לחודש בערב
19 שיבעת ימים שאור לוא ימצא בבתיכם כי
כל אוכל מחמצת וניכרתה הנפש ההיוא מעדת

ישראל בגר ובאזרח הארץ 20 כל מחמצת לוא
תואכלו בכול מושבותיכם תואכלו מצות 21 ויקרא
מושה לכול זיקני ישראל ויואמר אלהם
מישכו וקחו לכם צואן למישפחותיכם ושחטו
הפסח 22 ולקחתם אגודת אזוב וטבלתם בדם אשר
בסף והיגעתם אל המשקוף ואל שתי המזוזות
מין הדם אשר בסף ואתם לוא תצאו איש
מיפתח ביתו עד בוקר 23 ועבר יהוה לינגוף
את מיצריים וראה את הדם על המשקוף ועל
שתי המזוזות ופסח יהוה על הפתח ולוא יתן
המשחית לבוא אל בתיכם לינגו 24 ושמרתם את
הדבר הזה לחק לכה ולבניכה עד עולם 25 והיה כי
תבואו אל הארץ אשר יתן יהוה לכם כאשר דיבר
ושמרתם את העבודה הזואת 26 והיה כי יואמרו
אליכם בניכם מה העבודה הזואת לכם
27 ואמרתם זבח פסח הוא ליהוה אשר פסח על
בתי בני ישראל במיצריים בנגפו את
מיצריים ואת בתינו היציל ויקוד העם
וישתחוו 28 וילכו ויעשו בני ישראל כאשר
ציוה יהוה את מושה ואהרון כן עשו 29 ויהי
בחצי הלילה ויהוה היכה כל בכור בארץ
מיצריים מבכור פרעוה היושב על כיסאו
עד בכור השבי אשר בבית הבור וכול בכור בהמה
30 ויקם פרעוה לילה הוא וכל עבדיו וכל
מיצריים ותהי צעקה גדולה במיצריים
כי אין ביית אשר אין שם מת 31 ויקרא
למושה ולאהרון לילה ויואמר קומו צאו מיתוך
עמי גם אתם גם בני ישראל ולכו עיבדו את
יהוה כדברכם 32 גם צואנכם גם בקרכם קחו
כאשר דיברתם ולכו וברכתם גם אותי 33 ותחזק
מיצריים על העם למהר לשלחם מין הארץ
כי אמרו כולנו מתים 34 וישא העם את בצקו
טרם יחמץ מישארותם צרורות בשימלותם על
שיכמם 35 ובני ישראל עשו כדיבר מושה
וישאלו מימיצריים כלי כסף וכלי זהב
ושמלות 36 ויהוה נתן את חן העם בעיני
מיצריים וישאלום וינצלו את
מיצריים 37 ויסעו בני ישראל מרעמסס
סוכתה כשש מאות אלף רגלי הגברים לבד מיט
38 וגם ערב רב עלה איתם וצואן ובקר מיקנה
כבד מואד 39 ויואפו את הבצק אשר הוציאו

מימיצריים עוגות מצות כי לוא חמץ כי
גורשו מימיצריים ולוא יכלו להיתמהמה
וגם צדה לוא עסו להם 40 ומושב בני יסראל אשר
ישבו במיצריים שלושים שנה וארבע מאות
שנה 41 ויהי מיקץ שלושים שנה וארבע
מאות שנה ויהי בעצם היום הזה יצאו כל
ציבאות יהוה מארץ מיצריים 42 ליל
שימורים הוא ליהוה להוציאם מארץ
מיצריים הוא הלילה הזה ליהוה
שימורים לכל בני יסראל לדורותם 43 ויאמר
יהוה אל מושה ואהרון זואת חוקת הפסח כל בן
נכר לוא יואכל בו 44 וכל עבד איש מיקנת כסף
ומלתה אותו אז יואכל בו 45 תושב וסכיר לוא
יואכל בו 46 בביית אחד יאכל לוא תוציא מין
הביית מין הבסר חוצה ועצם לוא תישברו בו
47 כל עדת יסראל יעסו אותו 48 וכי יגור איתכה
גר ועסה פסח ליהוה הימול לו כל זכר ואז יקרב
לעסותו והיה כאזרח הארץ וכל ערל לוא יואכל בו
49 תורה אחת יהיה לאזרח ולגר הגר בתוככם
50 ויעסו כל בני יסראל כאשר ציוה יהוה את
מושה ואת אהרון כן עסו 51 ויהי בעצם היום
הזה הוציא יהוה את בני יסראל מארץ
מיצריים על ציבאותם

שמות פרק 13

1 וידבר יהוה אל מושה לאמור 2 קדש לי כל בכור
פטר כל רחם ביבני יסראל באדם ובבהמה לי
הוא 3 ויאמר מושה אל העם זכור את היום הזה
אשר יצאתם מימיצריים מיבית עבדים
כי בחוזק יד הוציא יהוה אתכם מיזה ולוא
יאכל חמץ 4 היום אתם יוצאים בחודש האבי
5 והיה כי יביאכה יהוה אל ארץ הכנעני
והחיתי והאמורי והחיוי והיבוסי אשר
נישבע לאבותיכה לתת לך ארץ זבת חלב ודבש
ועבדת את העבודה הזואת בחודש הזה 6 שיבעת
ימים תואכל מצות וביום השביעי חג ליהוה
7 מצות יאכל את שיבעת הימים ולוא יראה
לכה חמץ ולוא יראה לכה סאור בכל גבולכה
8 והיגדת לבינכה ביום ההוא לאמור בעבור זה
עסה יהוה לי בצאתי מימיצריים 9 והיה

10

11

12

13

14

15

16

17

18

19

20

21

22

14

1

2

3

4

[illegible]
[illegible] 5 [illegible]
[illegible]
[illegible]
[illegible] 6 [illegible]
[illegible] 7 [illegible]
[illegible] 8 [illegible]
[illegible]
[illegible]
[illegible] 9 [illegible]
[illegible]
[illegible]
[illegible] 10 [illegible]
[illegible]
[illegible]
[illegible] 11 [illegible]
[illegible]
[illegible]
[illegible] 12
[illegible]
[illegible]
[illegible] 13 [illegible]
[illegible]
[illegible]
[illegible]
[illegible] 14 [illegible]
[illegible] 15
[illegible] 16 [illegible]
[illegible]
[illegible] 17 [illegible]
[illegible]
[illegible]
[illegible] 18
[illegible] 19 [illegible]
[illegible]
[illegible]
[illegible] 20 [illegible]
[illegible]
[illegible]
[illegible] 21 [illegible]
[illegible]

[illegible] 22 [illegible]
[illegible]
[illegible] 23 [illegible]
[illegible]
[illegible] 24 [illegible]
[illegible]
[illegible]
[illegible] 25
[illegible]
[illegible] 26 [illegible]
[illegible]
[illegible]
[illegible] 27
[illegible]
[illegible]
[illegible] 28 [illegible]
[illegible]
[illegible] 29 [illegible]
[illegible]
[illegible] 30 [illegible]
[illegible]
[illegible] 31 [illegible]
[illegible]
[illegible]
[illegible]

15 [illegible]

[illegible] 1
[illegible]
[illegible] 2 [illegible]
[illegible]
[illegible] 3 [illegible]
[illegible] 4 [illegible]
[illegible] 5 [illegible]
[illegible] 6 [illegible]
[illegible]
[illegible] 7
[illegible] 8 [illegible]
[illegible]
[illegible] 9

נפשי אריק חרבי תורישמו ידי 10 נשפת
ברוחכה כסמו ים צללו כעופרת במיים
אדירים 11 מי כמוכה באלים יהוה מי
כמוכה נאדר בקודש נורא תהילות עוסה פלא
12 נטית ימינכה תיבלעמו ארץ 13 נחית
בחסדכה עם זו גאלת נהלת בעזכה אל נוה קדשכה
14 שמעו עמים ירגזון חיל אחז יושבי
פלשת 15 אז ניבהלו אלופי אדום אילי מואב
יואחזמו רעד נמוגו כול יושבי כנען
16 תיפול עליהם אימתה ופחד ביגדול
זרועכה ידמו כאבן עד יעבור עמכה יהוה עד
יעבור עם זו קנית 17 תביאמו ותיטעמו בהר
נחלתכה מכון לשיבתכה פעלת יהוה מיקדש
אדוני כוננו ידיכה 18 יהוה ימלוך לעולם
ועד 19 כי בא סוס פרעוה בריכבו ובפרשיו בים
וישב יהוה עליהם את מי הים ובני יסראל
הלכו ביבשה בתוך הים 20 ותיקח מירים
הנביאה אחות אהרון את התוף בידה ותצאן כל
הנשים אחריה בתופים ובימחולות 21 ותען
להם מירים שירו ליהוה כי גאוה גאה סוס
ורוכבו רמה בים 22 ויסע מושה את יסראל מים
סוף ויצאו אל מידבר שור וילכו שלושת ימים
במידבר ולוא מצאו מיים 23 ויבואו מרתה ולוא
יכלו לישתות מיים מימרה כי מרים הם
על כן קרא שמה מרה 24 וילונו העם על מושה
לאמור מה נישתה 25 ויצעק אל יהוה ויורהו
יהוה עץ וישלך אל המיים וימתקו המיים
שם סם לו חוק ומישפט ושם ניסהו 26 ויואמר
אם שמוע תישמע לקול יהוה אלוהיכה
והישר בעיניו תעסה והאזנת למיצותיו
ושמרת כל חוקיו כל המחלה אשר סמתי
במיצריים לוא אסים עליכה כי אני יהוה
רופאכה 27 ויבואו אילמה ושם שתים עסרה
עינות מיים ושיבעים תמרים ויחנו שם
על המיים

שמות פרק 16

1 ויסעו מאילים ויבואו כל עדת בני יסראל
אל מידבר סין אשר בין אילים ובין
סיני בחמישה עסר יום לחודש השני לצאתם
מארץ מיצריים 2 וילינו כל עדת בני

3
4
5
6
7
8
9
10
11
12
13
14
15
16
17
18
19
20

ויבאש ויקצוף עלהם מושה 21 וילקטו אותו
בבוקר בבוקר איש כפי אכלו וחם השמש ונמם
22 ויהי ביום השישי לקטו לחם מישנה
שני העומר לאחד ויבואו כל נסיאי העדה
ויגידו למושה 23 ויואמר אלהם הוא אשר דיבר
יהוה שבתון שבת קודש ליהוה מחר את אשר
תואפו אפו ואת אשר תבשלו בשלו ואת כל העודף
הניחו לכם למישמרת עד הבוקר 24 ויניחו
אותו עד הבוקר כאשר ציוה מושה ולוא היבאיש
ורימה לוא היתה בו 25 ויואמר מושה איכלוהו
היום כי שבת היום ליהוה היום לוא
תימצאוהו בסדה 26 ששת ימים תילקטוהו
וביום השביעי שבת לוא יהיה בו 27 ויהי
ביום השביעי יצאו מין העם לילקוט ולוא
מצאו 28 ויואמר יהוה אל מושה עד אנה
מאנתם לישמור מיצותי ותורותי 29 ראו כי
יהוה נתן לכם השבת על כן הוא נותן לכם
ביום השישי לחם יומים שבו איש תחתיו
אל יצא איש מימקומו ביום השביעי
30 וישבתו העם ביום השביעי 31 ויקראו בית
ישראל את שמו מן והוא כזרע גד לבן וטעמו
כצפיחית בידבש 32 ויואמר מושה זה הדבר
אשר ציוה יהוה מלוא העומר מימנו
למישמרת לדורותיכם למען יראו את הלחם
אשר האכלתי אתכם במידבר בהוציאי אתכם
מארץ מיצרים 33 ויואמר מושה אל אהרון
קח צינצנת אחת ותן שמה מלוא העומר מן
והנח אותו ליפני יהוה למישמרת
לדורותיכם 34 כאשר ציוה יהוה אל מושה
ויניחהו אהרון ליפני העדות למישמרת
35 ובני ישראל אכלו את המן ארבעים שנה עד
בואם אל ארץ נושבת את המן אכלו עד בואם אל
קצה ארץ כנען 36 והעומר עסירית האיפה
הוא

שמות פרק 17

1 ויסעו כל עדת בני ישראל מימידבר סין
למסעיהם על פי יהוה ויחנו בירפידים
ואין מים לישתות העם 2 ויריב העם עים
מושה ויואמרו תנו לנו מים ונישתה
ויואמר להם מושה מה תריבון עימדי מה

תנסון את יהוה 3 ויצמא שם העם למיים
וילן העם על מושה ויואמר למה זה העליתנו
מימיצריים להמית אותי ואת בני ואת
מיקני בצמא 4 ויצעק מושה אל יהוה לאמור
מה אעסה לעם הזה עוד מעט וסקלוני 5 ויואמר
יהוה אל מושה עבור ליפני העם וקח איתכה
מיזיקני יסראל ומטכה אשר היכית בו את
היאור קח בידכה והלכת 6 הינני עומד
לפניכה שם על הצור בחורב והיכית בצור
ויצאו מימנו מיים ושתה העם ויעס כן
מושה לעיני זיקני יסראל 7 ויקרא שם
המקום מסה ומריבה על ריב בני יסראל ועל
נסותם את יהוה לאמור היש יהוה בקירבנו
אים אין 8 ויבוא עמלק וילחם עים
יסראל בירפידים 9 ויואמר מושה אל
יהושוע בחר לנו אנשים וצא הילחם בעמלק
מחר אנוכי ניצב על רואש הגיבעה ומטה
האלוהים בידי 10 ויעס יהושוע כאשר אמר לו
מושה להילחם בעמלק ומושה אהרון וחור עלו
רואש הגיבעה 11 והיה כאשר ירים מושה ידו
וגבר יסראל וכאשר יניח ידו וגבר עמלק
12 וידי מושה כבדים ויקחו אבן ויסימו
תחתיו וישב עליה ואהרון וחור תמכו בידיו
מיזה אחד ומיזה אחד ויהי ידיו אמונה עד
בוא השמש 13 ויחלוש יהושוע את עמלק ואת עמו
לפי חר 14 ויואמר יהוה אל מושה כתוב זואת
זיכרון בספר וסים באזני יהושוע כי מחוה
אמחה את זכר עמלק מיתחת השמיים 15 ויבן
מושה מיזבח ויקרא שמו יהוה ניסי
16 ויואמר כי יד על כס יה מילחמה ליהוה
בעמלק מידור דור

שמות פרק 18

1 וישמע יתרו כוהן מידין חותן מושה את כל
אשר עסה אלוהים למושה וליסראל עמו כי
הוציא יהוה את יסראל מימיצריים 2 ויקח
יתרו חותן מושה את ציפורה אשת מושה אחר
שילוחיה 3 ואת שני בניה אשר שם האחד
גרשום כי אמר גר הייתי בארץ נכריה
4 ושם האחד אליעזר כי אלוהי אבי בעזרי
ויצילני מחרב פרעוה 5 ויבוא יתרו חותן

6

7

8

9

10

11

12

13

14

15

16

17

18

19

20

21

22

23

𐤅𐤂𐤌 𐤊𐤋 𐤄𐤏𐤌 𐤄𐤆𐤄 𐤏𐤋 𐤌𐤒𐤅𐤌𐤅 𐤉𐤁𐤅𐤀 𐤁𐤔𐤋𐤅𐤌
24 𐤅𐤉𐤔𐤌𐤏 𐤌𐤅𐤔𐤄 𐤋𐤒𐤅𐤋 𐤇𐤅𐤕𐤍𐤅 𐤅𐤉𐤏𐤎 𐤊𐤅𐤋 𐤀𐤔𐤓 𐤀𐤌𐤓
25 𐤅𐤉𐤁𐤇𐤓 𐤌𐤅𐤔𐤄 𐤀𐤍𐤔𐤉 𐤇𐤉𐤉𐤋 𐤌𐤉𐤊𐤋 𐤉𐤎𐤓𐤀𐤋
𐤅𐤉𐤕𐤍 𐤀𐤅𐤕𐤌 𐤓𐤀𐤔𐤉𐤌 𐤏𐤋 𐤄𐤏𐤌 𐤎𐤓𐤉 𐤀𐤋𐤐𐤉𐤌 𐤎𐤓𐤉
𐤌𐤀𐤅𐤕 𐤎𐤓𐤉 𐤇𐤌𐤉𐤔𐤉𐤌 𐤅𐤎𐤓𐤉 𐤏𐤎𐤓𐤅𐤕 26 𐤅𐤔𐤐𐤈𐤅 𐤀𐤕
𐤄𐤏𐤌 𐤁𐤊𐤋 𐤏𐤕 𐤀𐤕 𐤄𐤃𐤁𐤓 𐤄𐤒𐤔𐤄 𐤉𐤁𐤉𐤀𐤅𐤍 𐤀𐤋 𐤌𐤅𐤔𐤄
𐤅𐤊𐤋 𐤄𐤃𐤁𐤓 𐤄𐤒𐤈𐤅𐤍 𐤉𐤔𐤐𐤅𐤈𐤅 𐤄𐤌 27 𐤅𐤉𐤔𐤋𐤇 𐤌𐤅𐤔𐤄 𐤀𐤕
𐤇𐤅𐤕𐤍𐤅 𐤅𐤉𐤋𐤊 𐤋𐤅 𐤀𐤋 𐤀𐤓𐤑𐤅

𐤔𐤌𐤅𐤕 𐤐𐤓𐤒 19

1 𐤁𐤇𐤅𐤃𐤔 𐤄𐤔𐤋𐤉𐤔𐤉 𐤋𐤑𐤀𐤕 𐤁𐤍𐤉 𐤉𐤎𐤓𐤀𐤋 𐤌𐤀𐤓𐤑
𐤌𐤉𐤑𐤓𐤉𐤌 𐤁𐤉𐤅𐤌 𐤄𐤆𐤄 𐤁𐤀𐤅 𐤌𐤉𐤃𐤁𐤓 𐤎𐤉𐤍𐤉
2 𐤅𐤉𐤎𐤏𐤅 𐤌𐤓𐤐𐤉𐤃𐤉𐤌 𐤅𐤉𐤁𐤅𐤀𐤅 𐤌𐤉𐤃𐤁𐤓 𐤎𐤉𐤍𐤉
𐤅𐤉𐤇𐤍𐤅 𐤁𐤌𐤉𐤃𐤁𐤓 𐤅𐤉𐤇𐤍 𐤔𐤌 𐤉𐤎𐤓𐤀𐤋 𐤍𐤂𐤃 𐤄𐤄𐤓
3 𐤅𐤌𐤅𐤔𐤄 𐤏𐤋𐤄 𐤀𐤋 𐤄𐤀𐤋𐤅𐤄𐤉𐤌 𐤅𐤉𐤒𐤓𐤀 𐤀𐤋𐤉𐤅 𐤉𐤄𐤅𐤄
𐤌𐤉𐤍 𐤄𐤄𐤓 𐤋𐤀𐤌𐤅𐤓 𐤊𐤅𐤄 𐤕𐤅𐤀𐤌𐤓 𐤋𐤁𐤉𐤕 𐤉𐤏𐤒𐤅𐤁 𐤅𐤕𐤂𐤉𐤃
𐤋𐤁𐤍𐤉 𐤉𐤎𐤓𐤀𐤋 4 𐤀𐤕𐤌 𐤓𐤀𐤉𐤕𐤌 𐤀𐤔𐤓 𐤏𐤎𐤉𐤕𐤉
𐤋𐤌𐤉𐤑𐤓𐤉𐤌 𐤅𐤀𐤎𐤀 𐤀𐤕𐤊𐤌 𐤏𐤋 𐤊𐤍𐤐𐤉 𐤍𐤔𐤓𐤉𐤌
𐤅𐤀𐤁𐤉𐤀 𐤀𐤕𐤊𐤌 𐤀𐤋𐤉 5 𐤅𐤏𐤕𐤄 𐤀𐤌 𐤔𐤌𐤅𐤏 𐤕𐤉𐤔𐤌𐤏𐤅
𐤁𐤒𐤅𐤋𐤉 𐤅𐤔𐤌𐤓𐤕𐤌 𐤀𐤕 𐤁𐤓𐤉𐤕𐤉 𐤅𐤉𐤄𐤉𐤉𐤕𐤌 𐤋𐤉
𐤎𐤂𐤅𐤋𐤄 𐤌𐤉𐤊𐤋 𐤄𐤏𐤌𐤉𐤌 𐤊𐤉 𐤋𐤉 𐤊𐤋 𐤄𐤀𐤓𐤑 6 𐤅𐤀𐤕𐤌
𐤕𐤉𐤄𐤉𐤅 𐤋𐤉 𐤌𐤌𐤋𐤊𐤕 𐤊𐤅𐤄𐤍𐤉𐤌 𐤅𐤂𐤅𐤉 𐤒𐤃𐤅𐤔 𐤀𐤋𐤄
𐤄𐤃𐤁𐤓𐤉𐤌 𐤀𐤔𐤓 𐤕𐤃𐤁𐤓 𐤀𐤋 𐤁𐤍𐤉 𐤉𐤎𐤓𐤀𐤋 7 𐤅𐤉𐤁𐤅𐤀
𐤌𐤅𐤔𐤄 𐤅𐤉𐤒𐤓𐤀 𐤋𐤆𐤉𐤒𐤍𐤉 𐤄𐤏𐤌 𐤅𐤉𐤎𐤌 𐤋𐤉𐤐𐤍𐤉𐤄𐤌
𐤀𐤕 𐤊𐤋 𐤄𐤃𐤁𐤓𐤉𐤌 𐤄𐤀𐤋𐤄 𐤀𐤔𐤓 𐤑𐤉𐤅𐤄𐤅 𐤉𐤄𐤅𐤄 8 𐤅𐤉𐤏𐤍𐤅
𐤊𐤋 𐤄𐤏𐤌 𐤉𐤇𐤃𐤅 𐤅𐤉𐤅𐤀𐤌𐤓𐤅 𐤊𐤅𐤋 𐤀𐤔𐤓 𐤃𐤉𐤁𐤓 𐤉𐤄𐤅𐤄
𐤍𐤏𐤎𐤄 𐤅𐤉𐤔𐤁 𐤌𐤅𐤔𐤄 𐤀𐤕 𐤃𐤉𐤁𐤓𐤉 𐤄𐤏𐤌 𐤀𐤋 𐤉𐤄𐤅𐤄
9 𐤅𐤉𐤅𐤀𐤌𐤓 𐤉𐤄𐤅𐤄 𐤀𐤋 𐤌𐤅𐤔𐤄 𐤄𐤉𐤍𐤄 𐤀𐤍𐤅𐤊𐤉 𐤁𐤀
𐤀𐤋𐤉𐤊𐤄 𐤁𐤏𐤁 𐤄𐤏𐤍𐤍 𐤁𐤏𐤁𐤅𐤓 𐤉𐤔𐤌𐤏 𐤄𐤏𐤌 𐤁𐤃𐤁𐤓𐤉
𐤏𐤉𐤌𐤊 𐤅𐤂𐤌 𐤁𐤊𐤄 𐤉𐤀𐤌𐤉𐤍𐤅 𐤋𐤏𐤅𐤋𐤌 𐤅𐤉𐤂𐤃 𐤌𐤅𐤔𐤄 𐤀𐤕
𐤃𐤉𐤁𐤓𐤉 𐤄𐤏𐤌 𐤀𐤋 𐤉𐤄𐤅𐤄 10 𐤅𐤉𐤅𐤀𐤌𐤓 𐤉𐤄𐤅𐤄 𐤀𐤋 𐤌𐤅𐤔𐤄
𐤋𐤊 𐤀𐤋 𐤄𐤏𐤌 𐤅𐤒𐤉𐤃𐤔𐤕𐤌 𐤄𐤉𐤅𐤌 𐤅𐤌𐤇𐤓 𐤅𐤊𐤉𐤁𐤎𐤅
𐤎𐤉𐤌𐤋𐤅𐤕𐤌 11 𐤅𐤄𐤉𐤅 𐤍𐤊𐤅𐤍𐤉𐤌 𐤋𐤉𐤅𐤌 𐤄𐤔𐤋𐤉𐤔𐤉
𐤊𐤉 𐤁𐤉𐤅𐤌 𐤄𐤔𐤋𐤉𐤔𐤉 𐤉𐤓𐤃 𐤉𐤄𐤅𐤄 𐤋𐤏𐤉𐤍𐤉 𐤊𐤋 𐤄𐤏𐤌
𐤏𐤋 𐤄𐤓 𐤎𐤉𐤍𐤉 12 𐤅𐤄𐤉𐤂𐤁𐤋𐤕 𐤀𐤕 𐤄𐤏𐤌 𐤎𐤁𐤉𐤁 𐤋𐤀𐤌𐤅𐤓
𐤄𐤉𐤔𐤌𐤓𐤅 𐤋𐤊𐤌 𐤏𐤋𐤅𐤕 𐤁𐤄𐤓 𐤅𐤍𐤂𐤅𐤏 𐤁𐤒𐤑𐤄𐤅 𐤊𐤋 𐤄𐤍𐤅𐤂𐤏
𐤁𐤄𐤓 𐤌𐤅𐤕 𐤉𐤅𐤌𐤕 13 𐤋𐤅𐤀 𐤕𐤉𐤂𐤏 𐤁𐤅 𐤉𐤃 𐤊𐤉 𐤎𐤒𐤅𐤋 𐤉𐤎𐤒𐤋
𐤀𐤅 𐤉𐤓𐤅𐤄 𐤉𐤉𐤓𐤄 𐤀𐤉𐤌 𐤁𐤄𐤌𐤄 𐤀𐤉𐤌 𐤀𐤉𐤔 𐤋𐤅𐤀
𐤉𐤇𐤉𐤄 𐤁𐤌𐤔𐤅𐤊 𐤄𐤉𐤅𐤁𐤋 𐤄𐤌𐤄 𐤉𐤏𐤋𐤅 𐤁𐤄𐤓 14 𐤅𐤉𐤓𐤃
𐤌𐤅𐤔𐤄 𐤌𐤉𐤍 𐤄𐤄𐤓 𐤀𐤋 𐤄𐤏𐤌 𐤅𐤉𐤒𐤃𐤔 𐤀𐤕 𐤄𐤏𐤌 𐤅𐤉𐤊𐤁𐤎𐤅
𐤎𐤉𐤌𐤋𐤅𐤕𐤌 15 𐤅𐤉𐤅𐤀𐤌𐤓 𐤀𐤋 𐤄𐤏𐤌 𐤄𐤉𐤅 𐤍𐤊𐤅𐤍𐤉𐤌

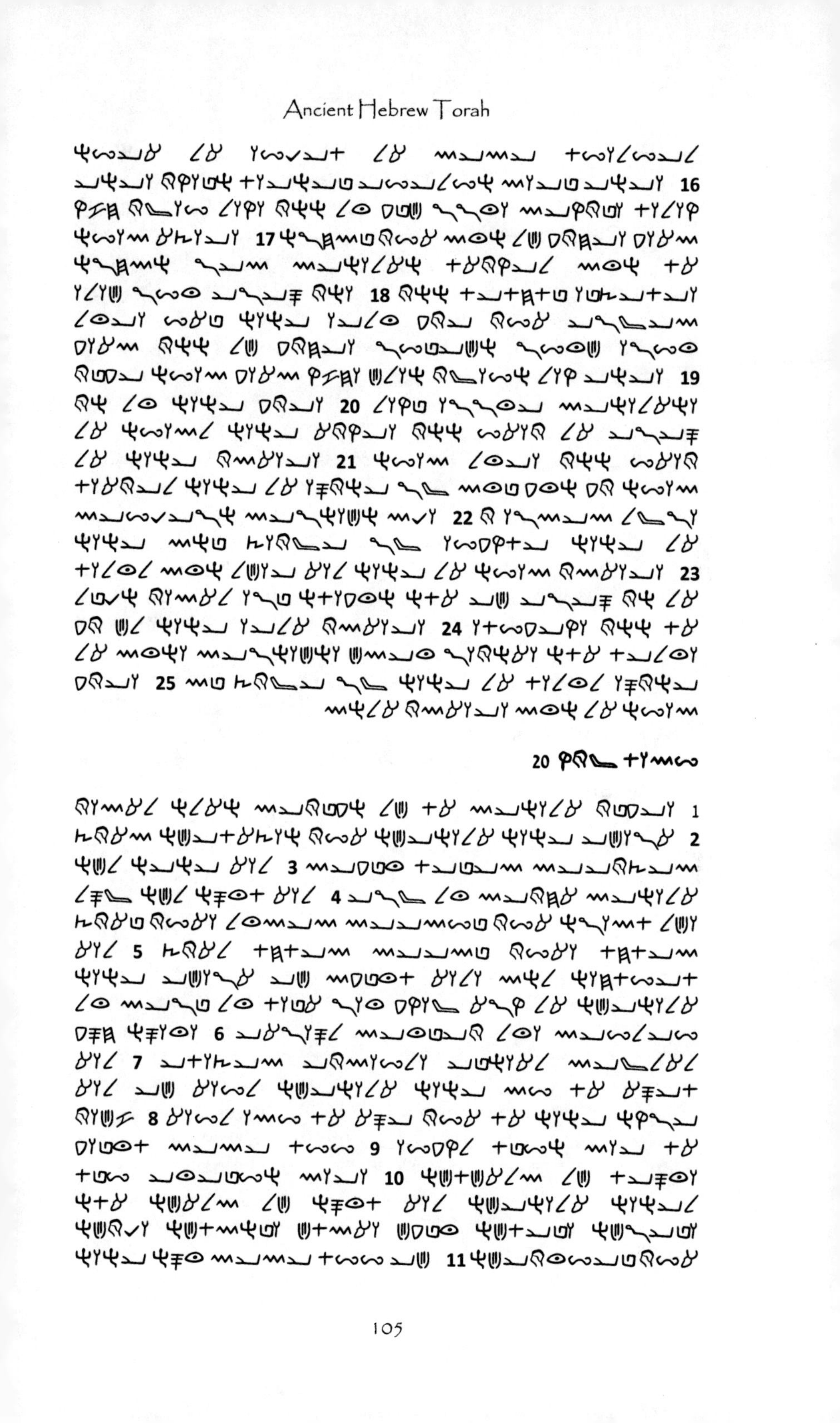

[illegible]
16 [illegible]
[illegible]
[illegible] 17 [illegible]
[illegible]
[illegible] 18 [illegible]
[illegible]
[illegible]
19 [illegible]
[illegible] 20 [illegible]
[illegible]
[illegible] 21 [illegible]
[illegible]
[illegible] 22 [illegible]
[illegible]
23 [illegible]
[illegible]
[illegible] 24 [illegible]
[illegible]
[illegible] 25 [illegible]
[illegible]

20 [illegible]

1 [illegible]
2 [illegible]
[illegible] 3 [illegible]
[illegible] 4 [illegible]
[illegible]
[illegible] 5 [illegible]
[illegible]
[illegible]
[illegible] 6 [illegible]
[illegible] 7 [illegible]
[illegible]
[illegible] 8 [illegible]
[illegible] 9 [illegible]
[illegible] 10 [illegible]
[illegible]
[illegible]
[illegible] 11 [illegible]

את השמיים ואת הארץ את הים ואת כל אשר בם
וינח ביום השביעי על כן ברך יהוה את יום
השבת ויקדשהו 12 כבד את אביכה ואת אימכה
למען יארכון ימיכה על האדמה אשר יהוה
אלוהיכה נותן לך 13 לוא תי-רצח 14 לוא
תי-נאף 15 לוא ת-יגנו 16 לוא תענה ברעכה עד
שקר 17 לוא תחמוד בית רעכה לוא תחמוד אשת
רעכה ועבדו ואמתו ושורו וחמורו וכול אשר לרעכה
18 וכול העם רואים את הקולות ואת הלפידים
ואת קול השופר ואת ההר עשן וירא העם וינועו
ויעמדו מרחוק 19 ויואמרו אל מושה דבר אתה
עימנו ונישמעה ואל ידבר עימנו אלוהים
פן נמות 20 ויואמר מושה אל העם אל תיראו
כי לבעבור נסות אתכם בא האלוהים ובעבור
תיהיה יראתו על פניכם לבילתי תחטאו
21 ויעמוד העם מרחוק ומושה ניגש אל הערפל
אשר שם האלוהים 22 ויואמר יהוה אל מושה
כוה תואמר אל בני יסראל אתם ראיתם כי
מין השמיים דיברתי עימכם 23 לוא
תעסון איתי אלוהי כסף ואלוהי זהב לוא תעסו
לכם 24 מיזבח אדמה תעסה לי וזבחת עליו את
עולותיכה ואת שלמיכה את צואנכה ואת בקרכה
בכל המקום אשר אזכיר את שמי אבוא אליכה
וברכתיכה 25 ואים מיזבח אבנים תעסה לי
לוא תיבנה אתהן גזית כי חרבכה הנפת עליה
ותחללה 26 ולוא תעלה במעלות על מיזבחי אשר
לוא תיגלה ערותכה עליו

שמות פרק 21

1 ואלה המישפטים אשר תסים ליפניהם
2 כי תיקנה עבד עברי שש שנים יעבוד
ובשביעית יצא לחפשי חינם 3 אים בגפו
יבוא בגפו יצא אים בעל אישה הוא ויצאה
אישתו עימו 4 אים אדוניו יתן לו אישה
וילדה לו בנים או בנות האישה וילדיה
תיהיה לאדוניה והוא יצא בגפו 5 ואים אמור
יואמר העבד אהבתי את אדוני את אישתי ואת
בני לוא אצא חפשי 6 והיגישו אדוניו אל
האלוהים והיגישו אל הדלת או אל המזוזה
ורצע אדוניו את אזנו במרצע ועבדו לעולם

7

8

9

10

11

12

13

14

15

16

17

18

19

20

21

22

23

24

25

26

27

28

29

30

31

32

33

בור או כי יכרה איש בור ולוא יכסנו ונפל שמה
שור או חמור 34 בעל הבור ישלם כסף ישיב
לבעליו והמת יהיה לו 35 וכי יגוף שור
איש את שור רעהו ומת ומכרו את השור החי וחצו
את כספו וגם את המת יחצון 36 או נודע כי שור
נגח הוא מיתמול שילשום ולוא ישמרנו
בעליו שלם ישלם שור תחת השור והמת יהיה
לו 37 כי יגנוב איש שור או סה וטבחו או מכרו
חמישה בקר ישלם תחת השור וארבע צאון תחת
הסה

שמות פרק 22

1 אים במחתרת ימצא הגנב והוכה ומת אין לו
דמים 2 אים זרחה השמש עליו דמים לו
שלם ישלם אים אין לו ונימכר ביגנבתו
3 אים הימצא תימצא בידו הגנבה מישור
עד חמור עד סה חיים שניים ישלם 4 כי
יבער איש סדה או כרם ושילח את בעירה
וביער ביסדה אחר מיטב סדהו ומיטב כרמו
ישלם 5 כי תצא אש ומצאה קוצים ונאכל
גדיש או הקמה או הסדה שלם ישלם המביער
את הבערה 6 כי יתן איש אל רעהו כסף או
כלים לישמור וגונב מיבית האיש אים
ימצא הגנב ישלם שניים 7 אים לוא
ימצא הגנב וניקרב בעל הבית אל האלוהים
אים לוא שלח ידו בימלאכת רעהו 8 על כל דבר
פשע על שור על חמור על סה על סלמה על כל אבדה
אשר יואמר כי הוא זה עד האלוהים יבוא דבר
שניהם אשר ירישעון אלוהים ישלם
שניים לרעהו 9 כי יתן איש אל רעהו חמור
או שור או סה וכל בהמה לישמור ומת או נישבר
או נישבה אין רואה 10 שבועת יהוה תיהיה
בין שניהם אים לוא שלח ידו בימלאכת
רעהו ולקח בעליו ולוא ישלם 11 ואים גנוב
יגנב מעימו ישלם לבעליו 12 אים טרוף
יטרף יביאהו עד הטרפה לוא ישלם 13 וכי
ישאל איש מעים רעהו ונישבר או מת בעליו
אין עימו שלם ישלם 14 אים בעליו עימו
לוא ישלם אים סכיר הוא בא ביסכרו 15 וכי
יפתה איש בתולה אשר לוא אורסה ושכב עימה

[illegible] 16 [illegible]
[illegible]
17 [illegible] 18 [illegible]
[illegible] 19 [illegible]
[illegible] 20 [illegible]
[illegible] 21 [illegible]
[illegible] 22 [illegible]
[illegible] 23 [illegible]
[illegible]
[illegible] 24 [illegible]
[illegible]
[illegible] 25 [illegible]
[illegible] 26 [illegible]
[illegible]
[illegible]
[illegible] 27 [illegible]
28 [illegible]
[illegible] 29 [illegible]
[illegible]
[illegible] 30 [illegible]
[illegible]

[illegible] 23

1 [illegible]
[illegible] 2 [illegible]
[illegible]
3 [illegible] 4 [illegible]
[illegible] 5 [illegible]
[illegible]
[illegible] 6 [illegible]
[illegible] 7 [illegible]
[illegible] 8 [illegible]
[illegible]
[illegible] 9 [illegible]
[illegible]
[illegible] 10 [illegible]
[illegible] 11 [illegible]
[illegible]
[illegible] 12 [illegible]
[illegible]

13

14

15

16

17

18

19

20

21

22

23

24

25

26

27

28

29

30

31

32

33

ישבו בארצכה פן יחטיאו אותכה לי כי תעבוד
את אלוהיהם כי יהיה לכה למוקש

שמות פרק 24

1 ואל מושה אמר עלה אל יהוה אתה ואהרון נדב
ואביהוא ושיבעים מיזיקני יסראל
והישתחויתם מרחוק 2 וניגש מושה לבדו אל
יהוה והם לוא יגשו והעם לוא יעלו עימו
3 ויבוא מושה ויספר לעם את כל דיברי יהוה
ואת כל המישפטים ויען כל העם קול אחד
ויאמרו כל הדברים אשר דיבר יהוה נעסה
4 ויכתוב מושה את כל דיברי יהוה וישכם
בבוקר ויבן מיזבח תחת ההר ושתים עסרה מצבה
לישנים עסר שיבטי יסראל 5 וישלח את
נערי בני יסראל ויעלו עולות ויזבחו זבחים
שלמים ליהוה פרים 6 ויקח מושה חצי הדם
ויסם באגנות וחצי הדם זרק על המיזבח 7 ויקח
ספר הברית ויקרא באוזני העם ויאמרו כול
אשר דיבר יהוה נעסה ונישמע 8 ויקח מושה
את הדם ויזרוק על העם ויאמר הינה דם
הברית אשר כרת יהוה עימכם על כל הדברים
האלה 9 ויעל מושה ואהרון נדב ואביהוא
ושיבעים מיזיקני יסראל 10 ויראו את
אלוהי יסראל ותחת רגליו כמעסה ליבנת
הספיר וכעצם השמיים לטוהר 11 ואל אצילי
בני יסראל לוא שלח ידו ויחזו את האלוהים
ויאכלו וישתו 12 ויאמר יהוה אל מושה עלה
אלי ההרה והיה שם ואתנה לכה את לוחות האבן
והתורה והמצוה אשר כתבתי להורותם 13 ויקם
מושה ויהושוע משרתו ויעל מושה אל הר
האלוהים 14 ואל הזקינים אמר שבו לנו בזה עד
אשר נשוב אליכם והינה אהרון וחור עימכם
מי בעל דברים יגש אלהם 15 ויעל מושה אל
ההר ויכס הענן את ההר 16 וישכון כבוד יהוה
על הר סיני ויכסהו הענן ששת ימים
ויקרא אל מושה ביום השביעי מיתוך הענן
17 ומראה כבוד יהוה כאש אוכלת ברואש ההר
לעיני בני יסראל 18 ויבוא מושה בתוך
הענן ויעל אל ההר ויהי מושה בהר ארבעים
יום וארבעים לילה

שמות פרק 25

1 וידבר יהוה אל מושה לאמור 2 דבר אל בני
יסראל ויקחו לי תרומה מאת כל איש אשר
ידבנו ליבו תיקחו את תרומתי 3 וזואת התרומה
אשר תיקחו מאיתם זהב וכסף ונחושת 4 ותכלת
וארגמן ותולעת שני ושש ועיזים 5 ועורות
אילים מאדמים ועורות תחשים ועצי
שיטים 6 שמן למאור בסמים לשמן
המישחה וליקטורת הסמים 7 אבני שוהם
ואבני מילואים לאפוד ולחושן 8 ועסו לי
מיקדש ושכנתי בתוכם 9 ככול אשר אני מראה
אותכה את תבנית המישכן ואת תבנית כל כליו
וכן תעסו 10 ועסו ארון עצי שיטים אמתים
וחצי ארכו ואמה וחצי רחבו ואמה וחצי קומתו
11 וציפית אותו זהב טהור מבית ומיחוץ
תצפנו ועסית עליו זר זהב סביב 12 ויצקת לו
ארבע טבעות זהב ונתתה על ארבע פעמותיו
ושתי טבעות על צלעו האחת ושתי טבעות על צלעו
השנית 13 ועסית בדי עצי שיטים
וציפית אותם זה 14 והבאת את הבדים בטבעות
על צלעות הארון לסאת את הארון בהם 15 בטבעות
הארון יהיו הבדים לוא יסורו מימנו 16 ונתת
אל הארון את העדות אשר אתן אליכה 17 ועסית
כפורת זהב טהור אמתים וחצי ארכה ואמה
וחצי רחבה 18 ועסית שנים כרובים זהב
מיקשה תעסה אותם מישני קצות הכפורת
19 ועסה כרוב אחד מיקצה מיזה וכרוב אחד
מיקצה מיזה מין הכפורת תעסו את הכרובים
על שני קצותיו 20 והיו הכרובים פורסי
כנפים למעלה סוככים בכנפיהם על
הכפורת ופניהם איש אל אחיו אל הכפורת
יהיו פני הכרובים 21 ונתת את הכפורת על
הארון מילמעלה ואל הארון תיתן את העדות
אשר אתן אליכה 22 ונועדתי לכה שם ודיברתי
איתכה מעל הכפורת מיבין שני הכרובים
אשר על ארון העדות את כל אשר אצוה אותכה אל
בני יסראל 23 ועסית שולחן עצי שיטים
אמתים ארכו ואמה רחבו ואמה וחצי קומתו
24 וציפית אותו זהב טהור ועסית לו זר זהב סביב
25 ועסית לו מסגרת טופח סביב ועסית זר זהב

[illegible] 26 [illegible]
[illegible]
[illegible] 27 [illegible]
[illegible] 28 [illegible]
[illegible]
[illegible] 29 [illegible]
[illegible]
[illegible] 30 [illegible]
[illegible] 31 [illegible]
[illegible]
[illegible]
[illegible] 32
[illegible]
[illegible] 33 [illegible]
[illegible]
[illegible]
[illegible]
[illegible] 34
[illegible] 35 [illegible]
[illegible]
[illegible]
[illegible]
[illegible] 36
[illegible] 37 [illegible]
[illegible]
[illegible] 38 [illegible]
[illegible] 39
[illegible] 40 [illegible]
[illegible]

26 [illegible]

[illegible] 1
[illegible]
[illegible] 2 [illegible]
[illegible]
[illegible] 3 [illegible]
[illegible]
[illegible] 4 [illegible]
[illegible]
[illegible]

השנית 5 חמישים לולאות תעשה ביריעה
האחת וחמישים לולאות תעשה ביקצה היריעה
אשר במחברת השנית מקבילות הלולאות אישה
אל אחותה 6 ועשית חמישים קרסי זהב וחיברת
את היריעות אישה אל אחותה בקרסים והיה
המישכן אחד 7 ועשית יריעות עיזים
לאוהל על המישכן עשתי עשרה יריעות תעשה
אותם 8 אורך היריעה האחת שלושים באמה
ורוחב ארבע באמה היריעה האחת מידה אחת
לעשתי עשרה יריעות 9 וחיברת את חמש
היריעות לבד ואת שש היריעות לבד וכפלת את
היריעה השישית אל מול פני האוהל
10 ועשית חמישים לולאות על שפת היריעה
האחת הקיצונה בחוברת וחמישים לולאות על
שפת היריעה החוברת השנית 11 ועשית קרסי
נחושת חמישים והבאת את הקרסים בלולאות
וחיברת את האוהל והיה אחד 12 וסרח העודף
ביריעות האוהל חצי היריעה העודפת תיסרח
על אחורי המישכן 13 והאמה מיזה והאמה
מיזה בעודף באורך יריעות האוהל יהיה סרוח
על צידי המישכן מיזה ומיזה לכסותו
14 ועשית מיכסה לאוהל עורות אילים
מאדמים ומיכסה עורות תחשים מילמעלה
15 ועשית את הקרשים למישכן עצי שיטים
עומדים 16 עשר אמות אורך הקרש ואמה וחצי
האמה רוחב הקרש האחד 17 שתי ידות לקרש האחד
משולבות אישה אל אחותה כן תעשה לכול קרשי
המישכן 18 ועשית את הקרשים למישכן
עשרים קרש ליפאת נגבה תימנה
19 וארבעים אדני כסף תעשה תחת עשרים
הקרש שני אדנים תחת הקרש האחד לשתי
ידותיו ושני אדנים תחת הקרש האחד לשתי
ידותיו 20 ולצלע המישכן השנית ליפאת
צפון עשרים קרש 21 וארבעים אדניהם כסף
שני אדנים תחת הקרש האחד ושני אדנים
תחת הקרש האחד 22 ולירכתי המישכן ימה
תעשה שישה קרשים 23 ושני קרשים תעשה
לימקוצעות המישכן בירכתיים
24 ויהיו תואמים מילמטה ויחדו יהיו
תמים על ראשו אל הטבעת האחת כן יהיה
לשניהם לשני המיקוצעות יהיו

25 והיו שמנה קרשים ואדניהם כסף ששה
עשר אדנים שני אדנים תחת הקרש האחד
ושני אדנים תחת הקרש האחד 26 ועשית
בריחם עצי שטים חמשה לקרשי צלע
המשכן האחד 27 וחמשה בריחם לקרשי
צלע המשכן השנית וחמשה בריחם
לקרשי צלע המשכן לירכתים ימה
28 והבריח התיכן בתוך הקרשים מבריח מן
הקצה אל הקצה 29 ואת הקרשים תצפה זהב ואת
טבעתיהם תעשה זהב בתים לבריחם
וצפית את הבריחם זהב 30 והקמת את
המשכן כמשפטו אשר הראית בהר
31 ועשית פרכת תכלת וארגמן ותולעת שני
ושש משזר מעשה חשב יעשה אתה כרבים
32 ונתתה אתה על ארבעה עמודי שטים
מצפים זהב וויהם זהב על ארבעה אדני כסף
33 ונתתה את הפרכת תחת הקרסים והבאת שמה
מבית לפרכת את ארון העדות והבדילה
הפרכת לכם בין הקדש ובין קדש הקדשים
34 ונתת את הכפרת על ארון העדות בקדש
הקדשים 35 ושמת את השלחן מחוץ לפרכת
ואת המנרה נכח השלחן על צלע המשכן
תימנה והשלחן תתן על צלע צפון
36 ועשית מסך לפתח האהל תכלת וארגמן ותולעת
שני ושש משזר מעשה רקם 37 ועשית למסך
חמשה עמודי שטים וצפית אתם זהב
וויהם זהב ויצקת להם חמשה אדני נחשת

שמות פרק 27

1 ועשית את המזבח עצי שטים חמש אמות
ארך וחמש אמות רחב רבוע יהיה המזבח
ושלש אמות קמתו 2 ועשית קרנתיו על ארבע
פנתיו ממנו תהיין קרנתיו
וצפית אתו נחשת 3 ועשית סירתיו לדשנו
ויעיו ומזרקתיו ומזלגתיו ומחתתיו
לכל כליו תעשה נחשת 4 ועשית לו מכבר מעשה
רשת נחשת ועשית על הרשת ארבע טבעת נחשת
על ארבע קצותיו 5 ונתתה אתה תחת כרכב
המזבח מלמטה והיתה הרשת עד חצי
המזבח 6 ועשית בדים למזבח בדי עצי

𐤔𐤉𐤈𐤉𐤌 𐤅𐤑𐤉𐤐𐤉𐤕 𐤀𐤅𐤕𐤌 𐤍𐤇𐤅𐤔𐤕 7 𐤅𐤄𐤅𐤁𐤀 𐤀𐤕
𐤁𐤃𐤉𐤅 𐤁𐤈𐤁𐤏𐤅𐤕 𐤅𐤄𐤉𐤅 𐤄𐤁𐤃𐤉𐤌 𐤏𐤋 𐤔𐤕𐤉 𐤑𐤋𐤏𐤅𐤕
𐤄𐤌𐤉𐤆𐤁𐤇 𐤁𐤉𐤎𐤀𐤕 𐤀𐤅𐤕𐤅 8 𐤍𐤁𐤅𐤁 𐤋𐤅𐤇𐤅𐤕 𐤕𐤏𐤎𐤄 𐤀𐤅𐤕𐤅
𐤊𐤀𐤔𐤓 𐤄𐤓𐤀𐤄 𐤀𐤅𐤕𐤊𐤄 𐤁𐤄𐤓 𐤊𐤍 𐤉𐤏𐤎𐤅 9 𐤅𐤏𐤎𐤉𐤕 𐤀𐤕 𐤇𐤑𐤓
𐤄𐤌𐤉𐤔𐤊𐤍 𐤋𐤉𐤐𐤀𐤕 𐤍𐤂𐤁 𐤕𐤉𐤌𐤍𐤄 𐤒𐤋𐤏𐤉𐤌 𐤋𐤇𐤑𐤓
𐤔𐤔 𐤌𐤔𐤆𐤓 𐤌𐤀𐤄 𐤁𐤀𐤌𐤄 𐤀𐤅𐤓𐤊 𐤋𐤐𐤀𐤄 𐤄𐤀𐤇𐤕
10 𐤅𐤏𐤌𐤅𐤃𐤉𐤅 𐤏𐤎𐤓𐤉𐤌 𐤅𐤀𐤃𐤍𐤉𐤄𐤌 𐤏𐤎𐤓𐤉𐤌 𐤍𐤇𐤅𐤔𐤕
𐤅𐤅𐤉 𐤄𐤏𐤌𐤅𐤃𐤉𐤌 𐤅𐤇𐤔𐤅𐤒𐤉𐤄𐤌 𐤊𐤎 11 𐤅𐤊𐤍 𐤋𐤉𐤐𐤀𐤕
𐤑𐤐𐤅𐤍 𐤁𐤀𐤅𐤓𐤊 𐤒𐤋𐤏𐤉𐤌 𐤌𐤀𐤄 𐤀𐤅𐤓𐤊 𐤅𐤏𐤌𐤃𐤅 𐤏𐤎𐤓𐤉𐤌
𐤅𐤀𐤃𐤍𐤉𐤄𐤌 𐤏𐤎𐤓𐤉𐤌 𐤍𐤇𐤅𐤔𐤕 𐤅𐤅𐤉 𐤄𐤏𐤌𐤅𐤃𐤉𐤌
𐤅𐤇𐤔𐤅𐤒𐤉𐤄𐤌 𐤊𐤎 12 𐤅𐤓𐤅𐤇𐤁 𐤄𐤇𐤑𐤓 𐤋𐤉𐤐𐤀𐤕 𐤉𐤌 𐤒𐤋𐤏𐤉𐤌
𐤇𐤌𐤉𐤔𐤉𐤌 𐤀𐤌𐤄 𐤏𐤌𐤅𐤃𐤉𐤄𐤌 𐤏𐤎𐤓𐤄 𐤅𐤀𐤃𐤍𐤉𐤄𐤌
𐤏𐤎𐤓𐤄 13 𐤅𐤓𐤅𐤇𐤁 𐤄𐤇𐤑𐤓 𐤋𐤉𐤐𐤀𐤕 𐤒𐤃𐤌𐤄 𐤌𐤉𐤆𐤓𐤇𐤄
𐤇𐤌𐤉𐤔𐤉𐤌 𐤀𐤌𐤄 14 𐤅𐤇𐤌𐤔 𐤏𐤎𐤓𐤄 𐤀𐤌𐤄 𐤒𐤋𐤏𐤉𐤌
𐤋𐤊𐤕𐤐 𐤏𐤌𐤅𐤃𐤉𐤄𐤌 𐤔𐤋𐤅𐤔𐤄 𐤅𐤀𐤃𐤍𐤉𐤄𐤌 𐤔𐤋𐤅𐤔𐤄
15 𐤅𐤋𐤊𐤕𐤐 𐤄𐤔𐤍𐤉𐤕 𐤇𐤌𐤔 𐤏𐤎𐤓𐤄 𐤒𐤋𐤏𐤉𐤌
𐤏𐤌𐤅𐤃𐤉𐤄𐤌 𐤔𐤋𐤅𐤔𐤄 𐤅𐤀𐤃𐤍𐤉𐤄𐤌 𐤔𐤋𐤅𐤔𐤄 16 𐤅𐤋𐤔𐤏𐤓
𐤄𐤇𐤑𐤓 𐤌𐤎𐤊 𐤏𐤎𐤓𐤉𐤌 𐤀𐤌𐤄 𐤕𐤊𐤋𐤕 𐤅𐤀𐤓𐤂𐤌𐤍 𐤅𐤕𐤅𐤋𐤏𐤕
𐤔𐤍𐤉 𐤅𐤔𐤔 𐤌𐤔𐤆𐤓 𐤌𐤏𐤎𐤄 𐤓𐤅𐤒𐤌 𐤏𐤌𐤅𐤃𐤉𐤄𐤌 𐤀𐤓𐤁𐤏𐤄
𐤅𐤀𐤃𐤍𐤉𐤄𐤌 𐤀𐤓𐤁𐤏𐤄 17 𐤊𐤋 𐤏𐤌𐤅𐤃𐤉 𐤄𐤇𐤑𐤓 𐤎𐤁𐤉𐤁
𐤌𐤇𐤅𐤔𐤒𐤉𐤌 𐤊𐤎𐤐 𐤅𐤅𐤉𐤄𐤌 𐤊𐤎𐤐 𐤅𐤀𐤃𐤍𐤉𐤄𐤌 𐤍𐤇𐤅𐤔𐤕
18 𐤀𐤅𐤓𐤊 𐤄𐤇𐤑𐤓 𐤌𐤀𐤄 𐤁𐤀𐤌𐤄 𐤅𐤓𐤅𐤇𐤁 𐤇𐤌𐤉𐤔𐤉𐤌
𐤁𐤇𐤌𐤉𐤔𐤉𐤌 𐤅𐤒𐤅𐤌𐤄 𐤇𐤌𐤔 𐤀𐤌𐤅𐤕 𐤔𐤔 𐤌𐤔𐤆𐤓
𐤅𐤀𐤃𐤍𐤉𐤄𐤌 𐤍𐤇𐤅𐤔𐤕 19 𐤋𐤊𐤅𐤋 𐤊𐤋𐤉 𐤄𐤌𐤉𐤔𐤊𐤍 𐤁𐤊𐤅𐤋
𐤏𐤁𐤅𐤃𐤕𐤅 𐤅𐤊𐤋 𐤉𐤕𐤃𐤅𐤕𐤉𐤅 𐤅𐤊𐤋 𐤉𐤕𐤃𐤅𐤕 𐤄𐤇𐤑𐤓 𐤍𐤇𐤅𐤔𐤕
20 𐤅𐤀𐤕𐤄 𐤕𐤑𐤅𐤄 𐤀𐤕 𐤁𐤍𐤉 𐤉𐤎𐤓𐤀𐤋 𐤅𐤉𐤉𐤒𐤇𐤅 𐤀𐤋𐤉𐤊𐤄
𐤔𐤌𐤍 𐤆𐤉𐤉𐤕 𐤆𐤊 𐤊𐤕𐤉𐤕 𐤋𐤌𐤀𐤅𐤓 𐤋𐤄𐤏𐤋𐤅𐤕 𐤍𐤓 𐤕𐤌𐤉𐤃
21 𐤁𐤀𐤅𐤄𐤋 𐤌𐤅𐤏𐤃 𐤌𐤉𐤇𐤅𐤑 𐤋𐤐𐤓𐤅𐤊𐤕 𐤀𐤔𐤓 𐤏𐤋 𐤄𐤏𐤃𐤅𐤕
𐤉𐤏𐤓𐤅𐤊 𐤀𐤅𐤕𐤅 𐤀𐤄𐤓𐤅𐤍 𐤅𐤁𐤍𐤉𐤅 𐤌𐤏𐤓𐤁 𐤏𐤃 𐤁𐤅𐤒𐤓
𐤋𐤉𐤐𐤍𐤉 𐤉𐤄𐤅𐤄 𐤇𐤅𐤒𐤕 𐤏𐤅𐤋𐤌 𐤋𐤃𐤅𐤓𐤅𐤕𐤌 𐤌𐤀𐤕 𐤁𐤍𐤉
𐤉𐤎𐤓𐤀𐤋

𐤔𐤌𐤅𐤕 𐤐𐤓𐤒 28

1 𐤅𐤀𐤕𐤄 𐤄𐤒𐤓𐤁 𐤀𐤋𐤉𐤊𐤄 𐤀𐤕 𐤀𐤄𐤓𐤅𐤍 𐤀𐤇𐤉𐤊𐤄 𐤅𐤀𐤕 𐤁𐤍𐤉𐤅
𐤀𐤉𐤕𐤅 𐤌𐤉𐤕𐤅𐤊 𐤁𐤍𐤉 𐤉𐤎𐤓𐤀𐤋 𐤋𐤊𐤄𐤍𐤅 𐤋𐤉 𐤀𐤄𐤓𐤅𐤍 𐤍𐤃𐤁
𐤅𐤀𐤁𐤉𐤄𐤅𐤀 𐤀𐤋𐤏𐤆𐤓 𐤅𐤀𐤉𐤕𐤌𐤓 𐤁𐤍𐤉 𐤀𐤄𐤓𐤅𐤍 2 𐤅𐤏𐤎𐤉𐤕
𐤁𐤉𐤂𐤃𐤉 𐤒𐤅𐤃𐤔 𐤋𐤀𐤄𐤓𐤅𐤍 𐤀𐤇𐤉𐤊𐤄 𐤋𐤊𐤁𐤅𐤃 𐤅𐤋𐤕𐤉𐤐𐤀𐤓𐤕
3 𐤅𐤀𐤕𐤄 𐤕𐤃𐤁𐤓 𐤀𐤋 𐤊𐤋 𐤇𐤊𐤌𐤉 𐤋𐤁 𐤀𐤔𐤓 𐤌𐤉𐤋𐤀𐤕𐤉𐤅 𐤓𐤅𐤇
𐤇𐤊𐤌𐤄 𐤅𐤏𐤎𐤅 𐤀𐤕 𐤁𐤉𐤂𐤃𐤉 𐤀𐤄𐤓𐤅𐤍 𐤋𐤒𐤃𐤔𐤅 𐤋𐤊𐤄𐤍𐤅 𐤋𐤉
4 𐤅𐤀𐤋𐤄 𐤄𐤁𐤂𐤃𐤉𐤌 𐤀𐤔𐤓 𐤉𐤏𐤎𐤅 𐤇𐤅𐤔𐤍 𐤅𐤀𐤐𐤅𐤃 𐤅𐤌𐤏𐤉𐤋
𐤅𐤊𐤕𐤅𐤍𐤕 𐤕𐤔𐤁𐤑 𐤌𐤉𐤑𐤍𐤐𐤕 𐤅𐤀𐤁𐤍𐤈 𐤅𐤏𐤎𐤅 𐤁𐤉𐤂𐤃𐤉

קודש לאהרון אחיכה ולבניו לכהנו לי 5 והם
יקחו את הזהב ואת התכלת ואת הארגמן ואת תולעת
השני ואת השש 6 ועשו את האפוד זהב תכלת
וארגמן תולעת שני ושש משזר מעשה חוש
7 שתי כתפות חוברות יהיה לו אל שני קצותיו
וחובר 8 וחשב אפודתו אשר עליו כמעשהו מימנו
יהיה זהב תכלת וארגמן ותולעת שני ושש
משזר 9 ולקחת את שתי אבני שוהם ופיתחת
עליהם שמות בני ישראל 10 שישה
משמותם על האבן האחת ואת שמות השישה
הנותרים על האבן השנית כתולדותם 11 מעשה
חרש אבן פיתוחי חותם תפתח את שתי
האבנים על שמות בני ישראל מוסבות
מישבצות זהב תעשה אותם 12 ושמת את שתי
האבנים על כיתפות האפוד אבני זיכרון
לבני ישראל ונשא אהרון את שמותם
לפני יהוה על שתי כתפיו לזיכרון
13 ועשית מישבצות זה 14 ושתי שרשרות זהב
טהור מיגבלות תעשה אותם מעשה עבות ונתתה את
שרשרות העבותות על המישבצות 15 ועשית
חושן מישפט מעשה חושב כמעשה אפוד תעשנו
זהב תכלת וארגמן ותולעת שני ושש משזר
תעשה אותו 16 רבוע יהיה כפול זרת ארכו וזרת
רחבו 17 ומילאת בו מילואת אבן ארבעה טורים
אבן טור אודם פיטדה וברקת הטור האחד 18 והטור
השני נופך ספיר ויהלום 19 והטור
השלישי לשם שבו ואחלמה 20 והטור הרביעי
תרשיש ושוהם וישפה משובצים זהב יהיו
במילואותם 21 והאבנים תיהיין על שמות
בני ישראל שתים עשרה על שמותם פיתוחי
חותם איש על שמו תיהיין לשני עשר
שבט 22 ועשית על החושן שרשרות גבלות מעשה
עבות זהב טהור 23 ועשית על החושן שתי טבעות
זהב ונתת את שתי הטבעות על שני קצות החושן
24 ונתתה את שתי עבותות הזהב על שתי הטבעות
אל קצות החושן 25 ואת שתי קצות שתי העבותות
תיתן על שתי המישבצות ונתתה על כיתפות
האפוד אל מול פניו 26 ועשית שתי טבעות זהב
ושמת אותם על שני קצות החושן על שפתו אשר
אל עבר האפוד ביתה 27 ועשית שתי טבעות זהב
ונתתה אותם על שתי כיתפות האפוד מילמטה

מימול פניו לעומת מחברתו מימעל לחשב
האפוד 28 ויירכסו את החושן מיטבעותו אל
טבעות האפוד ביפתיל תכלת ליהיות על חשב
האפוד ולוא יזח החושן מעל האפוד 29 ונסא
אהרון את שמות בני יסראל בחושן המישפט
על ליבו בבואו אל הקודש לזיכרון ליפני
יהוה תמיד 30 ונתת אל חושן המישפט את
האורים ואת התומים והיו על לב אהרון בבואו
ליפני יהוה ונסא אהרון את מישפט בני
יסראל על ליבו ליפני יהוה תמיד 31 ועסית
את מעיל האפוד כליל תכלת 32 והיה פי רואשו
בתוכו ספה יהיה לפיו סביב מעסה אורג כפי
תחרא יהיה לו לוא יקרע 33 ועסית על שוליו
רימוני תכלת וארגמן ותולעת שני על שוליו
סביב ופעמוני זהב בתוכם סביב 34 פעמון זהב
ורימון פעמון זהב ורימון על שולי
המעיל סביב 35 והיה על אהרון לשרת ונישמע
קולו בבואו אל הקודש ליפני יהוה ובצאתו ולוא
ימות 36 ועסית ציץ זהב טהור ופיתחת עליו
פיתוחי חותם קודש ליהוה 37 וסמת אותו על
פתיל תכלת והיה על המיצנפת אל מול פני
המיצנפת יהיה 38 והיה על מצח אהרון
ונסא אהרון את עון הקדשים אשר יקדישו
בני יסראל לכל מתנות קדשיהם והיה על
מיצחו תמיד לרצון להם ליפני יהוה
39 ושיבצת הכתונת שש ועסית מיצנפת שש
ואבנט תעסה מעסה רוקם 40 וליבני אהרון
תעסה כותנות ועסית להם אבנטים ומיגבעות
תעסה להם לכבוד ולתיפארת 41 והילבשת אותם
את אהרון אחיכה ואת בניו איתו ומשחת אותם
ומילאת את ידם וקידשת אותם וכיהנו לי
42 ועסה להם מיכנסי בד לכסות בסר ערוה
מימתניים ועד ירכיים יהיו 43 והיו על
אהרון ועל בניו בבואם אל אוהל מועד או
ביגישתם אל המיזבח לשרת בקודש ולוא יסאו
עון ומתו חוקת עולם לו ולזרעו אחריו

שמות פרק 29

1 וזה הדבר אשר תעסה להם לקדש אותם לכהן לי
לקח פר אחד בן בקר ואילים שניים
תמימים 2 ולחם מצות וחלות מצות בלולות

בשמן ורקיקי מצות משוחים בשמן סולת
חיטים תעסה אותם 3 ונתת אותם על סל אחד
והיקרבת אותם בסל ואת הפר ואת שני האילים
4 ואת אהרון ואת בניו תקריב אל פתח אוהל מועד
ורחצת אותם במיים 5 ולקחת את הבגדים
והילבשת את אהרון את הכותונת ואת מעיל
האפוד ואת האפוד ואת החושן ואפדת לו בחשב
האפוד 6 וסמת המיצנפת על רואשו ונתת את
נזר הקודש על המיצנפת 7 ולקחת את שמן
המישחה ויצקת על רואשו ומשחת אותו 8 ואת
בניו תקריב והילבשתם כותנות 9 וחגרת אותם
אבנט אהרון ובניו וחבשת להם מיגבעות
והיתה להם כהונה לחוקת עולם ומילאת יד
אהרון ויד בניו 10 והיקרבת את הפר ליפני
אוהל מועד וסמך אהרון ובניו את ידיהם על
רואש הפר 11 ושחטת את הפר ליפני יהוה
פתח אוהל מועד 12 ולקחת מידם הפר ונתתה על
קרנות המיזבח באצבעכה ואת כל הדם תישפוך
אל יסוד המיזבח 13 ולקחת את כל החלב המכסה את
הקרב ואת היתרת על הכבד ואת שתי הכליות ואת
החלב אשר עליהן והיקטרת המיזבחה 14 ואת
בסר הפר ואת עורו ואת פירשו תיסרוף באש
מיחוץ למחנה חטאת הוא 15 ואת האייל האחד
תיקח וסמכו אהרון ובניו את ידיהם על רואש
האייל 16 ושחטת את האייל ולקחת את דמו וזרקת
על המיזבח סביב 17 ואת האייל תנתח
לנתחיו ורחצת קירבו וכרעיו ונתת על נתחיו
ועל רואשו 18 והיקטרת את כל האייל המיזבחה
עלה הוא ליהוה ריח ניחוח אשה ליהוה הוא
19 ולקחת את האייל השני וסמך אהרון ובניו
את ידיהם על רואש האייל 20 ושחטת את
האייל ולקחת מידמו ונתתה על תנוך אוזן
אהרון ועל תנוך אוזן בניו הימנית ועל בוהן
ידם הימנית ועל בוהן רגלם הימנית
וזרקת את הדם על המיזבח סביב 21 ולקחת מין
הדם אשר על המיזבח ומישמן המישחה
והיזית על אהרון ועל בגדיו ועל בניו ועל
בגדי בניו איתו וקדש הוא ובגדיו ובניו
ובגדי בניו איתו 22 ולקחת מין האייל
החלב והאליה ואת החלב המכסה את הקרב ואת
יתרת הכבד ואת שתי הכליות ואת החלב אשר

איועד לכם שמה לדבר אליכה שם 43 ונועדתי
שמה ליבני יסראל וניקדש ביכבודי
44 וקידשתי את אוהל מועד ואת המיזבח ואת
אהרון ואת בניו אקדש לכהן לי 45 ושכנתי
בתוך בני יסראל והייתי להם לאלוהים
46 וידעו כי אני יהוה אלוהיהם אשר
הוצאתי אותם מארץ מיצריים לשכני
בתוכם אני יהוה אלוהיהם

שמות פרק 30

1 ועסית מיזבח מיקטר קטורת עצי שיטים
תעסה אותו 2 אמה ארכו ואמה רחבו רבוע ייהיה
ואמתיים קומתו מימנו קרנותיו 3 וציפית
אותו זהב טהור את גגו ואת קירותיו סביב ואת
קרנותיו ועסית לו זר זהב סבי 4 ושתי טבעות
זהב תעסה לו מיתחת לזרו על שתי צלעותיו
תעסה על שני צידיו והיה לבתים לבדים
לסאת אותו בהמה 5 ועסית את הבדים עצי
שיטים וציפית אותם זה 6 ונתתה אותו
ליפני הפרוכת אשר על ארון העדות ליפני
הכיפורת אשר על העדות אשר איועד לכה שמה
7 והיקטיר עליו אהרון קטורת סמים בבוקר
בבוקר בהיטיבו את הנרות יקטירנה 8 ובהעלות
אהרון את הנרות בין הערביים יקטירנה
קטורת תמיד ליפני יהוה לדורותיכם 9 לוא
תעלו עליו קטורת זרה ועולה ומינחה ונסך לוא
תיסכו עליו 10 וכיפר אהרון על קרנותיו אחת
בשנה מידם חטאת הכיפורים אחת בשנה
יכפר עליו לדורותיכם קודש קדשים הוא
ליהוה 11 וידבר יהוה אל מושה לאמור 12 כי
תיסא את רואש בני יסראל ליפקודיהם
ונתנו איש כופר נפשו ליהוה ביפקוד אותם
ולוא יהיה בהם נגף ביפקוד אותם 13 זה
יתנו כל העובר על הפקודים מחצית השקל
בשקל הקודש עסרים גרה השקל מחצית השקל
תרומה ליהוה 14 כול העובר על הפקודים מיבן
עסרים שנה ומעלה יתן תרומת יהוה
15 העשיר לוא ירבה והדל לוא ימעיט
מימחצית השקל לתת את תרומת יהוה לכפר על
נפשותיכם 16 ולקחת את כסף הכיפורים מאת
בני יסראל ונתת אותו על עבודת אוהל מועד

𐤅𐤄𐤉𐤄 𐤋𐤉𐤁𐤍𐤉 𐤉𐤎𐤓𐤀𐤋 𐤋𐤆𐤉𐤊𐤓𐤅𐤍 𐤋𐤉𐤐𐤍𐤉 𐤉𐤄𐤅𐤄
𐤋𐤊𐤐𐤓 𐤏𐤋 𐤍𐤐𐤔𐤅𐤕𐤉𐤊𐤌 17 𐤅𐤉𐤃𐤁𐤓 𐤉𐤄𐤅𐤄 𐤀𐤋 𐤌𐤅𐤔𐤄
𐤋𐤀𐤌𐤅𐤓 18 𐤅𐤏𐤎𐤉𐤕 𐤊𐤉𐤅𐤓 𐤍𐤇𐤅𐤔𐤕 𐤅𐤊𐤍𐤅 𐤍𐤇𐤅𐤔𐤕 𐤋𐤓𐤇𐤑𐤄
𐤅𐤍𐤕𐤕 𐤀𐤅𐤕𐤅 𐤁𐤉𐤍 𐤀𐤅𐤄𐤋 𐤌𐤅𐤏𐤃 𐤅𐤁𐤉𐤍 𐤄𐤌𐤉𐤆𐤁𐤇 𐤅𐤍𐤕𐤕
𐤔𐤌𐤄 𐤌𐤉𐤉𐤌 19 𐤅𐤓𐤇𐤑𐤅 𐤀𐤄𐤓𐤅𐤍 𐤅𐤁𐤍𐤉𐤅 𐤌𐤉𐤌𐤍𐤅 𐤀𐤕
𐤉𐤃𐤉𐤄𐤌 𐤅𐤀𐤕 𐤓𐤂𐤋𐤉𐤄𐤌 20 𐤁𐤁𐤅𐤀𐤌 𐤀𐤋 𐤀𐤅𐤄𐤋 𐤌𐤅𐤏𐤃
𐤉𐤓𐤇𐤑𐤅 𐤌𐤉𐤉𐤌 𐤅𐤋𐤅𐤀 𐤉𐤌𐤅𐤕𐤅 𐤀𐤅 𐤁𐤂𐤉𐤔𐤕𐤌 𐤀𐤋
𐤄𐤌𐤉𐤆𐤁𐤇 𐤋𐤔𐤓𐤕 𐤋𐤄𐤒𐤈𐤉𐤓 𐤀𐤉𐤔𐤄 𐤋𐤉𐤄𐤅𐤄 21 𐤅𐤓𐤇𐤑𐤅
𐤉𐤃𐤉𐤄𐤌 𐤅𐤓𐤂𐤋𐤉𐤄𐤌 𐤅𐤋𐤅𐤀 𐤉𐤌𐤅𐤕𐤅 𐤅𐤄𐤉𐤕𐤄 𐤋𐤄𐤌 𐤇𐤒
𐤏𐤅𐤋𐤌 𐤋𐤅 𐤅𐤋𐤆𐤓𐤏𐤅 𐤋𐤃𐤅𐤓𐤅𐤕𐤌 22 𐤅𐤉𐤃𐤁𐤓 𐤉𐤄𐤅𐤄 𐤀𐤋 𐤌𐤅𐤔𐤄
𐤋𐤀𐤌𐤅𐤓 23 𐤅𐤀𐤕𐤄 𐤒𐤇 𐤋𐤊𐤄 𐤁𐤎𐤌𐤉𐤌 𐤓𐤅𐤀𐤔 𐤌𐤓 𐤃𐤓𐤅𐤓
𐤇𐤌𐤔 𐤌𐤀𐤅𐤕 𐤅𐤒𐤉𐤍𐤌𐤍 𐤁𐤎𐤌 𐤌𐤇𐤑𐤉𐤕𐤅 𐤇𐤌𐤉𐤔𐤉𐤌
𐤅𐤌𐤀𐤕𐤉𐤉𐤌 𐤅𐤒𐤍𐤄 𐤁𐤅𐤎𐤌 𐤇𐤌𐤉𐤔𐤉𐤌 𐤅𐤌𐤀𐤕𐤉𐤉𐤌
24 𐤅𐤒𐤉𐤃𐤄 𐤇𐤌𐤔 𐤌𐤀𐤅𐤕 𐤁𐤔𐤒𐤋 𐤄𐤒𐤅𐤃𐤔 𐤅𐤔𐤌𐤍 𐤆𐤉𐤉𐤕
𐤄𐤉𐤍 25 𐤅𐤏𐤎𐤉𐤕 𐤀𐤅𐤕𐤅 𐤔𐤌𐤍 𐤌𐤉𐤔𐤇𐤕 𐤒𐤅𐤃𐤔 𐤓𐤅𐤒𐤇
𐤌𐤉𐤓𐤒𐤇𐤕 𐤌𐤏𐤎𐤄 𐤓𐤅𐤒𐤇 𐤔𐤌𐤍 𐤌𐤉𐤔𐤇𐤕 𐤒𐤅𐤃𐤔 𐤉𐤄𐤉𐤄
26 𐤅𐤌𐤔𐤇𐤕 𐤁𐤅 𐤀𐤕 𐤀𐤅𐤄𐤋 𐤌𐤅𐤏𐤃 𐤅𐤀𐤕 𐤀𐤓𐤅𐤍 𐤄𐤏𐤃𐤅𐤕 27 𐤅𐤀𐤕
𐤄𐤔𐤅𐤋𐤇𐤍 𐤅𐤀𐤕 𐤊𐤋 𐤊𐤋𐤉𐤅 𐤅𐤀𐤕 𐤄𐤌𐤍𐤅𐤓𐤄 𐤅𐤀𐤕 𐤊𐤋𐤉𐤄 𐤅𐤀𐤕
𐤌𐤉𐤆𐤁𐤇 𐤄𐤒𐤈𐤅𐤓𐤕 28 𐤅𐤀𐤕 𐤌𐤉𐤆𐤁𐤇 𐤄𐤏𐤅𐤋𐤄 𐤅𐤀𐤕 𐤊𐤋 𐤊𐤋𐤉𐤅
𐤅𐤀𐤕 𐤄𐤊𐤉𐤅𐤓 𐤅𐤀𐤕 𐤊𐤍𐤅 29 𐤅𐤒𐤉𐤃𐤔𐤕 𐤀𐤅𐤕𐤌 𐤅𐤄𐤉𐤅 𐤒𐤅𐤃𐤔
𐤒𐤃𐤔𐤉𐤌 𐤊𐤋 𐤄𐤍𐤅𐤂𐤏 𐤁𐤄𐤌 𐤉𐤒𐤃𐤔 30 𐤅𐤀𐤕 𐤀𐤄𐤓𐤅𐤍 𐤅𐤀𐤕
𐤁𐤍𐤉𐤅 𐤕𐤉𐤌𐤔𐤇 𐤅𐤒𐤉𐤃𐤔𐤕 𐤀𐤅𐤕𐤌 𐤋𐤊𐤄𐤍 𐤋𐤉 31 𐤅𐤀𐤋
𐤁𐤍𐤉 𐤉𐤎𐤓𐤀𐤋 𐤕𐤃𐤁𐤓 𐤋𐤀𐤌𐤅𐤓 𐤔𐤌𐤍 𐤌𐤉𐤔𐤇𐤕 𐤒𐤅𐤃𐤔
𐤉𐤄𐤉𐤄 𐤆𐤄 𐤋𐤉 𐤋𐤃𐤅𐤓𐤅𐤕𐤉𐤊𐤌 32 𐤏𐤋 𐤁𐤎𐤓 𐤀𐤃𐤌 𐤋𐤅𐤀
𐤉𐤉𐤎𐤊 𐤅𐤁𐤌𐤕𐤊𐤅𐤍𐤕𐤅 𐤋𐤅𐤀 𐤕𐤏𐤎𐤅 𐤊𐤌𐤅𐤄𐤅 𐤒𐤅𐤃𐤔 𐤄𐤅𐤀 𐤒𐤅𐤃𐤔
𐤉𐤄𐤉𐤄 𐤋𐤊𐤌 33 𐤀𐤉𐤔 𐤀𐤔𐤓 𐤉𐤓𐤒𐤇 𐤊𐤌𐤅𐤄𐤅 𐤅𐤀𐤔𐤓
𐤉𐤕𐤍 𐤌𐤉𐤌𐤍𐤅 𐤏𐤋 𐤆𐤓 𐤅𐤍𐤉𐤊𐤓𐤕 𐤌𐤏𐤌𐤉𐤅
34 𐤅𐤉𐤅𐤀𐤌𐤓 𐤉𐤄𐤅𐤄 𐤀𐤋 𐤌𐤅𐤔𐤄 𐤒𐤇 𐤋𐤊𐤄 𐤎𐤌𐤉𐤌 𐤍𐤈𐤐
𐤅𐤔𐤇𐤋𐤕 𐤅𐤇𐤋𐤁𐤍𐤄 𐤎𐤌𐤉𐤌 𐤅𐤋𐤁𐤅𐤍𐤄 𐤆𐤊𐤄 𐤁𐤃 𐤁𐤁𐤃 𐤉𐤄𐤉𐤄
35 𐤅𐤏𐤎𐤉𐤕 𐤀𐤅𐤕𐤄 𐤒𐤈𐤅𐤓𐤕 𐤓𐤅𐤒𐤇 𐤌𐤏𐤎𐤄 𐤓𐤅𐤒𐤇 𐤌𐤌𐤅𐤋𐤇 𐤈𐤄𐤅𐤓
𐤒𐤅𐤃𐤔 36 𐤅𐤔𐤇𐤒𐤕 𐤌𐤉𐤌𐤍𐤄 𐤄𐤃𐤒 𐤅𐤍𐤕𐤕𐤄 𐤌𐤉𐤌𐤍𐤄
𐤋𐤉𐤐𐤍𐤉 𐤄𐤏𐤃𐤅𐤕 𐤁𐤀𐤅𐤄𐤋 𐤌𐤅𐤏𐤃 𐤀𐤔𐤓 𐤀𐤉𐤅𐤏𐤃 𐤋𐤊𐤄
𐤔𐤌𐤄 𐤒𐤅𐤃𐤔 𐤒𐤃𐤔𐤉𐤌 𐤕𐤄𐤉𐤄 𐤋𐤊𐤌 37 𐤅𐤄𐤒𐤈𐤅𐤓𐤕 𐤀𐤔𐤓
𐤕𐤏𐤎𐤄 𐤁𐤌𐤕𐤊𐤅𐤍𐤕𐤄 𐤋𐤅𐤀 𐤕𐤏𐤎𐤅 𐤋𐤊𐤌 𐤒𐤅𐤃𐤔 𐤕𐤄𐤉𐤄 𐤋𐤊𐤄
𐤋𐤉𐤄𐤅𐤄 38 𐤀𐤉𐤔 𐤀𐤔𐤓 𐤉𐤏𐤎𐤄 𐤊𐤌𐤅𐤄 𐤋𐤄𐤓𐤉𐤇 𐤁𐤄
𐤅𐤍𐤉𐤊𐤓𐤕 𐤌𐤏𐤌𐤉𐤅

𐤔𐤌𐤅𐤕 𐤐𐤓𐤒 31

1 𐤅𐤉𐤃𐤁𐤓 𐤉𐤄𐤅𐤄 𐤀𐤋 𐤌𐤅𐤔𐤄 𐤋𐤀𐤌𐤅𐤓 2 𐤓𐤀𐤄 𐤒𐤓𐤀𐤕𐤉
𐤁𐤔𐤌 𐤁𐤑𐤋𐤀𐤋 𐤁𐤍 𐤀𐤅𐤓𐤉 𐤁𐤍 𐤇𐤅𐤓 𐤋𐤌𐤈𐤄 𐤉𐤄𐤅𐤃𐤄

[illegible] 3
[illegible] 4 [illegible]
[illegible] 5 [illegible]
[illegible] 6 [illegible]
[illegible]
[illegible]
[illegible] 7
[illegible] 8 [illegible]
[illegible]
[illegible] 9 [illegible]
[illegible] 10 [illegible]
[illegible]
[illegible] 11 [illegible]
[illegible] 12 [illegible]
[illegible] 13 [illegible]
[illegible]
[illegible]
[illegible] 14 [illegible]
[illegible]
[illegible]
[illegible] 15 [illegible]
[illegible]
[illegible] 16 [illegible]
[illegible]
[illegible] 17 [illegible]
[illegible]
[illegible]
[illegible] 18 [illegible]
[illegible]
[illegible]

32 [illegible]

[illegible] 1
[illegible]
[illegible]
[illegible]
[illegible] 2 [illegible]
[illegible]
[illegible] 3 [illegible]
[illegible]

אהרון 4 ויקח מידם ויצר אותו בחרט ויעשהו
עגל מסכה ויואמרו אלה אלוהיכה ישראל אשר
העלוכה מארץ מיצריים 5 וירא אהרון ויבן
מיזבח לפניו ויקרא אהרון ויואמר חג
ליהוה מחר 6 וישכימו מימחרת ויעלו עולות
ויגישו שלמים וישב העם לאכול ושתו
ויקומו לצחק 7 וידבר יהוה אל מושה לך רד כי
שיחת עמכה אשר העלית מארץ מיצריים
8 סרו מהר מין הדרך אשר ציויתים עשו להם
עגל מסכה וישתחוו לו ויזבחו לו ויואמרו אלה
אלוהיכה ישראל אשר העלוכה מארץ
מיצריים 9 ויואמר יהוה אל מושה ראיתי
את העם הזה והינה עם קשה עורף הוא 10 ועתה
הניחה לי וייחר אפי בהם ואכלם ואעשה
אותכה לגוי גדול 11 ויחל מושה את פני יהוה
אלוהיו ויואמר למה יהוה יחרה אפכה בעמכה
אשר הוצאת מארץ מיצריים בכוח גדול וביד
חזקה 12 למה יואמרו מיצריים לאמור ברעה
הוציאם להרוג אותם בהרים ולכלותם מעל
פני האדמה שוב מחרון אפכה והינחם על
הרעה לעמכה 13 זכור לאברהם לייצחק ולישראל
עבדיכה אשר נישבעת להם בך ותדבר אלהם
ארבה את זרעכם ככוכבי השמיים וכול הארץ
הזואת אשר אמרתי אתן לזרעכם ונחלו לעולם
14 וינחם יהוה על הרעה אשר דיבר לעשות
לעמו 15 ויפן וירד מושה מין ההר ושני
לוחות העדות בידו לוחות כתובים מישני
עבריהם מיזה ומיזה הם כתובים 16 והלוחות
מעשה אלוהים המה והמיכתב מיכתב אלוהים
הוא חרות על הלוחות 17 וישמע יהושוע את קול
העם ברעוה ויואמר אל מושה קול מילחמה
במחנה 18 ויואמר אין קול ענות גבורה ואין
קול ענות חלושה קול ענות אנוכי שומע 19 ויהי
כאשר קרב אל המחנה וירא את העגל ומחולות
ויחר אף מושה וישלך מידו את הלוחות וישבר
אותם תחת ההר 20 ויקח את העגל אשר עשו וישרוף
באש ויטחן עד אשר דק ויזר על פני המיים
וישק את בני ישראל 21 ויואמר מושה אל
אהרון מה עשה לכה העם הזה כי הבאת עליו
חטאה גדולה 22 ויואמר אהרון אל יחר אף
אדוני אתה ידעת את העם כי ברע הוא

23

24

25

26

27

28

29

30

31

32

33

34

35

33

1

2

3

4

5

𐤅𐤊𐤉𐤋𐤉𐤕𐤉𐤊𐤄 𐤅𐤏𐤕𐤄 𐤄𐤅𐤓𐤃 𐤏𐤃𐤉𐤊𐤄 𐤌𐤏𐤋𐤉𐤊𐤄 𐤅𐤀𐤃𐤏𐤄
𐤌𐤄 𐤀𐤏𐤎𐤄 𐤋𐤊 6 𐤅𐤉𐤕𐤍𐤑𐤋𐤅 𐤁𐤍𐤉 𐤉𐤎𐤓𐤀𐤋 𐤀𐤕 𐤏𐤃𐤉𐤌
𐤌𐤄𐤓 𐤇𐤅𐤓 7 𐤅𐤌𐤅𐤔𐤄 𐤉𐤒𐤇 𐤀𐤕 𐤄𐤀𐤅𐤄𐤋 𐤅𐤍𐤈𐤄 𐤋𐤅 𐤌𐤉𐤇𐤅𐤑
𐤋𐤌𐤇𐤍𐤄 𐤄𐤓𐤇𐤒 𐤌𐤉𐤍 𐤄𐤌𐤇𐤍𐤄 𐤅𐤒𐤓𐤀 𐤋𐤅 𐤀𐤅𐤄𐤋 𐤌𐤅𐤏𐤃
𐤅𐤄𐤉𐤄 𐤊𐤋 𐤌𐤁𐤒𐤔 𐤉𐤄𐤅𐤄 𐤉𐤑𐤀 𐤀𐤋 𐤀𐤅𐤄𐤋 𐤌𐤅𐤏𐤃 𐤀𐤔𐤓
𐤌𐤉𐤇𐤅𐤑 𐤋𐤌𐤇𐤍𐤄 8 𐤅𐤄𐤉𐤄 𐤊𐤑𐤀𐤕 𐤌𐤅𐤔𐤄 𐤀𐤋 𐤄𐤀𐤅𐤄𐤋
𐤉𐤒𐤅𐤌𐤅 𐤊𐤋 𐤄𐤏𐤌 𐤅𐤍𐤉𐤑𐤁𐤅 𐤀𐤉𐤔 𐤐𐤕𐤇 𐤀𐤄𐤋𐤅
𐤅𐤄𐤉𐤁𐤉𐤈𐤅 𐤀𐤇𐤓𐤉 𐤌𐤅𐤔𐤄 𐤏𐤃 𐤁𐤅𐤀𐤅 𐤄𐤀𐤅𐤄𐤋𐤄 9 𐤅𐤄𐤉𐤄
𐤊𐤁𐤅𐤀 𐤌𐤅𐤔𐤄 𐤄𐤀𐤅𐤄𐤋𐤄 𐤉𐤓𐤃 𐤏𐤌𐤅𐤃 𐤄𐤏𐤍𐤍 𐤅𐤏𐤌𐤃 𐤐𐤕𐤇
𐤄𐤀𐤅𐤄𐤋 𐤅𐤃𐤉𐤁𐤓 𐤏𐤉𐤌 𐤌𐤅𐤔𐤄 10 𐤅𐤓𐤀𐤄 𐤊𐤋 𐤄𐤏𐤌 𐤀𐤕
𐤏𐤌𐤅𐤃 𐤄𐤏𐤍𐤍 𐤏𐤅𐤌𐤃 𐤐𐤕𐤇 𐤄𐤀𐤅𐤄𐤋 𐤅𐤒𐤌 𐤊𐤋 𐤄𐤏𐤌
𐤅𐤄𐤉𐤔𐤕𐤇𐤅𐤅 𐤀𐤉𐤔 𐤐𐤕𐤇 𐤀𐤄𐤋𐤅 11 𐤅𐤃𐤉𐤁𐤓 𐤉𐤄𐤅𐤄 𐤀𐤋
𐤌𐤅𐤔𐤄 𐤐𐤍𐤉𐤌 𐤀𐤋 𐤐𐤍𐤉𐤌 𐤊𐤀𐤔𐤓 𐤉𐤃𐤁𐤓 𐤀𐤉𐤔 𐤀𐤋
𐤓𐤏𐤄𐤅 𐤅𐤔𐤁 𐤀𐤋 𐤄𐤌𐤇𐤍𐤄 𐤅𐤌𐤔𐤓𐤕𐤅 𐤉𐤄𐤅𐤔𐤅𐤏 𐤁𐤉𐤍 𐤍𐤅𐤍
𐤍𐤏𐤓 𐤋𐤅𐤀 𐤉𐤌𐤉𐤔 𐤌𐤉𐤕𐤅𐤊 𐤄𐤀𐤅𐤄𐤋 12 𐤅𐤉𐤅𐤀𐤌𐤓
𐤌𐤅𐤔𐤄 𐤀𐤋 𐤉𐤄𐤅𐤄 𐤓𐤀𐤄 𐤀𐤕𐤄 𐤀𐤅𐤌𐤓 𐤀𐤋𐤉 𐤄𐤏𐤋 𐤀𐤕 𐤄𐤏𐤌
𐤄𐤆𐤄 𐤅𐤀𐤕𐤄 𐤋𐤅𐤀 𐤄𐤅𐤃𐤏𐤕𐤍𐤉 𐤀𐤕 𐤀𐤔𐤓 𐤕𐤔𐤋𐤇 𐤏𐤉𐤌𐤉
𐤅𐤀𐤕𐤄 𐤀𐤌𐤓𐤕 𐤉𐤃𐤏𐤕𐤉𐤊𐤄 𐤁𐤔𐤌 𐤅𐤂𐤌 𐤌𐤑𐤀𐤕 𐤇𐤍
𐤁𐤏𐤉𐤍𐤉 13 𐤅𐤏𐤕𐤄 𐤀𐤉𐤌 𐤍𐤀 𐤌𐤑𐤀𐤕𐤉 𐤇𐤍
𐤁𐤏𐤉𐤍𐤉𐤊𐤄 𐤄𐤅𐤃𐤉𐤏𐤍𐤉 𐤍𐤀 𐤀𐤕 𐤃𐤓𐤊𐤊𐤄 𐤅𐤀𐤃𐤏𐤊𐤄
𐤋𐤌𐤏𐤍 𐤀𐤌𐤑𐤀 𐤇𐤍 𐤁𐤏𐤉𐤍𐤉𐤊𐤄 𐤅𐤓𐤀𐤄 𐤊𐤉 𐤏𐤌𐤊𐤄
𐤄𐤂𐤅𐤉 𐤄𐤆𐤄 14 𐤅𐤉𐤅𐤀𐤌𐤓 𐤐𐤍𐤉 𐤉𐤋𐤊𐤅 𐤅𐤄𐤍𐤉𐤇𐤅𐤕𐤉 𐤋𐤊
15 𐤅𐤉𐤅𐤀𐤌𐤓 𐤀𐤋𐤉𐤅 𐤀𐤉𐤌 𐤀𐤉𐤍 𐤐𐤍𐤉𐤊𐤄 𐤄𐤅𐤋𐤊𐤉𐤌
𐤀𐤋 𐤕𐤏𐤋𐤍𐤅 𐤌𐤉𐤆𐤄 16 𐤅𐤁𐤌𐤄 𐤉𐤅𐤃𐤏 𐤀𐤐𐤅𐤀 𐤊𐤉
𐤌𐤑𐤀𐤕𐤉 𐤇𐤍 𐤁𐤏𐤉𐤍𐤉𐤊𐤄 𐤀𐤍𐤉 𐤅𐤏𐤌𐤊𐤄 𐤄𐤋𐤅𐤀
𐤁𐤋𐤊𐤕𐤊𐤄 𐤏𐤉𐤌𐤍𐤅 𐤅𐤍𐤉𐤐𐤋𐤉𐤍𐤅 𐤀𐤍𐤉 𐤅𐤏𐤌𐤊𐤄
𐤌𐤉𐤊𐤋 𐤄𐤏𐤌 𐤀𐤔𐤓 𐤏𐤋 𐤐𐤍𐤉 𐤄𐤀𐤃𐤌𐤄 17 𐤅𐤉𐤅𐤀𐤌𐤓
𐤉𐤄𐤅𐤄 𐤀𐤋 𐤌𐤅𐤔𐤄 𐤂𐤌 𐤀𐤕 𐤄𐤃𐤁𐤓 𐤄𐤆𐤄 𐤀𐤔𐤓 𐤃𐤉𐤁𐤓𐤕
𐤀𐤏𐤎𐤄 𐤊𐤉 𐤌𐤑𐤀𐤕 𐤇𐤍 𐤁𐤏𐤉𐤍𐤉 𐤅𐤀𐤃𐤏𐤊𐤄 𐤁𐤔𐤌
18 𐤅𐤉𐤅𐤀𐤌𐤓 𐤄𐤓𐤀𐤍𐤉 𐤍𐤀 𐤀𐤕 𐤊𐤁𐤅𐤃𐤊𐤄 19 𐤅𐤉𐤅𐤀𐤌𐤓
𐤀𐤍𐤉 𐤀𐤏𐤁𐤉𐤓 𐤊𐤋 𐤈𐤅𐤁𐤉 𐤏𐤋 𐤐𐤍𐤉𐤊𐤄 𐤅𐤒𐤓𐤀𐤕𐤉 𐤁𐤔𐤌
𐤉𐤄𐤅𐤄 𐤋𐤐𐤍𐤉𐤊𐤄 𐤅𐤇𐤍𐤅𐤕𐤉 𐤀𐤕 𐤀𐤔𐤓 𐤀𐤇𐤅𐤍 𐤅𐤓𐤉𐤇𐤌𐤕𐤉
𐤀𐤕 𐤀𐤔𐤓 𐤀𐤓𐤇𐤌 20 𐤅𐤉𐤅𐤀𐤌𐤓 𐤋𐤅𐤀 𐤕𐤅𐤊𐤋 𐤋𐤉𐤓𐤀𐤅𐤕 𐤀𐤕
𐤐𐤍𐤉 𐤊𐤉 𐤋𐤅𐤀 𐤉𐤓𐤀𐤍𐤉 𐤄𐤀𐤃𐤌 𐤅𐤇𐤉 21 𐤅𐤉𐤅𐤀𐤌𐤓
𐤉𐤄𐤅𐤄 𐤄𐤉𐤍𐤄 𐤌𐤒𐤅𐤌 𐤀𐤉𐤕𐤉 𐤅𐤍𐤉𐤑𐤁𐤕 𐤏𐤋 𐤄𐤑𐤅𐤓
22 𐤅𐤄𐤉𐤄 𐤁𐤏𐤁𐤅𐤓 𐤊𐤁𐤅𐤃𐤉 𐤅𐤎𐤌𐤕𐤉𐤊𐤄 𐤁𐤍𐤉𐤒𐤓𐤕 𐤄𐤑𐤅𐤓
𐤅𐤎𐤊𐤅𐤕𐤉 𐤊𐤐𐤉 𐤏𐤋𐤉𐤊𐤄 𐤏𐤃 𐤏𐤁𐤓𐤉 23 𐤅𐤄𐤎𐤉𐤓𐤅𐤕𐤉 𐤀𐤕
𐤊𐤐𐤉 𐤅𐤓𐤀𐤉𐤕 𐤀𐤕 𐤀𐤇𐤅𐤓𐤉 𐤅𐤐𐤍𐤉 𐤋𐤅𐤀 𐤉𐤓𐤀𐤅

שמות פרק 34

1 ויואמר יהוה אל מושה פסל לכה שני לוחות
אבנים כריאשונים וכתבתי על הלוחות את
הדברים אשר היו על הלוחות הריאשונים אשר
שיברת 2 והיה נכון לבוקר ועלית בבוקר אל הר
סיני וניצבת לי שם על רואש ההר 3 ואיש
לוא יעלה עימך וגם איש אל ירא בכל ההר גם
הצואן והבקר אל ירעו אל מול ההר ההוא
4 ויפסול שני לוחות אבנים כריאשונים
וישכם מושה בבוקר ויעל אל הר סיני כאשר
ציוה יהוה אותו ויקח בידו שני לוחות אבנים
5 וירד יהוה בענן ויתיצב עימו שם ויקרא
בשם יהוה 6 ויעבור יהוה על פניו ויקרא
יהוה יהוה אל רחום וחנון ארך אפיים ורב חסד
ואמת 7 נוצר חסד לאלפים נוסא עון ופשע
וחטאה ונקה לוא ינקה פוקד עון אבות על בנים
ועל בני בנים על שילשים ועל רבעים
8 וימהר מושה ויקוד ארצה וישתחו 9 ויואמר
אים נא מצאתי חן בעיניכה אדוני ילך נא
אדוני בקירבנו כי עם קשה עורף הוא וסלחת
לעוננו ולחטאתנו ונחלתנו 10 ויואמר הינה
אנוכי כורת בירית נגד כל עמכה אעסה
ניפלאות אשר לוא ניבראו בכל הארץ ובכל
הגויים וראה כל העם אשר אתה בקירבו את
מעסה יהוה כי נורא הוא אשר אני עוסה עימך
11 שמר לכה את אשר אנוכי מצוכה היום
הינני גורש מיפניכה את האמורי
והכנעני והחיתי והפריזי והחיוי
והיבוסי 12 הישמר לכה פן תיכרות בירית
ליושב הארץ אשר אתה בא עליה פן יהיה
למוקש בקירבכה 13 כי את מיזבחותם תיתוצון
ואת מצבותם תשברון ואת אשריו תיכרותון
14 כי לוא תישתחוה לאל אחר כי יהוה קנא שמו
אל קנא הוא 15 פן תיכרות בירית ליושב הארץ
וזנו אחרי אלוהיהם וזבחו לאלוהיהם וקרא לכה
ואכלת מיזבחו 16 ולקחת מיבנותיו לבניכה
וזנו בנותיו אחרי אלוהיהן והיזנו את
בניכה אחרי אלוהיהן 17 אלוהי מסכה לוא
תעסה לך 18 את חג המצות תישמור שיבעת
ימים תאכל מצות אשר ציויתיכה למועד
חודש האביב כי בחודש האביב יצאת

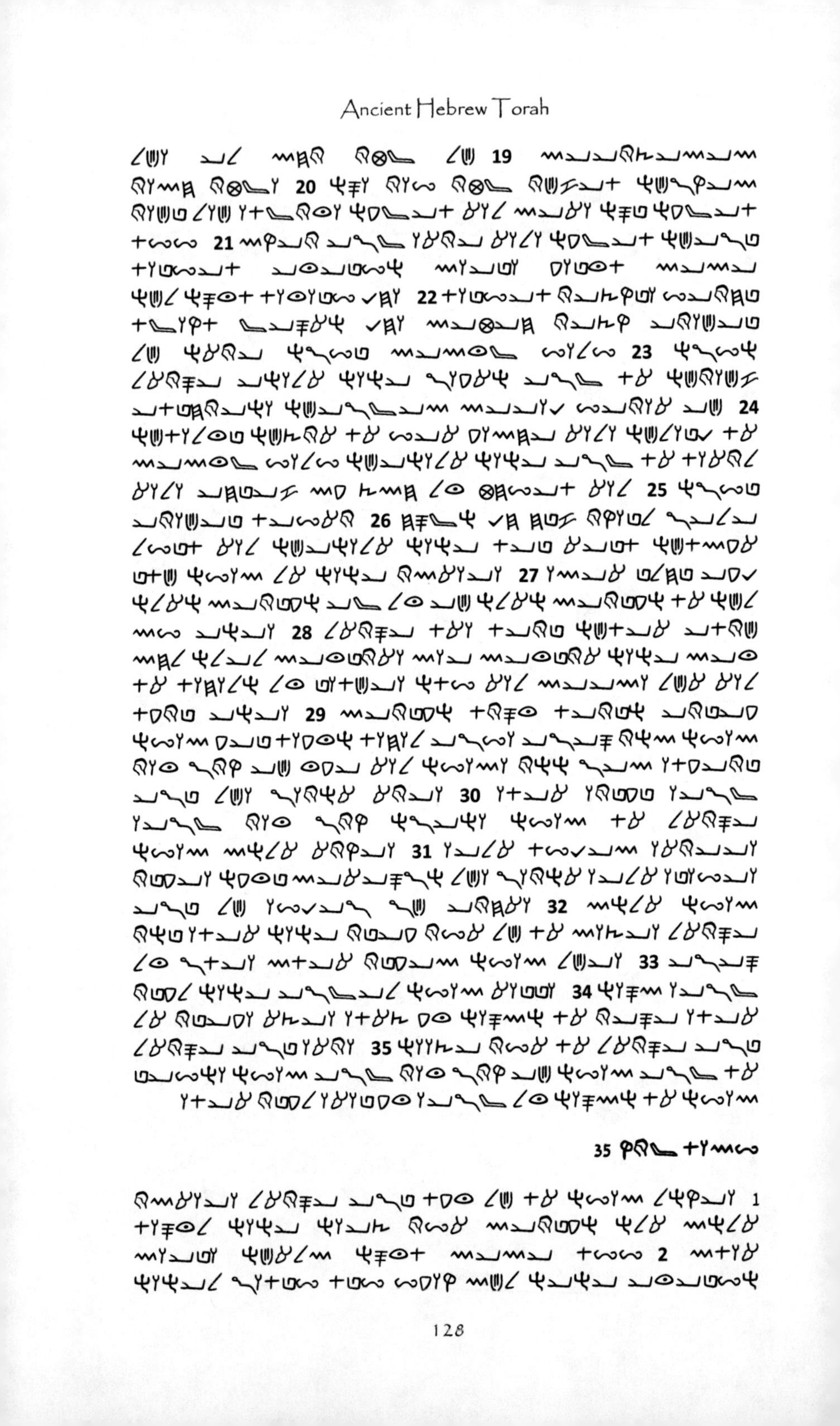

כל העוסה בו מלאכה יומת 3 לוא תבערו אש בכול
מושבותיכם ביום השבת 4 ויואמר מושה אל כל
עדת בני יסראל לאמור זה הדבר אשר ציוה
יהוה לאמור 5 קחו מאיתכם תרומה ליהוה כול
נדיב ליבו יביאה את תרומת יהוה זהב וכסף
ונחושת 6 ותכלת וארגמן ותולעת שני ושש
ועיזים 7 ועורות אילים מאדמים ועורות
תחשים ועצי שיטים 8 ושמן למאור
ובסמים לשמן המישחה וליקטורת הסמים
9 ואבני שוהם ואבני מילואים לאפוד
ולחושן 10 וכל חכם לב בכם יבואו ויעסו את כל
אשר ציוה יהוה 11 את המישכן את אהלו ואת
מיכסהו את קרסיו ואת קרשיו את בריחו את
עמודיו ואת אדניו 12 את הארון ואת בדיו את
הכפורת ואת פרוכת המסך 13 את השולחן ואת
בדיו ואת כל כליו ואת לחם הפנים 14 ואת
מנורת המאור ואת כליה ואת נרותיה ואת שמן
המאור 15 ואת מיזבח הקטורת ואת בדיו ואת שמן
המישחה ואת קטורת הסמים ואת מסך הפתח
לפתח המישכן 16 את מיזבח העולה ואת
מיכבר הנחושת אשר לו את בדיו ואת כל כליו את
הכיור ואת כנו 17 את קלעי החצר את עמודיו ואת
אדניה ואת מסך שער החצר 18 את יתדות
המישכן ואת יתדות החצר ואת מיתריהם
19 את ביגדי הסרד לשרת בקודש את ביגדי
הקודש לאהרון הכוהן ואת ביגדי בניו לכהן
20 ויצאו כל עדת בני יסראל מיליפני
מושה 21 ויבואו כל איש אשר נסאו ליבו וכל
אשר נדבה רוחו אותו הביאו את תרומת יהוה
לימלאכת אוהל מועד ולכל עבודתו ולביגדי
הקודש 22 ויבואו האנשים על הנשים כול
נדיב לב הביאו חח ונזם וטבעת וכומז כל כלי
זהב וכל איש אשר הניף תנופת זהב ליהוה
23 וכל איש אשר נימצא איתו תכלת וארגמן
ותולעת שני ושש ועיזים ועורות אילים
מאדמים ועורות תחשים הביאו 24 כל מרים
תרומת כסף ונחושת הביאו את תרומת יהוה וכול
אשר נימצא איתו עצי שיטים לכל מלאכת
העבודה הביאו 25 וכל אשה חכמת לב בידיה טוו
ויביאו מטוה את התכלת ואת הארגמן את תולעת
השני ואת השש 26 וכל הנשים אשר נסא

ליבן אותנה בחכמה טוו את העיזים
27 והנסיאים הביאו את אבני השוהם ואת
אבני המילואים לאפוד ולחושן 28 ואת הבוסם
ואת השמן למאור ולשמן המישחה וליקטורת
הסמים 29 כל איש ואישה אשר נדב ליבם
אותם להביא לכל המלאכה אשר ציוה יהוה
לעסות ביד מושה הביאו בני יסראל נדבה
ליהוה 30 ויואמר מושה אל בני יסראל ראו קרא
יהוה בשם בצלאל בן אורי בן חור למטה יהודה
31 וימלא אותו רוח אלוהים בחכמה ביתבונה
ובדעת ובכל מלאכה 32 ולחשוב מחשבות לעסות בזהב
ובכסף ובנחושת 33 ובחרושת אבן למלאות ובחרושת
עץ לעסות בכל מלאכת מחשבת 34 ולהורות נתן
בליבו הוא ואהליאב בן אחיסמך למטה דן
35 מילא אותם חכמת לב לעסות כל מלאכת חרש
וחושב ורוקם בתכלת ובארגמן בתולעת השני
ובשש ואורג עוסי כל מלאכה וחושבי מחשבות

שמות פרק 36

1 ועסה בצלאל ואהליאב וכול איש חכם לב אשר
נתן יהוה חכמה ותבונה בהמה לדעת לעסות את כל
מלאכת עבודת הקודש לכול אשר ציוה יהוה
2 ויקרא מושה אל בצלאל ואל אהליאב ואל כל
איש חכם לב אשר נתן יהוה חכמה בליבו כול
אשר נסאו ליבו לקרבה אל המלאכה לעסות אותה
3 ויקחו מיליפני מושה את כל התרומה אשר
הביאו בני יסראל למלאכת עבודת הקודש
לעסות אותה והם הביאו אליו עוד נדבה בבוקר
בבוקר 4 ויבואו כל החכמים העוסים את כל
מלאכת הקודש איש איש ממלאכתו אשר המה
עוסים 5 ויואמרו אל מושה לאמור מרבים
העם להביא מידי העבודה למלאכה אשר ציוה
יהוה לעסות אותה 6 ויצו מושה ויעבירו קול
במחנה לאמור איש ואישה אל יעסו עוד מלאכה
לתרומת הקודש ויכלא העם מהביא 7 והמלאכה
היתה דים לכל המלאכה לעסות אותה והותר
8 ויעסו כל חכם לב בעוסי המלאכה את המישכן
עסר יריעות שש מושזר ותכלת וארגמן ותולעת
שני כרובים מעסה חושב עסה אותם 9 אורך
היריעה האחת שמונה ועסרים באמה ורוחב
ארבע באמה היריעה האחת מידה אחת לכל

היריעות 10 ויחבר את חמש היריעות אחת אל
אחת וחמש יריעות חיבר אחת אל אחת 11 ויעש
לולאות תכלת על שפת היריעה האחת מיקצה
במחברת כן עשה בישפת היריעה הקיצונה
במחברת השנית 12 חמישים לולאות עשה
ביריעה האחת וחמישים לולאות עשה ביקצה
היריעה אשר במחברת השנית מקבילות
הלולאות אחת אל אחת 13 ויעש חמישים קרסי
זהב ויחבר את היריעות אחת אל אחת בקרסים
ויהי המישכן אחד 14 ויעש יריעות
עיזים לאוהל על המישכן עשתי עשרה
יריעות עשה אותם 15 אורך היריעה האחת
שלושים באמה וארבע אמות רוחב היריעה
האחת מידה אחת לעשתי עשרה יריעות
16 ויחבר את חמש היריעות לבד ואת שש
היריעות לבד 17 ויעש לולאות חמישים על
שפת היריעה הקיצונה במחברת וחמישים
לולאות עשה על שפת היריעה החוברת השנית
18 ויעש קרסי נחושת חמישים לחבר את האוהל
ליהיות אחד 19 ויעש מיכסה לאוהל עורות
אלים מאדמים ומיכסה עורות תחשים
מילמעלה 20 ויעש את הקרשים למישכן
עצי שיטים עומדים 21 עשר אמות אורך הקרש
ואמה וחצי האמה רוחב הקרש האחד 22 שתי ידות
לקרש האחד משולבות אחת אל אחת כן עשה לכול
קרשי המישכן 23 ויעש את הקרשים
למישכן עשרים קרשים ליפאת נגב
תימנה 24 וארבעים אדני כסף עשה תחת
עשרים הקרשים שני אדנים תחת הקרש האחד
לשתי ידותיו ושני אדנים תחת הקרש האחד
לשתי ידותיו 25 ולצלע המישכן השנית
ליפאת צפון עשה עשרים קרשים
26 וארבעים אדניהם כסף שני אדנים תחת
הקרש האחד ושני אדנים תחת הקרש האחד
27 ולירכתי המישכן ימה עשה שישה
קרשים 28 ושני קרשים עשה לימקוצעות
המישכן בירכתיים 29 והיו תואמים
מילמטה ויחדו יהיו תמים אל ראשו אל
הטבעת האחת כן עשה לישניהם לישני
המיקצועות 30 והיו שמונה קרשים ואדניהם
כסף שישה עשר אדנים שני אדנים שני

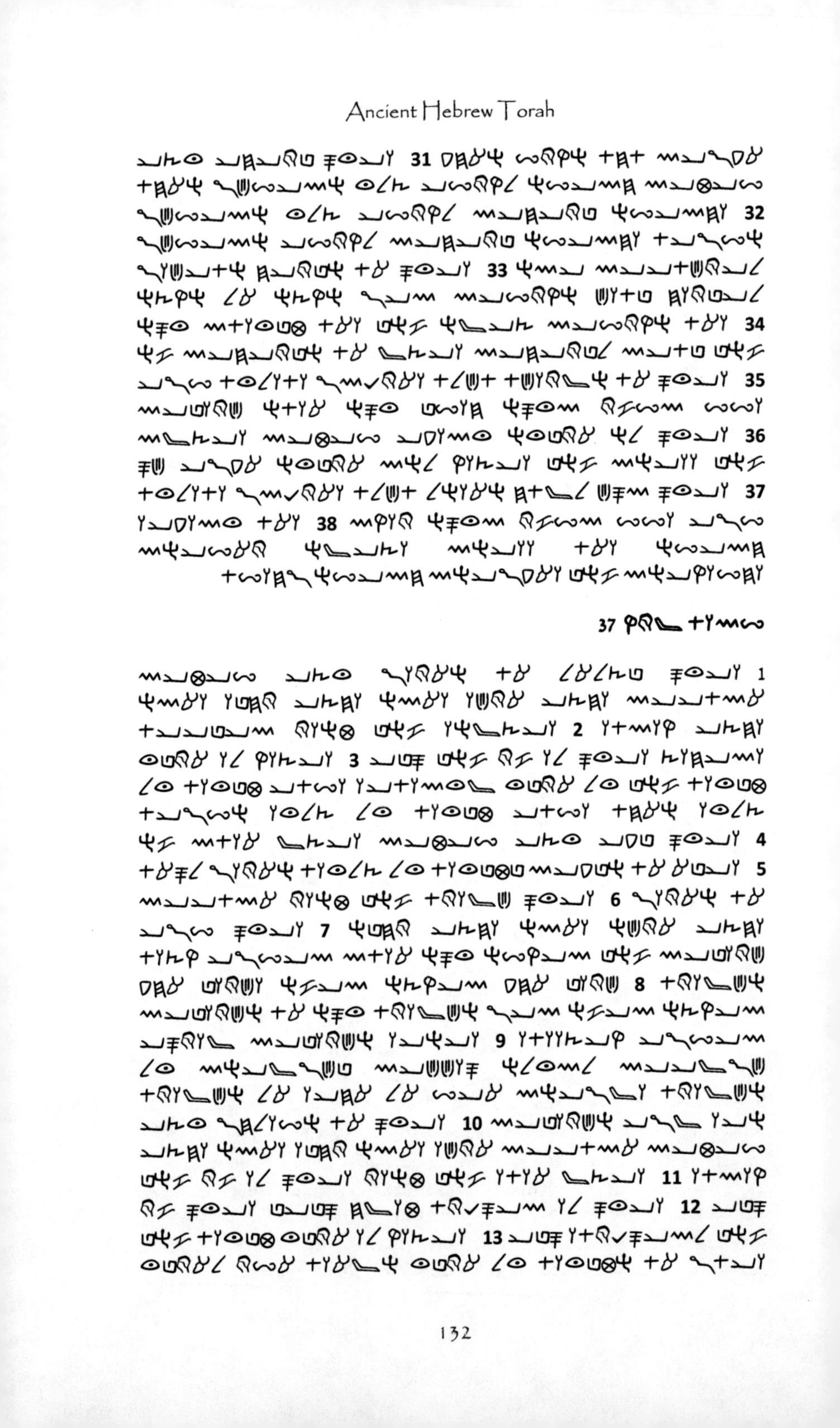

[illegible] 31 [illegible]
[illegible]
[illegible] 32
[illegible]
[illegible] 33 [illegible]
[illegible]
[illegible] 34
[illegible]
[illegible] 35
[illegible]
[illegible] 36
[illegible]
[illegible] 37
[illegible] 38 [illegible]
[illegible]
[illegible]

37 [illegible]

[illegible] 1
[illegible]
[illegible] 2 [illegible]
[illegible] 3 [illegible]
[illegible]
[illegible]
[illegible] 4
[illegible] 5
[illegible] 6 [illegible]
[illegible] 7 [illegible]
[illegible]
[illegible] 8 [illegible]
[illegible]
[illegible] 9 [illegible]
[illegible]
[illegible]
[illegible] 10 [illegible]
[illegible]
[illegible] 11 [illegible]
[illegible] 12 [illegible]
[illegible] 13 [illegible]
[illegible]

𐤓𐤂𐤋𐤉𐤅 14 𐤋𐤏𐤅𐤌𐤕 𐤄𐤌𐤉𐤎𐤂𐤓𐤕 𐤄𐤉𐤅 𐤄𐤈𐤁𐤏𐤅𐤕 𐤁𐤕𐤉𐤌
𐤋𐤁𐤃𐤉𐤌 𐤋𐤎𐤀𐤕 𐤀𐤕 𐤄𐤔𐤅𐤋𐤇𐤍 15 𐤅𐤉𐤏𐤎 𐤀𐤕 𐤄𐤁𐤃𐤉𐤌
𐤏𐤑𐤉 𐤔𐤉𐤈𐤉𐤌 𐤅𐤉𐤑𐤐 𐤀𐤅𐤕𐤌 𐤆𐤄𐤁 𐤋𐤎𐤀𐤕 𐤀𐤕
𐤄𐤔𐤅𐤋𐤇𐤍 16 𐤅𐤉𐤏𐤎 𐤀𐤕 𐤄𐤊𐤋𐤉𐤌 𐤀𐤔𐤓 𐤏𐤋 𐤄𐤔𐤅𐤋𐤇𐤍 𐤀𐤕
𐤒𐤏𐤓𐤅𐤕𐤉𐤅 𐤅𐤀𐤕 𐤊𐤐𐤅𐤕𐤉𐤅 𐤅𐤀𐤕 𐤌𐤍𐤒𐤉𐤅𐤕𐤉𐤅 𐤅𐤀𐤕 𐤄𐤒𐤎𐤅𐤕
𐤀𐤔𐤓 𐤉𐤅𐤎𐤊 𐤁𐤄𐤍 𐤆𐤄𐤁 𐤈𐤄𐤅𐤓 17 𐤅𐤉𐤏𐤎 𐤀𐤕 𐤄𐤌𐤍𐤅𐤓𐤄
𐤆𐤄𐤁 𐤈𐤄𐤅𐤓 𐤌𐤉𐤒𐤔𐤄 𐤏𐤎𐤄 𐤀𐤕 𐤄𐤌𐤍𐤅𐤓𐤄 𐤉𐤓𐤊𐤄 𐤅𐤒𐤍𐤄
𐤂𐤁𐤉𐤏𐤉𐤄 𐤊𐤐𐤕𐤅𐤓𐤉𐤄 𐤅𐤐𐤓𐤇𐤉𐤄 𐤌𐤉𐤌𐤍𐤄 𐤄𐤉𐤅
18 𐤅𐤔𐤉𐤔𐤄 𐤒𐤍𐤉𐤌 𐤉𐤅𐤑𐤀𐤉𐤌 𐤌𐤉𐤑𐤉𐤃𐤉𐤄 𐤔𐤋𐤅𐤔𐤄
𐤒𐤍𐤉 𐤌𐤍𐤅𐤓𐤄 𐤌𐤉𐤑𐤉𐤃𐤄 𐤄𐤀𐤇𐤃 𐤅𐤔𐤋𐤅𐤔𐤄 𐤒𐤍𐤉
𐤌𐤍𐤅𐤓𐤄 𐤌𐤉𐤑𐤉𐤃𐤄 𐤄𐤔𐤍𐤉 19 𐤔𐤋𐤅𐤔𐤄 𐤂𐤁𐤉𐤏𐤉𐤌
𐤌𐤔𐤅𐤒𐤃𐤉𐤌 𐤁𐤒𐤍𐤄 𐤄𐤀𐤇𐤃 𐤊𐤐𐤕𐤅𐤓 𐤅𐤐𐤓𐤇 𐤅𐤔𐤋𐤅𐤔𐤄
𐤂𐤁𐤉𐤏𐤉𐤌 𐤌𐤔𐤅𐤒𐤃𐤉𐤌 𐤁𐤒𐤍𐤄 𐤀𐤇𐤃 𐤊𐤐𐤕𐤅𐤓 𐤅𐤐𐤓𐤇 𐤊𐤍
𐤋𐤔𐤔𐤕 𐤄𐤒𐤍𐤉𐤌 𐤄𐤉𐤅𐤑𐤀𐤉𐤌 𐤌𐤉𐤍 𐤄𐤌𐤍𐤅𐤓𐤄
20 𐤅𐤁𐤌𐤍𐤅𐤓𐤄 𐤀𐤓𐤁𐤏𐤄 𐤂𐤁𐤉𐤏𐤉𐤌 𐤌𐤔𐤅𐤒𐤃𐤉𐤌
𐤊𐤐𐤕𐤅𐤓𐤉𐤄 𐤅𐤐𐤓𐤇𐤉𐤄 21 𐤅𐤊𐤐𐤕𐤅𐤓 𐤕𐤇𐤕 𐤔𐤍𐤉
𐤄𐤒𐤍𐤉𐤌 𐤌𐤉𐤌𐤍𐤄 𐤅𐤊𐤐𐤕𐤅𐤓 𐤕𐤇𐤕 𐤔𐤍𐤉 𐤄𐤒𐤍𐤉𐤌
𐤌𐤉𐤌𐤍𐤄 𐤅𐤊𐤐𐤕𐤅𐤓 𐤕𐤇𐤕 𐤔𐤍𐤉 𐤄𐤒𐤍𐤉𐤌 𐤌𐤉𐤌𐤍𐤄
𐤋𐤔𐤔𐤕 𐤄𐤒𐤍𐤉𐤌 𐤄𐤉𐤅𐤑𐤀𐤉𐤌 𐤌𐤉𐤌𐤍𐤄
22 𐤊𐤐𐤕𐤅𐤓𐤉𐤄𐤌 𐤅𐤒𐤍𐤅𐤕𐤌 𐤌𐤉𐤌𐤍𐤄 𐤄𐤉𐤅 𐤊𐤅𐤋𐤄
𐤌𐤉𐤒𐤔𐤄 𐤀𐤇𐤕 𐤆𐤄𐤁 𐤈𐤄𐤅𐤓 23 𐤅𐤉𐤏𐤎 𐤀𐤕 𐤍𐤓𐤅𐤕𐤉𐤄
𐤔𐤉𐤁𐤏𐤄 𐤅𐤌𐤋𐤒𐤇𐤉𐤄 𐤅𐤌𐤇𐤕𐤅𐤕𐤉𐤄 𐤆𐤄𐤁 𐤈𐤄𐤅𐤓 24 𐤊𐤉𐤊𐤓
𐤆𐤄𐤁 𐤈𐤄𐤅𐤓 𐤏𐤎𐤄 𐤀𐤅𐤕𐤄 𐤅𐤀𐤕 𐤊𐤋 𐤊𐤋𐤉𐤄 25 𐤅𐤉𐤏𐤎 𐤀𐤕
𐤌𐤉𐤆𐤁𐤇 𐤄𐤒𐤈𐤅𐤓𐤕 𐤏𐤑𐤉 𐤔𐤉𐤈𐤉𐤌 𐤀𐤌𐤄 𐤀𐤓𐤊𐤅 𐤅𐤀𐤌𐤄
𐤓𐤇𐤁𐤅 𐤓𐤁𐤅𐤏 𐤅𐤀𐤌𐤕𐤉𐤉𐤌 𐤒𐤅𐤌𐤕𐤅 𐤌𐤉𐤌𐤍𐤅 𐤄𐤉𐤅
𐤒𐤓𐤍𐤅𐤕𐤉𐤅 26 𐤅𐤉𐤑𐤐 𐤀𐤅𐤕𐤅 𐤆𐤄𐤁 𐤈𐤄𐤅𐤓 𐤀𐤕 𐤂𐤂𐤅 𐤅𐤀𐤕
𐤒𐤉𐤓𐤅𐤕𐤉𐤅 𐤎𐤁𐤉𐤁 𐤅𐤀𐤕 𐤒𐤓𐤍𐤅𐤕𐤉𐤅 𐤅𐤉𐤏𐤎 𐤋𐤅 𐤆𐤓 𐤆𐤄𐤁
𐤎𐤁𐤉 27 𐤅𐤔𐤕𐤉 𐤈𐤁𐤏𐤅𐤕 𐤆𐤄𐤁 𐤏𐤎𐤄 𐤋𐤅 𐤌𐤉𐤕𐤇𐤕 𐤋𐤆𐤓𐤅 𐤏𐤋
𐤔𐤕𐤉 𐤑𐤋𐤏𐤅𐤕𐤉𐤅 𐤏𐤋 𐤔𐤍𐤉 𐤑𐤉𐤃𐤉𐤅 𐤋𐤁𐤕𐤉𐤌 𐤋𐤁𐤃𐤉𐤌
𐤋𐤎𐤀𐤕 𐤀𐤅𐤕𐤅 𐤁𐤄𐤌 28 𐤅𐤉𐤏𐤎 𐤀𐤕 𐤄𐤁𐤃𐤉𐤌 𐤏𐤑𐤉
𐤔𐤉𐤈𐤉𐤌 𐤅𐤉𐤑𐤐 𐤀𐤅𐤕𐤌 𐤆𐤄 29 𐤅𐤉𐤏𐤎 𐤀𐤕 𐤔𐤌𐤍
𐤄𐤌𐤉𐤔𐤇𐤄 𐤒𐤅𐤃𐤔 𐤅𐤀𐤕 𐤒𐤈𐤅𐤓𐤕 𐤄𐤎𐤌𐤉𐤌 𐤈𐤄𐤅𐤓 𐤌𐤏𐤎𐤄
𐤓𐤅𐤒𐤇

𐤔𐤌𐤅𐤕 𐤐𐤓𐤒 38

1 𐤅𐤉𐤏𐤎 𐤀𐤕 𐤌𐤉𐤆𐤁𐤇 𐤄𐤏𐤅𐤋𐤄 𐤏𐤑𐤉 𐤔𐤉𐤈𐤉𐤌 𐤇𐤌𐤔
𐤀𐤌𐤅𐤕 𐤀𐤓𐤊𐤅 𐤅𐤇𐤌𐤔 𐤀𐤌𐤅𐤕 𐤓𐤇𐤁𐤅 𐤓𐤁𐤅𐤏 𐤅𐤔𐤋𐤅𐤔 𐤀𐤌𐤅𐤕
𐤒𐤅𐤌𐤕𐤅 2 𐤅𐤉𐤏𐤎 𐤒𐤓𐤍𐤅𐤕𐤉𐤅 𐤏𐤋 𐤀𐤓𐤁𐤏 𐤐𐤉𐤍𐤅𐤕𐤉𐤅
𐤌𐤉𐤌𐤍𐤅 𐤄𐤉𐤅 𐤒𐤓𐤍𐤅𐤕𐤉𐤅 𐤅𐤉𐤑𐤐 𐤀𐤅𐤕𐤅 𐤍𐤇𐤅𐤔𐤕
3 𐤅𐤉𐤏𐤎 𐤀𐤕 𐤊𐤋 𐤊𐤋𐤉 𐤄𐤌𐤉𐤆𐤁𐤇 𐤀𐤕 𐤄𐤎𐤉𐤓𐤅𐤕 𐤅𐤀𐤕
𐤄𐤉𐤏𐤉𐤌 𐤅𐤀𐤕 𐤄𐤌𐤉𐤆𐤓𐤒𐤅𐤕 𐤀𐤕 𐤄𐤌𐤉𐤆𐤋𐤂𐤅𐤕 𐤅𐤀𐤕

המחתות כל כליו עסה נחושת 4 ויעס למיזבח
מיכבר מעסה רשת נחושת תחת כרכובו מילמטה
עד חציו 5 ויצוק ארבע טבעות בארבע הקצות
למיכבר הנחושת בתים לבדים 6 ויעס את
הבדים עצי שיטים ויצף אותם נחושת
7 ויבא את הבדים בטבעות על צלעות המיזבח
לסאת אותו בהם נבוב לוחות עסה אותו 8 ויעס את
הכיור נחושת ואת כנו נחושת במראות הצובאות
אשר צבאו פתח אוהל מועד 9 ויעס את החצר
ליפאת נגב תימנה קלעי החצר שש משזר
מאה באמה 10 עמודיהם עסרים ואדניהם
עסרים נחושת ווי העמודים וחשוקיהם כס
11 וליפאת צפון מאה באמה עמודיהם
עסרים ואדניהם עסרים נחושת ווי
העמודים וחשוקיהם כס 12 וליפאת ים
קלעים חמישים באמה עמודיהם עסרה
ואדניהם עסרה ווי העמודים וחשוקיהם כס
13 וליפאת קדמה מיזרחה חמישים אמה
14 קלעים חמש עסרה אמה אל הכתף עמודיהם
שלושה ואדניהם שלושה 15 ולכתף השנית
מיזה ומיזה לשער החצר קלעים חמש עסרה
אמה עמודיהם שלושה ואדניהם שלושה 16 כל
קלעי החצר סביב שש משזר 17 והאדנים
לעמודים נחושת ווי העמודים וחשוקיהם
כסף וציפוי ראשיהם כסף והם מחושקים
כסף כול עמודי החצר 18 ומסך שער החצר מעסה
רוקם תכלת וארגמן ותולעת שני ושש משזר
ועסרים אמה אורך וקומה ברוחב חמש אמות
לעומת קלעי החצר 19 ועמודיהם ארבעה
ואדניהם ארבעה נחושת וויהם כסף וציפוי
ראשיהם וחשוקיהם כס 20 וכל היתדות
למישכן ולחצר סביב נחושת 21 אלה פקודי
המישכן מישכן העדות אשר פוקד על פי
מושה עבודת הלוים ביד איתמר בן אהרון
הכוהן 22 ובצלאל בן אורי בן חור למטה יהודה
עסה את כל אשר צוה יהוה את מושה 23 ואיתו
אהליאב בן אחיסמך למטה דן חרש וחושב ורוקם
בתכלת בארגמן בתולעת השני ובשש 24 כל
הזהב העסוי למלאכה בכול מלאכת הקודש ויהי
זהב התנופה תשע ועסרים כיכר ושבע מאות
ושלושים שקל בשקל הקודש 25 וכסף פקודי

26

27

28

29

30

31

39

1

2

3

4

5

6

7

8

9

10

11

12

13

[illegible] 14
[illegible]
[illegible] 15 [illegible]
[illegible] 16 [illegible]
[illegible]
[illegible] 17 [illegible]
[illegible]
[illegible] 18 [illegible]
[illegible]
[illegible] 19 [illegible]
[illegible]
[illegible] 20 [illegible]
[illegible]
[illegible]
[illegible] 21 [illegible]
[illegible]
[illegible]
[illegible] 22 [illegible]
[illegible] 23 [illegible]
[illegible] 24 [illegible]
[illegible]
[illegible] 25 [illegible]
[illegible]
[illegible]
[illegible] 26
[illegible]
[illegible] 27
[illegible] 28 [illegible]
[illegible]
[illegible] 29
[illegible]
[illegible] 30
[illegible]
[illegible] 31
[illegible] 32 [illegible]
[illegible]
[illegible]
[illegible] 33
[illegible]
[illegible] 34
[illegible] 35 [illegible]

ארון העדות ואת בדיו ואת הכפורת 36 את השולחן
את כל כליו ואת לחם הפנים 37 את המנורה
הטהורה את נרותיה נרות המערכה ואת כל כליה
ואת שמן המאור 38 ואת מיזבח הזהב ואת שמן
המישחה ואת קטורת הסמים ואת מסך פתח האוהל
39 את מיזבח הנחושת ואת מיכבר הנחושת אשר
לו את בדיו ואת כל כליו את הכיור ואת כנו 40 את
קלעי החצר את עמודיה ואת אדניה ואת המסך
לשער החצר את מיתריו ויתדותיה ואת כל כלי
עבודת המישכן לאוהל מועד 41 את ביגדי הסרד
לשרת בקודש את ביגדי הקודש לאהרון הכוהן
ואת ביגדי בניו לכהן 42 ככול אשר ציוה יהוה
את מושה כן עסו בני יסראל את כל העבודה
43 וירא מושה את כל המלאכה והינה עסו אותה
כאשר ציוה יהוה כן עסו ויברך אותם מושה

שמות פרק 40

1 וידבר יהוה אל מושה לאמור 2 ביום החודש
הראישון באחד לחודש תקים את המישכן אוהל
מועד 3 וסמת שם את ארון העדות וסכות על הארון
את הפרוכת 4 והבאת את השולחן וערכת את ערכו
והבאת את המנורה והעלית את נרותיה 5 ונתתה
את מיזבח הזהב ליקטורת ליפני ארון העדות
וסמת את מסך הפתח למישכן 6 ונתתה את
מיזבח העולה ליפני פתח מישכן אוהל
מועד 7 ונתת את הכיור בין אוהל מועד ובין
המיזבח ונתת שם מיים 8 וסמת את החצר
סביב ונתת את מסך שער החצר 9 ולקחת את שמן
המישחה ומשחת את המישכן ואת כל אשר בו
וקידשת אותו ואת כל כליו והיה קודש 10 ומשחת
את מיזבח העולה ואת כל כליו וקידשת את
המיזבח והיה המיזבח קודש קדשים 11 ומשחת
את הכיור ואת כנו וקידשת אותו 12 והיקרבת את
אהרון ואת בניו אל פתח אוהל מועד ורחצת אותם
במיים 13 והילבשת את אהרון את ביגדי
הקודש ומשחת אותו וקידשת אותו וכיהן לי
14 ואת בניו תקריב והילבשת אותם כותנות
15 ומשחת אותם כאשר משחת את אביהם וכיהנו
לי והיתה ליהיות להם משחתם ליכהונת
עולם לדורותם 16 ויעס מושה ככול אשר ציוה

יהוה אותו כן עסה 17 ויהי בחודש הריאשון
בשנה השנית באחד לחודש הוקם המישכן
18 ויקם מושה את המישכן ויתן את אדניו
וישם את קרשיו ויתן את בריחיו ויקם את
עמודיו 19 ויפרוס את האוהל על המישכן
וישם את מיכסה האוהל עליו מילמעלה כאשר
ציוה יהוה את מושה 20 ויקח ויתן את העדות אל
הארון וישם את הבדים על הארון ויתן את
הכפורת על הארון מילמעלה 21 ויבא את
הארון אל המישכן וישם את פרוכת המסך ויסך
על ארון העדות כאשר ציוה יהוה את מושה
22 ויתן את השולחן באוהל מועד על ירך
המישכן צפונה מיחוץ לפרוכת 23 ויערוך
עליו ערך לחם ליפני יהוה כאשר ציוה
יהוה את מושה 24 וישם את המנורה באוהל מועד
נוכח השולחן על ירך המישכן נגבה 25 ויעל
הנרות ליפני יהוה כאשר ציוה יהוה את
מושה 26 וישם את מיזבח הזהב באוהל מועד
ליפני הפרוכת 27 ויקטר עליו קטורת סמים
כאשר ציוה יהוה את מושה 28 וישם את מסך
הפתח למישכן 29 ואת מיזבח העולה סם פתח
מישכן אוהל מועד ויעל עליו את העולה ואת
המינחה כאשר ציוה יהוה את מושה 30 וישם
את הכיורבין אוהל מועד ובין המיזבח ויתן
שמה מים לרחצה 31 ורחצו מימנו מושה
ואהרון ובניו את ידיהם ואת רגליהם
32 בבואם אל אוהל מועד ובקרבתם אל המיזבח
ירחצו כאשר ציוה יהוה את מושה 33 ויקם את
החצר סביב למישכן ולמיזבח ויתן את מסך
שער החצר ויכל מושה את המלאכה 34 ויכס
הענן את אוהל מועד וכבוד יהוה מלא את
המישכן 35 ולוא יכול מושה לבוא אל אוהל מועד
כי שכן עליו הענן וכבוד יהוה מלא את
המישכן 36 ובהעלות הענן מעל המישכן
יסעו בני יסראל בכול מסעיהם 37 ואים לוא
יעלה הענן ולוא יסעו עד יום העלותו 38 כי
ענן יהוה על המישכן יומם ואש תיהיה
לילה בו לעיני כל בית יסראל בכול מסעיהם

𐤅𐤉𐤒𐤓𐤀

wayiqra / Leviticus

𐤅𐤉𐤒𐤓𐤀 𐤐𐤓𐤒 1

1 𐤅𐤉𐤒𐤓𐤀 𐤀𐤋 𐤌𐤅𐤔𐤄 𐤅𐤉𐤃𐤁𐤓 𐤉𐤄𐤅𐤄 𐤀𐤋𐤉𐤅 𐤌𐤀𐤅𐤄𐤋
𐤌𐤅𐤏𐤃 𐤋𐤀𐤌𐤅𐤓 2 𐤃𐤁𐤓 𐤀𐤋 𐤁𐤍𐤉 𐤉𐤎𐤓𐤀𐤋 𐤅𐤀𐤌𐤓𐤕 𐤀𐤋𐤄𐤌
𐤀𐤃𐤌 𐤊𐤉 𐤉𐤒𐤓𐤉𐤁 𐤌𐤉𐤊𐤌 𐤒𐤓𐤁𐤍 𐤋𐤉𐤄𐤅𐤄 𐤌𐤉𐤍
𐤄𐤁𐤄𐤌𐤄 𐤌𐤉𐤍 𐤄𐤁𐤒𐤓 𐤅𐤌𐤉𐤍 𐤄𐤑𐤅𐤀𐤍 𐤕𐤒𐤓𐤉𐤁𐤅 𐤀𐤕
𐤒𐤓𐤁𐤍𐤊𐤌 3 𐤀𐤉𐤌 𐤏𐤅𐤋𐤄 𐤒𐤓𐤁𐤍𐤅 𐤌𐤉𐤍 𐤄𐤁𐤒𐤓 𐤆𐤊𐤓
𐤕𐤌𐤉𐤌 𐤉𐤒𐤓𐤉𐤁𐤍𐤅 𐤀𐤋 𐤐𐤕𐤇 𐤀𐤅𐤄𐤋 𐤌𐤅𐤏𐤃 𐤉𐤒𐤓𐤉𐤁
𐤀𐤅𐤕𐤅 𐤋𐤉𐤓𐤑𐤅𐤍𐤅 𐤋𐤉𐤐𐤍𐤉 𐤉𐤄𐤅𐤄 4 𐤅𐤎𐤌𐤊 𐤉𐤃𐤅 𐤏𐤋
𐤓𐤅𐤀𐤔 𐤄𐤏𐤅𐤋𐤄 𐤅𐤍𐤉𐤓𐤑𐤄 𐤋𐤅 𐤋𐤊𐤐𐤓 𐤏𐤋𐤉𐤅 5 𐤅𐤔𐤇𐤈 𐤀𐤕
𐤁𐤍 𐤄𐤁𐤒𐤓 𐤋𐤉𐤐𐤍𐤉 𐤉𐤄𐤅𐤄 𐤅𐤄𐤉𐤒𐤓𐤉𐤁𐤅 𐤁𐤍𐤉 𐤀𐤄𐤓𐤅𐤍
𐤄𐤊𐤅𐤄𐤍𐤉𐤌 𐤀𐤕 𐤄𐤃𐤌 𐤅𐤆𐤓𐤒𐤅 𐤀𐤕 𐤄𐤃𐤌 𐤏𐤋 𐤄𐤌𐤉𐤆𐤁𐤇
𐤎𐤁𐤉𐤁 𐤀𐤔𐤓 𐤐𐤕𐤇 𐤀𐤅𐤄𐤋 𐤌𐤅𐤏𐤃 6 𐤅𐤄𐤉𐤐𐤔𐤉𐤈 𐤀𐤕
𐤄𐤏𐤅𐤋𐤄 𐤅𐤍𐤉𐤕𐤇 𐤀𐤅𐤕𐤄 𐤋𐤉𐤍𐤕𐤇𐤉𐤄 7 𐤅𐤍𐤕𐤍𐤅 𐤁𐤍𐤉
𐤀𐤄𐤓𐤅𐤍 𐤄𐤊𐤅𐤄𐤍 𐤀𐤔 𐤏𐤋 𐤄𐤌𐤉𐤆𐤁𐤇 𐤅𐤏𐤓𐤊𐤅 𐤏𐤑𐤉𐤌 𐤏𐤋
𐤄𐤀𐤔 8 𐤅𐤏𐤓𐤊𐤅 𐤁𐤍𐤉 𐤀𐤄𐤓𐤅𐤍 𐤄𐤊𐤅𐤄𐤍𐤉𐤌 𐤀𐤕
𐤄𐤍𐤕𐤇𐤉𐤌 𐤀𐤕 𐤄𐤓𐤅𐤀𐤔 𐤅𐤀𐤕 𐤄𐤐𐤃𐤓 𐤏𐤋 𐤄𐤏𐤑𐤉𐤌 𐤀𐤔𐤓
𐤏𐤋 𐤄𐤀𐤔 𐤀𐤔𐤓 𐤏𐤋 𐤄𐤌𐤉𐤆𐤁𐤇 9 𐤅𐤒𐤉𐤓𐤁𐤅 𐤅𐤊𐤓𐤏𐤉𐤅
𐤉𐤓𐤇𐤑 𐤁𐤌𐤉𐤉𐤌 𐤅𐤄𐤉𐤒𐤈𐤉𐤓 𐤄𐤊𐤅𐤄𐤍 𐤀𐤕 𐤄𐤊𐤅𐤋
𐤄𐤌𐤉𐤆𐤁𐤇𐤄 𐤏𐤅𐤋𐤄 𐤀𐤉𐤔𐤄 𐤓𐤉𐤇 𐤍𐤉𐤇𐤅𐤇 𐤋𐤉𐤄𐤅𐤄
10 𐤅𐤀𐤉𐤌 𐤌𐤉𐤍 𐤄𐤑𐤅𐤀𐤍 𐤒𐤓𐤁𐤍𐤅 𐤌𐤉𐤍 𐤄𐤊𐤎𐤁𐤉𐤌 𐤀𐤅
𐤌𐤉𐤍 𐤄𐤏𐤉𐤆𐤉𐤌 𐤋𐤏𐤅𐤋𐤄 𐤆𐤊𐤓 𐤕𐤌𐤉𐤌 𐤉𐤒𐤓𐤉𐤁𐤍𐤅
11 𐤅𐤔𐤇𐤈 𐤀𐤅𐤕𐤅 𐤏𐤋 𐤉𐤓𐤊 𐤄𐤌𐤉𐤆𐤁𐤇 𐤑𐤐𐤅𐤍𐤄 𐤋𐤉𐤐𐤍𐤉
𐤉𐤄𐤅𐤄 𐤅𐤆𐤓𐤒𐤅 𐤁𐤍𐤉 𐤀𐤄𐤓𐤅𐤍 𐤄𐤊𐤅𐤄𐤍𐤉𐤌 𐤀𐤕 𐤃𐤌𐤅 𐤏𐤋
𐤄𐤌𐤉𐤆𐤁𐤇 𐤎𐤁𐤉𐤁 12 𐤅𐤍𐤉𐤕𐤇 𐤀𐤅𐤕𐤅 𐤋𐤉𐤍𐤕𐤇𐤉𐤅 𐤅𐤀𐤕
𐤓𐤅𐤀𐤔𐤅 𐤅𐤀𐤕 𐤐𐤉𐤃𐤓𐤅 𐤅𐤏𐤓𐤊 𐤄𐤊𐤅𐤄𐤍 𐤀𐤅𐤕𐤌 𐤏𐤋 𐤄𐤏𐤑𐤉𐤌
𐤀𐤔𐤓 𐤏𐤋 𐤄𐤀𐤔 𐤀𐤔𐤓 𐤏𐤋 𐤄𐤌𐤉𐤆𐤁𐤇 13 𐤅𐤄𐤒𐤓𐤁
𐤅𐤄𐤊𐤓𐤏𐤉𐤉𐤌 𐤉𐤓𐤇𐤑 𐤁𐤌𐤉𐤉𐤌 𐤅𐤄𐤉𐤒𐤓𐤉𐤁 𐤄𐤊𐤅𐤄𐤍 𐤀𐤕
𐤄𐤊𐤅𐤋 𐤅𐤄𐤉𐤒𐤈𐤉𐤓 𐤄𐤌𐤉𐤆𐤁𐤇𐤄 𐤏𐤅𐤋𐤄 𐤄𐤅𐤀 𐤀𐤉𐤔𐤄 𐤓𐤉𐤇

הוא 16 והקטיר הכהן את אזכרתה מגרשה
ומשמנה על כל לבנתה אשה ליהוה

ויקרא פרק 3

1 ואם זבח שלמים קרבנו אם מן הבקר
הוא מקריב אם זכר אם נקבה תמים
יקריבנו לפני יהוה 2 וסמך ידו על ראש
קרבנו ושחטו פתח אהל מועד וזרקו בני אהרן
הכהנים את הדם על המזבח סביב 3 והקריב
מזבח השלמים אשה ליהוה את החלב המכסה
את הקרב ואת כל החלב אשר על הקרב 4 ואת שתי
הכלית ואת החלב אשר עלהן אשר על הכסלים
ואת היתרת על הכבד על הכליות יסירנה
5 והקטירו אתו בני אהרן המזבחה על
העלה אשר על העצים אשר על האש אשה
ריח ניחח ליהוה 6 ואם מן הצאן קרבנו
לזבח שלמים ליהוה זכר או נקבה תמים
יקריבנו 7 אם כשב הוא מקריב את קרבנו
והקריב אתו לפני יהוה 8 וסמך את ידו על
ראש קרבנו ושחט אתו לפני אהל מועד וזרקו
בני אהרן את דמו על המזבח סביב 9 והקריב
מזבח השלמים אשה ליהוה חלבו האליה
תמימה לעמת העצה יסירנה ואת החלב
המכסה את הקרב ואת כל החלב אשר על הקרב 10 ואת
שתי הכלית ואת החלב אשר עלהן אשר על
הכסלים ואת היתרת על הכבד על הכליות
יסירנה 11 והקטירו הכהן המזבחה לחם
אשה ליהוה 12 ואם עז קרבנו והקריבו
לפני יהוה 13 וסמך את ידו על ראשו ושחט
אתו לפני אהל מועד וזרקו בני אהרן את
דמו על המזבח סביב 14 והקריב ממנו
קרבנו אשה ליהוה את החלב המכסה את הקרב ואת
כל החלב אשר על הקרב 15 ואת שתי הכלית ואת
החלב אשר עלהן אשר על הכסלים ואת היתרת
על הכבד על הכליות יסירנה 16 והקטירם
הכהן המזבחה לחם אשה לריח ניחח כל חלב
ליהוה 17 חקת עולם לדרתיכם בכל
מושבתיכם כל חלב וכל דם לא תאכלו

ויקרא פרק 4

1 וידבר יהוה אל מושה לאמור 2 דבר אל בני
יסראל לאמור נפש כי תחטא בישגגה מיכול
מיצות יהוה אשר לוא תעסינה ועסה מאחת
מהנה 3 אים הכוהן המשיח יחטא לאשמת
העם והיקריב על חטאתו אשר חטא פר בן בקר
תימים ליהוה לחטאת 4 והביא את הפר אל פתח
אוהל מועד ליפני יהוה וסמך את ידו על רואש
הפר ושחט את הפר ליפני יהוה 5 ולקח הכוהן
המשיח מידם הפר והביא אותו אל אוהל מועד
6 וטבל הכוהן את אצבעו בדם והיזה מין הדם
שבע פעמים ליפני יהוה את פני פרוכת
הקודש 7 ונתן הכוהן מין הדם על קרנות
מיזבח קטורת הסמים ליפני יהוה אשר
באוהל מועד ואת כל דם הפר ישפוך אל יסוד
מיזבח העולה אשר פתח אוהל מועד 8 ואת כל חלב
פר החטאת ירים מימנו את החלב המכסה על
הקרב ואת כל החלב אשר על הקר 9 ואת שתי הכליות
ואת החלב אשר עליהן אשר על הכסלים ואת
היותרת על הכבד על הכליות יסירנה 10 כאשר
יורם מישור זבח השלמים והיקטירם הכוהן
על מיזבח העולה 11 ואת עור הפר ואת כל בסרו על
רואשו ועל כרעיו וקירבו ופירשו 12 והוציא את
כל הפר אל מיחוץ למחנה אל מקום טהור אל
שפך הדשן וסרף אותו על עצים באש על שפך
הדשן יסרף 13 ואים כל עדת יסראל ישגו
ונעלם דבר מעיני הקהל ועסו אחת מיכל
מיצות יהוה אשר לוא תעסינה ואשמו
14 ונודעה החטאת אשר חטאו עליה והיקריבו
הקהל פר בן בקר לחטאת והביאו אותו ליפני
אוהל מועד 15 וסמכו זיקני העדה את ידיהם
על רואש הפר ליפני יהוה ושחט את הפר
ליפני יהוה 16 והביא הכוהן המשיח מידם
הפר אל אוהל מועד 17 וטבל הכוהן אצבעו מין
הדם והיזה שבע פעמים ליפני יהוה את
פני הפרוכת 18 ומין הדם יתן על קרנות
המיזבח אשר ליפני יהוה אשר באוהל מועד
ואת כל הדם ישפוך אל יסוד מיזבח העולה אשר
פתח אוהל מועד 19 ואת כל חלבו ירים מימנו
והיקטיר המיזבחה 20 ועסה לפר כאשר עסה

לפר החטאת כן יעסה לו וכיפר עלהם הכוהן
וניסלח להם 21 והוציא את הפר אל מיחוץ
למחנה וסרף אותו כאשר סרף את הפר הריאשון
חטאת הקהל הוא 22 אשר נסיא יחטא ועסה אחת
מיכל מיצות יהוה אלוהיו אשר לוא תעסינה
בישגגה ואשם 23 או הודע אליו חטאתו אשר חטא
בה והביא את קרבנו סעיר עיזים זכר תמים
24 וסמך ידו על רואש הסעיר ושחט אותו בימקום
אשר ישחט את העולה ליפני יהוה חטאת הוא
25 ולקח הכוהן מידם החטאת באצבעו ונתן על
קרנות מיזבח העולה ואת דמו ישפוך אל יסוד
מיזבח העולה 26 ואת כל חלבו יקטיר המיזבחה
כחלב זבח השלמים וכיפר עליו הכוהן מחטאתו
וניסלח לו 27 ואים נפש אחת תחטא בישגגה
מעם הארץ בעסותה אחת מימיצות יהוה אשר
לוא תעסינה ואשם 28 או הודע אליו חטאתו אשר
חטא והביא קרבנו סעירת עיזים תמימה
נקבה על חטאתו אשר חטא 29 וסמך את ידו על רואש
החטאת ושחט את החטאת בימקום העולה 30 ולקח
הכוהן מידמה באצבעו ונתן על קרנות מיזבח
העולה ואת כל דמה ישפוך אל יסוד המיזבחה
31 ואת כל חלבה יסיר כאשר הוסר חלב מעל זבח
השלמים והקטיר הכוהן המיזבחה לריח
ניחוח ליהוה וכיפר עליו הכוהן וניסלח לו
32 ואים כבס יביא קרבנו לחטאת נקבה תמימה
יביאנה 33 וסמך את ידו על רואש החטאת ושחט
אותה לחטאת בימקום אשר ישחט את העולה
34 ולקח הכוהן מידם החטאת באצבעו ונתן על
קרנות מיזבח העולה ואת כל דמה ישפוך אל
יסוד המיזבחה 35 ואת כל חלבה יסיר כאשר יוסר
חלב הכסב מיזבח השלמים והקטיר הכוהן
אותם המיזבחה על אישי יהוה וכיפר עליו
הכוהן על חטאתו אשר חטא וניסלח לו

ויקרא פרק 5

1 ונפש כי תחטא ושמעה קול אלה והוא עד או ראה
או ידע אים לוא יגיד ונסא עונו 2 או נפש
אשר תיגע בכל דבר טמא או בניבלת חיה טמאה
או בניבלת בהמה טמאה או בניבלת שרץ טמא
ונעלם מימנו והוא טמא ואשם 3 או כי יגע
בטומאת אדם לכול טומאתו אשר יטמא בה ונעלם

[illegible] 4 [illegible]
[illegible]
[illegible]
[illegible] 5 [illegible]
[illegible] 6 [illegible]
[illegible]
[illegible]
[illegible] 7 [illegible]
[illegible]
[illegible]
[illegible] 8
[illegible]
[illegible] 9 [illegible]
[illegible]
[illegible] 10 [illegible]
[illegible]
[illegible] 11 [illegible]
[illegible]
[illegible]
[illegible]
[illegible] 12 [illegible]
[illegible]
[illegible] 13 [illegible]
[illegible]
[illegible] 14 [illegible]
[illegible] 15
[illegible]
[illegible]
[illegible] 16 [illegible]
[illegible]
[illegible]
[illegible] 17 [illegible]
[illegible]
[illegible] 18 [illegible]
[illegible]
[illegible]
[illegible] 19 [illegible]
[illegible] 21 [illegible] 20
[illegible]
[illegible]
[illegible] 22 [illegible]

שקר על אחת מיכול אשר יעסה האדם לחטוא
בהנה 23 והיה כי יחטא ואשם והשיב את הגזלה
אשר גזל או את העושק אשר עשק או את הפיקדון
אשר הפקד אתו או את האבדה אשר מצא 24 או
מיכול אשר ישבע עליו לשקר ושילם אותו
ברואשו וחמישיתיו יוסף עליו לאשר הוא לו
יתננו ביום אשמתו 25 ואת אשמו יביא
ליהוה אייל תמים מין הצואן בערככה
לאשם אל הכוהן 26 וכיפר עליו הכוהן
ליפני יהוה וניסלח לו על אחת מיכול אשר
יעסה לאשמה בה

ויקרא פרק 6

1 וידבר יהוה אל מושה לאמור 2 צו את אהרון
ואת בניו לאמור זואת תורת העולה הוא העולה
על מוקדה על המזבח כל הלילה עד הבוקר ואש
המזבח תוקד בו 3 ולבש הכוהן מידו בד
ומיכנסי בד ילבש על בסרו והרים את הדשן
אשר תאכל האש את העולה על המזבח ושמו אצל
המזבח 4 ופשט את בגדיו ולבש בגדים
אחרים והוציא את הדשן אל מיחוץ למחנה אל
מקום טהור 5 והאש על המזבח תוקד בו לוא
תיכבה וביער עליה הכוהן עצים בבוקר בבוקר
וערך עליה העולה והיקטיר עליה חלבי
השלמים 6 אש תמיד תוקד על המזבח לוא
תיכבה 7 וזואת תורת המינחה הקרב אותה בני
אהרון ליפני יהוה אל פני המזבח
8 והרים מימנו בקומצו מיסולת המינחה
ומישמנה ואת כל הלבונה אשר על המינחה
והיקטיר המזבח ריח ניחוח אזכרתה ליהוה
9 והנותרת מימנה יואכלו אהרון ובניו מצות
תאכל במקום קדוש בחצר אוהל מועד יואכלוה
10 לוא תאפה חמץ חלקם נתתי אותה מאישי
קודש קודשים היוא כחטאת וכאשם 11 כל זכר
בבני אהרון יואכלנה חק עולם לדורותיכם
מאישי יהוה כול אשר יגע בהם יקדש
12 וידבר יהוה אל מושה לאמור 13 זה קרבן
אהרון ובניו אשר יקריבו ליהוה ביום
הימשח אותו עסירית האפה סולת מינחה
תמיד מחציתהבבוקר ומחציתהבערב 14 על מחבת
בשמן תעסה מורבכת תביאנה תופיני

[illegible]
15 [illegible]
[illegible] 16 [illegible]
[illegible] 17 [illegible]
[illegible] 18 [illegible]
[illegible]
[illegible]
19 [illegible]
[illegible] 20 [illegible]
[illegible]
[illegible] 21 [illegible]
[illegible]
[illegible] 22 [illegible]
[illegible] 23 [illegible]
[illegible]
[illegible]

7 [illegible]

1 [illegible] 2 [illegible]
[illegible]
[illegible] 3 [illegible]
[illegible]
4 [illegible]
[illegible]
[illegible] 5 [illegible]
[illegible] 6 [illegible]
[illegible]
7 [illegible]
[illegible] 8 [illegible]
[illegible] 9 [illegible]
[illegible]
[illegible] 10 [illegible]
[illegible]
[illegible] 11 [illegible]
[illegible] 12 [illegible]
[illegible]
[illegible]
[illegible] 13 [illegible]
[illegible]
14 [illegible]

[illegible]
[illegible] 15
[illegible] 16 [illegible]
[illegible]
[illegible] 17 [illegible]
[illegible]
[illegible] 18
[illegible]
[illegible]
[illegible] 19 [illegible]
[illegible] 20 [illegible]
[illegible]
[illegible]
[illegible] 21 [illegible]
[illegible]
[illegible]
[illegible] 22 [illegible]
[illegible] 23 [illegible]
[illegible] 24 [illegible]
[illegible] 25 [illegible]
[illegible]
[illegible]
[illegible] 26 [illegible]
[illegible] 27 [illegible]
[illegible] 28 [illegible]
[illegible] 29 [illegible]
[illegible]
[illegible] 30 [illegible]
[illegible]
[illegible]
[illegible] 31 [illegible]
[illegible] 32 [illegible]
[illegible]
[illegible] 33 [illegible]
[illegible]
[illegible] 34
[illegible]
[illegible]
[illegible] 35 [illegible]
[illegible]
[illegible] 36 [illegible]

אותם מאת בני יסראל חוקת עולם לדורותם
37 זואת התורה לעולה למינחה ולחטאת ולאשם
ולמילואים ולזבח השלמים 38 אשר ציוה
יהוה את מושה בהר סיני ביום צותו את בני
יסראל להקריב את קרבניהם ליהוה במידבר
סיני

ויקרא פרק 8

1 וידבר יהוה אל מושה לאמור 2 קח את אהרון
ואת בניו איתו ואת הבגדים ואת שמן
המשחה ואת פר החטאת ואת שני האילים
ואת סל המצות 3 ואת כל העדה הקהל אל פתח אוהל
מועד 4 ויעס מושה כאשר ציוה יהוה אותו
ותיקהל העדה אל פתח אוהל מועד 5 ויואמר
מושה אל העדה זה הדבר אשר ציוה יהוה לעסות
6 ויקרב מושה את אהרון ואת בניו וירחץ אותם
במים 7 ויתן עליו את הכותונת ויחגור אותו
באבנט וילבש אותו את המעיל ויתן עליו את
האפוד ויחגור אותו בחשב האפוד ויאפוד לו בו
8 ויסם עליו את החושן ויתן אל החושן את
האורים ואת התומים 9 ויסם את המיצנפת
על רואשו ויסם על המיצנפת אל מול פניו
את ציץ הזהב נזר הקודש כאשר ציוה יהוה את
מושה 10 ויקח מושה את שמן המשחה וימשח
את המשכן ואת כל אשר בו ויקדש אותם 11 ויז
מימנו על המזבח שבע פעמים וימשח את
המזבח ואת כל כליו ואת הכיור ואת כנו לקדשם
12 ויצוק מישמן המשחה על רואש אהרון
וימשח אותו לקדשו 13 ויקרב מושה את בני
אהרון וילבישם כותנות ויחגור אותם אבנט
ויחבוש להם מיגבעות כאשר ציוה יהוה את
מושה 14 ויגש את פר החטאת ויסמוך אהרון
ובניו את ידיהם על רואש פר החטאת 15 וישחט
ויקח מושה את הדם ויתן על קרנות המזבח
סביב באצבעו ויחטא את המזבח ואת הדם יצק
אל יסוד המזבח ויקדשהו לכפר עליו 16 ויקח
את כל החלב אשר על הקרב ואת יותרת הכבד ואת
שתי הכליות ואת חלבהן ויקטר מושה המזבחה
17 ואת הפר ואת עורו ואת בסרו ואת פירשו סרף
באש מיחוץ למחנה כאשר ציוה יהוה את מושה

18 ויקרב את איל העולה ויסמכו אהרון ובניו
את ידיהם על רואש האייל 19 וישחט ויזרוק
מושה את הדם על המיזבח סביב 20 ואת האייל
ניתח לינתחיו ויקטר מושה את הרואש ואת
הנתחים ואת הפדר 21 ואת הקרב ואת הכרעיים
רחץ במיים ויקטר מושה את כל האייל
המיזבחה עולה הוא לריח ניחוח אישה הוא
ליהוה כאשר ציוה יהוה את מושה 22 ויקרב את
האייל השני איל המילואים ויסמכו
אהרון ובניו את ידיהם על רואש האייל
23 וישחט ויקח מושה מידמו ויתן על תנוך
אוזן אהרון הימנית ועל בוהן ידו הימנית
ועל בוהן רגלו הימנית 24 ויקרב את בני
אהרון ויתן מושה מין הדם על תנוך אזנם
הימנית ועל בוהן ידם הימנית ועל בוהן
רגלם הימנית ויזרוק מושה את הדם על
המיזבח סביב 25 ויקח את החלב ואת האליה ואת כל
החלב אשר על הקרב ואת יותרת הכבד ואת שתי
הכליות ואת חלבהן ואת שוק הימין 26 ומיסל
המצות אשר לפני יהוה לקח חלת מצה אחת
וחלת לחם שמן אחת ורקיק אחד ויסם על החלבים
ועל שוק הימין 27 ויתן את הכול על כפי
אהרון ועל כפי בניו ויניף אותם תנופה
לפני יהוה 28 ויקח מושה אותם מעל
כפיהם ויקטר המיזבחה על העולה מילואים
הם לריח ניחוח אישה הוא ליהוה 29 ויקח
מושה את החזה ויניפהו תנופה לפני
יהוה מאיל המילואים למושה היה למנה
כאשר ציוה יהוה את מושה 30 ויקח מושה
מישמן המישחה ומין הדם אשר על
המיזבח ויז על אהרון על בגדיו ועל בניו ועל
ביגדי בניו איתו ויקדש את אהרון את בגדיו
ואת בניו ואת ביגדי בניו איתו 31 ויואמר
מושה אל אהרון ואל בניו בשלו את הבסר פתח
אוהל מועד ושם תאכלו אותו ואת הלחם אשר בסל
המילואים כאשר ציויתי לאמור אהרון
ובניו יאכלוהו 32 והנותר בבסר ובלחם באש
תיסרופו 33 ומיפתח אוהל מועד לוא תצאו
שיבעת ימים עד יום מלואת ימי
מילואיכם כי שיבעת ימים ימלא את
ידכם 34 כאשר עסה ביום הזה ציוה יהוה

לעסות לכפר עליכם 35 ופתח אוהל מועד תשבו
יומם ולילה שיבעת ימים ושמרתם את
מישמרת יהוה ולוא תמותו כי כן צוויתי
36 ויעס אהרון ובניו את כל הדברים אשר ציוה
יהוה ביד מושה

ויקרא פרק 9

1 ויהי ביום השמיני קרא מושה לאהרון
ולבניו ולזיקני יסראל 2 ויואמר אל אהרון
קח לכה עגל בן בקר לחטאת ואייל לעולה
תמימים והקרב ליפני יהוה 3 ואל בני
יסראל תדבר לאמור קחו סעיר עיזים לחטאת
ועגל וכבס בני שנה תמימים לעולה 4 ושור
ואייל לישלמים ליזבוח ליפני יהוה
ומינחה בלולה בשמן כי היום יהוה ניראה
אליכם 5 ויקחו את אשר ציוה מושה אל פני
אוהל מועד ויקרבו כל העדה ויעמדו ליפני
יהוה 6 ויואמר מושה זה הדבר אשר ציוה יהוה
תעסו וירא אליכם כבוד יהוה 7 ויואמר מושה
אל אהרון קרב אל המיזבח ועסה את חטאתכה ואת
עולתכה וכפר בעדכה ובעד העם ועסה את קרבן
העם וכפר בעדם כאשר ציוה יהוה 8 ויקרב
אהרון אל המיזבח וישחט את עגל החטאת אשר לו
9 ויקרבו בני אהרון את הדם אליו ויטבול
אצבעו בדם ויתן על קרנות המיזבח ואת הדם
יצק אל יסוד המיזבח 10 ואת החלב ואת הכליות
ואת היותרת מין הכבד מין החטאת היקטיר
המיזבחה כאשר ציוה יהוה את מושה 11 ואת
הבסר ואת העור סרף באש מיחוץ למחנה
12 וישחט את העולה וימציאו בני אהרון
אליו את הדם ויזרקהו על המיזבח סבי 13 ואת
העולה הימציאו אליו לינתחיה ואת הרואש
ויקטר על המיזבח 14 וירחץ את הקרב ואת
הכרעיים ויקטר על העולה המיזבחה 15 ויקרב
את קרבן העם ויקח את סעיר החטאת אשר לעם
וישחטהו ויחטאהו כריאשון 16 ויקרב את העולה
ויעסה כמישפט 17 ויקרב את המינחה וימלא
כפו מימנה ויקטר על המיזבח מילבד עולת
הבוקר 18 וישחט את השור ואת האייל זבח
השלמים אשר לעם וימציאו בני אהרון את

הדם אליו ויזרקהו על המיזבח סביב 19 ואת
החלבים מין השור ומין האייל האליה
והמכסה והכליות ויותרת הכבד 20 ויסימו את
החלבים על החזות ויקטר החלבים המיזבחה
21 ואת החזות ואת שוק הימין הניף אהרון
תנופה ליפני יהוה כאשר ציוה מושה
22 ויסא אהרון את ידו אל העם ויברכם וירד
מעסות החטאת והעולה והשלמים 23 ויבוא מושה
ואהרון אל אוהל מועד ויצאו ויברכו את העם
וירא כבוד יהוה אל כל העם 24 ותצא אש
מיליפני יהוה ותואכל על המיזבח את
העולה ואת החלבים וירא כל העם וירונו ויפלו
על פניהם

ויקרא פרק 10

1 ויקחו בני אהרון נדב ואביהוא איש מחתתו
ויתנו בהן אש ויסימו עליה קטורת ויקריבו
ליפני יהוה אש זרה אשר לוא ציוה אותם
2 ותצא אש מיליפני יהוה ותואכל אותם
וימותו ליפני יהוה 3 ויאמר מושה אל
אהרון הוא אשר דיבר יהוה לאמור ביקרובי
אקדש ועל פני כל העם אכבד וידום אהרון
4 ויקרא מושה אל מישאל ואל אלצפן בני
עוזיאל דוד אהרון ויאמר אלהם קירבו סאו את
אחיכם מאת פני הקודש אל מיחוץ למחנה
5 ויקרבו ויסאום בכותנותם אל מיחוץ למחנה
כאשר דיבר מושה 6 ויאמר מושה אל אהרון
ולאלעזר ולאיתמר בניו ראשיכם אל תיפרעו
וביגדיכם לוא תיפרומו ולוא תמותו ועל כל
העדה יקצוף ואחיכם כל בית יסראל יבכו את
הסרפה אשר סרף יהוה 7 ומיפתח אוהל מועד
לוא תצאו פן תמותו כי שמן מישחת יהוה
עליכם ויעסו כידבר מושה 8 וידבר יהוה אל
אהרון לאמור 9 יין ושכר אל תשת אתה ובניכה
איתך בבואכם אל אוהל מועד ולוא תמותו חוקת
עולם לדורותיכם 10 ולהבדיל בין הקודש ובין
החול ובין הטמא ובין הטהור 11 ולהורות את בני
יסראל את כל החוקים אשר דיבר יהוה אליהם
ביד מושה 12 וידבר מושה אל אהרון ואל אלעזר
ואל איתמר בניו הנותרים קחו את המינחה
הנותרת מאישי יהוה ואיכלוה מצות אצל

𐤄𐤌𐤉𐤆𐤁𐤇 𐤊𐤉 𐤒𐤅𐤃𐤔 𐤒𐤃𐤔𐤉𐤌 𐤄𐤉𐤅𐤀 13 𐤅𐤀𐤊𐤋𐤕𐤌 𐤀𐤅𐤕𐤄
𐤁𐤌𐤒𐤅𐤌 𐤒𐤃𐤅𐤔 𐤊𐤉 𐤇𐤒𐤊𐤄 𐤅𐤇𐤒 𐤁𐤍𐤉𐤊𐤄 𐤄𐤉𐤅𐤀 𐤌𐤀𐤉𐤔𐤉
𐤉𐤄𐤅𐤄 𐤊𐤉 𐤊𐤍 𐤑𐤅𐤅𐤉𐤕𐤉 14 𐤅𐤀𐤕 𐤇𐤆𐤄 𐤄𐤕𐤍𐤅𐤐𐤄 𐤅𐤀𐤕
𐤔𐤅𐤒 𐤄𐤕𐤓𐤅𐤌𐤄 𐤕𐤅𐤀𐤊𐤋𐤅 𐤁𐤌𐤒𐤅𐤌 𐤈𐤄𐤅𐤓 𐤀𐤕𐤄 𐤅𐤁𐤍𐤉𐤊𐤄
𐤅𐤁𐤍𐤅𐤕𐤉𐤊𐤄 𐤀𐤉𐤕𐤊 𐤊𐤉 𐤇𐤒𐤊𐤄 𐤅𐤇𐤒 𐤁𐤍𐤉𐤊𐤄 𐤍𐤉𐤕𐤍𐤅
𐤌𐤉𐤆𐤉𐤁𐤇𐤉 𐤔𐤋𐤌𐤉 𐤁𐤍𐤉 𐤉𐤎𐤓𐤀𐤋 15 𐤔𐤅𐤒 𐤄𐤕𐤓𐤅𐤌𐤄
𐤅𐤇𐤆𐤄 𐤄𐤕𐤍𐤅𐤐𐤄 𐤏𐤋 𐤀𐤉𐤔𐤉 𐤄𐤇𐤋𐤁𐤉𐤌 𐤉𐤁𐤉𐤀𐤅
𐤋𐤄𐤍𐤉𐤐 𐤕𐤍𐤅𐤐𐤄 𐤋𐤉𐤐𐤍𐤉 𐤉𐤄𐤅𐤄 𐤅𐤄𐤉𐤄 𐤋𐤊𐤄
𐤅𐤋𐤁𐤍𐤉𐤊𐤄 𐤀𐤉𐤕𐤊𐤄 𐤋𐤇𐤒 𐤏𐤅𐤋𐤌 𐤊𐤀𐤔𐤓 𐤑𐤉𐤅𐤄 𐤉𐤄𐤅𐤄
16 𐤅𐤀𐤕 𐤎𐤏𐤉𐤓 𐤄𐤇𐤈𐤀𐤕 𐤃𐤓𐤅𐤔 𐤃𐤓𐤔 𐤌𐤅𐤔𐤄 𐤅𐤄𐤉𐤍𐤄
𐤎𐤅𐤓𐤐 𐤅𐤉𐤒𐤑𐤅𐤐 𐤏𐤋 𐤀𐤋𐤏𐤆𐤓 𐤅𐤏𐤋 𐤀𐤉𐤕𐤌𐤓 𐤁𐤍𐤉
𐤀𐤄𐤓𐤅𐤍 𐤄𐤍𐤅𐤕𐤓𐤉𐤌 𐤋𐤀𐤌𐤅𐤓 17 𐤌𐤃𐤅𐤏 𐤋𐤅𐤀 𐤀𐤊𐤋𐤕𐤌 𐤀𐤕
𐤄𐤇𐤈𐤀𐤕 𐤁𐤉𐤌𐤒𐤅𐤌 𐤄𐤒𐤅𐤃𐤔 𐤊𐤉 𐤒𐤅𐤃𐤔 𐤒𐤃𐤔𐤉𐤌 𐤄𐤉𐤅𐤀
𐤅𐤀𐤅𐤕𐤄 𐤍𐤕𐤍 𐤋𐤊𐤌 𐤋𐤎𐤀𐤕 𐤀𐤕 𐤏𐤅𐤍 𐤄𐤏𐤃𐤄 𐤋𐤊𐤐𐤓
𐤏𐤋𐤉𐤄𐤌 𐤋𐤉𐤐𐤍𐤉 𐤉𐤄𐤅𐤄 18 𐤄𐤍 𐤋𐤅𐤀 𐤄𐤅𐤁𐤀 𐤀𐤕 𐤃𐤌𐤄
𐤀𐤋 𐤄𐤒𐤅𐤃𐤔 𐤐𐤍𐤉𐤌𐤄 𐤀𐤊𐤅𐤋 𐤕𐤅𐤀𐤊𐤋𐤅 𐤀𐤅𐤕𐤄 𐤁𐤒𐤅𐤃𐤔
𐤊𐤀𐤔𐤓 𐤑𐤉𐤅𐤉𐤕𐤉 19 𐤅𐤉𐤃𐤁𐤓 𐤀𐤄𐤓𐤅𐤍 𐤀𐤋 𐤌𐤅𐤔𐤄 𐤄𐤍
𐤄𐤉𐤅𐤌 𐤄𐤉𐤒𐤓𐤉𐤁𐤅 𐤀𐤕 𐤇𐤈𐤀𐤕𐤌 𐤅𐤀𐤕 𐤏𐤅𐤋𐤕𐤌 𐤋𐤉𐤐𐤍𐤉
𐤉𐤄𐤅𐤄 𐤅𐤕𐤉𐤒𐤓𐤀𐤍𐤄 𐤀𐤅𐤕𐤉 𐤊𐤀𐤋𐤄 𐤅𐤀𐤊𐤋𐤕𐤉 𐤇𐤈𐤀𐤕
𐤄𐤉𐤅𐤌 𐤄𐤉𐤉𐤈𐤁 𐤁𐤏𐤉𐤍𐤉 𐤉𐤄𐤅𐤄 20 𐤅𐤉𐤔𐤌𐤏 𐤌𐤅𐤔𐤄
𐤅𐤉𐤉𐤈𐤁 𐤁𐤏𐤉𐤍𐤉𐤅

𐤅𐤉𐤒𐤓𐤀 𐤐𐤓𐤒 11

1 𐤅𐤉𐤃𐤁𐤓 𐤉𐤄𐤅𐤄 𐤀𐤋 𐤌𐤅𐤔𐤄 𐤅𐤀𐤋 𐤀𐤄𐤓𐤅𐤍 𐤋𐤀𐤌𐤅𐤓 𐤀𐤋𐤄𐤌
2 𐤃𐤁𐤓𐤅 𐤀𐤋 𐤁𐤍𐤉 𐤉𐤎𐤓𐤀𐤋 𐤋𐤀𐤌𐤅𐤓 𐤆𐤅𐤀𐤕 𐤄𐤇𐤉𐤄 𐤀𐤔𐤓
𐤕𐤅𐤀𐤊𐤋𐤅 𐤌𐤉𐤊𐤋 𐤄𐤁𐤄𐤌𐤄 𐤀𐤔𐤓 𐤏𐤋 𐤄𐤀𐤓𐤑 3 𐤊𐤅𐤋
𐤌𐤐𐤓𐤎𐤕 𐤐𐤓𐤎𐤄 𐤅𐤔𐤅𐤎𐤏𐤕 𐤔𐤎𐤏 𐤐𐤓𐤎𐤅𐤕 𐤌𐤏𐤋𐤕 𐤂𐤓𐤄
𐤁𐤁𐤄𐤌𐤄 𐤀𐤅𐤕𐤄 𐤕𐤅𐤀𐤊𐤋𐤅 4 𐤀𐤊 𐤀𐤕 𐤆𐤄 𐤋𐤅𐤀 𐤕𐤅𐤀𐤊𐤋𐤅
𐤌𐤉𐤌𐤏𐤋𐤉 𐤄𐤂𐤓𐤄 𐤅𐤌𐤉𐤌𐤐𐤓𐤉𐤎𐤉 𐤄𐤐𐤓𐤎𐤄 𐤀𐤕
𐤄𐤂𐤌𐤋 𐤊𐤉 𐤌𐤏𐤋𐤄 𐤂𐤓𐤄 𐤄𐤅𐤀 𐤅𐤐𐤓𐤎𐤄 𐤀𐤉𐤍𐤍𐤅
𐤌𐤐𐤓𐤉𐤎 𐤈𐤌𐤀 𐤄𐤅𐤀 𐤋𐤊𐤌 5 𐤅𐤀𐤕 𐤄𐤔𐤐𐤍 𐤊𐤉 𐤌𐤏𐤋𐤄
𐤂𐤓𐤄 𐤄𐤅𐤀 𐤅𐤐𐤓𐤎𐤄 𐤋𐤅𐤀 𐤉𐤐𐤓𐤉𐤎 𐤈𐤌𐤀 𐤄𐤅𐤀 𐤋𐤊𐤌 6 𐤅𐤀𐤕
𐤄𐤀𐤓𐤍𐤁𐤕 𐤊𐤉 𐤌𐤏𐤋𐤕 𐤂𐤓𐤄 𐤄𐤉𐤅𐤀 𐤅𐤐𐤓𐤎𐤄 𐤋𐤅𐤀
𐤄𐤉𐤐𐤓𐤉𐤎𐤄 𐤈𐤌𐤀𐤄 𐤄𐤉𐤅𐤀 𐤋𐤊𐤌 7 𐤅𐤀𐤕 𐤄𐤇𐤆𐤉𐤓 𐤊𐤉
𐤌𐤐𐤓𐤉𐤎 𐤐𐤓𐤎𐤄 𐤄𐤅𐤀 𐤅𐤔𐤅𐤎𐤏 𐤔𐤎𐤏 𐤐𐤓𐤎𐤄 𐤅𐤄𐤅𐤀 𐤂𐤓𐤄
𐤋𐤅𐤀 𐤉𐤂𐤓 𐤈𐤌𐤀 𐤄𐤅𐤀 𐤋𐤊𐤌 8 𐤌𐤉𐤁𐤎𐤓𐤌 𐤋𐤅𐤀 𐤕𐤅𐤀𐤊𐤋𐤅
𐤅𐤁𐤍𐤉𐤁𐤋𐤕𐤌 𐤋𐤅𐤀 𐤕𐤉𐤂𐤏𐤅 𐤈𐤌𐤀𐤉𐤌 𐤄𐤌 𐤋𐤊𐤌 9 𐤀𐤕 𐤆𐤄
𐤕𐤅𐤀𐤊𐤋𐤅 𐤌𐤉𐤊𐤅𐤋 𐤀𐤔𐤓 𐤁𐤌𐤉𐤉𐤌 𐤊𐤅𐤋 𐤀𐤔𐤓 𐤋𐤅𐤎𐤍𐤐𐤉𐤓
𐤅𐤒𐤎𐤒𐤎𐤕 𐤁𐤌𐤉𐤉𐤌 𐤁𐤉𐤌𐤉𐤌 𐤅𐤁𐤍𐤇𐤋𐤉𐤌 𐤀𐤅𐤕𐤌 𐤕𐤅𐤀𐤊𐤋𐤅
10 𐤅𐤊𐤅𐤋 𐤀𐤔𐤓 𐤀𐤉𐤍 𐤋𐤅 𐤎𐤍𐤐𐤉𐤓 𐤅𐤒𐤎𐤒𐤎𐤕 𐤁𐤉𐤌𐤉𐤌
𐤅𐤁𐤍𐤇𐤋𐤉𐤌 𐤌𐤉𐤊𐤅𐤋 𐤔𐤓𐤑 𐤄𐤌𐤉𐤉𐤌 𐤅𐤌𐤉𐤊𐤅𐤋 𐤍𐤐𐤔

החיה אשר במיים שקץ הם לכם 11 ושקץ יהיו
לכם מיבסרם לוא תואכלו ואת ניבלתם תשקצו
12 כול אשר אין לו סנפיר וקסקסת במיים
שקץ הוא לכם 13 ואת אלה תשקצו מין העוף לוא
יאכלו שקץ הם את הנשר ואת הפרס ואת
העזניה 14 ואת הדאה ואת האיה למינה 15 את
כל עורב למינו 16 ואת בת היענה ואת התחמס ואת
השחף ואת הנץ למינהו 17 ואת הכוס ואת השלך
ואת הינשו 18 ואת התינשמת ואת הקאת ואת
הרחם 19 ואת החסידה האנפה למינה ואת
הדוכיפת ואת העטל 20 כול שרץ העוף ההולך על
ארבע שקץ הוא לכם 21 אך את זה תואכלו מיכול
שרץ העוף ההולך על ארבע אשר לוא כרעיים
מימעל לרגליו לנתר בהן על הארץ 22 את אלה
מהם תואכלו את הארבה למינו ואת הסלעם
למינהו ואת החרגול למינהו ואת החגב
למינהו 23 וכול שרץ העוף אשר לו ארבע
רגליים שקץ הוא לכם 24 ולאלה תיטמאו כל
הנוגע בניבלתם יטמא עד הער 25 וכל הנוסא
מיניבלתם יכבס בגדיו וטמא עד הער 26 לכל
הבהמה אשר היוא מפרסת פרסה ושסע איננה
שוסעת וגרה איננה מעלה טמאים הם לכם כל
הנוגע בהם יטמא 27 וכול הולך על כפיו בכל
החיה ההולכת על ארבע טמאים הם לכם כל
הנוגע בניבלתם יטמא עד הער 28 והנוסא את
ניבלתם יכבס בגדיו וטמא עד הערב טמאים
המה לכם 29 וזה לכם הטמא בשרץ השורץ על
הארץ החולד והעכבר והצב למינהו 30 והאנקה
והכוח והלטאה והחומט והתינשמת 31 אלה
הטמאים לכם בכל השרץ כל הנוגע בהם במותם
יטמא עד הער 32 וכול אשר יפול עליו מהם
במותם יטמא מיכל כלי עץ או בגד או עור או סק
כל כלי אשר יעסה מלאכה בהם במיים יובא
וטמא עד הערב וטהר 33 וכל כלי חרס אשר יפול
מהם אל תוכו כול אשר בתוכו יטמא ואותו תישבורו
34 מיכל האוכל אשר יאכל אשר יבוא עליו
מיים יטמא וכל משקה אשר ישתה בכל כלי
יטמא 35 וכול אשר יפול מיניבלתם עליו
יטמא תנור וכיריים יותץ טמאים הם
וטמאים יהיו לכם 36 אך מעין בור מיקוה
מיים יהיה טהור ונוגע בניבלתם יטמא

37 וכי יפול מנבלתם על כל זרע זרוע אשר
יזרע טהור הוא 38 וכי יותן מים על זרע
ונפל מנבלתם עליו טמא הוא לכם 39 וכי
ימות מן הבהמה אשר היא לכם לאכלה
הנוגע בנבלתה יטמא עד הערב 40 והאוכל
מנבלתה יכבס בגדיו וטמא עד הערב והנושא
את נבלתה יכבס בגדיו וטמא עד הערב 41 וכל
השרץ השורץ על הארץ שקץ הוא לוא יאכל 42 כול
הולך על גחון וכול הולך על ארבע עד כל מרבה
רגלים לכל השרץ השורץ על הארץ לוא
תאכלום כי שקץ הם 43 אל תשקצו את
נפשותיכם בכל השרץ השורץ ולוא תטמאו
בהם ונטמתם בם 44 כי אני יהוה אלהיכם
והתקדשתם והייתם קדושים כי קדוש
אני ולוא תטמאו את נפשותיכם בכל השרץ
הרומש על הארץ 45 כי אני יהוה המעלה אתכם
מארץ מצרים להיות לכם לאלהים
והייתם קדושים כי קדוש אני 46 זואת תורת
הבהמה והעוף וכול נפש החיה הרומשת
במים ולכל נפש השורצת על הארץ
47 להבדיל בין הטמא ובין הטהור ובין החיה
הנאכלת ובין החיה אשר לוא תאכל

ויקרא פרק 12

1 וידבר יהוה אל משה לאמור 2 דבר אל בני
ישראל לאמור אשה כי תזריע וילדה זכר
וטמאה שבעת ימים כימי נדת דותה
תטמא 3 וביום השמיני ימול בשר ערלתו
4 ושלושים יום ושלושת ימים תשב בדמי
טהרה בכל קודש לוא תגע ואל המקדש לוא תבוא
עד מלאות ימי טהרה 5 ואם נקבה תלד וטמאה
שבועים כנדתה וששים יום וששת
ימים תשב על דמי טהרה 6 ובמלואת ימי
טהרה לבן או לבת תביא כבש בן שנתו לעולה ובן
יונה או תור לחטאת אל פתח אוהל מועד אל הכוהן
7 והקריבו לפני יהוה וכפר עליה
וטהרה ממקור דמיה זאת תורת היולדת לזכר
או לנקבה 8 ואם לוא תמצא ידה די שה ולקחה
שתי תורים או שני בני יונה אחד לעולה
ואחד לחטאת וכפר עליה הכוהן וטהרה

ויקרא פרק 13

1 וידבר יהוה אל מושה ואל אהרון לאמור 2 אדם
כי יהיה בעור בשרו שאת או ספחת או בהרת והיה
בעור בשרו לנגע צרעת והובא אל אהרון הכוהן או
אל אחד מיבניו הכוהנים 3 וראה הכוהן את
הנגע בעור הבשר ושער בנגע הפך לבן ומראה
הנגע עמוק מעור בשרו נגע צרעת הוא וראהו
הכוהן וטימא אותו 4 ואים בהרת לבנה היוא
בעור בשרו ועמוק אין מראה מין העור ושערה
לוא הפך לבן והיסגיר הכוהן את הנגע שיבעת
ימים 5 וראהו הכוהן ביום השביעי והינה
הנגע עמד בעיניו לוא פשה הנגע בעור
והיסגירו הכוהן שיבעת ימים שנית
6 וראה הכוהן אותו ביום השביעי שנית
והינה כהה הנגע ולוא פשה הנגע בעור וטיהרו
הכוהן מיספחת היא וכיבס בגדיו וטהר
7 ואים פשוה תיפשה המיספחת בעור אחרי
הראותו אל הכוהן לטהרתו וניראה שנית אל
הכוהן 8 וראה הכוהן והינה פשתה המיספחת
בעור וטימאו הכוהן צרעת היוא 9 נגע צרעת
כי תיהיה באדם והובא אל הכוהן 10 וראה הכוהן
והינה שאת לבנה בעור והיא הפכה שער לבן
ומיחית בשר חי בשאת 11 צרעת נושנת היוא
בעור בשרו וטימאו הכוהן לוא יסגירנו כי טמא
הוא 12 ואים פרוח תיפרח הצרעת בעור וכיסתה
הצרעת את כל עור הנגע מרואשו ועד רגליו לכל
מראה עיני הכוהן 13 וראה הכוהן והינה
כיסתה הצרעת את כל בשרו וטיהר את הנגע כולו
הפך לבן טהור הוא 14 וביום הראות בו בשר חי
יטמא 15 וראה הכוהן את הבשר החי וטימאו הבשר
החי טמא הוא צרעת הוא 16 או כי ישוב הבשר
החי ונהפך ללבן ובא אל הכוהן 17 וראהו הכוהן
והינה נהפך הנגע ללבן וטיהר הכוהן את
הנגע טהור הוא 18 ובשר כי יהיה בו בעורו
שחין ונירפא 19 והיה בימקום השחין שאת
לבנה או בהרת לבנה אדמדמת וניראה אל הכוהן
20 וראה הכוהן והינה מראה שפל מין העור
ושערה הפך לבן וטימאו הכוהן נגע צרעת היוא
בשחין פרחה 21 ואים יראנה הכוהן והינה
אין בה שער לבן ושפלה איננה מין העור

והיא כהה והיסגירו הכוהן שיבעת ימים
22 ואים פסוה תיפסה בעור וטימא הכוהן אותו
נגע היוא 23 ואים תחתיה תעמוד הבהרת לוא
פסתה צרבת השחין היוא וטיהרו הכוהן 24 או
בסר כי יהיה בעורו מיכות אש והיתה מיחית
המיכוה בהרת לבנה אדמדמת או לבנה 25 וראה
אותה הכוהן והינה נהפך סער לבן בבהרת
ומראה עמוק מין העור צרעת היוא במיכוה
פרחה וטימא אותו הכוהן נגע צרעת היוא
26 ואים יראנה הכוהן והינה אין בבהרת
סער לבן ושפלה איננה מין העור והיוא כהה
והיסגירו הכוהן שיבעת ימים 27 וראהו
הכוהן ביום השביעי אים פסוה תיפסה
בעור וטימא הכוהן אותו נגע צרעת היוא
28 ואים תחתיה תעמוד הבהרת לוא פסתה בעור
והיוא כהה סאת המיכוה היוא וטיהרו הכוהן כי
צרבת המיכוה היוא 29 ואיש או אישה כי
יהיה בו נגע בראוש או בזקן 30 וראה הכוהן את
הנגע והינה מראהו עמוק מין העור בו סער
צהוב דק וטימא אותו הכוהן נתק הוא צרעת הראוש
או הזקן הוא 31 וכי יראה הכוהן את נגע הנתק
והינה אין מראהו עמוק מין העור וסער שחור
אין בו והיסגיר הכוהן את נגע הנתק שיבעת
ימים 32 וראה הכוהן את הנגע ביום
השביעי והינה לוא פסה הנתק ולוא היה בו
סער צהוב ומראה הנתק אין עמוק מין העור
33 והיתגלח ואת הנתק לוא יגלח והיסגיר
הכוהן את הנתק שיבעת ימים שנית 34 וראה
הכוהן את הנתק ביום השביעי והינה לוא
פסה הנתק בעור ומראהו איננו עמוק מין
העור וטיהר אותו הכוהן וכיבס בגדיו וטהר
35 ואים פסוה יפסה הנתק בעור אחרי טהרתו
36 וראהו הכוהן והינה פסה הנתק בעור לוא
יבקר הכוהן לסער הצהוב טמא הוא 37 ואים
בעיניו עמד הנתק וסער שחור צמח בו נירפא
הנתק טהור הוא וטיהרו הכוהן 38 ואיש או אישה
כי יהיה בעור בסרם בהרות בהרות לבנות 39 וראה
הכוהן והינה בעור בסרם בהרות כהות לבנות בוהק
הוא פרח בעור טהור הוא 40 ואיש כי ימרט
ראושו קרח הוא טהור הוא 41 ואים מיפאת
פניו ימרט ראושו גיבח הוא טהור הוא 42 וכי

[illegible]
[illegible] 43 [illegible]
[illegible]
[illegible] 44 [illegible]
[illegible]
[illegible] 45 [illegible]
[illegible]
[illegible] 46 [illegible]
[illegible]
[illegible] 47
[illegible] 48 [illegible]
[illegible]
[illegible] 49
[illegible]
[illegible] 50 [illegible]
[illegible] 51 [illegible]
[illegible]
[illegible]
[illegible]
[illegible] 52
[illegible]
[illegible]
[illegible] 53
[illegible] 54 [illegible]
[illegible]
[illegible] 55 [illegible]
[illegible]
[illegible]
[illegible] 56 [illegible]
[illegible]
[illegible]
[illegible] 57 [illegible]
[illegible]
[illegible] 58 [illegible]
[illegible]
[illegible] 59 [illegible]
[illegible]
[illegible]

𐤅𐤉𐤒𐤓𐤀 𐤐𐤓𐤒 14

1 𐤅𐤉𐤃𐤁𐤓 𐤉𐤄𐤅𐤄 𐤀𐤋 𐤌𐤅𐤔𐤄 𐤋𐤀𐤌𐤅𐤓 2 𐤆𐤅𐤀𐤕 𐤕𐤉𐤄𐤉𐤄
𐤕𐤅𐤓𐤕 𐤄𐤌𐤑𐤅𐤓𐤏 𐤁𐤉𐤅𐤌 𐤈𐤄𐤓𐤕𐤅 𐤅𐤄𐤅𐤁𐤀 𐤀𐤋 𐤄𐤊𐤅𐤄𐤍
3 𐤅𐤉𐤑𐤀 𐤄𐤊𐤅𐤄𐤍 𐤀𐤋 𐤌𐤉𐤇𐤅𐤑 𐤋𐤌𐤇𐤍𐤄 𐤅𐤓𐤀𐤄 𐤄𐤊𐤅𐤄𐤍
𐤅𐤄𐤉𐤍𐤄 𐤍𐤉𐤓𐤐𐤀 𐤍𐤂𐤏 𐤄𐤑𐤓𐤏𐤕 𐤌𐤉𐤍 𐤄𐤑𐤓𐤅𐤏
4 𐤅𐤑𐤉𐤅𐤄 𐤄𐤊𐤅𐤄𐤍 𐤅𐤋𐤒𐤇 𐤋𐤌𐤉𐤈𐤄𐤓 𐤔𐤕𐤉 𐤑𐤉𐤐𐤓𐤉𐤌
𐤇𐤉𐤅𐤕 𐤈𐤄𐤅𐤓𐤅𐤕 𐤅𐤏𐤑 𐤀𐤓𐤆 𐤅𐤔𐤍𐤉 𐤕𐤅𐤋𐤏𐤕 𐤅𐤀𐤆𐤅 5 𐤅𐤑𐤉𐤅𐤄
𐤄𐤊𐤅𐤄𐤍 𐤅𐤔𐤇𐤈 𐤀𐤕 𐤄𐤑𐤉𐤐𐤅𐤓 𐤄𐤀𐤇𐤕 𐤀𐤋 𐤊𐤋𐤉 𐤇𐤓𐤎 𐤏𐤋
𐤌𐤉𐤉𐤌 𐤇𐤉𐤉𐤌 6 𐤀𐤕 𐤄𐤑𐤉𐤐𐤅𐤓 𐤄𐤇𐤉𐤄 𐤉𐤒𐤇 𐤀𐤅𐤕𐤄
𐤅𐤀𐤕 𐤏𐤑 𐤄𐤀𐤓𐤆 𐤅𐤀𐤕 𐤔𐤍𐤉 𐤄𐤕𐤅𐤋𐤏𐤕 𐤅𐤀𐤕 𐤄𐤀𐤆𐤅𐤁 𐤅𐤈𐤁𐤋
𐤀𐤅𐤕𐤌 𐤅𐤀𐤕 𐤄𐤑𐤉𐤐𐤅𐤓 𐤄𐤇𐤉𐤄 𐤁𐤃𐤌 𐤄𐤑𐤉𐤐𐤅𐤓 𐤄𐤔𐤇𐤅𐤈𐤄
𐤏𐤋 𐤄𐤌𐤉𐤉𐤌 𐤄𐤇𐤉𐤉𐤌 7 𐤅𐤄𐤉𐤆𐤄 𐤏𐤋 𐤄𐤌𐤉𐤈𐤄𐤓
𐤌𐤉𐤍 𐤄𐤑𐤓𐤏𐤕 𐤔𐤁𐤏 𐤐𐤏𐤌𐤉𐤌 𐤅𐤈𐤄𐤓𐤅 𐤅𐤔𐤉𐤋𐤇 𐤀𐤕
𐤄𐤑𐤉𐤐𐤅𐤓 𐤄𐤇𐤉𐤄 𐤏𐤋 𐤐𐤍𐤉 𐤄𐤎𐤃𐤄 8 𐤅𐤊𐤉𐤁𐤎
𐤄𐤌𐤉𐤈𐤄𐤓 𐤀𐤕 𐤁𐤂𐤃𐤉𐤅 𐤅𐤂𐤋𐤇 𐤀𐤕 𐤊𐤋 𐤎𐤏𐤓𐤅 𐤅𐤓𐤇𐤑
𐤁𐤌𐤉𐤉𐤌 𐤅𐤈𐤄𐤓 𐤅𐤀𐤇𐤓 𐤉𐤁𐤅𐤀 𐤀𐤋 𐤄𐤌𐤇𐤍𐤄 𐤅𐤉𐤔𐤁
𐤌𐤉𐤇𐤅𐤑 𐤋𐤀𐤄𐤋𐤅 𐤔𐤁𐤏𐤕 𐤉𐤌𐤉𐤌 9 𐤅𐤄𐤉𐤄 𐤁𐤉𐤅𐤌
𐤄𐤔𐤁𐤉𐤏𐤉 𐤉𐤂𐤋𐤇 𐤀𐤕 𐤊𐤋 𐤎𐤏𐤓𐤅 𐤀𐤕 𐤓𐤅𐤀𐤔𐤅 𐤅𐤀𐤕 𐤆𐤒𐤍𐤅
𐤅𐤀𐤕 𐤂𐤁𐤅𐤕 𐤏𐤉𐤍𐤉𐤅 𐤅𐤀𐤕 𐤊𐤋 𐤎𐤏𐤓𐤅 𐤉𐤂𐤋𐤇 𐤅𐤊𐤉𐤁𐤎 𐤀𐤕
𐤁𐤂𐤃𐤉𐤅 𐤅𐤓𐤇𐤑 𐤀𐤕 𐤁𐤎𐤓𐤅 𐤁𐤌𐤉𐤉𐤌 𐤅𐤈𐤄𐤓 10 𐤅𐤁𐤉𐤅𐤌
𐤄𐤔𐤌𐤉𐤍𐤉 𐤉𐤒𐤇 𐤔𐤍𐤉 𐤊𐤁𐤎𐤉𐤌 𐤕𐤌𐤉𐤌𐤉𐤌 𐤅𐤊𐤁𐤎𐤄
𐤀𐤇𐤕 𐤁𐤕 𐤔𐤍𐤕𐤄 𐤕𐤌𐤉𐤌𐤄 𐤅𐤔𐤋𐤅𐤔𐤄 𐤏𐤎𐤓𐤅𐤍𐤉𐤌 𐤎𐤅𐤋𐤕
𐤌𐤍𐤇𐤄 𐤁𐤋𐤅𐤋𐤄 𐤁𐤔𐤌𐤍 𐤅𐤋𐤅𐤂 𐤀𐤇𐤃 𐤔𐤌𐤍 11 𐤅𐤄𐤏𐤌𐤉𐤃
𐤄𐤊𐤅𐤄𐤍 𐤄𐤌𐤈𐤄𐤓 𐤀𐤕 𐤄𐤀𐤉𐤔 𐤄𐤌𐤉𐤈𐤄𐤓 𐤅𐤀𐤅𐤕𐤌
𐤋𐤐𐤍𐤉 𐤉𐤄𐤅𐤄 𐤐𐤕𐤇 𐤀𐤅𐤄𐤋 𐤌𐤅𐤏𐤃 12 𐤅𐤋𐤒𐤇 𐤄𐤊𐤅𐤄𐤍 𐤀𐤕
𐤄𐤊𐤁𐤎 𐤄𐤀𐤇𐤃 𐤅𐤄𐤉𐤒𐤓𐤉𐤁 𐤀𐤅𐤕𐤅 𐤋𐤀𐤔𐤌 𐤅𐤀𐤕 𐤋𐤅𐤂 𐤄𐤔𐤌𐤍
𐤅𐤄𐤍𐤉𐤐 𐤀𐤅𐤕𐤌 𐤕𐤍𐤅𐤐𐤄 𐤋𐤐𐤍𐤉 𐤉𐤄𐤅𐤄 13 𐤅𐤔𐤇𐤈
𐤀𐤕 𐤄𐤊𐤁𐤎 𐤁𐤉𐤌𐤒𐤅𐤌 𐤀𐤔𐤓 𐤉𐤔𐤇𐤈 𐤀𐤕 𐤄𐤇𐤈𐤀𐤕 𐤅𐤀𐤕
𐤄𐤏𐤅𐤋𐤄 𐤁𐤉𐤌𐤒𐤅𐤌 𐤄𐤒𐤅𐤃𐤔 𐤊𐤉 𐤊𐤇𐤈𐤀𐤕 𐤄𐤀𐤔𐤌 𐤄𐤅𐤀
𐤋𐤊𐤅𐤄𐤍 𐤒𐤅𐤃𐤔 𐤒𐤅𐤃𐤔𐤉𐤌 𐤄𐤅𐤀 14 𐤅𐤋𐤒𐤇 𐤄𐤊𐤅𐤄𐤍 𐤌𐤉𐤃𐤌
𐤄𐤀𐤔𐤌 𐤅𐤍𐤕𐤍 𐤄𐤊𐤅𐤄𐤍 𐤏𐤋 𐤕𐤍𐤅𐤊 𐤀𐤅𐤆𐤍 𐤄𐤌𐤉𐤈𐤄𐤓
𐤄𐤉𐤌𐤍𐤉𐤕 𐤅𐤏𐤋 𐤁𐤅𐤄𐤍 𐤉𐤃𐤅 𐤄𐤉𐤌𐤍𐤉𐤕 𐤅𐤏𐤋 𐤁𐤅𐤄𐤍
𐤓𐤂𐤋𐤅 𐤄𐤉𐤌𐤍𐤉𐤕 15 𐤅𐤋𐤒𐤇 𐤄𐤊𐤅𐤄𐤍 𐤌𐤉𐤋𐤅𐤂 𐤄𐤔𐤌𐤍
𐤅𐤉𐤑𐤒 𐤏𐤋 𐤊𐤐 𐤄𐤊𐤅𐤄𐤍 𐤄𐤎𐤌𐤀𐤋𐤉𐤕 16 𐤅𐤈𐤁𐤋 𐤄𐤊𐤅𐤄𐤍 𐤀𐤕
𐤀𐤑𐤁𐤏𐤅 𐤄𐤉𐤌𐤍𐤉𐤕 𐤌𐤉𐤍 𐤄𐤔𐤌𐤍 𐤀𐤔𐤓 𐤏𐤋 𐤊𐤐𐤅
𐤄𐤎𐤌𐤀𐤋𐤉𐤕 𐤅𐤄𐤉𐤆𐤄 𐤌𐤉𐤍 𐤄𐤔𐤌𐤍 𐤁𐤀𐤑𐤁𐤏𐤅 𐤔𐤁𐤏
𐤐𐤏𐤌𐤉𐤌 𐤋𐤐𐤍𐤉 𐤉𐤄𐤅𐤄 17 𐤅𐤌𐤉𐤕𐤓 𐤄𐤔𐤌𐤍
𐤀𐤔𐤓 𐤏𐤋 𐤊𐤐𐤅 𐤉𐤕𐤍 𐤄𐤊𐤅𐤄𐤍 𐤏𐤋 𐤕𐤍𐤅𐤊 𐤀𐤅𐤆𐤍
𐤄𐤌𐤉𐤈𐤄𐤓 𐤄𐤉𐤌𐤍𐤉𐤕 𐤅𐤏𐤋 𐤁𐤅𐤄𐤍 𐤉𐤃𐤅 𐤄𐤉𐤌𐤍𐤉𐤕
𐤅𐤏𐤋 𐤁𐤅𐤄𐤍 𐤓𐤂𐤋𐤅 𐤄𐤉𐤌𐤍𐤉𐤕 𐤏𐤋 𐤃𐤌 𐤄𐤀𐤔𐤌
18 𐤅𐤄𐤍𐤅𐤕𐤓 𐤁𐤔𐤌𐤍 𐤀𐤔𐤓 𐤏𐤋 𐤊𐤐 𐤄𐤊𐤅𐤄𐤍 𐤉𐤕𐤍 𐤏𐤋

[illegible]
[illegible] 19 [illegible]
[illegible]
[illegible] 20
[illegible] 21 [illegible]
[illegible]
[illegible]
[illegible] 22 [illegible]
[illegible]
[illegible] 23 [illegible]
[illegible]
[illegible] 24 [illegible]
[illegible]
[illegible] 25
[illegible]
[illegible]
[illegible] 26
[illegible] 27 [illegible]
[illegible]
[illegible] 28 [illegible]
[illegible]
[illegible]
[illegible] 29 [illegible]
[illegible]
[illegible] 30 [illegible]
[illegible]
[illegible] 31 [illegible]
[illegible]
[illegible] 32 [illegible]
[illegible]
[illegible] 34 [illegible] 33
[illegible]
[illegible]
[illegible] 35
[illegible] 36 [illegible]
[illegible]
[illegible]
[illegible] 37 [illegible]
[illegible]
[illegible]
[illegible] 38 [illegible]

הבית והסגיר את הבית שבעת ימים
39 ושב הכוהן ביום השביעי וראה והנה פשה
הנגע בקירות הבית 40 וצוה הכוהן וחלצו
את האבנים אשר בהן הנגע והשליכו אתהן
אל מחוץ לעיר אל מקום טמא 41 ואת הבית
יקצע מבית סביב ושפכו את העפר אשר
הקצו אל מחוץ לעיר אל מקום טמא 42 ולקחו
אבנים אחרות והביאו אל תחת האבנים ועפר
אחר יקח וטח את הבית 43 ואם ישוב הנגע
ופרח בבית אחר חלץ את האבנים ואחרי
הקצות את הבית ואחרי הטוח 44 ובא הכוהן
וראה והנה פשה הנגע בבית צרעת ממארת
היא בבית טמא הוא 45 ונתץ את הבית את
אבניו ואת עציו ואת כל עפר הבית והוציא
אל מחוץ לעיר אל מקום טמא 46 והבא אל
הבית כל ימי הסגיר אותו יטמא עד הערב
47 והשכב בבית יכבס את בגדיו והאכל בבית
יכבס את בגדיו 48 ואם בוא יבוא הכוהן וראה
והנה לוא פשה הנגע בבית אחרי הטוח את
הבית וטהר הכוהן את הבית כי נרפא
הנגע 49 ולקח לחטא את הבית שתי צפרים
ועץ ארז ושני תולעת ואזוב 50 ושחט את הצפור
האחת אל כלי חרש על מים חיים 51 ולקח את
עץ הארז ואת האזוב ואת שני התולעת ואת
הצפור החיה וטבל אותם בדם הצפור השחוטה
ובמים החיים והזה אל הבית שבע
פעמים 52 וחטא את הבית בדם הצפור
ובמים החיים ובצפור החיה ובעץ הארז
ובאזוב ובשני התולעת 53 ושלח את הצפור
החיה אל מחוץ לעיר אל פני השדה וכפר
על הבית וטהר 54 זואת התורה לכל נגע הצרעת
ולנתק 55 ולצרעת הבגד ולבית 56 ולשאת ולספחת
57 להורות ביום הטמא וביום הטהור זואת
תורת הצרעת

ויקרא פרק 15

1 וידבר יהוה אל משה ואל אהרון לאמור 2 דברו
אל בני ישראל ואמרתם אלהם איש איש כי
יהיה זב מבשרו זובו טמא הוא 3 וזואת תהיה
טמאתו בזובו רר בשרו את זובו או החתים בשרו

[illegible] 4 [illegible]
[illegible]
[illegible] 5 [illegible]
[illegible] 6 [illegible]
[illegible]
[illegible] 7 [illegible]
[illegible] 8 [illegible]
[illegible]
[illegible] 10 [illegible] 9
[illegible]
[illegible]
[illegible] 11 [illegible]
[illegible]
[illegible] 12 [illegible]
[illegible] 13 [illegible]
[illegible]
[illegible] 14 [illegible]
[illegible]
[illegible]
[illegible] 15 [illegible]
[illegible]
[illegible] 16 [illegible]
[illegible] 17 [illegible]
[illegible]
[illegible] 18 [illegible]
[illegible]
[illegible] 19 [illegible]
[illegible]
[illegible] 20 [illegible]
[illegible]
[illegible] 21 [illegible]
[illegible] 22 [illegible]
[illegible]
[illegible] 23 [illegible]
[illegible]
[illegible] 24
[illegible]
[illegible] 25 [illegible]
[illegible]
[illegible]
[illegible] 26 [illegible]

תישכב עליו כל ימי זובה כמישכב נידתה
יהיה לה וכל הכלי אשר תשב עליו טמא יהיה
כטומאת נידתה 27 וכל הנוגע בם יטמא וכיבס
בגדיו ורחץ במיים וטמא עד הער 28 ואים
טהרה מיזובה וספרה לה שיבעת ימים ואחר
תיטהר 29 וביום השמיני תיקח לה שתי
תורים או שני בני יונה והביאה אותם אל
הכוהן אל פתח אוהל מועד 30 ועסה הכוהן את
האחד חטאת ואת האחד עולה וכיפר עליה הכוהן
ליפני יהוה מיזוב טומאתה 31 והיזרתם את
בני יסראל מיטומאתם ולוא ימותו בטומאתם
בטמאם את מישכני אשר בתוכם 32 זואת תורת
הזב ואשר תצא מימנו שיכבת זרע לטמאה בה
33 והדוה בנידתה והזב את זובו לזכר ולנקבה
ולאיש אשר ישכב עים טמאה

ויקרא פרק 16

1 וידבר יהוה אל מושה אחרי מות שני בני
אהרון בקרבתם ליפני יהוה וימותו
2 ויואמר יהוה אל מושה דבר אל אהרון אחיכה
ואל יבוא בכל עת אל הקודש מיבית לפרוכת אל
פני הכפורת אשר על הארון ולוא ימות כי
בענן אראה על הכפורת 3 בזואת יבוא אהרון אל
הקודש בפר בן בקר לחטאת ואיל לעולה 4 כותנת
בד קודש ילבש ומיכנסי בד יהיו על בסרו
ובאבנט בד יחגור ובמיצנפת בד יצנוף
ביגדי קודש הם ורחץ במיים את בסרו ולבשם
5 ומאת עדת בני יסראל יקח שני סעירי
עיזים לחטאת ואיל אחד לעולה 6 והיקריב
אהרון את פר החטאת אשר לו וכיפר בעדו ובעד
ביתו 7 ולקח את שני הסעירים והעמיד אותם
ליפני יהוה פתח אוהל מועד 8 ונתן אהרון
על שני הסעירים גורלות גורל אחד ליהוה
וגורל אחד לעזאזל 9 והיקריב אהרון את הסעיר
אשר עלה עליו הגורל ליהוה ועסהו חטאת
10 והסעיר אשר עלה עליו הגורל לעזאזל
יעמד חי ליפני יהוה לכפר עליו לשלח
אותו לעזאזל המידברה 11 והיקריב אהרון את
פר החטאת אשר לו וכיפר בעדו ובעד ביתו ושחט
את פר החטאת אשר לו 12 ולקח מלוא המחתה גחלי
אש מעל המזבח מליפני יהוה ומלוא

𐤇𐤐𐤍𐤉𐤅 𐤒𐤈𐤅𐤓𐤕 𐤎𐤌𐤉𐤌 𐤃𐤒𐤄 𐤅𐤄𐤁𐤉𐤀 𐤌𐤉𐤁𐤉𐤕
𐤋𐤐𐤓𐤅𐤊𐤕 13 𐤅𐤍𐤕𐤍 𐤀𐤕 𐤄𐤒𐤈𐤅𐤓𐤕 𐤏𐤋 𐤄𐤀𐤔 𐤋𐤉𐤐𐤍𐤉
𐤉𐤄𐤅𐤄 𐤅𐤊𐤉𐤎𐤄 𐤏𐤍𐤍 𐤄𐤒𐤈𐤅𐤓𐤕 𐤀𐤕 𐤄𐤊𐤐𐤅𐤓𐤕 𐤀𐤔𐤓 𐤏𐤋
𐤄𐤏𐤃𐤅𐤕 𐤅𐤋𐤅𐤀 𐤉𐤌𐤅𐤕 14 𐤅𐤋𐤒𐤇 𐤌𐤉𐤃𐤌 𐤄𐤐𐤓 𐤅𐤄𐤉𐤆𐤄
𐤁𐤀𐤑𐤁𐤏𐤅 𐤏𐤋 𐤐𐤍𐤉 𐤄𐤊𐤐𐤅𐤓𐤕 𐤒𐤃𐤌𐤄 𐤅𐤋𐤉𐤐𐤍𐤉
𐤄𐤊𐤐𐤅𐤓𐤕 𐤉𐤆𐤄 𐤔𐤁𐤏 𐤐𐤏𐤌𐤉𐤌 𐤌𐤉𐤍 𐤄𐤃𐤌 𐤁𐤀𐤑𐤁𐤏𐤅
15 𐤅𐤔𐤇𐤈 𐤀𐤕 𐤎𐤏𐤉𐤓 𐤄𐤇𐤈𐤀𐤕 𐤀𐤔𐤓 𐤋𐤏𐤌 𐤅𐤄𐤁𐤉𐤀 𐤀𐤕 𐤃𐤌𐤅
𐤀𐤋 𐤌𐤉𐤁𐤉𐤕 𐤋𐤐𐤓𐤅𐤊𐤕 𐤅𐤏𐤎𐤄 𐤀𐤕 𐤃𐤌𐤅 𐤊𐤀𐤔𐤓 𐤏𐤎𐤄 𐤋𐤃𐤌
𐤄𐤐𐤓 𐤅𐤄𐤉𐤆𐤄 𐤀𐤅𐤕𐤅 𐤏𐤋 𐤄𐤊𐤐𐤅𐤓𐤕 𐤅𐤋𐤉𐤐𐤍𐤉 𐤄𐤊𐤐𐤅𐤓𐤕
16 𐤅𐤊𐤉𐤐𐤓 𐤏𐤋 𐤄𐤒𐤅𐤃𐤔 𐤌𐤉𐤈𐤅𐤌𐤀𐤅𐤕 𐤁𐤍𐤉 𐤉𐤎𐤓𐤀𐤋
𐤅𐤌𐤉𐤐𐤉𐤔𐤏𐤉𐤄𐤌 𐤋𐤊𐤋 𐤇𐤈𐤅𐤀𐤕𐤌 𐤅𐤊𐤍 𐤉𐤏𐤎𐤄 𐤋𐤀𐤅𐤄𐤋
𐤌𐤅𐤏𐤃 𐤄𐤔𐤅𐤊𐤍 𐤀𐤉𐤕𐤌 𐤁𐤕𐤅𐤊 𐤈𐤅𐤌𐤀𐤅𐤕𐤌 17 𐤅𐤊𐤋 𐤀𐤃𐤌
𐤋𐤅𐤀 𐤉𐤄𐤉𐤄 𐤁𐤀𐤅𐤄𐤋 𐤌𐤅𐤏𐤃 𐤁𐤁𐤅𐤀𐤅 𐤋𐤊𐤐𐤓 𐤁𐤒𐤅𐤃𐤔 𐤏𐤃
𐤑𐤀𐤕𐤅 𐤅𐤊𐤉𐤐𐤓 𐤁𐤏𐤃𐤅 𐤅𐤁𐤏𐤃 𐤁𐤉𐤕𐤅 𐤅𐤁𐤏𐤃 𐤊𐤋 𐤒𐤄𐤋 𐤉𐤎𐤓𐤀𐤋
18 𐤅𐤉𐤑𐤀 𐤀𐤋 𐤄𐤌𐤉𐤆𐤁𐤇 𐤀𐤔𐤓 𐤋𐤉𐤐𐤍𐤉 𐤉𐤄𐤅𐤄
𐤅𐤊𐤉𐤐𐤓 𐤏𐤋𐤉𐤅 𐤅𐤋𐤒𐤇 𐤌𐤉𐤃𐤌 𐤄𐤐𐤓 𐤅𐤌𐤉𐤃𐤌 𐤄𐤎𐤏𐤉𐤓
𐤅𐤍𐤕𐤍 𐤏𐤋 𐤒𐤓𐤍𐤅𐤕 𐤄𐤌𐤉𐤆𐤁𐤇 𐤎𐤁𐤉𐤁 19 𐤅𐤄𐤉𐤆𐤄 𐤏𐤋𐤉𐤅
𐤌𐤉𐤍 𐤄𐤃𐤌 𐤁𐤀𐤑𐤁𐤏𐤅 𐤔𐤁𐤏 𐤐𐤏𐤌𐤉𐤌 𐤅𐤈𐤉𐤄𐤓𐤅
𐤅𐤒𐤉𐤃𐤔𐤅 𐤌𐤉𐤈𐤅𐤌𐤀𐤅𐤕 𐤁𐤍𐤉 𐤉𐤎𐤓𐤀𐤋 20 𐤅𐤊𐤉𐤋𐤄
𐤌𐤉𐤊𐤐𐤓 𐤀𐤕 𐤄𐤒𐤅𐤃𐤔 𐤅𐤀𐤕 𐤀𐤅𐤄𐤋 𐤌𐤅𐤏𐤃 𐤅𐤀𐤕 𐤄𐤌𐤉𐤆𐤁𐤇
𐤅𐤄𐤉𐤒𐤓𐤉𐤁 𐤀𐤕 𐤄𐤎𐤏𐤉𐤓 𐤄𐤇𐤉 21 𐤅𐤎𐤌𐤊 𐤀𐤄𐤓𐤅𐤍 𐤀𐤕
𐤔𐤕𐤉 𐤉𐤃𐤅 𐤏𐤋 𐤓𐤅𐤀𐤔 𐤄𐤎𐤏𐤉𐤓 𐤄𐤇𐤉 𐤅𐤄𐤉𐤕𐤅𐤃𐤄 𐤏𐤋𐤉𐤅
𐤀𐤕 𐤊𐤋 𐤏𐤅𐤍𐤅𐤕 𐤁𐤍𐤉 𐤉𐤎𐤓𐤀𐤋 𐤅𐤀𐤕 𐤊𐤋 𐤐𐤉𐤔𐤏𐤉𐤄𐤌
𐤋𐤊𐤋 𐤇𐤈𐤅𐤀𐤕𐤌 𐤅𐤍𐤕𐤍 𐤀𐤅𐤕𐤌 𐤏𐤋 𐤓𐤅𐤀𐤔 𐤄𐤎𐤏𐤉𐤓 𐤅𐤔𐤉𐤋𐤇
𐤁𐤉𐤃 𐤀𐤉𐤔 𐤏𐤉𐤕𐤉 𐤄𐤌𐤉𐤃𐤁𐤓𐤄 22 𐤅𐤍𐤎𐤀 𐤄𐤎𐤏𐤉𐤓
𐤏𐤋𐤉𐤅 𐤀𐤕 𐤊𐤋 𐤏𐤅𐤍𐤅𐤕𐤌 𐤀𐤋 𐤀𐤓𐤑 𐤂𐤆𐤓𐤄 𐤅𐤔𐤉𐤋𐤇 𐤀𐤕
𐤄𐤎𐤏𐤉𐤓 𐤁𐤌𐤉𐤃𐤁𐤓 23 𐤅𐤁𐤀 𐤀𐤄𐤓𐤅𐤍 𐤀𐤋 𐤀𐤅𐤄𐤋 𐤌𐤅𐤏𐤃
𐤅𐤐𐤔𐤈 𐤀𐤕 𐤁𐤉𐤂𐤃𐤉 𐤄𐤁𐤃 𐤀𐤔𐤓 𐤋𐤁𐤔 𐤁𐤁𐤅𐤀𐤅 𐤀𐤋 𐤄𐤒𐤅𐤃𐤔
𐤅𐤄𐤉𐤍𐤉𐤇𐤌 𐤔𐤌 24 𐤅𐤓𐤇𐤑 𐤀𐤕 𐤁𐤎𐤓𐤅 𐤁𐤌𐤉𐤉𐤌 𐤁𐤌𐤒𐤅𐤌
𐤒𐤃𐤅𐤔 𐤅𐤋𐤁𐤔 𐤀𐤕 𐤁𐤂𐤃𐤉𐤅 𐤅𐤉𐤑𐤀 𐤅𐤏𐤎𐤄 𐤀𐤕 𐤏𐤅𐤋𐤕𐤅 𐤅𐤀𐤕
𐤏𐤅𐤋𐤕 𐤄𐤏𐤌 𐤅𐤊𐤉𐤐𐤓 𐤁𐤏𐤃𐤅 𐤅𐤁𐤏𐤃 𐤄𐤏𐤌 25 𐤅𐤀𐤕 𐤇𐤋𐤁
𐤄𐤇𐤈𐤀𐤕 𐤉𐤒𐤈𐤉𐤓 𐤄𐤌𐤉𐤆𐤁𐤇𐤄 26 𐤅𐤄𐤌𐤔𐤋𐤇 𐤀𐤕 𐤄𐤎𐤏𐤉𐤓
𐤋𐤏𐤆𐤀𐤆𐤋 𐤉𐤊𐤁𐤎 𐤁𐤂𐤃𐤉𐤅 𐤅𐤓𐤇𐤑 𐤀𐤕 𐤁𐤎𐤓𐤅 𐤁𐤌𐤉𐤉𐤌
𐤅𐤀𐤇𐤓𐤉 𐤊𐤍 𐤉𐤁𐤅𐤀 𐤀𐤋 𐤄𐤌𐤇𐤍𐤄 27 𐤅𐤀𐤕 𐤄𐤐𐤓 𐤄𐤇𐤈𐤀𐤕 𐤅𐤀𐤕
𐤎𐤏𐤉𐤓 𐤄𐤇𐤈𐤀𐤕 𐤀𐤔𐤓 𐤄𐤅𐤁𐤀 𐤀𐤕 𐤃𐤌𐤌 𐤋𐤊𐤐𐤓 𐤁𐤒𐤅𐤃𐤔
𐤉𐤅𐤑𐤉𐤀 𐤀𐤋 𐤌𐤉𐤇𐤅𐤑 𐤋𐤌𐤇𐤍𐤄 𐤅𐤎𐤓𐤐𐤅 𐤁𐤀𐤔 𐤀𐤕
𐤏𐤅𐤓𐤅𐤕𐤌 𐤅𐤀𐤕 𐤁𐤎𐤓𐤌 𐤅𐤀𐤕 𐤐𐤉𐤓𐤔𐤌 28 𐤅𐤄𐤎𐤅𐤓𐤐 𐤀𐤅𐤕𐤌
𐤉𐤊𐤁𐤎 𐤁𐤂𐤃𐤉𐤅 𐤅𐤓𐤇𐤑 𐤀𐤕 𐤁𐤎𐤓𐤅 𐤁𐤌𐤉𐤉𐤌 𐤅𐤀𐤇𐤓𐤉 𐤊𐤍
𐤉𐤁𐤅𐤀 𐤀𐤋 𐤄𐤌𐤇𐤍𐤄 29 𐤅𐤄𐤉𐤕𐤄 𐤋𐤊𐤌 𐤋𐤇𐤅𐤒𐤕 𐤏𐤅𐤋𐤌
𐤁𐤇𐤅𐤃𐤔 𐤄𐤔𐤁𐤉𐤏𐤉 𐤁𐤏𐤎𐤅𐤓 𐤋𐤇𐤅𐤃𐤔 𐤕𐤏𐤍𐤅 𐤀𐤕
𐤍𐤐𐤔𐤅𐤕𐤉𐤊𐤌 𐤅𐤊𐤋 𐤌𐤋𐤀𐤊𐤄 𐤋𐤅𐤀 𐤕𐤏𐤎𐤅 𐤄𐤀𐤆𐤓𐤇 𐤅𐤄𐤂𐤓

הגר בתוככם 30 כי ביום הזה יכפר עליכם
לטהר אתכם מיכול חטואתיכם ליפני יהוה
תיטהרו 31 שבת שבתון היא לכם ועיניתם את
נפשותיכם חוקת עולם 32 וכיפר הכוהן אשר
ימשח אותו ואשר ימלא את ידו לכהן תחת אביו
ולבש את ביגדי הבד ביגדי הקודש 33 וכיפר את
מיקדש הקודש ואת אוהל מועד ואת המיזבח
יכפר ועל הכוהנים ועל כל עם הקהל יכפר
34 והיתה זואת לכם לחוקת עולם לכפר על בני
ישראל מיכל חטואתם אחת בשנה ויעש כאשר
ציוה יהוה את משה

ויקרא פרק 17

1 וידבר יהוה אל מושה לאמור 2 דבר אל אהרון
ואל בניו ואל כל בני ישראל ואמרת אליהם זה
הדבר אשר ציוה יהוה לאמור 3 איש איש
מיבית ישראל אשר ישחט שור או כשב או עז
במחנה או אשר ישחט מיחוץ למחנה 4 ואל פתח
אוהל מועד לוא הביאו להקריב קרבן ליהוה
ליפני מישכן יהוה דם יחשב לאיש ההוא
דם שפך וניכרת האיש ההוא מיקרב עמו
5 למען אשר יביאו בני ישראל את
זיבחיהם אשר הם זובחים על פני השדה
והביאום ליהוה אל פתח אוהל מועד אל הכוהן
וזבחו זיבחי שלמים ליהוה אותם 6 וזרק
הכוהן את הדם על מיזבח יהוה פתח אוהל מועד
והיקטיר החלב לריח ניחוח ליהוה 7 ולוא יזבחו
עוד את זיבחיהם לשעירים אשר הם זונים
אחריהם חוקת עולם תיהיה זואת להם לדורותם
8 ואלהם תאמר איש איש מיבית ישראל
ומין הגר אשר יגור בתוכם אשר יעלה עולה או
זבח 9 ואל פתח אוהל מועד לוא יביאנו לעשות
אותו ליהוה וניכרת האיש ההוא מעמיו
10 ואיש איש מיבית ישראל ומין הגר הגר
בתוכם אשר יואכל כל דם ונתתי פני בנפש
האוכלת את הדם והיכרתי אותה מיקרב עמה
11 כי נפש הבשר בדם הוא ואני נתתיו לכם
על המיזבח לכפר על נפשותיכם כי הדם הוא
בנפש יכפר 12 על כן אמרתי ליבני ישראל
כל נפש מיכם לוא תואכל דם והגר הגר בתוככם
לוא יואכל דם 13 ואיש איש מיבני ישראל

ומין הגר הגר בתוכם אשר יצוד ציד חיה או
עוף אשר יאכל ושפך את דמו וכיסהו בעפר
14 כי נפש כל בשר דמו בנפשו הוא ואמר
לבני ישראל דם כל בשר לוא תאכלו כי נפש
כל בשר דמו היוא כל אכליו יכרת 15 וכל נפש
אשר תאכל נבלה וטרפה באזרח ובגר וכיבס
בגדיו ורחץ במיים וטמא עד הערב וטהר
16 ואים לוא יכבס ובשרו לוא ירחץ ונשא עונו

ויקרא פרק 18

1 וידבר יהוה אל מושה לאמור 2 דבר אל בני
ישראל ואמרת אלהם אני יהוה אלוהיכם
3 כמעשה ארץ מיצריים אשר ישבתם בה לוא
תעשו וכמעשה ארץ כנען אשר אני מביא אתכם
שמה לוא תעשו ובחוקותיהם לוא תלכו 4 את
משפטי תעשו ואת חוקותי תישמרו ללכת בהם
אני יהוה אלוהיכם 5 ושמרתם את חוקותי ואת
משפטי אשר יעשה אותם האדם וחי בהם
אני יהוה 6 איש איש אל כל שאר בשרו לוא
תיקרבו לגלות ערוה אני יהוה 7 ערות אביכה
וערות אמכה לוא תגלה אמכה היוא לוא תגלה
ערותה 8 ערות אשת אביכה לוא תגלה ערות אביכה
היוא 9 ערות אחותכה בת אביכה או בת אמכה
מולדת ביית או מולדת חוץ לוא תגלה ערותן
10 ערות בת בינכה או בת ביתכה לוא תגלה ערותן
כי ערותכה הנה 11 ערות בת אשת אביכה מולדת
אביכה אחותכה היוא לוא תגלה ערותה 12 ערות
אחות אביכה לוא תגלה שאר אביכה היוא 13 ערות
אחות אמכה לוא תגלה כי שאר אמכה היוא
14 ערות אחי אביכה לוא תגלה אל אישתו לוא
תיקרב דודתכה היוא 15 ערות כלתכה לוא תגלה
אשת בינכה היוא לוא תגלה ערותה 16 ערות אשת
אחיכה לוא תגלה ערות אחיכה היוא 17 ערות
אישה וביתה לוא תגלה את בת בנה ואת בת ביתה
לוא תיקח לגלות ערותה שארה הנה זימה היוא
18 ואישה אל אחותה לוא תיקח ליצרור לגלות
ערותה עליה בחייה 19 ואל אישה בנידת
טומאתה לוא תיקרב לגלות ערותה 20 ואל אשת
עמיתכה לוא תיתן שכבתכה לזרע לטמאה בה
21 ומיזרעכה לוא תיתן להעביר למולך ולוא

22
23
24
25
26
27
28
29
30

19

2 1
3
4
5
6
7
8
9
10
11
12
13

[illegible] 14
[illegible] 15 [illegible]
[illegible]
[illegible] 16 [illegible]
[illegible]
[illegible] 17 [illegible]
[illegible] 18 [illegible]
[illegible]
[illegible] 19 [illegible]
[illegible]
[illegible]
[illegible] 20 [illegible]
[illegible]
[illegible]
[illegible]
[illegible] 21
[illegible] 22 [illegible]
[illegible]
[illegible] 23 [illegible]
[illegible]
[illegible] 24 [illegible]
[illegible]
[illegible] 25 [illegible]
[illegible]
[illegible] 26
[illegible] 27
[illegible] 28 [illegible]
[illegible]
[illegible] 29 [illegible]
[illegible] 30 [illegible]
[illegible]
[illegible] 31 [illegible]
[illegible]
[illegible] 32
[illegible] 33 [illegible]
[illegible] 34 [illegible]
[illegible]
[illegible]
[illegible]
[illegible] 35 [illegible]
[illegible] 36 [illegible]
[illegible]

𐤀𐤍𐤉 𐤉𐤄𐤅𐤄 𐤀𐤋𐤅𐤄𐤉𐤊𐤌 𐤀𐤔𐤓 𐤄𐤅𐤑𐤀𐤕𐤉 𐤀𐤕𐤊𐤌 𐤌𐤀𐤓𐤑
𐤌𐤉𐤑𐤓𐤉𐤉𐤌 37 𐤅𐤔𐤌𐤓𐤕𐤌 𐤀𐤕 𐤊𐤋 𐤇𐤅𐤒𐤅𐤕𐤉 𐤅𐤀𐤕 𐤊𐤋
𐤌𐤉𐤔𐤐𐤈𐤉𐤉 𐤅𐤏𐤎𐤉𐤕𐤌 𐤀𐤅𐤕𐤌 𐤀𐤍𐤉 𐤉𐤄𐤅𐤄

𐤅𐤉𐤒𐤓𐤀 𐤐𐤓𐤒 20

1 𐤅𐤉𐤃𐤁𐤓 𐤉𐤄𐤅𐤄 𐤀𐤋 𐤌𐤅𐤔𐤄 𐤋𐤀𐤌𐤅𐤓 2 𐤅𐤀𐤋 𐤁𐤍𐤉
𐤉𐤎𐤓𐤀𐤋 𐤕𐤅𐤀𐤌𐤓 𐤀𐤉𐤔 𐤀𐤉𐤔 𐤌𐤉𐤁𐤍𐤉 𐤉𐤎𐤓𐤀𐤋
𐤅𐤌𐤉𐤍 𐤄𐤂𐤓 𐤄𐤂𐤓 𐤁𐤉𐤎𐤓𐤀𐤋 𐤀𐤔𐤓 𐤉𐤕𐤍 𐤌𐤉𐤆𐤓𐤏𐤅
𐤋𐤌𐤅𐤋𐤊 𐤌𐤅𐤕 𐤉𐤅𐤌𐤕 𐤏𐤌 𐤄𐤀𐤓𐤑 𐤉𐤓𐤂𐤌𐤅𐤄𐤅 𐤁𐤀𐤁𐤍
3 𐤅𐤀𐤍𐤉 𐤀𐤕𐤍 𐤀𐤕 𐤐𐤍𐤉 𐤁𐤀𐤉𐤔 𐤄𐤄𐤅𐤀 𐤅𐤄𐤉𐤊𐤓𐤕𐤉
𐤀𐤅𐤕𐤅 𐤌𐤉𐤒𐤓𐤁 𐤏𐤌𐤅 𐤊𐤉 𐤌𐤉𐤆𐤓𐤏𐤅 𐤍𐤕𐤍 𐤋𐤌𐤅𐤋𐤊
𐤋𐤌𐤏𐤍 𐤈𐤌𐤀 𐤀𐤕 𐤌𐤉𐤒𐤃𐤔𐤉 𐤅𐤋𐤇𐤋𐤋 𐤀𐤕 𐤔𐤌 𐤒𐤃𐤔𐤉
4 𐤅𐤀𐤉𐤌 𐤄𐤏𐤋𐤌 𐤉𐤏𐤋𐤉𐤌𐤅 𐤏𐤌 𐤄𐤀𐤓𐤑 𐤀𐤕
𐤏𐤉𐤍𐤉𐤄𐤌 𐤌𐤉𐤍 𐤄𐤀𐤉𐤔 𐤄𐤄𐤅𐤀 𐤁𐤉𐤕𐤕𐤅 𐤌𐤉𐤆𐤓𐤏𐤅
𐤋𐤌𐤅𐤋𐤊 𐤋𐤁𐤉𐤋𐤕𐤉 𐤄𐤌𐤉𐤕 𐤀𐤅𐤕𐤅 5 𐤅𐤎𐤌𐤕𐤉 𐤀𐤍𐤉 𐤀𐤕
𐤐𐤍𐤉 𐤁𐤀𐤉𐤔 𐤄𐤄𐤅𐤀 𐤅𐤁𐤌𐤉𐤔𐤐𐤇𐤕𐤅 𐤅𐤄𐤉𐤊𐤓𐤕𐤉 𐤀𐤅𐤕𐤅
𐤅𐤀𐤕 𐤊𐤋 𐤄𐤆𐤅𐤍𐤉𐤌 𐤀𐤇𐤓𐤉𐤅 𐤋𐤉𐤆𐤍𐤅𐤕 𐤀𐤇𐤓𐤉 𐤄𐤌𐤅𐤋𐤊
𐤌𐤉𐤒𐤓𐤁 𐤏𐤌𐤌 6 𐤅𐤄𐤍𐤐𐤔 𐤀𐤔𐤓 𐤕𐤉𐤐𐤍𐤄 𐤀𐤋 𐤄𐤀𐤅𐤁𐤅𐤕
𐤅𐤀𐤋 𐤄𐤉𐤃𐤏𐤅𐤍𐤉𐤌 𐤋𐤉𐤆𐤍𐤅𐤕 𐤀𐤇𐤓𐤉𐤄𐤌 𐤅𐤍𐤕𐤕𐤉 𐤀𐤕
𐤐𐤍𐤉 𐤁𐤍𐤐𐤔 𐤄𐤄𐤉𐤅𐤀 𐤅𐤄𐤉𐤊𐤓𐤕𐤉 𐤀𐤅𐤕𐤅 𐤌𐤉𐤒𐤓𐤁
𐤏𐤌𐤅 7 𐤅𐤄𐤉𐤕𐤒𐤃𐤉𐤔𐤕𐤌 𐤅𐤉𐤄𐤉𐤉𐤕𐤌 𐤒𐤃𐤅𐤔𐤉𐤌 𐤊𐤉
𐤀𐤍𐤉 𐤉𐤄𐤅𐤄 𐤀𐤋𐤅𐤄𐤉𐤊𐤌 8 𐤅𐤔𐤌𐤓𐤕𐤌 𐤀𐤕 𐤇𐤅𐤒𐤅𐤕𐤉
𐤅𐤏𐤎𐤉𐤕𐤌 𐤀𐤅𐤕𐤌 𐤀𐤍𐤉 𐤉𐤄𐤅𐤄 𐤌𐤒𐤃𐤉𐤔𐤊𐤌 9 𐤊𐤉
𐤀𐤉𐤔 𐤀𐤉𐤔 𐤀𐤔𐤓 𐤉𐤒𐤋𐤋 𐤀𐤕 𐤀𐤁𐤉𐤅 𐤅𐤀𐤕 𐤀𐤉𐤌𐤅 𐤌𐤅𐤕
𐤉𐤅𐤌𐤕 𐤀𐤁𐤉𐤅 𐤅𐤀𐤉𐤌𐤅 𐤒𐤉𐤋𐤋 𐤃𐤌𐤉𐤅 𐤁𐤅 10 𐤅𐤀𐤉𐤔 𐤀𐤔𐤓
𐤉𐤍𐤀𐤐 𐤀𐤕 𐤀𐤔𐤕 𐤀𐤉𐤔 𐤀𐤔𐤓 𐤉𐤍𐤀𐤐 𐤀𐤕 𐤀𐤔𐤕 𐤓𐤏𐤄𐤅
𐤌𐤅𐤕 𐤉𐤅𐤌𐤕 𐤄𐤍𐤅𐤀𐤐 𐤅𐤄𐤍𐤅𐤀𐤐𐤕 11 𐤅𐤀𐤉𐤔 𐤀𐤔𐤓
𐤉𐤔𐤊𐤁 𐤀𐤕 𐤀𐤔𐤕 𐤀𐤁𐤉𐤅 𐤏𐤓𐤅𐤕 𐤀𐤁𐤉𐤅 𐤂𐤉𐤋𐤄 𐤌𐤅𐤕
𐤉𐤅𐤌𐤕𐤅 𐤔𐤍𐤉𐤄𐤌 𐤃𐤌𐤉𐤄𐤌 𐤁𐤌 12 𐤅𐤀𐤉𐤔 𐤀𐤔𐤓
𐤉𐤔𐤊𐤁 𐤀𐤕 𐤊𐤋𐤕𐤅 𐤌𐤅𐤕 𐤉𐤅𐤌𐤕𐤅 𐤔𐤍𐤉𐤄𐤌 𐤕𐤁𐤋 𐤏𐤎𐤅
𐤃𐤌𐤉𐤄𐤌 𐤁𐤌 13 𐤅𐤀𐤉𐤔 𐤀𐤔𐤓 𐤉𐤔𐤊𐤁 𐤀𐤕 𐤆𐤊𐤓
𐤌𐤉𐤔𐤊𐤁𐤉 𐤀𐤉𐤔𐤄 𐤕𐤅𐤏𐤁𐤄 𐤏𐤎𐤅 𐤔𐤍𐤉𐤄𐤌 𐤌𐤅𐤕
𐤉𐤅𐤌𐤕𐤅 𐤃𐤌𐤉𐤄𐤌 𐤁𐤌 14 𐤅𐤀𐤉𐤔 𐤀𐤔𐤓 𐤉𐤒𐤇 𐤀𐤕 𐤀𐤉𐤔𐤄
𐤅𐤀𐤕 𐤀𐤉𐤌𐤄 𐤆𐤉𐤌𐤄 𐤄𐤉𐤅𐤀 𐤁𐤀𐤔 𐤉𐤎𐤓𐤐𐤅 𐤀𐤅𐤕𐤅 𐤅𐤀𐤕𐤄𐤍
𐤅𐤋𐤅𐤀 𐤕𐤉𐤄𐤉𐤄 𐤆𐤉𐤌𐤄 𐤁𐤕𐤅𐤊𐤊𐤌 15 𐤅𐤀𐤉𐤔 𐤀𐤔𐤓 𐤉𐤕𐤍
𐤔𐤊𐤁𐤕𐤅 𐤁𐤉𐤁𐤄𐤌𐤄 𐤌𐤅𐤕 𐤉𐤅𐤌𐤕 𐤅𐤀𐤕 𐤄𐤁𐤄𐤌𐤄 𐤕𐤄𐤓𐤅𐤂𐤅
16 𐤅𐤀𐤉𐤔𐤄 𐤀𐤔𐤓 𐤕𐤉𐤒𐤓𐤁 𐤀𐤋 𐤊𐤋 𐤁𐤄𐤌𐤄 𐤋𐤓𐤉𐤁𐤏𐤄
𐤀𐤅𐤕𐤄 𐤅𐤄𐤓𐤂𐤕 𐤀𐤕 𐤄𐤀𐤉𐤔𐤄 𐤅𐤀𐤕 𐤄𐤁𐤄𐤌𐤄 𐤌𐤅𐤕 𐤉𐤅𐤌𐤕𐤅
𐤃𐤌𐤉𐤄𐤌 𐤁𐤌 17 𐤅𐤀𐤉𐤔 𐤀𐤔𐤓 𐤉𐤒𐤇 𐤀𐤕 𐤀𐤇𐤅𐤕𐤅 𐤁𐤕 𐤀𐤁𐤉𐤅
𐤀𐤅 𐤁𐤕 𐤀𐤉𐤌𐤅 𐤅𐤓𐤀𐤄 𐤀𐤕 𐤏𐤓𐤅𐤕𐤄 𐤅𐤄𐤉𐤀 𐤕𐤉𐤓𐤀𐤄 𐤀𐤕
𐤏𐤓𐤅𐤕𐤅 𐤇𐤎𐤃 𐤄𐤅𐤀 𐤅𐤍𐤉𐤊𐤓𐤕𐤅 𐤋𐤏𐤉𐤍𐤉 𐤁𐤍𐤉 𐤏𐤌𐤌 𐤏𐤓𐤅𐤕

[illegible] 18 [illegible]
[illegible]
[illegible]
[illegible] 19 [illegible]
[illegible]
[illegible] 20
[illegible] 21 [illegible]
[illegible]
[illegible] 22 [illegible]
[illegible]
[illegible]
[illegible] 23
[illegible]
[illegible] 24
[illegible]
[illegible]
[illegible] 25 [illegible]
[illegible]
[illegible]
[illegible] 26 [illegible]
[illegible]
[illegible] 27 [illegible]
[illegible]
[illegible]

21 [illegible]

[illegible] 1
[illegible]
[illegible] 2 [illegible]
[illegible] 3 [illegible]
[illegible]
[illegible] 5 [illegible] 4
[illegible]
[illegible] 6 [illegible]
[illegible]
[illegible] 7 [illegible]
[illegible]
[illegible] 8 [illegible]
[illegible]
[illegible] 9 [illegible]
[illegible]

10 והכוהן הגדול מאחיו אשר יוצק על רואשו
שמן המישחה ומילא את ידו לילבוש את
הבגדים את רואשו לוא יפרע ובגדיו לוא
יפרום 11 ועל כל נפשות מת לוא יבוא לאביו
ולאימו לוא יטמא 12 ומין המיקדש לוא יצא
ולוא יחלל את מיקדש אלוהיו כי נזר שמן
מישחת אלוהיו עליו אני יהוה 13 והוא
אישה ביבתוליה יקח 14 אלמנה וגרושה וחללה
זונה את אלה לוא יקח כי אים בתולה מעמיו
יקח אישה 15 ולוא יחלל זרעו בעמיו כי אני
יהוה מקדשו 16 וידבר יהוה אל מושה לאמור
17 דבר אל אהרון לאמור איש מיזרעכה
לדורותם אשר יהיה בו מום לוא יקרב להקריב
לחם אלוהיו 18 כי כל איש אשר בו מום לוא
יקרב איש עיור או פיסח או חרום או סרוע 19 או
איש אשר יהיה בו שבר רגל או שבר יד 20 או
גיבן או דק או תבלול בעינו או גרב או ילפת או
מרוח אשך 21 כל איש אשר בו מום מיזרע
אהרון הכוהן לוא יגש להקריב את אישי
יהוה מום בו את לחם אלוהיו לוא יגש להקריב
22 לחם אלוהיו מיקדשי הקדשים ומין
הקדשים יואכל 23 אך אל הפרוכת לוא יבוא ואל
המיזבח לוא יגש כי מום בו ולוא יחלל את
מיקדשי כי אני יהוה מקדשם 24 וידבר
מושה אל אהרון ואל בניו ואל כל בני יסראל

ויקרא פרק 22

1 וידבר יהוה אל מושה לאמור 2 דבר אל אהרון
ואל בניו וינזרו מיקדשי בני יסראל ולוא
יחללו את שם קדשי אשר הם מקדישים לי
אני יהוה 3 אמור אלהם לדורותיכם כל איש
אשר יקרב מיכל זרעכם אל הקדשים אשר
יקדישו בני יסראל ליהוה וטומאתו עליו
ונכרתה הנפש ההוא מלפני אני
יהוה 4 איש איש מיזרע אהרון והוא צרוע או
זב בקדשים לוא יואכל עד אשר יטהר והנוגע
בכל טמא נפש או איש אשר תצא ממנו
שיכבת זרע 5 או איש אשר יגע בכל שרץ אשר
יטמא לו או באדם אשר יטמא לו לכול טומאתו
6 נפש אשר תיגע בו וטמאה עד הערב ולוא

יואכל מין הקדשים כי אים רחץ בסרו
במים 7 ובא השמש וטהר ואחר יואכל מין
הקדשים כי לחמו הוא 8 נבלה וטרפה לוא יואכל
לטמאה בה אני יהוה 9 ושמרו את מישמרתי
ולוא יסאו עליו חטא ומתו בו כי יחללוהו אני
יהוה מקדשם 10 וכל זר לוא יואכל קודש תושב
כוהן וסכיר לוא יואכל קודש 11 וכוהן כי יקנה
נפש קינין כספו הוא יואכל בו ויליד ביתו
הם יואכלו בלחמו 12 ובת כוהן כי תיהיה לאיש
זר הוא ביתרומת הקדשים לוא תואכל 13 ובת
כוהן כי תיהיה אלמנה וגרושה וזרע אין לה
ושבה אל בית אביה כינעוריה מילחם אביה
תואכל וכל זר לוא יואכל בו 14 ואיש כי יואכל
קודש בישגגה ויסף חמישיתו עליו ונתן
לכוהן את הקודש 15 ולוא יחללו את קדשי בני
יסראל את אשר ירימו ליהוה 16 והיסיאו
אותם עון אשמה באכלם את קדשיהם כי אני
יהוה מקדשם 17 וידבר יהוה אל מושה לאמור
18 דבר אל אהרון ואל בניו ואל כל בני יסראל
ואמרת אלהם איש איש מבית יסראל ומין
הגר ביסראל אשר יקריב קרבנו לכל נידריהם
ולכל נידבותם אשר יקריבו ליהוה לעולה
19 לירצונכם תמים זכר בבקר בכסבים
ובעיזים 20 כול אשר בו מום לוא תקריבו כי לוא
לרצון יהיה לכם 21 ואיש כי יקריב זבח
שלמים ליהוה לפלא נדר או לינדבה בבקר או
בצואן תמים יהיה לרצון כל מום לוא יהיה
בו 22 עורת או שבור או חרוץ או יבלת או גרב או
ילפת לוא תקריבו אלה ליהוה ואישה לוא
תיתנו מהם על המיזבח ליהוה 23 ושור וסה
סרוע וקלוט נדבה תעסה אותו ולנדר לוא ירצה
24 ומעוך וכתות ונתוק וכרות לוא תקריבו ליהוה
ובארצכם לוא תעסו 25 ומיד בן נכר לוא תקריבו
את לחם אלהיכם מיכל אלה כי משחתם בהם
מום בם לוא ירצו לכם 26 וידבר יהוה אל מושה
לאמור 27 שור או כסב או עז כי יולד והיה
שיבעת ימים תחת אימו ומיום השמיני
והלאה ירצה לקרבן אישה ליהוה 28 ושור או סה
אותו ואת בנו לוא תישחטו ביום אחד 29 וכי
תיזבחו זבח תודה ליהוה לירצונכם תיזבחו
30 ביום ההוא יאכל לוא תותירו מימנו עד בוקר

אני יהוה 31 ושמרתם מיצותי ועסיתם אותם
אני יהוה 32 ולוא תחללו את שם קדשי
וניקדשתי בתוך בני יסראל אני יהוה
מקדישכם 33 המוציא אתכם מארץ
מיצריים ליהיות לכם לאלהים אני
יהוה

ויקרא פרק 23

1 וידבר יהוה אל מושה לאמור 2 דבר אל בני
יסראל ואמרת אלהם מועדי יהוה אשר תיקראו
אותם מיקראי קודש אלה הם מועדי 3 ששת
ימים תעסה מלאכה וביום השביעי שבת
שבתון מיקרא קודש כל מלאכה לוא תעסו שבת
היוא ליהוה בכול מושבותיכם 4 אלה מועדי
יהוה מיקראי קודש אשר תיקראו אותם
במועדם 5 בחודש הריאשון בארבעה עסר לחודש
בין הערביים פסח ליהוה 6 ובחמישה עסר
יום לחודש הזה חג המצות ליהוה שיבעת
ימים מצות תואכלו 7 ביום הריאשון מיקרא
קודש יהיה לכם כל מלאכת עבודה לוא תעסו
8 והיקרבתם אישה ליהוה שיבעת ימים
ביום השביעי מיקרא קודש כל מלאכת עבודה
לוא תעסו 9 וידבר יהוה אל מושה לאמור 10 דבר
אל בני יסראל ואמרת אלהם כי תבואו אל הארץ
אשר אני נותן לכם וקצרתם את קצירה והבאתם
את עומר ראשית קצירכם אל הכוהן 11 והניף
את העומר ליפני יהוה לירצונכם מימחרת
השבת יניפנו הכוהן 12 ועסיתם ביום
הניפכם את העומר כבס תמים בן שנתו לעולה
ליהוה 13 ומינחתו שני עסרינים סולת בלולה
בשמן אישה ליהוה ריח ניחוח וניסכוה
יין רביעית ההין 14 ולחם וקלי וכרמל לוא
תואכלו עד עצם היום הזה עד הביאכם את קרבן
אלוהיכם חוקת עולם לדורותיכם בכול
מושבותיכם 15 וספרתם לכם מימחרת השבת
מיום הביאכם את עומר התנופה שבע שבתות
תמימות תיהיינה 16 עד מימחרת השבת
השביעית תיספרו חמישים יום
והיקרבתם מינחה חדשה ליהוה
17 מימושבותיכם תביאו לחם תנופה
שתיים שני עסרינים סולת תיהיינה

[illegible] 18 [illegible]
[illegible]
[illegible]
[illegible]
[illegible] 19 [illegible]
[illegible]
[illegible] 20
[illegible]
[illegible] 21 [illegible]
[illegible]
[illegible]
[illegible] 22
[illegible]
[illegible] 23 [illegible]
[illegible] 24 [illegible]
[illegible]
[illegible] 25 [illegible]
[illegible]
[illegible] 27 [illegible] 26
[illegible]
[illegible]
[illegible] 28 [illegible]
[illegible]
[illegible]
[illegible] 29 [illegible]
[illegible] 30 [illegible]
[illegible]
[illegible] 31 [illegible]
[illegible]
[illegible] 32 [illegible]
[illegible]
[illegible] 33 [illegible]
[illegible] 34 [illegible]
[illegible]
[illegible] 35 [illegible]
[illegible]
[illegible] 36
[illegible]
[illegible]
[illegible] 37 [illegible]
[illegible]

𐤅𐤌𐤉𐤍𐤇𐤄 𐤆𐤁𐤇 𐤅𐤍𐤎𐤊𐤉𐤌 𐤃𐤁𐤓 𐤉𐤅𐤌 𐤁𐤉𐤅𐤌𐤅 38 𐤌𐤉𐤋𐤁𐤃
𐤔𐤁𐤕𐤅𐤕 𐤉𐤄𐤅𐤄 𐤅𐤌𐤉𐤋𐤁𐤃 𐤌𐤕𐤍𐤅𐤕𐤉𐤊𐤌 𐤅𐤌𐤉𐤋𐤁𐤃 𐤊𐤋
𐤍𐤉𐤃𐤓𐤉𐤊𐤌 𐤅𐤌𐤉𐤋𐤁𐤃 𐤊𐤋 𐤍𐤉𐤃𐤁𐤅𐤕𐤉𐤊𐤌 𐤀𐤔𐤓
𐤕𐤉𐤕𐤍𐤅 𐤋𐤉𐤄𐤅𐤄 39 𐤀𐤊 𐤁𐤇𐤌𐤉𐤔𐤄 𐤏𐤎𐤓 𐤉𐤅𐤌 𐤋𐤇𐤅𐤃𐤔
𐤄𐤔𐤁𐤉𐤏𐤉 𐤁𐤀𐤎𐤐𐤊𐤌 𐤀𐤕 𐤕𐤁𐤅𐤀𐤕 𐤄𐤀𐤓𐤑 𐤕𐤇𐤅𐤂𐤅 𐤀𐤕 𐤇𐤂
𐤉𐤄𐤅𐤄 𐤔𐤉𐤁𐤏𐤕 𐤉𐤌𐤉𐤌 𐤁𐤉𐤅𐤌 𐤄𐤓𐤉𐤀𐤔𐤅𐤍 𐤔𐤁𐤕𐤅𐤍
𐤅𐤁𐤉𐤅𐤌 𐤄𐤔𐤌𐤉𐤍𐤉 𐤔𐤁𐤕𐤅𐤍 40 𐤅𐤋𐤒𐤇𐤕𐤌 𐤋𐤊𐤌 𐤁𐤉𐤅𐤌
𐤄𐤓𐤉𐤀𐤔𐤅𐤍 𐤐𐤓𐤉 𐤏𐤑 𐤄𐤃𐤓 𐤊𐤐𐤅𐤕 𐤕𐤌𐤓𐤉𐤌 𐤅𐤏𐤍𐤐
𐤏𐤑 𐤏𐤁𐤅𐤕 𐤅𐤏𐤓𐤁𐤉 𐤍𐤇𐤋 𐤅𐤎𐤌𐤇𐤕𐤌 𐤋𐤉𐤐𐤍𐤉 𐤉𐤄𐤅𐤄
𐤀𐤋𐤅𐤄𐤉𐤊𐤌 𐤔𐤉𐤁𐤏𐤕 𐤉𐤌𐤉𐤌 41 𐤅𐤇𐤂𐤅𐤕𐤌 𐤀𐤅𐤕𐤅 𐤇𐤂
𐤋𐤉𐤄𐤅𐤄 𐤔𐤉𐤁𐤏𐤕 𐤉𐤌𐤉𐤌 𐤁𐤔𐤍𐤄 𐤇𐤅𐤒𐤕 𐤏𐤅𐤋𐤌
𐤋𐤃𐤅𐤓𐤅𐤕𐤉𐤊𐤌 𐤁𐤇𐤅𐤃𐤔 𐤄𐤔𐤁𐤉𐤏𐤉 𐤕𐤇𐤅𐤂𐤅 𐤀𐤅𐤕𐤅 42 𐤁𐤎𐤅𐤊𐤅𐤕
𐤕𐤔𐤁𐤅 𐤔𐤉𐤁𐤏𐤕 𐤉𐤌𐤉𐤌 𐤊𐤋 𐤄𐤀𐤆𐤓𐤇 𐤁𐤉𐤎𐤓𐤀𐤋 𐤉𐤔𐤁𐤅
𐤁𐤎𐤅𐤊𐤅𐤕 43 𐤋𐤌𐤏𐤍 𐤉𐤃𐤏𐤅 𐤃𐤅𐤓𐤅𐤕𐤉𐤊𐤌 𐤊𐤉 𐤁𐤎𐤅𐤊𐤅𐤕
𐤄𐤅𐤔𐤁𐤕𐤉 𐤀𐤕 𐤁𐤍𐤉 𐤉𐤎𐤓𐤀𐤋 𐤁𐤄𐤅𐤑𐤉𐤀𐤉 𐤀𐤅𐤕𐤌 𐤌𐤀𐤓𐤑
𐤌𐤉𐤑𐤓𐤉𐤉𐤌 𐤀𐤍𐤉 𐤉𐤄𐤅𐤄 𐤀𐤋𐤅𐤄𐤉𐤊𐤌 44 𐤅𐤉𐤃𐤁𐤓
𐤌𐤅𐤔𐤄 𐤀𐤕 𐤌𐤅𐤏𐤃𐤉 𐤉𐤄𐤅𐤄 𐤀𐤋 𐤁𐤍𐤉 𐤉𐤎𐤓𐤀𐤋

𐤅𐤉𐤒𐤓𐤀 𐤐𐤓𐤒 24

1 𐤅𐤉𐤃𐤁𐤓 𐤉𐤄𐤅𐤄 𐤀𐤋 𐤌𐤅𐤔𐤄 𐤋𐤀𐤌𐤅𐤓 2 𐤑𐤅 𐤀𐤕 𐤁𐤍𐤉
𐤉𐤎𐤓𐤀𐤋 𐤅𐤉𐤒𐤇𐤅 𐤀𐤋𐤉𐤊𐤄 𐤔𐤌𐤍 𐤆𐤉𐤉𐤕 𐤆𐤊 𐤊𐤕𐤉𐤕
𐤋𐤌𐤀𐤅𐤓 𐤋𐤄𐤏𐤋𐤅𐤕 𐤍𐤓 𐤕𐤌𐤉𐤃 3 𐤌𐤉𐤇𐤅𐤑 𐤋𐤐𐤓𐤅𐤊𐤕
𐤄𐤏𐤃𐤅𐤕 𐤁𐤀𐤅𐤄𐤋 𐤌𐤅𐤏𐤃 𐤉𐤏𐤓𐤅𐤊 𐤀𐤅𐤕𐤅 𐤀𐤄𐤓𐤅𐤍 𐤌𐤏𐤓𐤁 𐤏𐤃
𐤁𐤅𐤒𐤓 𐤋𐤉𐤐𐤍𐤉 𐤉𐤄𐤅𐤄 𐤕𐤌𐤉𐤃 𐤇𐤅𐤒𐤕 𐤏𐤅𐤋𐤌
𐤋𐤃𐤅𐤓𐤅𐤕𐤉𐤊𐤌 4 𐤏𐤋 𐤄𐤌𐤍𐤅𐤓𐤄 𐤄𐤈𐤄𐤅𐤓𐤄 𐤉𐤏𐤓𐤅𐤊 𐤀𐤕
𐤄𐤍𐤓𐤅𐤕 𐤋𐤉𐤐𐤍𐤉 𐤉𐤄𐤅𐤄 𐤕𐤌𐤉𐤃 5 𐤅𐤋𐤒𐤇𐤕 𐤎𐤅𐤋𐤕
𐤅𐤀𐤐𐤉𐤕 𐤀𐤅𐤕𐤄 𐤔𐤕𐤉𐤌 𐤏𐤎𐤓𐤄 𐤇𐤋𐤅𐤕 𐤔𐤍𐤉 𐤏𐤎𐤓𐤅𐤍𐤉𐤌
𐤉𐤄𐤉𐤄 𐤄𐤇𐤋𐤄 𐤄𐤀𐤇𐤕 6 𐤅𐤎𐤌𐤕 𐤀𐤅𐤕𐤌 𐤔𐤕𐤉𐤉𐤌
𐤌𐤏𐤓𐤊𐤅𐤕 𐤔𐤔 𐤄𐤌𐤏𐤓𐤊𐤕 𐤏𐤋 𐤄𐤔𐤅𐤋𐤇𐤍 𐤄𐤈𐤄𐤅𐤓
𐤋𐤉𐤐𐤍𐤉 𐤉𐤄𐤅𐤄 7 𐤅𐤍𐤕𐤕 𐤏𐤋 𐤄𐤌𐤏𐤓𐤊𐤕 𐤋𐤁𐤅𐤍𐤄 𐤆𐤊𐤄
𐤅𐤄𐤉𐤕𐤄 𐤋𐤋𐤇𐤌 𐤋𐤀𐤆𐤊𐤓𐤄 𐤀𐤉𐤔𐤄 𐤋𐤉𐤄𐤅𐤄 8 𐤁𐤉𐤅𐤌
𐤄𐤔𐤁𐤕 𐤁𐤉𐤅𐤌 𐤄𐤔𐤁𐤕 𐤉𐤏𐤓𐤊𐤍𐤅 𐤋𐤉𐤐𐤍𐤉 𐤉𐤄𐤅𐤄
𐤕𐤌𐤉𐤃 𐤌𐤀𐤕 𐤁𐤍𐤉 𐤉𐤎𐤓𐤀𐤋 𐤁𐤓𐤉𐤕 𐤏𐤅𐤋𐤌 9 𐤅𐤄𐤉𐤕𐤄
𐤋𐤀𐤄𐤓𐤅𐤍 𐤅𐤋𐤁𐤍𐤉𐤅 𐤅𐤀𐤊𐤋𐤅𐤄𐤅 𐤁𐤌𐤒𐤅𐤌 𐤒𐤃𐤅𐤔 𐤊𐤉 𐤒𐤅𐤃𐤔
𐤒𐤃𐤔𐤉𐤌 𐤄𐤅𐤀 𐤋𐤅 𐤌𐤀𐤉𐤔𐤉 𐤉𐤄𐤅𐤄 𐤇𐤒 𐤏𐤅𐤋𐤌 10 𐤅𐤉𐤑𐤀
𐤁𐤍 𐤀𐤉𐤔𐤄 𐤉𐤎𐤓𐤀𐤋𐤉𐤕 𐤅𐤄𐤅𐤀 𐤁𐤍 𐤀𐤉𐤔 𐤌𐤉𐤑𐤓𐤉
𐤁𐤕𐤅𐤊 𐤁𐤍𐤉 𐤉𐤎𐤓𐤀𐤋 𐤅𐤉𐤍𐤑𐤅 𐤁𐤌𐤇𐤍𐤄 𐤁𐤍 𐤄𐤉𐤎𐤓𐤀𐤋𐤉𐤕
𐤅𐤀𐤉𐤔 𐤄𐤉𐤎𐤓𐤀𐤋𐤉 11 𐤅𐤉𐤒𐤅𐤁 𐤁𐤍 𐤄𐤀𐤉𐤔𐤄
𐤄𐤉𐤎𐤓𐤀𐤋𐤉𐤕 𐤀𐤕 𐤄𐤔𐤌 𐤅𐤉𐤒𐤋𐤋 𐤅𐤉𐤁𐤉𐤀𐤅 𐤀𐤅𐤕𐤅 𐤀𐤋
𐤌𐤅𐤔𐤄 𐤅𐤔𐤌 𐤀𐤉𐤌𐤅 𐤔𐤋𐤅𐤌𐤉𐤕 𐤁𐤕 𐤃𐤉𐤁𐤓𐤉 𐤋𐤌𐤈𐤄 𐤃𐤍
12 𐤅𐤉𐤍𐤉𐤇𐤅𐤄𐤅 𐤁𐤌𐤉𐤔𐤌𐤓 𐤋𐤉𐤐𐤓𐤅𐤔 𐤋𐤄𐤌 𐤏𐤋 𐤐𐤉

יהוה 13 וידבר יהוה אל מושה לאמור 14 הוצא את
המקלל אל מיחוץ למחנה וסמכו כל השומעים
את ידיהם על ראושו ורגמו אותו כל העדה 15 ואל
בני יסראל תדבר לאמור איש איש כי יקלל
אלוהיו ונסא חטאו 16 ונוקב שם יהוה מות יומת
רגום ירגמו בו כל העדה כגר כאזרח בנקבו שם
יומת 17 ואיש כי יכה כל נפש אדם מות יומת
18 ומכה נפש בהמה ישלמנה נפש תחת נפש
19 ואיש כי יתן מום בעמיתו כאשר עסה כן
יעסה לו 20 שבר תחת שבר עיין תחת עיין
שן תחת שן כאשר יתן מום באדם כן ינתן בו
21 ומכה בהמה ישלמנה ומכה אדם יומת
22 מישפט אחד יהיה לכם כגר כאזרח יהיה
כי אני יהוה אלוהיכם 23 וידבר מושה אל
בני יסראל ויוציאו את המקלל אל מיחוץ
למחנה וירגמו אותו אבן ובני יסראל עסו
כאשר ציוה יהוה את מושה

ויקרא פרק 25

1 וידבר יהוה אל מושה בהר סיני לאמור 2 דבר
אל בני יסראל ואמרת אלהם כי תבואו אל הארץ
אשר אני נותן לכם ושבתה הארץ שבת ליהוה
3 שש שנים תיזרע סדכה ושש שנים
תיזמור כרמכה ואספת את תבואתה 4 ובשנה
השביעית שבת שבתון יהיה לארץ שבת
ליהוה סדכה לוא תיזרע וכרמכה לוא תיזמור
5 את ספיח קצירכה לוא תיקצור ואת עינבי
נזירכה לוא תיבצור שנת שבתון יהיה לארץ
6 והיתה שבת הארץ לכם לאכלה לכה ולעבדכה
ולאמתכה וליסכירכה ולתושובכה הגרים עימך
7 וליבהמתכה ולחיה אשר בארצכה תיהיה כל
תבואתה לאכול 8 וספרת לכה שבע שבתות שנים
שבע שנים שבע פעמים והיו לכה ימי
שבע שבתות השנים תשע וארבעים שנה
9 והעברת שופר תרועה בחודש השביעי בעסור
לחודש ביום הכיפורים תעבירו שופר בכל
ארצכם 10 וקדשתם את שנת החמישים שנה
וקראתם דרור בארץ לכל יושביה יובל היוא
תיהיה לכם ושבתם איש אל אחוזתו ואיש אל
מישפחתו תשובו 11 יובל היוא שנת

12

13

14

15

16

17

18

19

20

21

22

23

24

25

26

27

28

29

30

31

32

33

עבדי הם אשר הוצאתי אותם מארץ
מיצריים אני יהוה אלוהיכם

ויקרא פרק 26

1 לוא תעסו לכם אלילים ופסל ומצבה לוא
תקימו לכם ואבן מסכית לוא תיתנו בארצכם
להישתחות עליה כי אני יהוה אלוהיכם 2 את
שבתותי תישמרו ומיקדשי תיראו אני
יהוה 3 אים בחוקותי תלכו ואת מיצותי
תישמרו ועסיתם אותם 4 ונתתי גישמיכם
בעיתם ונתנה הארץ יבולה ועץ הסדה יתן
פיריו 5 והיסיג לכם דייש את בציר ובציר
יסיג את זרע ואכלתם לחמכם לסובע וישבתם
לבטח בארצכם 6 ונתתי שלום בארץ ושכבתם
ואין מחריד והישבתי חיה רעה מין הארץ
וחרב לוא תעבור בארצכם 7 ורדפתם את אויביכם
ונפלו ליפניכם לחרב 8 ורדפו מיכם חמישה
מאה ומאה מיכם רבבה ירדופו ונפלו
אויביכם ליפניכם לחרב 9 ופניתי אליכם
והיפריתי אתכם והירביתי אתכם
והקימותי את בריתי איתכם 10 ואכלתם ישן
נושן וישן מיפני חדש תוציאו 11 ונתתי
מישכני בתוככם ולוא תיגעל נפשי אתכם
12 והיתהלכתי בתוככם והייתי לכם לאלוהים
ואתם תיהיו לי לעם 13 אני יהוה אלוהיכם
אשר הוצאתי אתכם מארץ מיצריים
מיהיות להם עבדים ואשבור מוטות עולכם
ואולך אתכם קוממיות 14 ואים לוא תישמעו לי
ולוא תעסו את כל המיצות האלה 15 ואים בחוקותי
תימאסו ואים את מישפטי תיגעל נפשכם
לבילתי עסות את כל מיצותי להפרכם את
בריתי 16 אף אני אעסה זאת לכם
והיפקדתי עליכם בהלה את השחפת ואת הקדחת
מכלות עיניים ומדיבות נפש וזרעתם
לריק זרעכם ואכלוהו אויביכם 17 ונתתי
פני בכם וניגפתם ליפני אויביכם ורדו
בכם סונאיכם ונסתם ואין רודף אתכם
18 ואים עד אלה לוא תישמעו לי ויספתי
ליסרה אתכם שבע על חטאותיכם 19 ושברתי את
גאון עוזכם ונתתי את שמיכם כברזל ואת

[illegible] 20 [illegible]
[illegible]
[illegible] 21
[illegible]
[illegible] 22
[illegible]
[illegible] 23 [illegible]
[illegible] 24 [illegible]
[illegible]
[illegible] 25 [illegible]
[illegible]
[illegible] 26 [illegible]
[illegible]
[illegible]
[illegible] 27
[illegible] 28 [illegible]
[illegible]
[illegible] 29
[illegible] 30
[illegible]
[illegible] 31 [illegible]
[illegible]
[illegible] 32 [illegible]
[illegible]
[illegible] 33
[illegible]
[illegible] 34
[illegible]
[illegible] 35 [illegible]
[illegible]
[illegible] 36 [illegible]
[illegible]
[illegible]
[illegible] 37
[illegible]
[illegible] 38 [illegible]
[illegible] 39 [illegible]
[illegible]
[illegible] 40 [illegible]
[illegible]
[illegible] 41 [illegible]

אותם בארץ אויביהם או אז יכנע לבבם הערל
ואז ירצו את עונם 42 וזכרתי את בריתי
יעקוב ואף את בריתי יצחק ואף את בריתי
אברהם אזכור והארץ אזכור 43 והארץ תעזב מהם
ותירץ את שבתותיה בהשמה מהם והם ירצו את
עונם יען וביען במשפטי מאסו ואת
חוקותי געלה נפשם 44 ואף גם זואת
ביהיותם בארץ אויביהם לוא מאסתים ולוא
געלתים לכלותם להפר בריתי איתם כי
אני יהוה אלוהיהם 45 וזכרתי להם ברית
ריאשונים אשר הוצאתי אותם מארץ
מצרים לעיני הגוים להיות להם
לאלוהים אני יהוה 46 אלה החוקים
והמשפטים והתורות אשר נתן יהוה בינו
ובין בני ישראל בהר סיני ביד מושה

ויקרא פרק 27

1 וידבר יהוה אל מושה לאמור 2 דבר אל בני
ישראל ואמרת אלהם איש כי יפליא נדר
בערככה נפשות ליהוה 3 והיה ערככה הזכר
מיבן עשרים שנה ועד בן שישים שנה
והיה ערככה חמשים שקל כסף בשקל הקודש
4 ואים נקבה היוא והיה ערככה שלושים שקל
5 ואים מיבן חמש שנים ועד בן עשרים
שנה והיה ערככה הזכר עשרים שקלים ולנקבה
עשרת שקלים 6 ואים מיבן חודש ועד בן חמש
שנים והיה ערככה הזכר חמשה שקלים
כסף ולנקבה ערככה שלושת שקלים כס 7 ואים
מיבן שישים שנה ומעלה אים זכר והיה
ערככה חמשה עשר שקל ולנקבה עשרה שקלים
8 ואים מך הוא מערככה והעמידו ליפני
הכוהן והעריך אותו הכוהן על פי אשר תסיג
יד הנודר יעריכנו הכוהן 9 ואים בהמה אשר
יקריבו מימנה קרבן ליהוה כול אשר יתן
מימנו ליהוה יהיה קודש 10 לוא יחליפנו
ולוא ימיר אותו טוב ברע או רע בטוב ואים המר
ימיר בהמה ביבהמה והיה הוא ותמורתו
יהיה קודש 11 ואים כל בהמה טמאה אשר לוא
יקריבו מימנה קרבן ליהוה והעמיד את
הבהמה ליפני הכוהן 12 והעריך הכוהן אותה
בין טוב ובין רע כערככה הכוהן כן יהיה

13 𐤅𐤀𐤉𐤌 𐤂𐤀𐤅𐤋 𐤉𐤂𐤀𐤋𐤍𐤄 𐤅𐤉𐤎𐤐 𐤇𐤌𐤉𐤔𐤉𐤕𐤅 𐤏𐤋
𐤏𐤓𐤊𐤊𐤄 14 𐤅𐤀𐤉𐤔 𐤊𐤉 𐤉𐤒𐤃𐤉𐤔 𐤀𐤕 𐤁𐤉𐤕𐤅 𐤒𐤅𐤃𐤔
𐤋𐤉𐤄𐤅𐤄 𐤅𐤄𐤏𐤓𐤉𐤊𐤅 𐤄𐤊𐤅𐤄𐤍 𐤁𐤉𐤍 𐤈𐤅𐤁 𐤅𐤁𐤉𐤍 𐤓𐤏 𐤊𐤀𐤔𐤓
𐤉𐤏𐤓𐤉𐤊 𐤀𐤅𐤕𐤅 𐤄𐤊𐤅𐤄𐤍 𐤊𐤍 𐤉𐤒𐤅𐤌 15 𐤅𐤀𐤉𐤌 𐤄𐤌𐤒𐤃𐤉𐤔
𐤉𐤂𐤀𐤋 𐤀𐤕 𐤁𐤉𐤕𐤅 𐤅𐤉𐤎𐤐 𐤇𐤌𐤉𐤔𐤉𐤕 𐤊𐤎𐤐 𐤏𐤓𐤊𐤊𐤄
𐤏𐤋𐤉𐤅 𐤅𐤄𐤉𐤄 𐤋𐤅 16 𐤅𐤀𐤉𐤌 𐤌𐤉𐤎𐤃𐤄 𐤀𐤇𐤅𐤆𐤕𐤅 𐤉𐤒𐤃𐤉𐤔
𐤀𐤉𐤔 𐤋𐤉𐤄𐤅𐤄 𐤅𐤄𐤉𐤄 𐤏𐤓𐤊𐤊𐤄 𐤋𐤐𐤉 𐤆𐤓𐤏𐤅 𐤆𐤓𐤏 𐤇𐤅𐤌𐤓
𐤎𐤏𐤅𐤓𐤉𐤌 𐤁𐤇𐤌𐤉𐤔𐤉𐤌 𐤔𐤒𐤋 𐤊𐤎 17 𐤀𐤉𐤌 𐤌𐤉𐤔𐤍𐤕
𐤄𐤉𐤅𐤁𐤋 𐤉𐤒𐤃𐤉𐤔 𐤎𐤃𐤄𐤅 𐤊𐤏𐤓𐤊𐤊𐤄 𐤉𐤒𐤅𐤌 18 𐤅𐤀𐤉𐤌 𐤀𐤇𐤓
𐤄𐤉𐤅𐤁𐤋 𐤉𐤒𐤃𐤉𐤔 𐤎𐤃𐤄𐤅 𐤅𐤇𐤉𐤔𐤁 𐤋𐤅 𐤄𐤊𐤅𐤄𐤍 𐤀𐤕 𐤄𐤊𐤎𐤐
𐤏𐤋 𐤐𐤉 𐤄𐤔𐤍𐤉𐤌 𐤄𐤍𐤅𐤕𐤓𐤅𐤕 𐤏𐤃 𐤔𐤍𐤕 𐤄𐤉𐤅𐤁𐤋
𐤅𐤍𐤉𐤂𐤓𐤏 𐤌𐤏𐤓𐤊𐤊𐤄 19 𐤅𐤀𐤉𐤌 𐤂𐤀𐤅𐤋 𐤉𐤂𐤀𐤋 𐤀𐤕 𐤄𐤎𐤃𐤄
𐤄𐤌𐤒𐤃𐤉𐤔 𐤀𐤅𐤕𐤅 𐤅𐤉𐤎𐤐 𐤇𐤌𐤉𐤔𐤉𐤕 𐤊𐤎𐤐 𐤏𐤓𐤊𐤊𐤄
𐤏𐤋𐤉𐤅 𐤅𐤒𐤌 𐤋𐤅 20 𐤅𐤀𐤉𐤌 𐤋𐤅𐤀 𐤉𐤂𐤀𐤋 𐤀𐤕 𐤄𐤎𐤃𐤄 𐤅𐤀𐤉𐤌
𐤌𐤊𐤓 𐤀𐤕 𐤄𐤎𐤃𐤄 𐤋𐤀𐤉𐤔 𐤀𐤇𐤓 𐤋𐤅𐤀 𐤉𐤂𐤀𐤋 𐤏𐤅𐤃 21 𐤅𐤄𐤉𐤄
𐤄𐤎𐤃𐤄 𐤁𐤑𐤀𐤕𐤅 𐤁𐤉𐤅𐤁𐤋 𐤒𐤅𐤃𐤔 𐤋𐤉𐤄𐤅𐤄 𐤊𐤉𐤎𐤃𐤄 𐤄𐤇𐤓𐤌
𐤋𐤊𐤅𐤄𐤍 𐤕𐤉𐤄𐤉𐤄 𐤀𐤇𐤅𐤆𐤕𐤅 22 𐤅𐤀𐤉𐤌 𐤀𐤕 𐤎𐤃𐤄 𐤌𐤉𐤒𐤍𐤕𐤅
𐤀𐤔𐤓 𐤋𐤅𐤀 𐤌𐤉𐤎𐤃𐤄 𐤀𐤇𐤅𐤆𐤕𐤅 𐤉𐤒𐤃𐤉𐤔 𐤋𐤉𐤄𐤅𐤄
23 𐤅𐤇𐤉𐤔𐤁 𐤋𐤅 𐤄𐤊𐤅𐤄𐤍 𐤀𐤕 𐤌𐤉𐤊𐤎𐤕 𐤄𐤏𐤓𐤊𐤊𐤄 𐤏𐤃 𐤔𐤍𐤕
𐤄𐤉𐤅𐤁𐤋 𐤅𐤍𐤕𐤍 𐤀𐤕 𐤄𐤏𐤓𐤊𐤊𐤄 𐤁𐤉𐤅𐤌 𐤄𐤄𐤅𐤀 𐤒𐤅𐤃𐤔 𐤋𐤉𐤄𐤅𐤄
24 𐤁𐤉𐤔𐤍𐤕 𐤄𐤉𐤅𐤁𐤋 𐤉𐤔𐤅𐤁 𐤄𐤎𐤃𐤄 𐤋𐤀𐤔𐤓 𐤒𐤍𐤄𐤅
𐤌𐤀𐤉𐤕𐤅 𐤋𐤀𐤔𐤓 𐤋𐤅 𐤀𐤇𐤅𐤆𐤕 𐤄𐤀𐤓𐤑 25 𐤅𐤊𐤋 𐤏𐤓𐤊𐤊𐤄
𐤉𐤄𐤉𐤄 𐤁𐤔𐤒𐤋 𐤄𐤒𐤅𐤃𐤔 𐤏𐤎𐤓𐤉𐤌 𐤂𐤓𐤄 𐤉𐤄𐤉𐤄 𐤄𐤔𐤒𐤋
26 𐤀𐤊 𐤁𐤊𐤅𐤓 𐤀𐤔𐤓 𐤉𐤁𐤅𐤊𐤓 𐤋𐤉𐤄𐤅𐤄 𐤁𐤉𐤁𐤄𐤌𐤄 𐤋𐤅𐤀
𐤉𐤒𐤃𐤉𐤔 𐤀𐤉𐤔 𐤀𐤅𐤕𐤅 𐤀𐤉𐤌 𐤔𐤅𐤓 𐤀𐤉𐤌 𐤎𐤄 𐤋𐤉𐤄𐤅𐤄
𐤄𐤅𐤀 27 𐤅𐤀𐤉𐤌 𐤁𐤁𐤄𐤌𐤄 𐤄𐤈𐤌𐤀𐤄 𐤅𐤐𐤃𐤄 𐤁𐤏𐤓𐤊𐤊𐤄 𐤅𐤉𐤎𐤐
𐤇𐤌𐤉𐤔𐤉𐤕𐤅 𐤏𐤋𐤉𐤅 𐤅𐤀𐤉𐤌 𐤋𐤅𐤀 𐤉𐤂𐤀𐤋 𐤅𐤍𐤉𐤌𐤊𐤓
𐤁𐤏𐤓𐤊𐤊𐤄 28 𐤀𐤊 𐤊𐤋 𐤇𐤓𐤌 𐤀𐤔𐤓 𐤉𐤇𐤓𐤉𐤌 𐤀𐤉𐤔 𐤋𐤉𐤄𐤅𐤄
𐤌𐤉𐤊𐤋 𐤀𐤔𐤓 𐤋𐤅 𐤌𐤀𐤃𐤌 𐤅𐤁𐤄𐤌𐤄 𐤅𐤌𐤉𐤎𐤃𐤄 𐤀𐤇𐤅𐤆𐤕𐤅 𐤋𐤅𐤀
𐤉𐤌𐤊𐤓 𐤅𐤋𐤅𐤀 𐤉𐤂𐤀𐤋 𐤊𐤋 𐤇𐤓𐤌 𐤒𐤅𐤃𐤔 𐤒𐤅𐤃𐤔𐤉𐤌 𐤄𐤅𐤀
𐤋𐤉𐤄𐤅𐤄 29 𐤊𐤋 𐤇𐤓𐤌 𐤀𐤔𐤓 𐤉𐤇𐤓𐤌 𐤌𐤉𐤍 𐤄𐤀𐤃𐤌 𐤋𐤅𐤀
𐤉𐤐𐤃𐤄 𐤌𐤅𐤕 𐤉𐤅𐤌𐤕 30 𐤅𐤊𐤋 𐤌𐤏𐤎𐤓 𐤄𐤀𐤓𐤑 𐤌𐤉𐤆𐤓𐤏
𐤄𐤀𐤓𐤑 𐤌𐤉𐤐𐤓𐤉 𐤄𐤏𐤑 𐤋𐤉𐤄𐤅𐤄 𐤄𐤅𐤀 𐤒𐤅𐤃𐤔 𐤋𐤉𐤄𐤅𐤄
31 𐤅𐤀𐤉𐤌 𐤂𐤀𐤅𐤋 𐤉𐤂𐤀𐤋 𐤀𐤉𐤔 𐤌𐤉𐤌𐤏𐤎𐤓𐤅
𐤇𐤌𐤉𐤔𐤉𐤕𐤅 𐤉𐤅𐤎𐤐 𐤏𐤋𐤉𐤅 32 𐤅𐤊𐤋 𐤌𐤏𐤎𐤓 𐤁𐤒𐤓 𐤅𐤑𐤀𐤅𐤍
𐤊𐤅𐤋 𐤀𐤔𐤓 𐤉𐤏𐤁𐤅𐤓 𐤕𐤇𐤕 𐤄𐤔𐤁𐤈 𐤄𐤏𐤎𐤉𐤓𐤉 𐤉𐤄𐤉𐤄 𐤒𐤅𐤃𐤔
𐤋𐤉𐤄𐤅𐤄 33 𐤋𐤅𐤀 𐤉𐤁𐤒𐤓 𐤁𐤉𐤍 𐤈𐤅𐤁 𐤋𐤓𐤏 𐤅𐤋𐤅𐤀 𐤉𐤌𐤉𐤓𐤍𐤅
𐤅𐤀𐤉𐤌 𐤄𐤌𐤓 𐤉𐤌𐤉𐤓𐤍𐤅 𐤅𐤄𐤉𐤄 𐤄𐤅𐤀 𐤅𐤕𐤌𐤅𐤓𐤕𐤅 𐤉𐤄𐤉𐤄
𐤒𐤅𐤃𐤔 𐤋𐤅𐤀 𐤉𐤂𐤀𐤋 34 𐤀𐤋𐤄 𐤄𐤌𐤉𐤑𐤅𐤕 𐤀𐤔𐤓 𐤑𐤉𐤅𐤄 𐤉𐤄𐤅𐤄
𐤀𐤕 𐤌𐤅𐤔𐤄 𐤀𐤋 𐤁𐤍𐤉 𐤉𐤎𐤓𐤀𐤋 𐤁𐤄𐤓 𐤎𐤉𐤍𐤉

במידבר

bemidbar / Numbers

במידבר פרק 1

1 וידבר יהוה אל מושה במידבר סיני באוהל
מועד באחד לחודש השני בשנה השנית לצאתם
מארץ מיצריים לאמור 2 סאו את רואש כל עדת
בני יסראל למישפחותם לבית אבותם
במיספר שמות כל זכר לגולגלותם 3 מיבן
עסרים שנה ומעלה כל יוצא צבא ביסראל
תיפקדו אותם לציבאותם אתה ואהרון
4 ואיתכם יהיו איש איש למטה איש רואש
לבית אבותיו הוא 5 ואלה שמות האנשים אשר
יעמדו איתכם ליראובן אליצור בן שדיאור
6 לשימעון שלומיאל בן צורישדי
7 ליהודה נחשון בן עמינד 8 לייסשכר
נתנאל בן צוער 9 ליזבולון אליאב בן חלון
10 ליבני יוסף לאפריים אלישמע בן
עמיהוד לימנשה גמליאל בן פדהצור
11 לבינימין אבידן בן גידעוני 12 לדן
אחיעזר בן עמישדי 13 לאשר פגעיאל בן
עכרן 14 לגד אליסף בן דעואל 15 לנפתלי
אחירע בן עינן 16 אלה קריאי העדה
נסיאי מטות אבותם ראשי אלפי יסראל הם
17 ויקח מושה ואהרון את האנשים האלה אשר
ניקבו בשמות 18 ואת כל העדה היקהילו באחד
לחודש השני ויתילדו על מישפחותם לבית
אבותם במיספר שמות מיבן עסרים שנה
ומעלה לגולגלותם 19 כאשר צוה יהוה את

מושה ויפקדם במידבר סיני 20 ויהיו בני
ראובן בכור יסראל תולדותם למישפחותם לבית
אבותם במיספר שמות לגולגלותם כל זכר מיבן
עסרים שנה ומעלה כול יוצא צבא 21 פקודיהם
למטה ראובן שישה וארבעים אלף וחמש מאות
22 ליבני שימעון תולדותם למישפחותם
לבית אבותם פקודיו במיספר שמות
לגולגלותם כל זכר מיבן עסרים שנה ומעלה
כול יוצא צבא 23 פקודיהם למטה שימעון
תישעה וחמישים אלף ושלוש מאות
24 ליבני גד תולדותם למישפחותם לבית
אבותם במיספר שמות מיבן עסרים שנה
ומעלה כול יוצא צבא 25 פקודיהם למטה גד
חמישה וארבעים אלף ושש מאות וחמישים
26 ליבני יהודה תולדותם למישפחותם לבית
אבותם במיספר שמות מיבן עסרים שנה
ומעלה כול יוצא צבא 27 פקודיהם למטה יהודה
ארבעה ושבעים אלף ושש מאות 28 ליבני
יסשכר תולדותם למישפחותם לבית אבותם
במיספר שמות מיבן עסרים שנה ומעלה כול
יוצא צבא 29 פקודיהם למטה יסשכר ארבעה
וחמישים אלף וארבע מאות 30 ליבני זבולון
תולדותם למישפחותם לבית אבותם במיספר
שמות מיבן עסרים שנה ומעלה כול יוצא צבא
31 פקודיהם למטה זבולון שיבעה וחמישים
אלף וארבע מאות 32 ליבני יוסף ליבני
אפרים תולדותם למישפחותם לבית אבותם
במיספר שמות מיבן עסרים שנה ומעלה כול
יוצא צבא 33 פקודיהם למטה אפרים
ארבעים אלף וחמש מאות 34 ליבני מנשה
תולדותם למישפחותם לבית אבותם במיספר
שמות מיבן עסרים שנה ומעלה כול יוצא צבא
35 פקודיהם למטה מנשה שנים ושלושים
אלף ומאתים 36 ליבני בנימין
תולדותם למישפחותם לבית אבותם במיספר
שמות מיבן עסרים שנה ומעלה כול יוצא צבא
37 פקודיהם למטה בנימין חמישה
ושלושים אלף וארבע מאות 38 ליבני דן
תולדותם למישפחותם לבית אבותם במיספר
שמות מיבן עסרים שנה ומעלה כול יוצא צבא
39 פקודיהם למטה דן שנים ושישים

40
41
42
43
44
45
46
47
48
49
50
51
52
53
54

2

1
2
3
4
5
6

פקודי בני ישראל לבית אבותם כל פקודי
המחנות לציבאותם שש מאות אלף ושלושת
אלפים וחמש מאות וחמישים 33 והלוים לוא
התפקדו בתוך בני ישראל כאשר ציוה יהוה את
מושה 34 ויעשו בני ישראל ככול אשר ציוה
יהוה את מושה כן חנו לדיגליהם וכן נסעו
איש למישפחותיו על בית אבותיו

במידבר פרק 3

1 ואלה תולדות אהרון ומושה ביום דיבר יהוה
את מושה בהר סיני 2 ואלה שמות בני אהרון
הבכור נדב ואביהוא אלעזר ואיתמר 3 אלה שמות
בני אהרון הכוהנים המשוחים אשר מילא
ידם לכהן 4 וימת נדב ואביהוא לפני
יהוה בהקריבם אש זרה לפני יהוה
במידבר סיני ובנים לוא היו להם ויכהן
אלעזר ואיתמר על פני אהרון אביהם
5 וידבר יהוה אל מושה לאמור 6 הקרב את מטה
לוי והעמדת אותו לפני אהרון הכוהן ושרתו
אותו 7 ושמרו את מישמרתו ואת מישמרת כל
העדה לפני אוהל מועד לעבוד את עבודת
המישכן 8 ושמרו את כל כלי אוהל מועד ואת
מישמרת בני ישראל לעבוד את עבודת
המישכן 9 ונתתה את הלוים לאהרון ולבניו
נתונים נתונים המה לו מאת בני ישראל
10 ואת אהרון ואת בניו תיפקוד ושמרו את
כהונתם והזר הקרב יומת 11 וידבר יהוה אל
מושה לאמור 12 ואני הינה לקחתי את הלוים
מיתוך בני ישראל תחת כל בכור פטר רחם
מבני ישראל והיו לי הלוים 13 כי לי כל
בכור ביום הכותי כל בכור בארץ מיצריים
הקדשתי לי כל בכור בישראל מאדם עד בהמה
לי יהיו אני יהוה 14 וידבר יהוה אל מושה
במידבר סיני לאמור 15 פקוד את בני לוי
לבית אבותם למישפחותם כל זכר מיבן חודש
ומעלה תיפקדם 16 ויפקוד אותם מושה על פי
יהוה כאשר צווה 17 ויהיו אלה בני לוי
בשמותם גרשון וקהת ומררי 18 ואלה שמות
בני גרשון למישפחותם ליבני ושימעי
19 ובני קהת למישפחותם עמרם וייצהר

[illegible] 20 [illegible]
[illegible]
[illegible] 21 [illegible]
[illegible]
[illegible] 22 [illegible]
[illegible]
[illegible] 23 [illegible]
[illegible] 24 [illegible]
[illegible] 25 [illegible]
[illegible]
[illegible] 26 [illegible]
[illegible]
[illegible] 27 [illegible]
[illegible]
[illegible]
[illegible] 28 [illegible]
[illegible]
[illegible] 29 [illegible]
[illegible] 30 [illegible]
[illegible]
[illegible] 31
[illegible]
[illegible] 32 [illegible]
[illegible]
[illegible] 33
[illegible]
[illegible] 34
[illegible] 35 [illegible]
[illegible]
[illegible]
[illegible] 36
[illegible]
[illegible] 37 [illegible]
[illegible] 38 [illegible]
[illegible]
[illegible]
[illegible]
[illegible] 39 [illegible]
[illegible]
[illegible]
[illegible] 40

ליבני יסראל מיבן חודש ומעלה וסא את
מיספר שמותם 41 ולקחת את הלויים לי אני
יהוה תחת כל בכור ביבני יסראל ואת בהמת
הלויים תחת כל בכור בבהמת בני יסראל
42 ויפקוד מושה כאשר ציוה יהוה אותו את כל
בכור ביבני יסראל 43 ויהי כל בכור זכר
במיספר שמות מיבן חודש ומעלה
ליפקודיהם שניים ועסרים אלף שלושה
ושיבעים ומאתיים 44 וידבר יהוה אל מושה
לאמור 45 קח את הלויים תחת כל בכור ביבני
יסראל ואת בהמת הלויים תחת בהמתם והיו לי
הלויים אני יהוה 46 ואת פדויי השלושה
והשיבעים והמאתיים העודפים על
הלויים מיבכור בני יסראל 47 ולקחת חמשת
חמשת שקלים לגולגולת בשקל הקודש תיקח
עסרים גרה השקל 48 ונתתה הכסף לאהרון
ולבניו פדויי העודפים בהם 49 ויקח מושה
את כסף הפידיום מאת העודפים על פדויי
הלויים 50 מאת בכור בני יסראל לקח את הכסף
חמישה ושישים ושלוש מאות ואלף בשקל
הקודש 51 ויתן מושה את כסף הפדויים
לאהרון ולבניו על פי יהוה כאשר ציוה יהוה
את מושה

במידבר פרק 4

1 וידבר יהוה אל מושה ואל אהרון לאמור 2 נסוא
את ראוש בני קהת מיתוך בני לוי
למישפחותם לבית אבותם 3 מיבן שלושים
שנה ומעלה ועדבן חמישים שנה כלבא לצבא
לעסות מלאכה באוהל מועד 4 זואת עבודת בני קהת
באוהל מועד קודש הקדשים 5 ובא אהרון ובניו
בינסוע המחנה והורידו את פרוכת המסך וכיסו
בה את ארון העדות 6 ונתנו עליו כסוי עור תחש
ופרסו בגד כליל תכלת מילמעלה וסמו בדיו
7 ועל שולחן הפנים יפרסו בגד תכלת ונתנו
עליו את הקערות ואת הכפות ואת המנקיות ואת
קסות הנסך ולחם התמיד עליו יהיה 8 ופרסו
עליהם בגד תולעת שני וכיסו אותו במיכסה
עור תחש וסמו את בדיו 9 ולקחו בגד תכלת וכיסו את
מנורת המאור ואת נרותיה ואת מלקחיה ואת

מחתותיה ואת כל כלי שמנה אשר ישרתו לה
בהם 10 ונתנו אותה ואת כל כליה אל מיכסה עור
תחש ונתנו על המוט 11 ועל מיזבח הזהב יפרסו
בגד תכלת וכיסו אותו במיכסה עור תחש וסמו את
בדיו 12 ולקחו את כל כלי השרת אשר ישרתו בם
בקודש ונתנו אל בגד תכלת וכיסו אותם במיכסה
עור תחש ונתנו על המוט 13 ודישנו את המיזבח
ופרסו עליו בגד ארגמן 14 ונתנו עליו את כל
כליו אשר ישרתו עליו בהם את המחתות את
המיזלגות ואת היעים ואת המיזרקות כול כלי
המיזבח ופרסו עליו כסוי עור תחש וסמו בדיו
15 וכילה אהרון ובניו לכסות את הקודש ואת כל
כלי הקודש בינסוע המחנה ואחרי כן יבואו
בני קהת לסאת ולוא יגעו אל הקודש ומתו אלה
מסא בני קהת באוהל מועד 16 ופקודת אלעזר בן
אהרון הכוהן שמן המאור וקטורת הסמים
ומנחת התמיד ושמן המישחה פקודת כל
המישכן וכל אשר בו בקודש ובכליו 17 וידבר
יהוה אל מושה ואל אהרון לאמור 18 אל תכריתו
את שבט מישפחות הקהתי מיתוך הלוים
19 וזואת עסו להם וחיו ולוא ימותו ביגשתם את
קודש הקדשים אהרון ובניו יבואו וסמו אותם
איש איש על עבודתו ואל מסאו 20 ולוא יבואו
ליראות כבלע את הקודש ומתו 21 וידבר יהוה אל
מושה לאמור 22 נסא את רואש בני גרשון גם
הם לבית אבותם למשפחותם 23 מיבן
שלושים שנה ומעלה עד בן חמישים שנה
תיפקוד אותם כל הבא ליצבוא צבא לעבוד עבודה
באוהל מועד 24 זואת עבודת מישפחות
הגרשוני לעבוד ולמסא 25 ונסאו את יריעות
המישכן ואת אוהל מועד מיכסהו ומיכסה
התחש אשר עליו מילמעלה ואת מסך פתח אוהל
מועד 26 ואת קלעי החצר ואת מסך פתח שער החצר
אשר על המישכן ועל המיזבח סביב ואת
מיתריהם ואת כל כלי עבודתם ואת כל אשר
יעסה להם ועבדו 27 על פי אהרון ובניו
תהיה כל עבודת בני הגרשוני לכל מסאם
ולכול עבודתם ופקדתם עלהם במשמרת את כל
מסאם 28 זואת עבודת מישפחות בני
הגרשוני באוהל מועד ומשמרתם ביד
איתמר בן אהרון הכוהן 29 בני מררי

30

31

32

33

34

35

36

37

38

39

40

41

42

43

44

45

46

47

48

49

במידבר פרק 5

1 וידבר יהוה אל מושה לאמור 2 צו את בני
ישראל וישלחו מין המחנה כל צרוע וכל זב וכול
טמא לנפש 3 מיזכר עד נקבה תשלחו אל מיחוץ
למחנה תשלחום ולוא יטמאו את מחניהם אשר
אני שוכן בתוכם 4 ויעשו כן בני ישראל
וישלחו אותם אל מיחוץ למחנה כאשר דיבר
יהוה אל מושה כן עשו בני ישראל 5 וידבר
יהוה אל מושה לאמור 6 דבר אל בני ישראל
איש או אשה כי יעשו מיכל חטואת האדם
לימעול מעל ביהוה ואשמה הנפש ההיוא
7 והיתודו את חטאתם אשר עשו והשיב את אשמו
בראשו וחמישיתו יוסף עליו ונתן לאשר
אשם לו 8 ואם אין לאיש גואל להשיב
האשם אליו האשם המושב ליהוה לכוהן
מילבד איל הכיפורים אשר יכפר בו עליו
9 וכל תרומה לכל קדשי בני ישראל אשר
יקריבו לכוהן לו יהיה 10 ואיש את קדשיו לו
יהיו איש אשר יתן לכוהן לו יהיה 11 וידבר
יהוה אל מושה לאמור 12 דבר אל בני ישראל
ואמרת אלהם איש איש כי תישטה אישתו
ומעלה בו מעל 13 ושכב איש אותה שיכבת זרע
ונעלם מעיני אישה ונסתרה והיא
נטמאה ועד אין בה והוא לוא ניתפשה
14 ועבר עליו רוח קינאה וקינא את אישתו
והוא נטמאה או עבר עליו רוח קינאה
וקינא את אישתו והיא לוא נטמאה 15 והביא
האיש את אישתו אל הכוהן והביא את קרבנה
עליה עשירת האיפה קמח שעורים לוא יצוק
עליו שמן ולוא יתן עליו לבונה כי מנחת
קינאת הוא מנחת זיכרון מזכרת עון
16 והקריב אותה הכוהן והעמידה ליפני
יהוה 17 ולקח הכוהן מיים קדושים ביכלי
חרש ומין העפר אשר יהיה בקרקע המישכן
יקח הכוהן ונתן אל המיים 18 והעמיד
הכוהן את האישה ליפני יהוה ופרע את
רואש האישה ונתן על כפיה את מנחת
הזיכרון מנחת קינאת הוא וביד הכוהן
יהיו מי המרים המאררים 19 והשביע
אותה הכוהן ואמר אל האישה אים לוא שכב

20
21
22
23
24
25
26
27
28
29
30
31

6

1
2
3
4
5

גדל פרע סער רואשו 6 כל ימי הזירו ליהוה
על נפש מת לוא יבוא 7 לאביו ולאימו לאחיו
ולאחותו לוא יטמא להם במותם כי נזר אלוהיו
על רואשו 8 כול ימי ניזרו קדוש הוא ליהוה
9 וכי ימות מת עליו בפתע פיתאום וטימא
רואש ניזרו וגילח רואשו ביום טהרתו ביום
השביעי יגלחנו 10 וביום השמיני יביא
שתי תורים או שני בני יונה אל הכוהן אל
פתח אוהל מועד 11 ועסה הכוהן אחד לחטאת ואחד
לעולה וכיפר עליו מאשר חטא על הנפש
וקידש את רואשו ביום ההוא 12 והיזיר ליהוה
את ימי ניזרו והביא כבס בן שנתו לאשם
והימים הריאשונים יפלו כי טמא ניזרו
13 וזואת תורת הנזיר ביום מלואת ימי
ניזרו יביא אותו אל פתח אוהל מועד
14 והיקריב את קרבנו ליהוה כבס בן שנתו
תמים אחד לעולה וכבסה אחת בת שנתה תמימה
לחטאת ואייל אחד תמים לישלמים 15 וסל
מצות סולת חלות בלולות בשמן ורקיקי מצות
משוחים בשמן ומינחתם וניסכיהם
16 והיקריב הכוהן ליפני יהוה ועסה את
חטאתו ואת עולתו 17 ואת האייל יעסה זבח
שלמים ליהוה על סל המצות ועסה הכוהן את
מינחתו ואת ניסכו 18 וגילח הנזיר פתח אוהל
מועד את רואש ניזרו ולקח את סער רואש ניזרו
ונתן על האש אשר תחת זבח השלמים 19 ולקח
הכוהן את הזרוע בשלה מין האייל וחלת מצה
אחת מן הסל ורקיק מצה אחד ונתן על כפי
הנזיר אחר היתגלחו את ניזרו 20 והניף
אותם הכוהן תנופה ליפני יהוה קודש הוא
לכוהן על חזה התנופה ועל שוק התרומה ואחר
ישתה הנזיר יין 21 זואת תורת הנזיר אשר
ידור קרבנו ליהוה על ניזרו מילבד אשר
תסיג ידו כפי נידרו אשר ידור כן יעסה על
תורת ניזרו 22 וידבר יהוה אל מושה לאמור
23 דבר אל אהרון ואל בניו לאמור כוה תברכו את
בני יסראל אמור להם 24 יברככה יהוה
וישמרכה 25 יאר יהוה פניו אליכה
ויחנכה 26 יסא יהוה פניו אליכה ויסם לכה
שלום 27 וסמו את שמי על בני יסראל ואני
אברכם

𐤁𐤌𐤉𐤃𐤁𐤓 𐤐𐤓𐤒 7

1 𐤅𐤉𐤄𐤉 𐤁𐤉𐤅𐤌 𐤊𐤋𐤅𐤕 𐤌𐤅𐤔𐤄 𐤋𐤄𐤒𐤉𐤌 𐤀𐤕 𐤄𐤌𐤉𐤔𐤊𐤍
𐤅𐤉𐤌𐤔𐤇 𐤀𐤅𐤕𐤅 𐤅𐤉𐤒𐤃𐤔 𐤀𐤅𐤕𐤅 𐤅𐤀𐤕 𐤊𐤋 𐤊𐤋𐤉𐤅 𐤅𐤀𐤕
𐤄𐤌𐤉𐤆𐤁𐤇 𐤅𐤀𐤕 𐤊𐤋 𐤊𐤋𐤉𐤅 𐤅𐤉𐤌𐤔𐤇𐤌 𐤅𐤉𐤒𐤃𐤔 𐤀𐤅𐤕𐤌
2 𐤅𐤉𐤒𐤓𐤉𐤁𐤅 𐤍𐤎𐤉𐤀𐤉 𐤉𐤎𐤓𐤀𐤋 𐤓𐤀𐤔𐤉 𐤁𐤉𐤕 𐤀𐤁𐤅𐤕𐤌
𐤄𐤌 𐤍𐤎𐤉𐤀𐤉 𐤄𐤌𐤈𐤅𐤕 𐤄𐤌 𐤄𐤏𐤅𐤌𐤃𐤉𐤌 𐤏𐤋 𐤄𐤐𐤒𐤅𐤃𐤉𐤌
3 𐤅𐤉𐤁𐤉𐤀𐤅 𐤀𐤕 𐤒𐤓𐤁𐤍𐤌 𐤋𐤉𐤐𐤍𐤉 𐤉𐤄𐤅𐤄 𐤔𐤔 𐤏𐤂𐤋𐤅𐤕
𐤑𐤁 𐤅𐤔𐤍𐤉 𐤏𐤎𐤓 𐤁𐤒𐤓 𐤏𐤂𐤋𐤄 𐤏𐤋 𐤔𐤍𐤉 𐤄𐤍𐤎𐤉𐤀𐤉𐤌
𐤅𐤔𐤅𐤓 𐤋𐤀𐤇𐤃 𐤅𐤉𐤒𐤓𐤉𐤁𐤅 𐤀𐤅𐤕𐤌 𐤋𐤉𐤐𐤍𐤉 𐤄𐤌𐤉𐤔𐤊𐤍
4 𐤅𐤉𐤅𐤀𐤌𐤓 𐤉𐤄𐤅𐤄 𐤀𐤋 𐤌𐤅𐤔𐤄 𐤋𐤀𐤌𐤅𐤓 5 𐤒𐤇 𐤌𐤀𐤉𐤕𐤌
𐤅𐤄𐤉𐤅 𐤋𐤏𐤁𐤅𐤃 𐤀𐤕 𐤏𐤁𐤅𐤃𐤕 𐤀𐤅𐤄𐤋 𐤌𐤅𐤏𐤃 𐤅𐤍𐤕𐤕𐤄 𐤀𐤅𐤕𐤌 𐤀𐤋
𐤄𐤋𐤅𐤉𐤌 𐤀𐤉𐤔 𐤊𐤐𐤉 𐤏𐤁𐤅𐤃𐤕𐤅 6 𐤅𐤉𐤒𐤇 𐤌𐤅𐤔𐤄 𐤀𐤕
𐤄𐤏𐤂𐤋𐤅𐤕 𐤅𐤀𐤕 𐤄𐤁𐤒𐤓 𐤅𐤉𐤕𐤍 𐤀𐤅𐤕𐤌 𐤀𐤋 𐤄𐤋𐤅𐤉𐤌 7 𐤀𐤕
𐤔𐤕𐤉 𐤄𐤏𐤂𐤋𐤅𐤕 𐤅𐤀𐤕 𐤀𐤓𐤁𐤏𐤕 𐤄𐤁𐤒𐤓 𐤍𐤕𐤍 𐤋𐤉𐤁𐤍𐤉
𐤂𐤓𐤔𐤅𐤍 𐤊𐤐𐤉 𐤏𐤁𐤅𐤃𐤕𐤌 8 𐤅𐤀𐤕 𐤀𐤓𐤁𐤏 𐤄𐤏𐤂𐤋𐤅𐤕 𐤅𐤀𐤕
𐤔𐤌𐤅𐤍𐤕 𐤄𐤁𐤒𐤓 𐤍𐤕𐤍 𐤋𐤉𐤁𐤍𐤉 𐤌𐤓𐤓𐤉 𐤊𐤐𐤉 𐤏𐤁𐤅𐤃𐤕𐤌
𐤁𐤉𐤃 𐤀𐤉𐤕𐤌𐤓 𐤁𐤍 𐤀𐤄𐤓𐤅𐤍 𐤄𐤊𐤅𐤄𐤍 9 𐤅𐤋𐤉𐤁𐤍𐤉 𐤒𐤄𐤕
𐤋𐤅𐤀 𐤍𐤕𐤍 𐤊𐤉 𐤏𐤁𐤅𐤃𐤕 𐤄𐤒𐤅𐤃𐤔 𐤏𐤋𐤄𐤌 𐤁𐤊𐤕𐤐 𐤉𐤎𐤀𐤅
10 𐤅𐤉𐤒𐤓𐤉𐤁𐤅 𐤄𐤍𐤎𐤉𐤀𐤉𐤌 𐤀𐤕 𐤇𐤍𐤅𐤊𐤕 𐤄𐤌𐤉𐤆𐤁𐤇
𐤁𐤉𐤅𐤌 𐤄𐤉𐤌𐤔𐤇 𐤀𐤅𐤕𐤅 𐤅𐤉𐤒𐤓𐤉𐤁𐤅 𐤄𐤍𐤎𐤉𐤀𐤉𐤌 𐤀𐤕
𐤒𐤓𐤁𐤍𐤌 𐤋𐤉𐤐𐤍𐤉 𐤄𐤌𐤉𐤆𐤁𐤇 11 𐤅𐤉𐤅𐤀𐤌𐤓 𐤉𐤄𐤅𐤄 𐤀𐤋
𐤌𐤅𐤔𐤄 𐤍𐤎𐤉𐤀 𐤀𐤇𐤃 𐤋𐤉𐤅𐤌 𐤍𐤎𐤉𐤀 𐤀𐤇𐤃 𐤋𐤉𐤅𐤌
𐤉𐤒𐤓𐤉𐤁𐤅 𐤀𐤕 𐤒𐤓𐤁𐤍𐤌 𐤋𐤇𐤍𐤅𐤊𐤕 𐤄𐤌𐤉𐤆𐤁𐤇 12 𐤅𐤉𐤄𐤉
𐤄𐤌𐤒𐤓𐤉𐤁 𐤁𐤉𐤅𐤌 𐤄𐤓𐤀𐤔𐤅𐤍 𐤀𐤕 𐤒𐤓𐤁𐤍𐤅 𐤍𐤇𐤔𐤅𐤍 𐤁𐤍
𐤏𐤌𐤉𐤍𐤃𐤁 𐤋𐤌𐤈𐤄 𐤉𐤄𐤅𐤃𐤄 13 𐤅𐤒𐤓𐤁𐤍𐤅 𐤒𐤏𐤓𐤕 𐤊𐤎𐤐 𐤀𐤇𐤕
𐤔𐤋𐤅𐤔𐤉𐤌 𐤅𐤌𐤀𐤄 𐤌𐤉𐤔𐤒𐤋𐤄 𐤌𐤉𐤆𐤓𐤒 𐤀𐤇𐤃 𐤊𐤎𐤐
𐤔𐤉𐤁𐤏𐤉𐤌 𐤔𐤒𐤋 𐤁𐤔𐤒𐤋 𐤄𐤒𐤅𐤃𐤔 𐤔𐤍𐤉𐤄𐤌 𐤌𐤋𐤀𐤉𐤌
𐤎𐤅𐤋𐤕 𐤁𐤋𐤅𐤋𐤄 𐤁𐤔𐤌𐤍 𐤋𐤌𐤉𐤍𐤇𐤄 14 𐤊𐤐 𐤀𐤇𐤕 𐤏𐤎𐤓𐤄 𐤆𐤄𐤁
𐤌𐤋𐤀𐤄 𐤒𐤈𐤅𐤓𐤕 15 𐤐𐤓 𐤀𐤇𐤃 𐤁𐤍 𐤁𐤒𐤓 𐤀𐤉𐤉𐤋 𐤀𐤇𐤃 𐤊𐤁𐤎 𐤀𐤇𐤃
𐤁𐤍 𐤔𐤍𐤕𐤅 𐤋𐤏𐤅𐤋𐤄 16 𐤎𐤏𐤉𐤓 𐤏𐤉𐤆𐤉𐤌 𐤀𐤇𐤃 𐤋𐤇𐤈𐤀𐤕
17 𐤅𐤋𐤆𐤁𐤇 𐤄𐤔𐤋𐤌𐤉𐤌 𐤁𐤒𐤓 𐤔𐤍𐤉𐤉𐤌 𐤀𐤉𐤋𐤉𐤌
𐤇𐤌𐤉𐤔𐤄 𐤏𐤕𐤅𐤃𐤉𐤌 𐤇𐤌𐤉𐤔𐤄 𐤊𐤁𐤎𐤉𐤌 𐤁𐤍𐤉 𐤔𐤍𐤄
𐤇𐤌𐤉𐤔𐤄 𐤆𐤄 𐤒𐤓𐤁𐤍 𐤍𐤇𐤔𐤅𐤍 𐤁𐤍 𐤏𐤌𐤉𐤍𐤃𐤁 18 𐤁𐤉𐤅𐤌
𐤄𐤔𐤍𐤉 𐤄𐤒𐤓𐤉𐤁 𐤍𐤕𐤍𐤀𐤋 𐤁𐤍 𐤑𐤅𐤏𐤓 𐤍𐤎𐤉𐤀 𐤉𐤎𐤔𐤊𐤓
19 𐤄𐤒𐤓𐤉𐤁 𐤀𐤕 𐤒𐤓𐤁𐤍𐤅 𐤒𐤏𐤓𐤕 𐤊𐤎𐤐 𐤀𐤇𐤕 𐤔𐤋𐤅𐤔𐤉𐤌
𐤅𐤌𐤀𐤄 𐤌𐤉𐤔𐤒𐤋𐤄 𐤌𐤉𐤆𐤓𐤒 𐤀𐤇𐤃 𐤊𐤎𐤐 𐤔𐤉𐤁𐤏𐤉𐤌 𐤔𐤒𐤋
𐤁𐤔𐤒𐤋 𐤄𐤒𐤅𐤃𐤔 𐤔𐤍𐤉𐤄𐤌 𐤌𐤋𐤀𐤉𐤌 𐤎𐤅𐤋𐤕 𐤁𐤋𐤅𐤋𐤄 𐤁𐤔𐤌𐤍
𐤋𐤌𐤉𐤍𐤇𐤄 20 𐤊𐤐 𐤀𐤇𐤕 𐤏𐤎𐤓𐤄 𐤆𐤄𐤁 𐤌𐤋𐤀𐤄 𐤒𐤈𐤅𐤓𐤕
21 𐤐𐤓 𐤀𐤇𐤃 𐤁𐤍 𐤁𐤒𐤓 𐤀𐤉𐤉𐤋 𐤀𐤇𐤃 𐤊𐤁𐤎 𐤀𐤇𐤃 𐤁𐤍 𐤔𐤍𐤕𐤅
𐤋𐤏𐤅𐤋𐤄 22 𐤎𐤏𐤉𐤓 𐤏𐤉𐤆𐤉𐤌 𐤀𐤇𐤃 𐤋𐤇𐤈𐤀𐤕 23 𐤅𐤋𐤆𐤁𐤇

השלמים בקר שניים אילים חמישה
עתודים חמישה כבסים בני שנה חמישה זה
קרבן נתנאל בן צוער 24 ביום השלישי
נסיא ליבני זבולון אליאב בן חלון 25 קרבנו
קערת כסף אחת שלושים ומאה מישקלה מיזרק
אחד כסף שיבעים שקל בשקל הקודש שניהם
מלאים סולת בלולה בשמן למינחה 26 כף אחת
עסרה זהב מלאה קטורת 27 פר אחד בן בקר אייל
אחד כבס אחד בן שנתו לעולה 28 סעיר עיזים
אחד לחטאת 29 ולזבח השלמים בקר שניים
אילים חמישה עתודים חמישה כבסים בני
שנה חמישה זה קרבן אליאב בן חלון 30 ביום
הרביעי נסיא ליבני ראובן אליצור בן
שדיאור 31 קרבנו קערת כסף אחת שלושים ומאה
מישקלה מיזרק אחד כסף שיבעים שקל בשקל
הקודש שניהם מלאים סולת בלולה בשמן
למינחה 32 כף אחת עסרה זהב מלאה קטורת
33 פר אחד בן בקר אייל אחד כבס אחד בן שנתו
לעולה 34 סעיר עיזים אחד לחטאת 35 ולזבח
השלמים בקר שניים אילים חמישה
עתודים חמישה כבסים בני שנה חמישה זה
קרבן אליצור בן שדיאור 36 ביום החמישי
נסיא ליבני שימעון שלומיאל בן
צורישדי 37 קרבנו קערת כסף אחת שלושים
ומאה מישקלה מיזרק אחד כסף שיבעים שקל
בשקל הקודש שניהם מלאים סולת בלולה בשמן
למינחה 38 כף אחת עסרה זהב מלאה קטורת
39 פר אחד בן בקר אייל אחד כבס אחד בן שנתו
לעולה 40 סעיר עיזים אחד לחטאת 41 ולזבח
השלמים בקר שניים אילים חמישה
עתודים חמישה כבסים בני שנה חמישה זה
קרבן שלומיאל בן צורישדי 42 ביום
השישי נסיא ליבני גד אליסף בן דעואל
43 קרבנו קערת כסף אחת שלושים ומאה
מישקלה מיזרק אחד כסף שיבעים שקל בשקל
הקודש שניהם מלאים סולת בלולה בשמן
למינחה 44 כף אחת עסרה זהב מלאה קטורת
45 פר אחד בן בקר אייל אחד כבס אחד בן שנתו
לעולה 46 סעיר עיזים אחד לחטאת 47 ולזבח
השלמים בקר שניים אילים חמישה
עתודים חמישה כבסים בני שנה חמישה זה

[illegible] 48 [illegible]
[illegible]
[illegible] 49 [illegible]
[illegible]
[illegible]
[illegible] 50 [illegible]
[illegible] 51
[illegible] 53 [illegible] 52 [illegible]
[illegible]
[illegible]
[illegible] 54 [illegible]
[illegible]
[illegible] 55 [illegible]
[illegible]
[illegible]
[illegible] 56 [illegible]
[illegible] 57
[illegible] 59 [illegible] 58 [illegible]
[illegible]
[illegible]
[illegible] 60 [illegible]
[illegible]
[illegible] 61 [illegible]
[illegible]
[illegible]
[illegible] 62 [illegible]
[illegible] 63
[illegible] 65 [illegible] 64 [illegible]
[illegible]
[illegible]
[illegible] 66 [illegible]
[illegible]
[illegible] 67
[illegible]
[illegible]
[illegible] 68 [illegible]
[illegible] 69
[illegible] 71 [illegible] 70 [illegible]
[illegible]
[illegible]
[illegible] 72 [illegible]

עשר יום נשיא ליבני אשר פגעיאל בן
עכרן 73 קרבנו קערת כסף אחת שלושים ומאה
מישקלה מיזרק אחד כסף שיבעים שקל בשקל
הקודש שניהם מלאים סולת בלולה בשמן
למינחה 74 כף אחת עשרה זהב מלאה קטורת
75 פר אחד בן בקר אייל אחד כבש אחד בן שנתו
לעולה 76 שעיר עיזים אחד לחטאת 77 ולזבח
השלמים בקר שניים אילים חמישה
עתודים חמישה כבשים בני שנה חמישה זה
קרבן פגעיאל בן עכרן 78 ביום שניים עשר
יום נשיא ליבני נפתלי אחירע בן עינן
79 קרבנו קערת כסף אחת שלושים ומאה
מישקלה מיזרק אחד כסף שיבעים שקל בשקל
הקודש שניהם מלאים סולת בלולה בשמן
למינחה 80 כף אחת עשרה זהב מלאה קטורת
81 פר אחד בן בקר אייל אחד כבש אחד בן שנתו
לעולה 82 שעיר עיזים אחד לחטאת 83 ולזבח
השלמים בקר שניים אילים חמישה
עתודים חמישה כבשים בני שנה חמישה זה
קרבן אחירע בן עינן 84 זואת חנוכת המיזבח
ביום הימשח אותו מאת נשיאי ישראל קערות
כסף שתים עשרה מיזרקי כסף שניים עשר
כפות זהב שתים עשרה 85 שלושים ומאה
הקערה האחת כסף ושיבעים המיזרק האחד כול
כסף הכלים אלפים וארבע מאות בשקל
הקודש 86 כפות זהב שתים עשרה מלאות קטורת
עשרה עשרה הכף בשקל הקודש כל זהב הכפות
עשרים ומאה 87 כל הבקר לעולה שניים עשר
פרים אילים שניים עשר כבשים בני שנה
שניים עשר ומינחתם ושעירי עיזים
שניים עשר לחטאת 88 וכול בקר זבח השלמים
עשרים וארבעה פרים אילים שישים
עתודים שישים כבשים בני שנה שישים
זואת חנוכת המיזבח אחרי הימשח אותו 89 ובבוא
מושה אל אוהל מועד לדבר איתו וישמע את הקול
מידבר אליו מעל הכפורת אשר על ארון העדות
מבין שני הכרובים וידבר אליו

במידבר פרק 8

1 וידבר יהוה אל מושה לאמור 2 דבר אל אהרון
ואמרת אליו בהעלותכה את הנרות אל מול פני

[illegible] 3 [illegible]
[illegible]
[illegible] 4 [illegible]
[illegible]
[illegible]
[illegible] 6 [illegible] 5 [illegible]
[illegible] 7 [illegible]
[illegible]
[illegible]
[illegible] 8 [illegible]
[illegible] 9 [illegible]
[illegible]
[illegible] 10 [illegible]
[illegible]
[illegible] 11 [illegible]
[illegible]
[illegible] 12 [illegible]
[illegible]
[illegible] 13 [illegible]
[illegible]
[illegible] 14 [illegible]
[illegible] 15 [illegible]
[illegible]
[illegible] 16 [illegible]
[illegible]
[illegible]
[illegible] 17
[illegible]
[illegible] 18 [illegible]
[illegible] 19 [illegible]
[illegible]
[illegible]
[illegible]
[illegible] 20 [illegible]
[illegible]
[illegible]
[illegible] 21 [illegible]
[illegible]
[illegible]
[illegible]
[illegible] 22
[illegible]

יהיה על המישכן כמראה אש עד בוקר 16 כן
יהיה תמיד הענן יכסנו ומראה אש לילה
17 ולפי העלות הענן מעל האוהל ואחרי כן
יסעו בני יסראל ובימקום אשר ישכן שם
הענן שם יחנו בני יסראל 18 על פי יהוה
יסעו בני יסראל ועל פי יהוה יחנו כל ימי
אשר ישכון הענן על המישכן יחנו
19 ובהאריך הענן על המישכן ימים רבים
ושמרו בני יסראל את מישמרת יהוה ולוא
יסעו 20 ויש אשר יהיה הענן ימים
מיספר על המישכן על פי יהוה יחנו ועל
פי יהוה יסעו 21 ויש אשר יהיה הענן
מערב עד בוקר ונעלה הענן בבוקר ונסעו או
יומם ולילה ונעלה הענן ונסעו 22 או
יומיים או חודש או ימים בהאריך הענן על
המישכן לישכון עליו יחנו בני יסראל ולוא
יסעו ובהעלותו יסעו 23 על פי יהוה יחנו
ועל פי יהוה יסעו את מישמרת יהוה שמרו
על פי יהוה ביד מושה

במידבר פרק 10

1 וידבר יהוה אל מושה לאמור 2 עסה לכה שתי
חצוצרות כסף מיקשה תעסה אותם והיו לכה
למיקרא העדה ולמסע את המחנות 3 ותקעו בהן
ונועדו אליכה כל העדה אל פתח אוהל מועד
4 ואים באחת יתקעו ונועדו אליכה הנסיאים
ראשי אלפי יסראל 5 ותקעתם תרועה ונסעו
המחנות החונים קדמה 6 ותקעתם תרועה שנית
ונסעו המחנות החונים תימנה תרועה יתקעו
למסעיהם 7 ובהקהיל את הקהל תיתקעו ולוא
תריעו 8 ובני אהרון הכוהנים יתקעו
בחצוצרות והיו לכם לחוקת עולם לדורותיכם
9 וכי תבואו מילחמה בארצכם על הצר הצורר
אתכם והרעותם בחצוצרות וניזכרתם ליפני
יהוה אלוהיכם ונושעתם מאויביכם
10 וביום שמחתכם ובמועדיכם ובראשי
חדשיכם ותקעתם בחצוצרות על עולותיכם ועל
זבחי שלמיכם והיו לכם לזיכרון ליפני
אלוהיכם אני יהוה אלוהיכם 11 ויהי בשנה
השנית בחודש השני בעסרים בחודש נעלה

[illegible] 12 [illegible]
[illegible]
[illegible] 13 [illegible]
[illegible] 14 [illegible]
[illegible]
[illegible] 15 [illegible]
[illegible] 16 [illegible]
[illegible] 17 [illegible]
[illegible] 18 [illegible]
[illegible]
[illegible] 19 [illegible]
[illegible] 20 [illegible]
[illegible] 21 [illegible]
[illegible] 22 [illegible]
[illegible]
[illegible] 23 [illegible]
[illegible] 24 [illegible]
[illegible]
[illegible] 25
[illegible]
[illegible] 26
[illegible] 27
[illegible] 28 [illegible]
[illegible] 29 [illegible]
[illegible]
[illegible]
[illegible]
[illegible] 30
[illegible] 31 [illegible]
[illegible]
[illegible] 32 [illegible]
[illegible]
[illegible] 33
[illegible]
[illegible] 34 [illegible]
[illegible]
[illegible] 35
[illegible]
[illegible] 36 [illegible]
[illegible]

11 [illegible]

1 [illegible]
[illegible]
[illegible] 2 [illegible]
[illegible] 3 [illegible]
[illegible]
4 [illegible]
[illegible]
[illegible] 5 [illegible]
[illegible]
[illegible] 6 [illegible]
[illegible]
[illegible] 7 [illegible]
[illegible] 8 [illegible]
[illegible]
[illegible] 9 [illegible]
[illegible] 10 [illegible]
[illegible]
[illegible] 11 [illegible]
[illegible]
[illegible]
12 [illegible]
[illegible]
[illegible]
[illegible] 13 [illegible]
[illegible]
[illegible] 14 [illegible]
[illegible] 15 [illegible]
[illegible]
[illegible] 16 [illegible]
[illegible]
[illegible]
[illegible]
[illegible] 17 [illegible]
[illegible]
[illegible]
[illegible] 18 [illegible]
[illegible]
[illegible]
[illegible]

19 לוא יום אחד תואכלון ולוא יומים ולוא
חמישה ימים ולוא עסרה ימים ולוא עסרים
יום 20 עד חודש ימים עד אשר יצא מאפכם
והיה לכם לזרא יען כי מאסתם את יהוה אשר
בקירבכם ותיבכו לפניו לאמור למה זה
יצאנו מימיצריים 21 ויואמר מושה שש
מאות אלף רגלי העם אשר אנוכי בקירבו ואתה
אמרת בסר אתן להם ואכלו חודש ימים
22 הצואן ובקר ישחט להם ומצא להם אים את כל
דגי הים יאסף להם ומצא להם 23 ויואמר
יהוה אל מושה היד יהוה תיקצר עתה תיראה
היקרכה דברי אים לוא 24 ויצא מושה וידבר
אל העם את דברי יהוה ויאסוף שיבעים
איש מיזיקני העם ויעמד אותם סביבות
האוהל 25 וירד יהוה בענן וידבר אליו ויאצל
מין הרוח אשר עליו ויתן על שיבעים איש
הזקנים ויהי כנוח עליהם הרוח ויתנבאו
ולוא יספו 26 וישארו שני אנשים במחנה
שם האחד אלדד ושם השני מידד ותנח עליהם
הרוח והמה בכתבים ולוא יצאו האוהלה ויתנבאו
במחנה 27 וירץ הנער ויגד למושה ויואמר
אלדד ומידד מיתנבאים במחנה 28 ויען
יהושוע בין נון משרת מושה מבחוריו
ויואמר אדוני מושה כלאם 29 ויואמר לו מושה
המקנא אתה לי ומי יתן כל עם יהוה
נביאים כי יתן יהוה את רוחו עליהם
30 ויאסף מושה אל המחנה הוא וזיקני
יסראל 31 ורוח נסע מאת יהוה ויגז סלוים
מין הים ויטוש על המחנה כדרך יום כוה
וכדרך יום כוה סביבות המחנה וכאמתים על
פני הארץ 32 ויקם העם כל היום ההוא וכל
הלילה וכל יום המחרת ויאספו את הסלו
הממעיט אסף עסרה חמרים וישטחו להם שטוח
סביבות המחנה 33 הבסר עודנו בין שיניהם
טרם יכרת ואף יהוה חרה בעם ויך יהוה בעם
מכה רבה מאוד 34 ויקרא את שם המקום ההוא
קיברות התאוה כי שם קברו את העם המיתאוים
35 מיקיברות התאוה נסעו העם חצרות ויהיו
בחצרות

12 [illegible]

1 [illegible]
[illegible]
2 [illegible]
[illegible] 3 [illegible]
[illegible]
4 [illegible]
[illegible]
[illegible] 5 [illegible]
[illegible]
6 [illegible]
[illegible]
[illegible] 7 [illegible]
8 [illegible]
[illegible]
[illegible] 9 [illegible] 10 [illegible]
[illegible]
[illegible]
11 [illegible]
[illegible]
12 [illegible]
[illegible] 13 [illegible]
[illegible] 14 [illegible]
[illegible]
[illegible]
[illegible] 15 [illegible]
[illegible]
[illegible] 16 [illegible]
[illegible]

13 [illegible]

1 [illegible] 2 [illegible]
[illegible]
[illegible]
[illegible] 3 [illegible]
[illegible]
[illegible] 4 [illegible]
[illegible] 5 [illegible]
[illegible] 6 [illegible]

יפנה 7 למטה יששכר יגאל בן יוסף 8 למטה
אפרים הושע בן נון 9 למטה
בנימן פלטי בן רפוא 10 למטה זבולן
גדיאל בן סודי 11 למטה יוסף למטה מנשה
גדי בן סוסי 12 למטה דן עמיאל בן גמלי
13 למטה אשר סתור בן מיכאל 14 למטה נפתלי
נחבי בן ופסי 15 למטה גד גאואל בן מכי
16 אלה שמות האנשים אשר שלח משה לתור את
הארץ ויקרא משה להושע בן נון יהושע
17 וישלח אותם משה לתור את ארץ כנען
ויאמר אלהם עלו זה בנגב ועליתם את ההר
18 וראיתם את הארץ מה הוא ואת העם היושב
עליה החזק הוא הרפה המעט הוא אם רב 19 ומה
הארץ אשר הוא יושב בה הטובה הוא אם רעה
ומה הערים אשר הוא יושב בהנה הבמחנים
אם במבצרים 20 ומה הארץ השמנה הוא
אם רזה היש בה עץ אם אין והתחזקתם
ולקחתם מפרי הארץ והימים ימי
בכורי ענבים 21 ויעלו ויתרו את הארץ
ממדבר צן עד רחב לבא חמת 22 ויעלו
בנגב ויבוא עד חברון ושם אחימן ששי
ותלמי בני הענק וחברון שבע שנים
נבנתה לפני צען מצרים
23 ויבואו עד נחל אשכל ויכרתו משם זמורה
ואשכול ענבים אחד וישאהו במוט בשנים
ומן הרמנים ומן התאנים 24 למקום
ההוא קרא נחל אשכול על אודות האשכול אשר כרתו
משם בני ישראל 25 וישבו מתור הארץ
מקץ ארבעים יום 26 וילכו ויבואו אל משה
ואל אהרן ואל כל עדת בני ישראל אל מדבר
פארן קדשה וישיבו אותם דבר ואת כל העדה
ויראום את פרי הארץ 27 ויספרו לו ויאמרו
באנו אל הארץ אשר שלחתנו וגם זבת חלב ודבש
הוא וזה פריה 28 אפס כי עז העם היושב
בארץ והערים בצרות גדולות מאוד וגם ילדי
הענק ראינו שם 29 עמלק יושב בארץ הנגב
והחתי והיבוסי והאמורי יושב בהר
והכנעני יושב על הים ועל יד הירדן
30 ויהס כלב את העם אל משה ויאמר עלה
נעלה וירשנו אתה כי יכול נוכל לה
31 והאנשים אשר עלו עמו אמרו לא נוכל

𐤋𐤏𐤋𐤅𐤕 𐤀𐤋 𐤄𐤏𐤌 𐤊𐤉 𐤇𐤆𐤒 𐤄𐤅𐤀 𐤌𐤌𐤍𐤅 32 𐤅𐤉𐤑𐤉𐤀𐤅
𐤃𐤁𐤕 𐤄𐤀𐤓𐤑 𐤀𐤔𐤓 𐤕𐤓𐤅 𐤀𐤕𐤄 𐤀𐤋 𐤁𐤍𐤉 𐤉𐤔𐤓𐤀𐤋 𐤋𐤀𐤌𐤓
𐤄𐤀𐤓𐤑 𐤀𐤔𐤓 𐤏𐤁𐤓𐤍𐤅 𐤁𐤄 𐤋𐤕𐤅𐤓 𐤀𐤕𐤄 𐤀𐤓𐤑 𐤀𐤊𐤋𐤕
𐤉𐤅𐤔𐤁𐤉𐤄 𐤄𐤅𐤀 𐤅𐤊𐤋 𐤄𐤏𐤌 𐤀𐤔𐤓 𐤓𐤀𐤉𐤍𐤅 𐤁𐤕𐤅𐤊𐤄
𐤀𐤍𐤔𐤉 𐤌𐤃𐤅𐤕 33 𐤅𐤔𐤌 𐤓𐤀𐤉𐤍𐤅 𐤀𐤕 𐤄𐤍𐤐𐤉𐤋𐤉𐤌
𐤁𐤍𐤉 𐤏𐤍𐤒 𐤌𐤍 𐤄𐤍𐤐𐤋𐤉𐤌 𐤅𐤍𐤄𐤉 𐤁𐤏𐤉𐤍𐤉𐤍𐤅
𐤊𐤇𐤂𐤁𐤉𐤌 𐤅𐤊𐤍 𐤄𐤉𐤉𐤍𐤅 𐤁𐤏𐤉𐤍𐤉𐤄𐤌

𐤁𐤌𐤃𐤁𐤓 𐤐𐤓𐤒 14

1 𐤅𐤕𐤔𐤀 𐤊𐤋 𐤄𐤏𐤃𐤄 𐤅𐤉𐤕𐤍𐤅 𐤀𐤕 𐤒𐤅𐤋𐤌 𐤅𐤉𐤁𐤊𐤅 𐤄𐤏𐤌
𐤁𐤋𐤉𐤋𐤄 𐤄𐤄𐤅𐤀 2 𐤅𐤉𐤋𐤍𐤅 𐤏𐤋 𐤌𐤔𐤄 𐤅𐤏𐤋 𐤀𐤄𐤓𐤍 𐤊𐤋
𐤁𐤍𐤉 𐤉𐤔𐤓𐤀𐤋 𐤅𐤉𐤀𐤌𐤓𐤅 𐤀𐤋𐤄𐤌 𐤊𐤋 𐤄𐤏𐤃𐤄 𐤋𐤅 𐤌𐤕𐤍𐤅
𐤁𐤀𐤓𐤑 𐤌𐤑𐤓𐤉𐤌 𐤀𐤅 𐤁𐤌𐤃𐤁𐤓 𐤄𐤆𐤄 𐤋𐤅 𐤌𐤕𐤍𐤅
3 𐤅𐤋𐤌𐤄 𐤉𐤄𐤅𐤄 𐤌𐤁𐤉𐤀 𐤀𐤕𐤍𐤅 𐤀𐤋 𐤄𐤀𐤓𐤑 𐤄𐤆𐤀𐤕
𐤋𐤍𐤐𐤋 𐤁𐤇𐤓𐤁 𐤍𐤔𐤉𐤍𐤅 𐤅𐤈𐤐𐤍𐤅 𐤉𐤄𐤉𐤅 𐤋𐤁𐤆 𐤄𐤋𐤅𐤀
𐤈𐤅𐤁 𐤋𐤍𐤅 𐤔𐤅𐤁 𐤌𐤑𐤓𐤉𐤌𐤄 4 𐤅𐤉𐤀𐤌𐤓𐤅 𐤀𐤉𐤔 𐤀𐤋
𐤀𐤇𐤉𐤅 𐤍𐤕𐤍𐤄 𐤓𐤀𐤔 𐤅𐤍𐤔𐤅𐤁𐤄 𐤌𐤑𐤓𐤉𐤌𐤄
5 𐤅𐤉𐤐𐤋𐤅 𐤌𐤔𐤄 𐤅𐤀𐤄𐤓𐤍 𐤏𐤋 𐤐𐤍𐤉𐤄𐤌 𐤋𐤐𐤍𐤉
𐤊𐤋 𐤒𐤄𐤋 𐤏𐤃𐤕 𐤁𐤍𐤉 𐤉𐤔𐤓𐤀𐤋 6 𐤅𐤉𐤄𐤅𐤔𐤏 𐤁𐤍 𐤍𐤅𐤍
𐤅𐤊𐤋𐤁 𐤁𐤍 𐤉𐤐𐤍𐤄 𐤌𐤍 𐤄𐤕𐤓𐤉𐤌 𐤀𐤕 𐤄𐤀𐤓𐤑 𐤒𐤓𐤏𐤅
𐤁𐤂𐤃𐤉𐤄𐤌 7 𐤅𐤉𐤀𐤌𐤓𐤅 𐤀𐤋 𐤊𐤋 𐤏𐤃𐤕 𐤁𐤍𐤉 𐤉𐤔𐤓𐤀𐤋
𐤋𐤀𐤌𐤓 𐤄𐤀𐤓𐤑 𐤀𐤔𐤓 𐤏𐤁𐤓𐤍𐤅 𐤁𐤄 𐤋𐤕𐤅𐤓 𐤀𐤕𐤄 𐤈𐤅𐤁𐤄 𐤄𐤀𐤓𐤑
𐤌𐤀𐤃 𐤌𐤀𐤃 8 𐤀𐤌 𐤇𐤐𐤑 𐤁𐤍𐤅 𐤉𐤄𐤅𐤄 𐤅𐤄𐤁𐤉𐤀 𐤀𐤕𐤍𐤅
𐤀𐤋 𐤄𐤀𐤓𐤑 𐤄𐤆𐤀𐤕 𐤅𐤍𐤕𐤍𐤄 𐤋𐤍𐤅 𐤀𐤓𐤑 𐤀𐤔𐤓 𐤄𐤅𐤀 𐤆𐤁𐤕
𐤇𐤋𐤁 𐤅𐤃𐤁𐤔 9 𐤀𐤊 𐤁𐤉𐤄𐤅𐤄 𐤀𐤋 𐤕𐤌𐤓𐤃𐤅 𐤅𐤀𐤕𐤌 𐤀𐤋
𐤕𐤉𐤓𐤀𐤅 𐤀𐤕 𐤏𐤌 𐤄𐤀𐤓𐤑 𐤊𐤉 𐤋𐤇𐤌𐤍𐤅 𐤄𐤌 𐤎𐤓 𐤑𐤋𐤌
𐤌𐤏𐤋𐤉𐤄𐤌 𐤅𐤉𐤄𐤅𐤄 𐤀𐤕𐤍𐤅 𐤀𐤋 𐤕𐤉𐤓𐤀𐤌
10 𐤅𐤉𐤀𐤌𐤓𐤅 𐤊𐤋 𐤄𐤏𐤃𐤄 𐤋𐤓𐤂𐤅𐤌 𐤀𐤕𐤌 𐤁𐤀𐤁𐤍𐤉𐤌
𐤅𐤊𐤁𐤅𐤃 𐤉𐤄𐤅𐤄 𐤍𐤓𐤀𐤄 𐤁𐤀𐤄𐤋 𐤌𐤅𐤏𐤃 𐤀𐤋 𐤊𐤋 𐤁𐤍𐤉
𐤉𐤔𐤓𐤀𐤋 11 𐤅𐤉𐤀𐤌𐤓 𐤉𐤄𐤅𐤄 𐤀𐤋 𐤌𐤔𐤄 𐤏𐤃 𐤀𐤍𐤄
𐤉𐤍𐤀𐤑𐤍𐤉 𐤄𐤏𐤌 𐤄𐤆𐤄 𐤅𐤏𐤃 𐤀𐤍𐤄 𐤋𐤀 𐤉𐤀𐤌𐤉𐤍𐤅 𐤁𐤉
𐤁𐤊𐤋 𐤄𐤀𐤕𐤅𐤕 𐤀𐤔𐤓 𐤏𐤔𐤉𐤕𐤉 𐤁𐤒𐤓𐤁𐤅 12 𐤀𐤊𐤍𐤅 𐤁𐤃𐤁𐤓
𐤅𐤀𐤅𐤓𐤔𐤍𐤅 𐤅𐤀𐤏𐤔𐤄 𐤀𐤕𐤊 𐤋𐤂𐤅𐤉 𐤂𐤃𐤅𐤋 𐤅𐤏𐤑𐤅𐤌
𐤌𐤌𐤍𐤅 13 𐤅𐤉𐤀𐤌𐤓 𐤌𐤔𐤄 𐤀𐤋 𐤉𐤄𐤅𐤄 𐤅𐤔𐤌𐤏𐤅
𐤌𐤑𐤓𐤉𐤌 𐤊𐤉 𐤄𐤏𐤋𐤉𐤕 𐤁𐤊𐤇𐤊 𐤀𐤕 𐤄𐤏𐤌 𐤄𐤆𐤄
𐤌𐤒𐤓𐤁𐤅 14 𐤅𐤀𐤌𐤓𐤅 𐤀𐤋 𐤉𐤅𐤔𐤁 𐤄𐤀𐤓𐤑 𐤄𐤆𐤀𐤕 𐤔𐤌𐤏𐤅
𐤊𐤉 𐤀𐤕𐤄 𐤉𐤄𐤅𐤄 𐤁𐤒𐤓𐤁 𐤄𐤏𐤌 𐤄𐤆𐤄 𐤀𐤔𐤓 𐤏𐤉𐤍
𐤁𐤏𐤉𐤍 𐤍𐤓𐤀𐤄 𐤀𐤕𐤄 𐤉𐤄𐤅𐤄 𐤅𐤏𐤍𐤍𐤊 𐤏𐤌𐤃
𐤏𐤋𐤄𐤌 𐤅𐤁𐤏𐤌𐤃 𐤏𐤍𐤍 𐤀𐤕𐤄 𐤄𐤋𐤊 𐤋𐤐𐤍𐤉𐤄𐤌
𐤉𐤅𐤌𐤌 𐤅𐤁𐤏𐤌𐤅𐤃 𐤀𐤔 𐤋𐤉𐤋𐤄 15 𐤅𐤄𐤌𐤕𐤄 𐤀𐤕 𐤄𐤏𐤌 𐤄𐤆𐤄
𐤊𐤀𐤉𐤔 𐤀𐤇𐤃 𐤅𐤀𐤌𐤓𐤅 𐤄𐤂𐤅𐤉𐤌 𐤀𐤔𐤓 𐤔𐤌𐤏𐤅 𐤀𐤕

𐤔𐤉𐤌𐤏𐤊𐤄 𐤋𐤀𐤌𐤅𐤓 16 𐤌𐤉𐤁𐤉𐤋𐤕𐤉 𐤉𐤊𐤅𐤋𐤕 𐤉𐤄𐤅𐤄
𐤋𐤄𐤁𐤉𐤀 𐤀𐤕 𐤄𐤏𐤌 𐤄𐤆𐤄 𐤀𐤋 𐤄𐤀𐤓𐤑 𐤀𐤔𐤓 𐤍𐤉𐤔𐤁𐤏 𐤋𐤄𐤌
𐤅𐤉𐤔𐤇𐤈𐤌 𐤁𐤌𐤉𐤃𐤁𐤓 17 𐤅𐤏𐤕𐤄 𐤉𐤂𐤃𐤋 𐤍𐤀 𐤊𐤅𐤇 𐤀𐤃𐤅𐤍𐤉
𐤊𐤀𐤔𐤓 𐤃𐤉𐤁𐤓𐤕 𐤋𐤀𐤌𐤅𐤓 18 𐤉𐤄𐤅𐤄 𐤀𐤓𐤊 𐤀𐤐𐤉𐤉𐤌 𐤅𐤓𐤁
𐤇𐤎𐤃 𐤍𐤅𐤎𐤀 𐤏𐤅𐤍 𐤅𐤐𐤔𐤏 𐤅𐤍𐤒𐤄 𐤋𐤅𐤀 𐤉𐤍𐤒𐤄 𐤐𐤅𐤒𐤃 𐤏𐤅𐤍
𐤀𐤁𐤅𐤕 𐤏𐤋 𐤁𐤍𐤉𐤌 𐤏𐤋 𐤔𐤉𐤋𐤔𐤉𐤌 𐤅𐤏𐤋 𐤓𐤉𐤁𐤏𐤉𐤌
19 𐤎𐤋𐤇 𐤍𐤀 𐤋𐤏𐤅𐤍 𐤄𐤏𐤌 𐤄𐤆𐤄 𐤊𐤂𐤅𐤃𐤋 𐤇𐤎𐤃𐤊𐤄 𐤅𐤊𐤀𐤔𐤓
𐤍𐤎𐤀𐤕𐤄 𐤋𐤏𐤌 𐤄𐤆𐤄 𐤌𐤉𐤌𐤉𐤑𐤓𐤉𐤉𐤌 𐤅𐤏𐤃 𐤄𐤍𐤄
20 𐤅𐤉𐤅𐤀𐤌𐤓 𐤉𐤄𐤅𐤄 𐤎𐤋𐤇𐤕𐤉 𐤊𐤉𐤃𐤁𐤓𐤊𐤄 21 𐤅𐤀𐤅𐤋𐤌 𐤇𐤉
𐤀𐤍𐤉 𐤅𐤉𐤌𐤋𐤀 𐤊𐤁𐤅𐤃 𐤉𐤄𐤅𐤄 𐤀𐤕 𐤊𐤋 𐤄𐤀𐤓𐤑 22 𐤊𐤉 𐤊𐤋
𐤄𐤀𐤍𐤔𐤉𐤌 𐤄𐤓𐤅𐤀𐤉𐤌 𐤀𐤕 𐤊𐤁𐤅𐤃𐤉 𐤅𐤀𐤕 𐤀𐤅𐤕𐤅𐤕𐤉 𐤀𐤔𐤓
𐤏𐤎𐤉𐤕𐤉 𐤁𐤌𐤉𐤑𐤓𐤉𐤉𐤌 𐤅𐤁𐤌𐤉𐤃𐤁𐤓 𐤅𐤉𐤍𐤎𐤅 𐤀𐤅𐤕𐤉 𐤆𐤄
𐤏𐤎𐤓 𐤐𐤏𐤌𐤉𐤌 𐤅𐤋𐤅𐤀 𐤔𐤌𐤏𐤅 𐤁𐤒𐤅𐤋𐤉 23 𐤀𐤉𐤌 𐤉𐤓𐤀𐤅
𐤀𐤕 𐤄𐤀𐤓𐤑 𐤀𐤔𐤓 𐤍𐤉𐤔𐤁𐤏𐤕𐤉 𐤋𐤀𐤁𐤅𐤕𐤌 𐤅𐤊𐤋 𐤌𐤍𐤀𐤑𐤉
𐤋𐤅𐤀 𐤉𐤓𐤀𐤅𐤄 24 𐤅𐤏𐤁𐤃𐤉 𐤊𐤋𐤁 𐤏𐤒𐤁 𐤄𐤉𐤕𐤄 𐤓𐤅𐤇 𐤀𐤇𐤓𐤕
𐤏𐤌𐤅 𐤅𐤉𐤌𐤋𐤀 𐤀𐤇𐤓𐤉 𐤅𐤄𐤁𐤉𐤀𐤅𐤕𐤉𐤅 𐤀𐤋 𐤄𐤀𐤓𐤑 𐤀𐤔𐤓
𐤁𐤀 𐤔𐤌𐤄 𐤅𐤆𐤓𐤏𐤅 𐤉𐤅𐤓𐤉𐤔𐤍𐤄 25 𐤅𐤄𐤏𐤌𐤋𐤒𐤉
𐤅𐤄𐤊𐤍𐤏𐤍𐤉 𐤉𐤅𐤔𐤁 𐤁𐤏𐤌𐤒 𐤌𐤇𐤓 𐤐𐤍𐤅 𐤅𐤎𐤏𐤅 𐤋𐤊𐤌
𐤄𐤌𐤉𐤃𐤁𐤓 𐤃𐤓𐤊 𐤉𐤌 𐤎𐤅𐤐 26 𐤅𐤉𐤃𐤁𐤓 𐤉𐤄𐤅𐤄 𐤀𐤋 𐤌𐤅𐤔𐤄
𐤅𐤀𐤋 𐤀𐤄𐤓𐤅𐤍 𐤋𐤀𐤌𐤅𐤓 27 𐤏𐤃 𐤌𐤕𐤉 𐤋𐤏𐤃𐤄 𐤄𐤓𐤏𐤄 𐤄𐤆𐤅𐤀𐤕
𐤀𐤔𐤓 𐤄𐤌𐤄 𐤌𐤋𐤉𐤍𐤉𐤌 𐤏𐤋𐤉 𐤀𐤕 𐤕𐤋𐤅𐤍𐤅𐤕 𐤁𐤍𐤉
𐤉𐤎𐤓𐤀𐤋 𐤀𐤔𐤓 𐤄𐤌𐤄 𐤌𐤋𐤉𐤍𐤉𐤌 𐤏𐤋𐤉 𐤔𐤌𐤏𐤕𐤉
28 𐤀𐤌𐤅𐤓 𐤀𐤋𐤄𐤌 𐤇𐤉 𐤀𐤍𐤉 𐤍𐤀𐤅𐤌 𐤉𐤄𐤅𐤄 𐤀𐤉𐤌 𐤋𐤅𐤀
𐤊𐤀𐤔𐤓 𐤃𐤉𐤁𐤓𐤕𐤌 𐤁𐤀𐤆𐤍𐤉 𐤊𐤍 𐤀𐤏𐤎𐤄 𐤋𐤊𐤌
29 𐤁𐤌𐤉𐤃𐤁𐤓 𐤄𐤆𐤄 𐤉𐤐𐤋𐤅 𐤐𐤉𐤂𐤓𐤉𐤊𐤌 𐤅𐤊𐤋
𐤐𐤒𐤅𐤃𐤉𐤊𐤌 𐤋𐤊𐤋 𐤌𐤉𐤎𐤐𐤓𐤊𐤌 𐤌𐤉𐤁𐤍 𐤏𐤎𐤓𐤉𐤌 𐤔𐤍𐤄
𐤅𐤌𐤏𐤋𐤄 𐤀𐤔𐤓 𐤄𐤋𐤉𐤍𐤅𐤕𐤌 𐤏𐤋𐤉 30 𐤀𐤉𐤌 𐤀𐤕𐤌 𐤕𐤁𐤅𐤀𐤅
𐤀𐤋 𐤄𐤀𐤓𐤑 𐤀𐤔𐤓 𐤍𐤎𐤀𐤕𐤉 𐤀𐤕 𐤉𐤃𐤉 𐤋𐤔𐤊𐤍 𐤀𐤕𐤊𐤌 𐤁𐤄
𐤊𐤉 𐤀𐤉𐤌 𐤊𐤋𐤁 𐤁𐤍 𐤉𐤐𐤅𐤍𐤄 𐤅𐤉𐤄𐤅𐤔𐤅𐤏 𐤁𐤉𐤍 𐤍𐤅𐤍
31 𐤅𐤈𐤐𐤊𐤌 𐤀𐤔𐤓 𐤀𐤌𐤓𐤕𐤌 𐤋𐤁𐤆 𐤉𐤄𐤉𐤄 𐤅𐤄𐤁𐤉𐤀𐤕𐤉
𐤀𐤅𐤕𐤌 𐤅𐤉𐤃𐤏𐤅 𐤀𐤕 𐤄𐤀𐤓𐤑 𐤀𐤔𐤓 𐤌𐤀𐤎𐤕𐤌 𐤁𐤄
32 𐤅𐤐𐤉𐤂𐤓𐤉𐤊𐤌 𐤀𐤕𐤌 𐤉𐤐𐤋𐤅 𐤁𐤌𐤉𐤃𐤁𐤓 𐤄𐤆𐤄
33 𐤅𐤁𐤍𐤉𐤊𐤌 𐤉𐤄𐤉𐤅 𐤓𐤅𐤏𐤉𐤌 𐤁𐤌𐤉𐤃𐤁𐤓 𐤀𐤓𐤁𐤏𐤉𐤌
𐤔𐤍𐤄 𐤅𐤍𐤎𐤀𐤅 𐤀𐤕 𐤆𐤍𐤅𐤕𐤉𐤊𐤌 𐤏𐤃 𐤕𐤅𐤌 𐤐𐤉𐤂𐤓𐤉𐤊𐤌
𐤁𐤌𐤉𐤃𐤁𐤓 34 𐤁𐤌𐤉𐤎𐤐𐤓 𐤄𐤉𐤌𐤉𐤌 𐤀𐤔𐤓 𐤕𐤓𐤕𐤌 𐤀𐤕
𐤄𐤀𐤓𐤑 𐤀𐤓𐤁𐤏𐤉𐤌 𐤉𐤅𐤌 𐤉𐤅𐤌 𐤋𐤔𐤍𐤄 𐤉𐤅𐤌 𐤋𐤔𐤍𐤄
𐤕𐤉𐤎𐤀𐤅 𐤀𐤕 𐤏𐤅𐤍𐤅𐤕𐤉𐤊𐤌 𐤀𐤓𐤁𐤏𐤉𐤌 𐤔𐤍𐤄 𐤅𐤉𐤃𐤏𐤕𐤌
𐤀𐤕 𐤕𐤍𐤅𐤀𐤕𐤉 35 𐤀𐤍𐤉 𐤉𐤄𐤅𐤄 𐤃𐤉𐤁𐤓𐤕𐤉 𐤀𐤉𐤌 𐤋𐤅𐤀
𐤆𐤅𐤀𐤕 𐤀𐤏𐤎𐤄 𐤋𐤊𐤋 𐤄𐤏𐤃𐤄 𐤄𐤓𐤏𐤄 𐤄𐤆𐤅𐤀𐤕 𐤄𐤍𐤅𐤏𐤃𐤉𐤌
𐤏𐤋𐤉 𐤁𐤌𐤉𐤃𐤁𐤓 𐤄𐤆𐤄 𐤉𐤕𐤌𐤅 𐤅𐤔𐤌 𐤉𐤌𐤅𐤕𐤅
36 𐤅𐤄𐤀𐤍𐤔𐤉𐤌 𐤀𐤔𐤓 𐤔𐤋𐤇 𐤌𐤅𐤔𐤄 𐤋𐤕𐤅𐤓 𐤀𐤕 𐤄𐤀𐤓𐤑

וישובו וילונו עליו את כל העדה להוציא דיבה
על הארץ 37 וימותו האנשים מוציאי דיבת
הארץ רעה במגפה ליפני יהוה 38 ויהושוע
בין נון וכלב בן יפונה חיו מין האנשים
ההם ההולכים לתור את הארץ 39 וידבר מושה את
הדברים האלה אל כל בני יסראל ויתאבלו העם
מאוד 40 וישכימו בבוקר ויעלו אל רואש ההר
לאמור היננו ועלינו אל המקום אשר אמר
יהוה כי חטאנו 41 ויואמר מושה למה זה אתם
עוברים את פי יהוה והיוא לוא 42 תיצלח אל
תעלו כי אין יהוה בקירבכם ולוא תינגפו
ליפני אויביכם 43 כי העמלקי והכנעני
שם ליפניכם ונפלתם בחרב כי על כן שבתם
מאחרי יהוה ולוא יהיה יהוה עימכם
44 ויעפילו לעלות אל רואש ההר וארון ברית
יהוה ומושה לוא משו מיקרב המחנה 45 וירד
העמלקי והכנעני היושב בהר ההוא ויכום
ויכתום עד החרמה

במידבר פרק 15

1 וידבר יהוה אל מושה לאמור 2 דבר אל בני
יסראל ואמרת אלהם כי תבואו אל ארץ
מושבותיכם אשר אני נותן לכם 3 ועסיתם
אישה ליהוה עולה או זבח לפלא נדר או בינדבה
או במועדיכם לעסות ריח ניחוח ליהוה מין
הבקר או מין הצואן 4 והיקריב המקריב קרבנו
ליהוה מינחה סולת עיסרון בלול בירביעית
ההין שמן 5 וייין לנסך רביעית ההין
תעסה על העולה או לזבח לכבס האחד 6 או לאייל
תעסה מינחה סולת שני עסרונים בלולה
בשמן שלישית ההין 7 וייין לנסך
שלישית ההין תקריב ריח ניחוח ליהוה
8 וכי תעסה בן בקר עולה או זבח לפלא נדר או
שלמים ליהוה 9 והיקריב על בן הבקר
מינחה סולת שלושה עסרונים בלול בשמן חצי
ההין 10 וייין תקריב לנסך חצי ההין
אישה ריח ניחוח ליהוה 11 ככה יעסה לשור
האחד או לאייל האחד או לסה בכבסים או
בעיזים 12 כמיספר אשר תעסו ככה תעסו לאחד
כמיספרם 13 כל האזרח יעסה ככה את אלה

להקריב אישה ריח ניחוח ליהוה 14 וכי יגור
איתכם גר או אשר בתוככם לדורותיכם ועשה
אישה ריח ניחוח ליהוה כאשר תעשו כן יעשה
15 הקהל חוקה אחת לכם ולגר הגר חוקת עולם
לדורותיכם ככם כגר יהיה ליפני יהוה
16 תורה אחת ומישפט אחד יהיה לכם ולגר הגר
איתכם 17 וידבר יהוה אל מושה לאמור 18 דבר
אל בני ישראל ואמרת אלהם בבואכם אל הארץ
אשר אני מביא אתכם שמה 19 והיה באכלכם
מילחם הארץ תרימו תרומה ליהוה 20 ראשית
עריסותכם חלה תרימו תרומה כיתרומת גורן
כן תרימו אותה 21 מראשית עריסותיכם
תיתנו ליהוה תרומה לדורותיכם 22 וכי תישגו
ולוא תעשו את כל המיצות האלה אשר דיבר יהוה
אל מושה 23 את כל אשר ציוה יהוה אליכם ביד
מושה מן היום אשר ציוה יהוה והלאה
לדורותיכם 24 והיה אם מעיני העדה
נעשתה לישגגה ועשו כל העדה פר בן בקר אחד
לעולה לריח ניחוח ליהוה ומינחתו וניסכו
כמישפט ושעיר עיזים אחד לחטאת 25 וכיפר
הכוהן על כל עדת בני ישראל וניסלח להם כי
שגגה היוא והם הביאו את קרבנם אישה
ליהוה וחטאתם ליפני יהוה על שיגגתם
26 וניסלח לכל עדת בני ישראל ולגר הגר בתוכם
כי לכל העם בישגגה 27 ואים נפש אחת תחטא
בישגגה והקריבה עז בת שנתה לחטאת
28 וכיפר הכוהן על הנפש השוגגת בחטאה
בישגגה ליפני יהוה לכפר עליו וניסלח לו
29 האזרח ביבני ישראל ולגר הגר בתוכם תורה
אחת יהיה לכם לעושה בישגגה 30 והנפש אשר
תעשה ביד רמה מין האזרח ומין הגר את
יהוה הוא מגדף וניכרתה הנפש ההיוא
מיקרב עמה 31 כי דבר יהוה בזה ואת מיצותו
הפר היכרת תיכרת הנפש ההיוא עונה בה
32 ויהיו בני ישראל במידבר וימצאו איש
מקושש עצים ביום השבת 33 ויקריבו אותו
המוצאים אותו מקושש עצים אל מושה ואל
אהרון ואל כל העדה 34 ויניחו אותו במישמר
כי לוא פורש מה יעשה לו 35 ויואמר יהוה אל
מושה מות יומת האיש רגום אותו באבנים כל
העדה מיחוץ למחנה 36 ויוציאו אותו כל העדה

𐤀𐤋 𐤌𐤉𐤇𐤅𐤑 𐤋𐤌𐤇𐤍𐤄 𐤅𐤉𐤓𐤂𐤌𐤅 𐤀𐤅𐤕𐤅 𐤁𐤀𐤁𐤍𐤉𐤌 𐤅𐤉𐤌𐤅𐤕
𐤊𐤀𐤔𐤓 𐤑𐤉𐤅𐤄 𐤉𐤄𐤅𐤄 𐤀𐤕 𐤌𐤅𐤔𐤄 37 𐤅𐤉𐤅𐤀𐤌𐤓 𐤉𐤄𐤅𐤄 𐤀𐤋
𐤌𐤅𐤔𐤄 𐤋𐤀𐤌𐤅𐤓 38 𐤃𐤁𐤓 𐤀𐤋 𐤁𐤍𐤉 𐤉𐤎𐤓𐤀𐤋 𐤅𐤀𐤌𐤓𐤕 𐤀𐤋𐤄𐤌
𐤅𐤏𐤎𐤅 𐤋𐤄𐤌 𐤑𐤉𐤑𐤉𐤕 𐤏𐤋 𐤊𐤍𐤐𐤉 𐤁𐤉𐤂𐤃𐤉𐤄𐤌
𐤋𐤃𐤅𐤓𐤅𐤕𐤌 𐤅𐤍𐤕𐤍𐤅 𐤏𐤋 𐤑𐤉𐤑𐤉𐤕 𐤄𐤊𐤍𐤐 𐤐𐤕𐤉𐤋 𐤕𐤊𐤋𐤕
39 𐤅𐤄𐤉𐤄 𐤋𐤊𐤌 𐤋𐤑𐤉𐤑𐤉𐤕 𐤅𐤓𐤀𐤉𐤕𐤌 𐤀𐤅𐤕𐤅 𐤅𐤆𐤊𐤓𐤕𐤌 𐤀𐤕
𐤊𐤋 𐤌𐤉𐤑𐤅𐤕 𐤉𐤄𐤅𐤄 𐤅𐤏𐤎𐤉𐤕𐤌 𐤀𐤅𐤕𐤌 𐤅𐤋𐤅𐤀 𐤕𐤕𐤅𐤓𐤅 𐤀𐤇𐤓𐤉
𐤋𐤁𐤁𐤊𐤌 𐤅𐤀𐤇𐤓𐤉 𐤏𐤉𐤍𐤉𐤊𐤌 𐤀𐤔𐤓 𐤀𐤕𐤌 𐤆𐤅𐤍𐤉𐤌
𐤀𐤇𐤓𐤉𐤄𐤌 40 𐤋𐤌𐤏𐤍 𐤕𐤉𐤆𐤊𐤓𐤅 𐤅𐤏𐤎𐤉𐤕𐤌 𐤀𐤕 𐤊𐤋
𐤌𐤉𐤑𐤅𐤕𐤉 𐤅𐤄𐤉𐤉𐤕𐤌 𐤒𐤃𐤅𐤔𐤉𐤌 𐤋𐤀𐤋𐤅𐤄𐤉𐤊𐤌
41 𐤀𐤍𐤉 𐤉𐤄𐤅𐤄 𐤀𐤋𐤅𐤄𐤉𐤊𐤌 𐤀𐤔𐤓 𐤄𐤅𐤑𐤀𐤕𐤉 𐤀𐤕𐤊𐤌
𐤌𐤀𐤓𐤑 𐤌𐤉𐤑𐤓𐤉𐤉𐤌 𐤋𐤄𐤉𐤅𐤕 𐤋𐤊𐤌 𐤋𐤀𐤋𐤅𐤄𐤉𐤌
𐤀𐤍𐤉 𐤉𐤄𐤅𐤄 𐤀𐤋𐤅𐤄𐤉𐤊𐤌

𐤁𐤌𐤉𐤃𐤁𐤓 𐤐𐤓𐤒 16

1 𐤅𐤉𐤒𐤇 𐤒𐤅𐤓𐤇 𐤁𐤍 𐤉𐤑𐤄𐤓 𐤁𐤍 𐤒𐤄𐤕 𐤁𐤍 𐤋𐤅𐤉 𐤅𐤃𐤕𐤍
𐤅𐤀𐤁𐤉𐤓𐤌 𐤁𐤍𐤉 𐤀𐤋𐤉𐤀𐤁 𐤅𐤀𐤅𐤍 𐤁𐤍 𐤐𐤋𐤕 𐤁𐤍𐤉 𐤓𐤀𐤅𐤁𐤍
2 𐤅𐤉𐤒𐤅𐤌𐤅 𐤋𐤐𐤍𐤉 𐤌𐤅𐤔𐤄 𐤅𐤀𐤍𐤔𐤉𐤌 𐤌𐤉𐤁𐤍𐤉
𐤉𐤎𐤓𐤀𐤋 𐤇𐤌𐤉𐤔𐤉𐤌 𐤅𐤌𐤀𐤕𐤉𐤉𐤌 𐤍𐤎𐤉𐤀𐤉 𐤏𐤃𐤄
𐤒𐤓𐤉𐤀𐤉 𐤌𐤅𐤏𐤃 𐤀𐤍𐤔𐤉 𐤔𐤌 3 𐤅𐤉𐤒𐤄𐤋𐤅 𐤏𐤋 𐤌𐤅𐤔𐤄 𐤅𐤏𐤋
𐤀𐤄𐤓𐤅𐤍 𐤅𐤉𐤀𐤌𐤓𐤅 𐤀𐤋𐤄𐤌 𐤓𐤁 𐤋𐤊𐤌 𐤊𐤉 𐤊𐤋 𐤄𐤏𐤃𐤄 𐤊𐤅𐤋𐤌
𐤒𐤃𐤅𐤔𐤉𐤌 𐤅𐤁𐤕𐤅𐤊𐤌 𐤉𐤄𐤅𐤄 𐤅𐤌𐤃𐤅𐤏 𐤕𐤉𐤕𐤍𐤎𐤀𐤅 𐤏𐤋 𐤒𐤄𐤋
𐤉𐤄𐤅𐤄 4 𐤅𐤉𐤔𐤌𐤏 𐤌𐤅𐤔𐤄 𐤅𐤉𐤐𐤅𐤋 𐤏𐤋 𐤐𐤍𐤉𐤅
5 𐤅𐤉𐤃𐤁𐤓 𐤀𐤋 𐤒𐤅𐤓𐤇 𐤅𐤀𐤋 𐤊𐤋 𐤏𐤃𐤕𐤅 𐤋𐤀𐤌𐤅𐤓 𐤁𐤅𐤒𐤓 𐤅𐤉𐤅𐤃𐤏
𐤉𐤄𐤅𐤄 𐤀𐤕 𐤀𐤔𐤓 𐤋𐤅 𐤅𐤀𐤕 𐤄𐤒𐤃𐤅𐤔 𐤅𐤄𐤉𐤒𐤓𐤉𐤁 𐤀𐤋𐤉𐤅 𐤅𐤀𐤕
𐤀𐤔𐤓 𐤉𐤁𐤇𐤓 𐤁𐤅 𐤉𐤒𐤓𐤉𐤁 𐤀𐤋𐤉𐤅 6 𐤆𐤅𐤀𐤕 𐤏𐤎𐤅 𐤒𐤇𐤅 𐤋𐤊𐤌
𐤌𐤇𐤕𐤅𐤕 𐤒𐤅𐤓𐤇 𐤅𐤊𐤋 𐤏𐤃𐤕𐤅 7 𐤅𐤕𐤍𐤅 𐤁𐤄𐤍 𐤀𐤔 𐤅𐤎𐤉𐤌𐤅
𐤏𐤋𐤉𐤄𐤍 𐤒𐤈𐤅𐤓𐤕 𐤋𐤐𐤍𐤉 𐤉𐤄𐤅𐤄 𐤌𐤇𐤓 𐤅𐤄𐤉𐤄 𐤄𐤀𐤉𐤔
𐤀𐤔𐤓 𐤉𐤁𐤇𐤓 𐤉𐤄𐤅𐤄 𐤄𐤅𐤀 𐤄𐤒𐤃𐤅𐤔 𐤓𐤁 𐤋𐤊𐤌 𐤁𐤍𐤉 𐤋𐤅𐤉
8 𐤅𐤉𐤅𐤀𐤌𐤓 𐤌𐤅𐤔𐤄 𐤀𐤋 𐤒𐤅𐤓𐤇 𐤔𐤉𐤌𐤏𐤅 𐤍𐤀 𐤁𐤍𐤉 𐤋𐤅𐤉
9 𐤄𐤌𐤏𐤈 𐤌𐤉𐤊𐤌 𐤊𐤉 𐤄𐤉𐤁𐤃𐤉𐤋 𐤀𐤋𐤅𐤄𐤉 𐤉𐤎𐤓𐤀𐤋
𐤀𐤕𐤊𐤌 𐤌𐤏𐤃𐤕 𐤉𐤎𐤓𐤀𐤋 𐤋𐤄𐤒𐤓𐤉𐤁 𐤀𐤕𐤊𐤌 𐤀𐤋𐤉𐤅 𐤋𐤏𐤁𐤅𐤃
𐤀𐤕 𐤏𐤁𐤅𐤃𐤕 𐤌𐤉𐤔𐤊𐤍 𐤉𐤄𐤅𐤄 𐤅𐤋𐤏𐤌𐤅𐤃 𐤋𐤐𐤍𐤉 𐤄𐤏𐤃𐤄
𐤋𐤔𐤓𐤕𐤌 10 𐤅𐤉𐤒𐤓𐤁 𐤀𐤅𐤕𐤊𐤄 𐤅𐤀𐤕 𐤊𐤋 𐤀𐤇𐤉𐤊𐤄 𐤁𐤍𐤉 𐤋𐤅𐤉
𐤀𐤉𐤕𐤊 𐤅𐤁𐤉𐤒𐤔𐤕𐤌 𐤂𐤌 𐤊𐤄𐤅𐤍𐤄 11 𐤋𐤊𐤍 𐤀𐤕𐤄 𐤅𐤊𐤋
𐤏𐤃𐤕𐤊𐤄 𐤄𐤍𐤅𐤏𐤃𐤉𐤌 𐤏𐤋 𐤉𐤄𐤅𐤄 𐤅𐤀𐤄𐤓𐤅𐤍 𐤌𐤄 𐤄𐤅𐤀 𐤊𐤉
𐤕𐤉𐤋𐤅𐤍𐤅 𐤏𐤋𐤉𐤅 12 𐤅𐤉𐤔𐤋𐤇 𐤌𐤅𐤔𐤄 𐤋𐤉𐤒𐤓𐤅𐤀 𐤋𐤃𐤕𐤍
𐤅𐤋𐤀𐤁𐤉𐤓𐤌 𐤁𐤍𐤉 𐤀𐤋𐤉𐤀𐤁 𐤅𐤉𐤀𐤌𐤓𐤅 𐤋𐤅𐤀 𐤍𐤏𐤋𐤄
13 𐤄𐤌𐤏𐤈 𐤊𐤉 𐤄𐤏𐤋𐤉𐤕𐤍𐤅 𐤌𐤀𐤓𐤑 𐤆𐤁𐤕 𐤇𐤋𐤁 𐤅𐤃𐤁𐤔
𐤋𐤄𐤌𐤉𐤕𐤍𐤅 𐤁𐤌𐤃𐤁𐤓 𐤊𐤉 𐤕𐤉𐤎𐤕𐤓𐤓 𐤏𐤋𐤉𐤍𐤅 𐤂𐤌
𐤄𐤉𐤎𐤕𐤓𐤓 14 𐤀𐤐 𐤋𐤅𐤀 𐤀𐤋 𐤀𐤓𐤑 𐤆𐤁𐤕 𐤇𐤋𐤁 𐤅𐤃𐤁𐤔

הביאותנו ותיתן לנו נחלת סדה וכרם העיני
האנשים ההם תנקר לוא נעלה 15 ויחר למושה
מאוד ויואמר אל יהוה אל תפן אל מינחתם
לוא חמור אחד מהם נסאתי ולוא הרעותי את אחד
מהם 16 ויואמר מושה אל קורח אתה וכל עדתכה
היו ליפני יהוה אתה והם ואהרון מחר 17 וקחו
איש מחתתו ונתתם עליהם קטורת והקרבתם
ליפני יהוה איש מחתתו חמישים
ומאתיים מחתות ואתה ואהרון איש מחתתו
18 ויקחו איש מחתתו ויתנו עליהם אש
ויסימו עליהם קטורת ויעמדו פתח אוהל מועד
ומושה ואהרון 19 ויקהל עליהם קורח את כל
העדה אל פתח אוהל מועד וירא כבוד יהוה אל כל
העדה 20 וידבר יהוה אל מושה ואל אהרון לאמור
21 היבדלו מיתוך העדה הזואת ואכלה אותם כרגע
22 ויפלו על פניהם ויואמרו אל אלוהי
הרוחות לכל בסר האיש אחד יחטא ועל כל העדה
תיקצוף 23 וידבר יהוה אל מושה לאמור 24 דבר
אל העדה לאמור העלו מיסביב למישכן קורח
דתן ואבירם 25 ויקם מושה וילך אל דתן
ואבירם וילכו אחריו זיקני יסראל 26 וידבר
אל העדה לאמור סורו נא מעל אהלי האנשים
הרשעים האלה ואל תיגעו בכל אשר להם פן
תיספו בכל חטואתם 27 ויעלו מעל מישכן קורח
דתן ואבירם מיסביב ודתן ואבירם יצאו
ניצבים פתח אהליהם ונשיהם ובניהם
וטפם 28 ויואמר מושה בזואת תדעון כי יהוה
שלחני לעסות את כל המעסים האלה כי לוא
מיליבי 29 אים כמות כל האדם ימותון אלה
ופקודת כל האדם יפקד עליהם לוא יהוה
שלחני 30 ואים בריאה יברא יהוה ופצתה
האדמה את פיה ובלעה אותם ואת כל אשר להם
וירדו חיים שאולה וידעתם כי ניאצו
האנשים האלה את יהוה 31 ויהי ככלותו לדבר
את כל הדברים האלה ותיבקע האדמה אשר
תחתיהם 32 ותיפתח הארץ את פיה ותיבלע
אותם ואת בתיהם ואת כל האדם אשר לקורח ואת כל
הרכוש 33 וירדו הם וכל אשר להם חיים שאולה
ותכס עליהם הארץ ויאבדו מיתוך הקהל 34 וכל
יסראל אשר סביבותיהם נסו לקולם כי אמרו
פן תבלענו הארץ 35 ואש יצאה מאת יהוה

17

1
2
3
4
5
6
7
8
9
10
11
12
13
14
15
16
17
18
19

איועד לכם שמה 20 והיה האיש אשר אבחר בו
מטהו יפרח והשיכותי מעלי את תלונות בני
יסראל אשר הם מלינים עליכם 21 וידבר
מושה אל בני יסראל ויתנו אליו כל
נסיאיהם מטה לנסיא אחד מטה לנסיא אחד
לבית אבותם שנים עסר מטות ומטה אהרון בתוך
מטותם 22 ויניח מושה את המטות ליפני יהוה
באוהל העדות 23 ויהי מימחרת ויבוא מושה אל
אוהל העדות והינה פרח מטה אהרון לבית לוי
ויוצא פרח ויצץ ציץ ויגמול שקדים
24 ויוצא מושה את כל המטות מיליפני יהוה
אל כל בני יסראל ויראו ויקחו איש מטהו
25 ויואמר יהוה אל מושה השב את מטה אהרון
ליפני העדות למישמרת לאות ליבני מרי
ותכל תלונותם מעלי ולוא ימותו 26 ויעס מושה
כאשר ציוה יהוה אותו כן עסה 27 ויואמרו בני
יסראל אל מושה לאמור הן גוענו אבדנו כולנו
אבדנו 28 כול הקרב הקרב אל מישכן יהוה ימות
האים תמנו ליגוע

במידבר פרק 18

1 ויואמר יהוה אל אהרון אתה ובניכה ובית
אביכה איתך תיסאו את עון המיקדש ואתה
ובניכה איתך תיסאו את עון כהונתכם 2 וגם
את אחיכה מטה לוי שבט אביכה הקרב איתך
ויילוו עליכה וישרתוכה ואתה ובניכה איתך
ליפני אוהל העדות 3 ושמרו מישמרתכה
ומישמרת כל האוהל אך אל כלי הקודש ואל
המיזבח לוא יקרבו ולוא ימותו גם הם גם אתם
4 ונילוו עליכה ושמרו את מישמרת אוהל
מועד לכול עבודת האוהל וזר לוא יקרב אליכם
5 ושמרתם את מישמרת הקודש ואת מישמרת
המיזבח ולוא יהיה עוד קצף על בני יסראל
6 ואני הינה לקחתי את אחיכם הלוים
מיתוך בני יסראל לכם מתנה נתונים
ליהוה לעבוד את עבודת אוהל מועד 7 ואתה
ובניכה איתכה תישמרו את כהונתכם לכל דבר
המיזבח ולמיבית לפרוכת ועבדתם עבודת
מתנה אתן את כהונתכם והזר הקרב יומת
8 וידבר יהוה אל אהרון ואני הינה נתתי
לכה את מישמרת תרומותי לכל קדשי בני

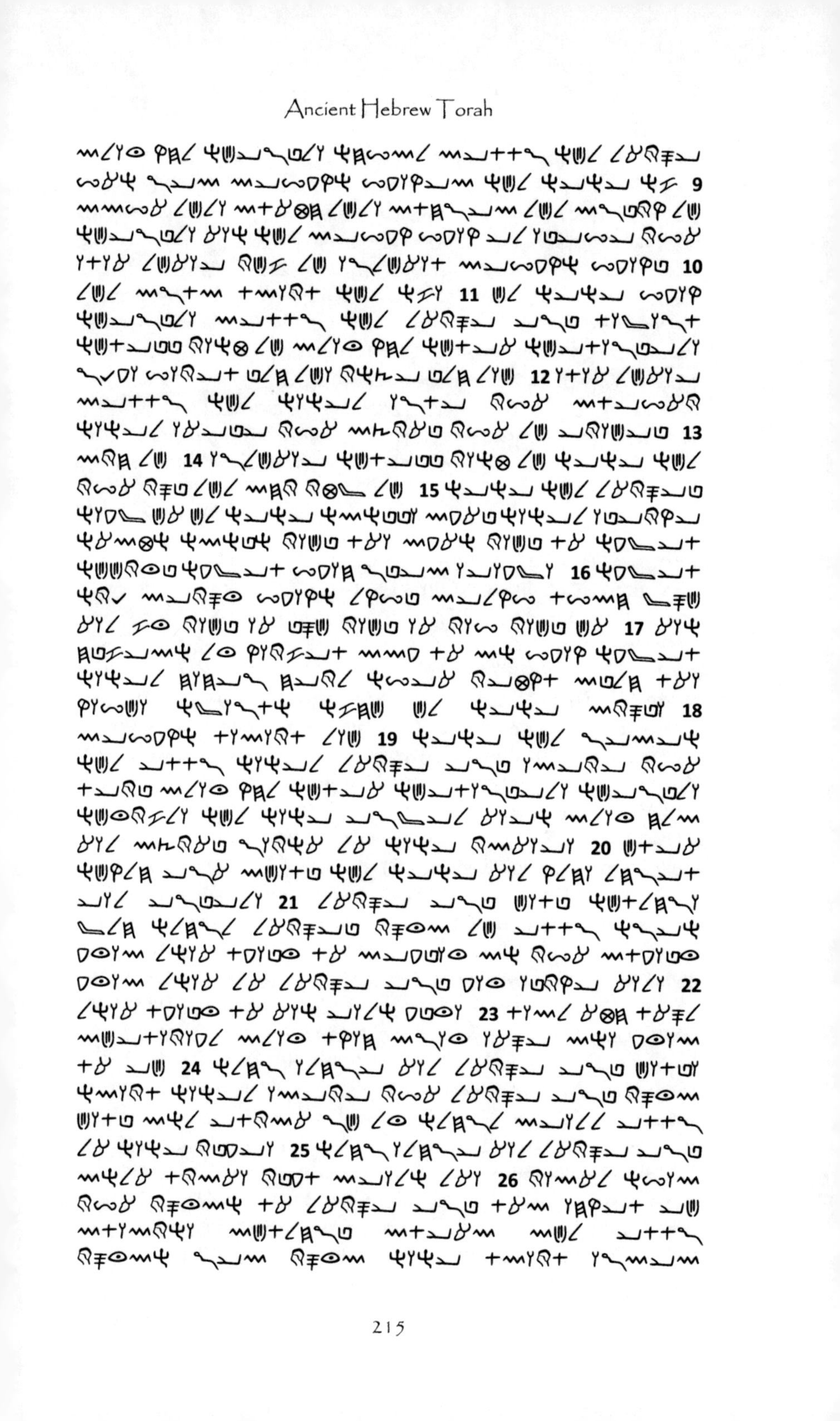

27 ונחשב לכם תרומתכם כדגן מין הגורן
וכמלאה מין היק 28 כן תרימו גם אתם תרומת
יהוה מיכול מעסרותיכם אשר תיקחו מאת
בני יסראל ונתתם מימנו את תרומת יהוה
לאהרון הכוהן 29 מיכול מתנותיכם תרימו את
כל תרומת יהוה מיכל חלבו את מיקדשו מימנו
30 ואמרת אלהם בהרימכם את חלבו מימנו
ונחשב ללוים כיתבואת גורן וכיתבואת יק
31 ואכלתם אותו בכל מקום אתם וביתכם כי סכר
הוא לכם חלף עבודתכם באוהל מועד 32 ולוא תיסאו
עליו חטא בהרימכם את חלבו מימנו ואת קדשי
בני יסראל לוא תחללו ולוא תמותו

במידבר פרק 19

1 וידבר יהוה אל מושה ואל אהרון לאמור 2 זואת
חוקת התורה אשר ציוה יהוה לאמור דבר אל בני
יסראל וייקחו אליכה פרה אדומה תמימה
אשר אין בה מום אשר לוא עלה עליה עול
3 ונתתם אותה אל אלעזר הכוהן והוציא אותה אל
מיחוץ למחנה ושחט אותה לפניו 4 ולקח אלעזר
הכוהן מידמה באצבעו והיזה אל נוכח פני
אוהל מועד מידמה שבע פעמים 5 וסרף את
הפרה לעיניו את עורה ואת בסרה ואת דמה על
פירשה יסרו 6 ולקח הכוהן עץ ארז ואזוב
ושני תולעת והישליך אל תוך סרפת הפרה
7 וכיבס בגדיו הכוהן ורחץ בסרו במיים ואחר
יבוא אל המחנה וטמא הכוהן עד הער 8 והסורף
אותה יכבס בגדיו במיים ורחץ בסרו במיים
וטמא עד הער 9 ואסף איש טהור את אפר הפרה
והיניח מיחוץ למחנה במקום טהור והיתה
לעדת בני יסראל למשמרת למי נידה חטאת
הוא 10 וכיבס האסף את אפר הפרה את בגדיו
וטמא עד הערב והיתה לבני יסראל ולגר הגר
בתוכם לחוקת עולם 11 הנוגע במת לכל נפש אדם
וטמא שיבעת ימים 12 הוא יתחטא בו ביום
השלישי ביום השביעי יטהר ואים לוא
יתחטא ביום השלישי ביום השביעי לוא
יטהר 13 כל הנוגע במת בנפש האדם אשר ימות
ולוא יתחטא את מישכן יהוה טימא וניכרתה
הנפש ההיוא מיסראל כי מי נידה לוא זורק

14

15

16

17

18

19

20

21

22

20

1

2

3

4

5

6

7 8

9

10

להם שמעו נא המורים המן הסלע הזה
נוציא לכם מים 11 וירם משה את ידו ויך
את הסלע במטהו פעמים ויצאו מים
רבים ותשת העדה ובעירם 12 ויאמר יהוה אל
משה ואל אהרן יען לוא האמנתם בי
להקדישני לעיני בני ישראל לכן לוא
תביאו את הקהל הזה אל הארץ אשר נתתי להם
13 המה מי מריבה אשר רבו בני ישראל את
יהוה ויקדש בם 14 וישלח משה מלאכים
מקדש אל מלך אדום כה אמר אחיך ישראל
אתה ידעת את כל התלאה אשר מצאתנו 15 וירדו
אבותינו מצרימה ונשב במצרים
ימים רבים וירעו לנו מצרים
ולאבותינו 16 ונצעק אל יהוה וישמע קלנו
וישלח מלאך ויצאנו ממצרים
והנה אנחנו בקדש עיר קצה גבולך 17 נעברה
נא בארצך לוא נעבר בשדה ובכרם ולוא נשתה
מי באר דרך המלך נלך לוא נטה ימין
ושמאול עד אשר נעבר גבולך 18 ויאמר אליו
אדום לוא תעבור בי פן בחרב אצא לקראתך
19 ויאמרו אליו בני ישראל במסלה נעלה
ואם מימיך נשתה אני ומקני
ונתתי מכרם רק אין דבר ברגלי אעבורה
20 ויאמר לוא תעבור ויצא אדום לקראתו בעם
כבד וביד חזקה 21 וימאן אדום נתן את ישראל
עבור בגבולו ויט ישראל מעליו 22 ויסעו
מקדש ויבואו בני ישראל כל העדה הור ההר
23 ויאמר יהוה אל משה ואל אהרן בהור ההר
על גבול ארץ אדום לאמר 24 יאסף אהרן אל
עמיו כי לוא יבוא אל הארץ אשר נתתי
לבני ישראל על אשר מריתם את פי למי
מריבה 25 קח את אהרן ואת אלעזר בנו והעל
אתם הור ההר 26 והפשט את אהרן את בגדיו
והלבשתם את אלעזר בנו ואהרן יאסף ומת
שם 27 ויעש משה כאשר צוה יהוה ויעלו אל
הור ההר לעיני כל העדה 28 ויפשט משה את
אהרן את בגדיו וילבש אתם את אלעזר בנו
וימת אהרן שם בראש ההר וירד משה ואלעזר
מן ההר 29 ויראו כל העדה כי גוע אהרן
ויבכו את אהרן שלשים יום כל בית ישראל

במידבר פרק 21

1 וישמע הכנעני מלך ערד יושב הנגב כי בא
יסראל דרך האתרים וילחם ביסראל וישב
מימנו שבי 2 וידר יסראל נדר ליהוה
ויואמר אים נתון תיתן את העם הזה בידי
והחרמתי את עריהם 3 וישמע יהוה בקול
יסראל ויתן את הכנעני ויחרם אתהם ואת
עריהם ויקרא שם המקום חרמה 4 ויסעו מהור
ההר דרך ים סוף ליסבוב את ארץ אדום ותיקצר
נפש העם בדרך 5 וידבר העם באלוהים
ובמושה למה העליתינו מימיצריים למות
במידבר כי אין לחם ואין מיים ונפשנו
קצה בלחם הקלוקל 6 וישלח יהוה בעם את
הנחשים הסרפים וינשכו את העם וימת עם
רב מיסראל 7 ויבוא העם אל מושה ויואמרו
חטאנו כי דיברנו ביהוה ובך היתפלל אל יהוה
ויסר מעלינו את הנחש ויתפלל מושה בעד
העם 8 ויואמר יהוה אל מושה עסה לכה סרף
וסים אותו על נס והיה כל הנשוך וראה אותו וחי
9 ויעס מושה נחש נחושת ויסימהו על הנס
והיה אים נשך הנחש את איש והיביט אל
נחש הנחושת וחי 10 ויסעו בני יסראל ויחנו
באובות 11 ויסעו מאובות ויחנו בעיי העבריים
במידבר אשר על פני מואב מימיזרח
השמש 12 מישם נסעו ויחנו בנחל זרד
13 מישם נסעו ויחנו מעבר ארנון אשר
במידבר היוצא מיגבול האמורי כי ארנון
גבול מואב בין מואב ובין האמורי 14 על כן
יאמר בספר מילחמות יהוה את והב בסופה ואת
הנחלים ארנון 15 ואשד הנחלים אשר נטה
לשבת ער ונישען ליגבול מוא 16 ומישם
בארה היוא הבאר אשר אמר יהוה למושה אסוף
את העם ואתנה להם מיים 17 אז יישיר
יסראל את השירה הזואת עלי באר ענו לה
18 באר חפרוה סרים כרוה נדיבי העם בימחוקק
במישענותם ומימידבר מתנה 19 ומימתנה
נחליאל ומינחליאל במות 20 ומיבמות הגיא
אשר ביסדה מואב רואש הפסגה ונשקפה על
פני הישימון 21 וישלח יסראל מלאכים
אל סיחון מלך האמורי לאמור 22 אעברה

23

24

25

26

27

28

29

30

31

32

33

34

35

22

1

2

3

4

5

[illegible] 6
[illegible]
[illegible]
[illegible] 7 [illegible]
[illegible]
[illegible] 8 [illegible]
[illegible]
[illegible] 9 [illegible]
[illegible]
[illegible] 10 [illegible]
[illegible] 11 [illegible]
[illegible]
[illegible]
[illegible] 12 [illegible]
[illegible]
[illegible] 13
[illegible]
[illegible] 14 [illegible]
[illegible] 15 [illegible]
[illegible]
[illegible] 16
[illegible] 17 [illegible]
[illegible]
[illegible] 18 [illegible]
[illegible]
[illegible]
[illegible] 19 [illegible]
[illegible]
[illegible] 20
[illegible]
[illegible]
[illegible] 21
[illegible] 22 [illegible]
[illegible]
[illegible] 23 [illegible]
[illegible]
[illegible]
[illegible] 24 [illegible]
[illegible]
[illegible] 25
[illegible]

26 ויוסף מלאך יהוה עבור ויעמד במקום צר
אשר אין דרך לנטות ימין ושמאול 27 ותרא
האתון את מלאך יהוה ותרבץ תחת בלעם ויחר
אף בלעם ויך את האתון במקל 28 ויפתח
יהוה את פי האתון ותאמר לבלעם מה
עשיתי לך כי הכיתני זה שלש רגלים
29 ויאמר בלעם לאתון כי התעללת בי לו
יש חרב בידי כי עתה הרגתיך 30 ותאמר
האתון אל בלעם הלוא אנכי אתנך אשר
רכבת עלי מעודך עד היום הזה ההסכן
הסכנתי לעשות לך כה ויאמר לא 31 ויגל
יהוה את עיני בלעם וירא את מלאך יהוה
נצב בדרך וחרבו שלפה בידו ויקד וישתחו
לאפיו 32 ויאמר אליו מלאך יהוה על מה
הכית את אתנך זה שלוש רגלים הנה
אנכי יצאתי לשטן כי ירט הדרך לנגדי
33 ותראני האתון ותט לפני זה שלש
רגלים אולי נטתה מפני כי עתה גם
אתכה הרגתי ואותה החייתי 34 ויאמר
בלעם אל מלאך יהוה חטאתי כי לא ידעתי
כי אתה נצב לקראתי בדרך ועתה אם רע
בעיניך אשובה לי 35 ויאמר מלאך יהוה אל
בלעם לך עם האנשים ואפס את הדבר אשר
אדבר אליך אתו תדבר וילך בלעם עם שרי
בלק 36 וישמע בלק כי בא בלעם ויצא
לקראתו אל עיר מואב אשר על גבול ארנן אשר
בקצה הגבול 37 ויאמר בלק אל בלעם הלא
שלח שלחתי אליך לקרא לך למה לא הלכת
אלי האמנם לא אוכל כבדך 38 ויאמר
בלעם אל בלק הנה באתי אליך עתה היכל
אוכל דבר מאומה הדבר אשר ישים אלהים
בפי אתו אדבר 39 וילך בלעם עם בלק
ויבאו קרית חצות 40 ויזבח בלק בקר וצאן
וישלח לבלעם ולשרים אשר אתו 41 ויהי
בבקר ויקח בלק את בלעם ויעלהו במות בעל
וירא משם קצה העם

במדבר פרק 23

1 ויאמר בלעם אל בלק בנה לי בזה שבעה
מזבחת והכן לי בזה שבעה פרים
ושבעה אילים 2 ויעש בלק כאשר דבר

בילעם ויעל בלק ובילעם פר ואייל במיזבח
3 ויואמר בילעם לבלק היתיצב על עולתכה
ואלכה אולי יקרה יהוה ליקראתי ודבר מה
יראני והיגדתי לך וילך שפי 4 ויקר
אלוהים אל בילעם ויואמר אליו את שיבעת
המיזבחות ערכתי ואעל פר ואייל במיזבח
5 וישם יהוה דבר בפי בילעם ויואמר שוב אל
בלק וכוה תדבר 6 וישב אליו והינה ניצב על
עולתו הוא וכל שרי מואב 7 וישא משלו ויואמר
מין ארם ינחני בלק מלך מואב מהררי קדם
לכה ארה לי יעקוב ולכה זועמה ישראל 8 מה
אקוב לוא קבוה אל ומה אזעום לוא זעם יהוה 9 כי
מרואש צורים אראנו ומיגבעות אשורנו הן
עם לבדד ישכון ובגויים לוא יתחשב 10 מי
מנה עפר יעקוב ומספר את רבע ישראל
תמות נפשי מות ישרים ותהי אחריתי
כמוהו 11 ויואמר בלק אל בילעם מה עשית לי
לקוב אויבי לקחתיכה והינה ברכת ברך 12 ויען
ויואמר הלוא את אשר ישים יהוה בפי אותו
אשמור לדבר 13 ויואמר אליו בלק לכה נא איתי
אל מקום אחר אשר תיראנו מישם אפס קצהו
תיראה וכולו לוא תיראה וקבנו לי מישם
14 ויקחהו שדה צפים אל רואש הפיסגה ויבן
שיבעה מיזבחות ויעל פר ואייל במיזבח
15 ויואמר אל בלק היתיצב כוה על עולתכה
ואנוכי איקרה כוה 16 ויקר יהוה אל בילעם
וישם דבר בפיו ויואמר שוב אל בלק וכוה תדבר
17 ויבוא אליו והינו ניצב על עולתו ושרי
מואב איתו ויואמר לו בלק מה דבר יהוה
18 וישא משלו ויואמר קום בלק ושמע האזינה
עדי בנו ציפור 19 לוא איש אל ויכזב ובן אדם
ויתנחם ההוא אמר ולוא יעשה ודבר ולוא
יקימנה 20 הינה ברך לקחתי וברך ולוא
אשיבנה 21 לוא הביט און ביעקוב ולוא ראה
עמל בישראל יהוה אלוהיו עימו ותרועת מלך בו
22 אל מוציאם מימיצריים כתועפות ראם
לו 23 כי לוא נחש ביעקוב ולוא קסם בישראל כעת
יאמר ליעקוב ולישראל מה פעל אל 24 הן עם
כלביא יקום וכארי יתנשא לוא ישכב עד
יאכל טרף ודם חללים ישתה 25 ויואמר בלק
אל בילעם גם קוב לוא תיקבנו גם ברך לוא

𐤕𐤁𐤓𐤊𐤍𐤅 26 𐤅𐤉𐤏𐤍 𐤁𐤉𐤋𐤏𐤌 𐤅𐤉𐤅𐤀𐤌𐤓 𐤀𐤋 𐤁𐤋𐤒 𐤄𐤋𐤅𐤀
𐤃𐤉𐤁𐤓𐤕𐤉 𐤀𐤋𐤉𐤊𐤄 𐤋𐤀𐤌𐤅𐤓 𐤊𐤅𐤋 𐤀𐤔𐤓 𐤉𐤃𐤁𐤓 𐤉𐤄𐤅𐤄 𐤀𐤅𐤕𐤅
𐤀𐤏𐤎𐤄 27 𐤅𐤉𐤅𐤀𐤌𐤓 𐤁𐤋𐤒 𐤀𐤋 𐤁𐤉𐤋𐤏𐤌 𐤋𐤊𐤄 𐤍𐤀 𐤀𐤒𐤇𐤊𐤄
𐤀𐤋 𐤌𐤒𐤅𐤌 𐤀𐤇𐤓 𐤀𐤅𐤋𐤉 𐤉𐤉𐤔𐤓 𐤁𐤏𐤉𐤍𐤉 𐤄𐤀𐤋𐤅𐤄𐤉𐤌
𐤅𐤒𐤁𐤅𐤕𐤅 𐤋𐤉 𐤌𐤉𐤔𐤌 28 𐤅𐤉𐤒𐤇 𐤁𐤋𐤒 𐤀𐤕 𐤁𐤉𐤋𐤏𐤌 𐤓𐤅𐤀𐤔
𐤄𐤐𐤏𐤅𐤓 𐤄𐤍𐤉𐤔𐤒𐤐 𐤏𐤋 𐤐𐤍𐤉 𐤄𐤉𐤔𐤉𐤌𐤅𐤍
29 𐤅𐤉𐤅𐤀𐤌𐤓 𐤁𐤉𐤋𐤏𐤌 𐤀𐤋 𐤁𐤋𐤒 𐤁𐤍𐤄 𐤋𐤉 𐤁𐤆𐤄 𐤔𐤉𐤁𐤏𐤄
𐤌𐤉𐤆𐤁𐤇𐤅𐤕 𐤅𐤄𐤊𐤍 𐤋𐤉 𐤁𐤆𐤄 𐤔𐤉𐤁𐤏𐤄 𐤐𐤓𐤉𐤌
𐤅𐤔𐤉𐤁𐤏𐤄 𐤀𐤉𐤋𐤉𐤌 30 𐤅𐤉𐤏𐤎 𐤁𐤋𐤒 𐤊𐤀𐤔𐤓 𐤀𐤌𐤓
𐤁𐤉𐤋𐤏𐤌 𐤅𐤉𐤏𐤋 𐤐𐤓 𐤅𐤀𐤉𐤉𐤋 𐤁𐤌𐤉𐤆𐤁𐤇

𐤁𐤌𐤉𐤃𐤁𐤓 𐤐𐤓𐤒 24

1 𐤅𐤉𐤓𐤀 𐤁𐤉𐤋𐤏𐤌 𐤊𐤉 𐤈𐤅𐤁 𐤁𐤏𐤉𐤍𐤉 𐤉𐤄𐤅𐤄 𐤋𐤁𐤓𐤊 𐤀𐤕
𐤉𐤎𐤓𐤀𐤋 𐤅𐤋𐤅𐤀 𐤄𐤋𐤊 𐤊𐤐𐤏𐤌 𐤁𐤐𐤏𐤌 𐤋𐤉𐤒𐤓𐤀𐤕 𐤍𐤇𐤔𐤉𐤌
𐤅𐤉𐤔𐤕 𐤀𐤋 𐤄𐤌𐤉𐤃𐤁𐤓 𐤐𐤍𐤉𐤅 2 𐤅𐤉𐤎𐤀 𐤁𐤉𐤋𐤏𐤌 𐤀𐤕
𐤏𐤉𐤍𐤉𐤅 𐤅𐤉𐤓𐤀 𐤀𐤕 𐤉𐤎𐤓𐤀𐤋 𐤔𐤅𐤊𐤍 𐤋𐤉𐤔𐤁𐤈𐤉𐤅 𐤅𐤕𐤄𐤉
𐤏𐤋𐤉𐤅 𐤓𐤅𐤇 𐤀𐤋𐤅𐤄𐤉𐤌 3 𐤅𐤉𐤎𐤀 𐤌𐤔𐤋𐤅 𐤅𐤉𐤅𐤀𐤌𐤓 𐤍𐤀𐤅𐤌
𐤁𐤉𐤋𐤏𐤌 𐤁𐤍𐤅 𐤁𐤏𐤅𐤓 𐤅𐤍𐤀𐤅𐤌 𐤄𐤂𐤁𐤓 𐤔𐤕𐤅𐤌 𐤄𐤏𐤉𐤉𐤍
4 𐤍𐤀𐤅𐤌 𐤔𐤅𐤌𐤏 𐤀𐤉𐤌𐤓𐤉 𐤀𐤋 𐤀𐤔𐤓 𐤌𐤇𐤆𐤄 𐤔𐤃𐤉
𐤉𐤇𐤆𐤄 𐤍𐤅𐤐𐤋 𐤅𐤂𐤋𐤅𐤉 𐤏𐤉𐤍𐤉𐤉𐤌 5 𐤌𐤄 𐤈𐤅𐤁𐤅
𐤀𐤅𐤄𐤋𐤉𐤊𐤄 𐤉𐤏𐤒𐤅𐤁 𐤌𐤉𐤔𐤊𐤍𐤅𐤕𐤉𐤊𐤄 𐤉𐤎𐤓𐤀𐤋
6 𐤊𐤉𐤍𐤇𐤋𐤉𐤌 𐤍𐤉𐤈𐤉𐤅 𐤊𐤂𐤍𐤅𐤕 𐤏𐤋𐤉 𐤍𐤄𐤓 𐤊𐤀𐤄𐤋𐤉𐤌
𐤍𐤈𐤏 𐤉𐤄𐤅𐤄 𐤊𐤀𐤓𐤆𐤉𐤌 𐤏𐤋𐤉 𐤌𐤉𐤉𐤌 7 𐤉𐤆𐤋
𐤌𐤉𐤉𐤌 𐤌𐤉𐤃𐤋𐤉𐤅 𐤅𐤆𐤓𐤏𐤅 𐤁𐤌𐤉𐤉𐤌 𐤓𐤁𐤉𐤌 𐤅𐤉𐤓𐤅𐤌
𐤌𐤀𐤂𐤂 𐤌𐤋𐤊𐤅 𐤅𐤕𐤉𐤍𐤎𐤀 𐤌𐤋𐤊𐤅𐤕𐤅 8 𐤀𐤋 𐤌𐤅𐤑𐤉𐤀𐤅
𐤌𐤉𐤌𐤉𐤑𐤓𐤉𐤉𐤌 𐤊𐤕𐤅𐤏𐤐𐤅𐤕 𐤓𐤀𐤌 𐤋𐤅 𐤉𐤅𐤀𐤊𐤋
𐤂𐤅𐤉𐤉𐤌 𐤑𐤓𐤉𐤅 𐤅𐤏𐤑𐤌𐤅𐤕𐤉𐤄𐤌 𐤉𐤂𐤓𐤌 𐤅𐤇𐤉𐤑𐤉𐤅
𐤉𐤌𐤇𐤑 9 𐤊𐤓𐤏 𐤔𐤊𐤁 𐤊𐤀𐤓𐤉 𐤅𐤊𐤋𐤁𐤉𐤀 𐤌𐤉 𐤉𐤒𐤉𐤌𐤍𐤅
𐤌𐤁𐤓𐤊𐤉𐤊𐤄 𐤁𐤓𐤅𐤊 𐤅𐤀𐤅𐤓𐤓𐤉𐤊𐤄 𐤀𐤓𐤅𐤓 10 𐤅𐤉𐤇𐤓 𐤀𐤐 𐤁𐤋𐤒
𐤀𐤋 𐤁𐤉𐤋𐤏𐤌 𐤅𐤉𐤎𐤐𐤅𐤒 𐤀𐤕 𐤊𐤐𐤉𐤅 𐤅𐤉𐤅𐤀𐤌𐤓 𐤁𐤋𐤒 𐤀𐤋
𐤁𐤉𐤋𐤏𐤌 𐤋𐤒𐤁 𐤀𐤅𐤉𐤁𐤉 𐤒𐤓𐤀𐤕𐤉𐤊𐤄 𐤅𐤄𐤉𐤍𐤄 𐤁𐤓𐤊𐤕 𐤁𐤓𐤊
𐤆𐤄 𐤔𐤋𐤅𐤔 𐤐𐤏𐤌𐤉𐤌 11 𐤅𐤏𐤕𐤄 𐤁𐤓𐤇 𐤋𐤊𐤄 𐤀𐤋 𐤌𐤒𐤅𐤌𐤊𐤄
𐤀𐤌𐤓𐤕𐤉 𐤊𐤁𐤃 𐤀𐤊𐤁𐤃𐤊𐤄 𐤅𐤄𐤉𐤍𐤄 𐤌𐤍𐤏𐤊𐤄 𐤉𐤄𐤅𐤄
𐤌𐤉𐤊𐤁𐤅𐤃 12 𐤅𐤉𐤅𐤀𐤌𐤓 𐤁𐤉𐤋𐤏𐤌 𐤀𐤋 𐤁𐤋𐤒 𐤄𐤋𐤅𐤀 𐤂𐤌 𐤀𐤋
𐤌𐤋𐤀𐤊𐤉𐤊𐤄 𐤀𐤔𐤓 𐤔𐤋𐤇𐤕 𐤀𐤋𐤉 𐤃𐤉𐤁𐤓𐤕𐤉 𐤋𐤀𐤌𐤅𐤓
13 𐤀𐤉𐤌 𐤉𐤕𐤍 𐤋𐤉 𐤁𐤋𐤒 𐤌𐤋𐤅𐤀 𐤁𐤉𐤕𐤅 𐤊𐤎𐤐 𐤅𐤆𐤄𐤁 𐤋𐤅𐤀
𐤀𐤅𐤊𐤋 𐤋𐤏𐤁𐤅𐤓 𐤀𐤕 𐤐𐤉 𐤉𐤄𐤅𐤄 𐤋𐤏𐤎𐤅𐤕 𐤈𐤅𐤁𐤄 𐤀𐤅 𐤓𐤏𐤄
𐤌𐤉𐤋𐤉𐤁𐤉 𐤀𐤔𐤓 𐤉𐤃𐤁𐤓 𐤉𐤄𐤅𐤄 𐤀𐤅𐤕𐤅 𐤀𐤃𐤁𐤓 14 𐤅𐤏𐤕𐤄
𐤄𐤉𐤍𐤍𐤉 𐤄𐤅𐤋𐤊 𐤋𐤏𐤌𐤉 𐤋𐤊𐤄 𐤀𐤉𐤏𐤑𐤊𐤄 𐤀𐤔𐤓 𐤉𐤏𐤎𐤄
𐤄𐤏𐤌 𐤄𐤆𐤄 𐤋𐤏𐤌𐤊𐤄 𐤁𐤀𐤇𐤓𐤉𐤕 𐤄𐤉𐤌𐤉𐤌 15 𐤅𐤉𐤎𐤀

16
17
18
19
20
21
22
23
24
25

25

1
2
3
4
5
6
7
8
9
10
11

[illegible] 12 [illegible]
[illegible] 13 [illegible]
[illegible]
[illegible] 14 [illegible]
[illegible]
[illegible] 15 [illegible]
[illegible]
[illegible] 16 [illegible]
[illegible] 17 [illegible]
[illegible] 18 [illegible]
[illegible]
[illegible]
[illegible] 19 [illegible]

26 [illegible]

[illegible] 1
[illegible] 2 [illegible]
[illegible]
[illegible] 3 [illegible]
[illegible]
[illegible] 4
[illegible]
[illegible] 5 [illegible]
[illegible]
[illegible] 6 [illegible]
[illegible] 7 [illegible]
[illegible]
[illegible] 9 [illegible] 8 [illegible]
[illegible]
[illegible]
[illegible] 10 [illegible]
[illegible]
[illegible]
[illegible] 12 [illegible] 11
[illegible]
[illegible]
[illegible] 13 [illegible]
[illegible] 14 [illegible]
[illegible]
[illegible] 15 [illegible]

[illegible]
[illegible] 16 [illegible]
[illegible]
[illegible] 17
[illegible] 18 [illegible]
[illegible]
[illegible] 19
[illegible] 20 [illegible]
[illegible]
[illegible] 21 [illegible]
[illegible]
[illegible] 22 [illegible]
[illegible]
[illegible] 23 [illegible]
[illegible]
[illegible] 24
[illegible] 25 [illegible]
[illegible]
[illegible] 26 [illegible]
[illegible]
[illegible] 27 [illegible]
[illegible]
[illegible] 28 [illegible]
[illegible] 29 [illegible]
[illegible]
[illegible] 30 [illegible]
[illegible]
[illegible] 31 [illegible]
[illegible]
[illegible] 32
[illegible] 33 [illegible]
[illegible]
[illegible] 34 [illegible]
[illegible]
[illegible] 35 [illegible]
[illegible]
[illegible]
[illegible] 36
[illegible] 37
[illegible]
[illegible] 38 [illegible]

בינימין למישפחותם לבלע מישפחת
הבלעי לאשבל מישפחת האשבלי לאחירם
מישפחת האחירמי 39 לישפופם
מישפחת השופמי לחופם מישפחת
החופמי 40 ויהיו בני בלע ארד ונעמן
מישפחת הארדי לנעמן מישפחת הנעמי
41 אלה בני בינימין למישפחותם
ופקודיהם חמישה וארבעים אלף ושש מאות
42 אלה בני דן למישפחותם לשוחם מישפחת
השוחמי אלה מישפחות דן למישפחותם
43 כל מישפחות השוחמי ליפקודיהם ארבעה
ושישים אלף וארבע מאות 44 בני אשר
למישפחותם ליימנה מישפחת הימנה
ליישוי מישפחת הישוי ליבריעה
מישפחת הבריעי 45 ליבני בריעה לחבר
מישפחת החברי למלכיאל מישפחת
המלכיאלי 46 ושם בת אשר סרח 47 אלה
מישפחות בני אשר ליפקודיהם שלושה
וחמישים אלף וארבע מאות 48 בני נפתלי
למישפחותם ליחצאל מישפחת היחצאלי
לגוני מישפחת הגוני 49 ליצר מישפחת
היצרי לשילם מישפחת השילמי 50 אלה
מישפחות נפתלי למישפחותם ופקודיהם
חמישה וארבעים אלף וארבע מאות 51 אלה
פקודי בני יסראל שש מאות אלף ואלף שבע
מאות ושלושים 52 וידבר יהוה אל מושה לאמור
53 לאלה תחלק הארץ בנחלה במיספר שמות
54 לרב תרבה נחלתו ולמעט תמעיט נחלתו איש
לפי פקודיו יתן נחלתו 55 אךבגורל יחלק את
הארץ לשמות מטות אבותם ינחלו 56 על פי
הגורל תחלק נחלתו בין רב לימעט 57 ואלה
פקודי הלוי למישפחותם לגרשון מישפחת
הגרשוני ליקהת מישפחת הקהתי לימררי
מישפחת המררי 58 אלה מישפחות לוי
מישפחת הליבני מישפחת החברוני
מישפחת המחלי מישפחת המושי
מישפחת הקרחי וקהת הוליד את עמרם 59 ושם
אשת עמרם יוכבד בת לוי אשר ילדה אותה ללוי
במיצרים ותלד לעמרם את אהרון ואת מושה
ואת מירים אחותם 60 ויולד לאהרון את נדב ואת
אביהוא את אלעזר ואת איתמר 61 וימת נדב

62

63

64

65

27

1

2

3

4

5

6

7

8

9

10

11

12

13

14

15

אל יהוה לאמור 16 יפקוד יהוה אלוהי הרוחות
לכל בסר איש על העדה 17 אשר יצא ליפניהם
ואשר יבוא ליפניהם ואשר יוציאם ואשר
יביאם ולוא תהיה עדת יהוה כצואן אשר
אין להם רועה 18 ויואמר יהוה אל מושה קח
לכה את יהושוע בין נון איש אשר רוח בו
וסמכת את ידכה עליו 19 והעמדת אותו ליפני
אלעזר הכוהן וליפני כל העדה וציויתה אותו
לעיניהם 20 ונתתה מהודכה עליו למען
ישמעו כל עדת בני יסראל 21 וליפני
אלעזר הכוהן יעמוד ושאל לו במישפט
האורים ליפני יהוה על פיו יצאו ועל
פיו יבואו הוא וכל בני יסראל איתו וכל העדה
22 ויעס מושה כאשר ציוה יהוה אותו ויקח את
יהושוע ויעמידהו ליפני אלעזר הכוהן
וליפני כל העדה 23 ויסמוך את ידיו עליו
ויצוהו כאשר דבר יהוה ביד מושה

במידבר פרק 28

1 וידבר יהוה אל מושה לאמור 2 צו את בני
יסראל ואמרת אליהם את קרבני לחמי לאישי
ריח ניחוחי תישמרו להקריב לי במועדו
3 ואמרת להם זה האישה אשר תקריבו ליהוה
כבסים בני שנה תמימים שניים ליום
עולה תמיד 4 את הכבס אחד תעסה בבוקר ואת הכבס
השני תעסה בין הערביים 5 ועסירית
האיפה סולת למינחה בלולה בשמן כתית
רביעית ההין 6 עולת תמיד העסויה בהר
סיני לריח ניחוח אישה ליהוה 7 וניסכו
רביעית ההין לכבס האחד בקודש הסך נסך שכר
ליהוה 8 ואת הכבס השני תעסה בין הערביים
כמינחת הבוקר וכניסכו תעסה אישה ריח
ניחוח ליהוה 9 וביום השבת שני כבסים בני
שנה תמימים ושני עסרונים סולת מינחה
בלולה בשמן וניסכו 10 עולת שבת בשבתו על עולת
התמיד וניסכה 11 ובראשי חדשיכם תקריבו
עולה ליהוה פרים בני בקר שניים ואייל
אחד כבסים בני שנה שיבעה תמימים
12 ושלושה עסרונים סולת מינחה בלולה בשמן
לפר האחד ושני עסרונים סולת מינחה בלולה

[illegible] 13 [illegible]
[illegible]
[illegible] 14 [illegible]
[illegible]
[illegible]
[illegible] 15 [illegible]
[illegible]
[illegible] 16
[illegible] 17 [illegible]
[illegible] 18 [illegible]
[illegible]
[illegible] 19
[illegible]
[illegible] 20 [illegible]
[illegible]
[illegible] 21 [illegible]
[illegible] 22 [illegible]
[illegible] 23 [illegible]
[illegible] 24 [illegible]
[illegible]
[illegible] 25 [illegible]
[illegible]
[illegible] 26 [illegible]
[illegible]
[illegible]
[illegible] 27
[illegible]
[illegible] 28 [illegible]
[illegible]
[illegible] 29 [illegible]
[illegible] 30 [illegible]
[illegible] 31 [illegible]
[illegible]

29 [illegible]

[illegible] 1
[illegible]
[illegible] 2 [illegible]
[illegible]
[illegible] 3 [illegible]

24
25
26
27
28
29
30
31
32
33
34
35
36
37
38
39

30

1
2
3
4
5

אביה את נידרה ואסרה אשר אסרה על נפשה
והחריש לה אביה וקמו כל נדריה וכל איסר אשר
אסרה על נפשה יקום 6 ואים הניא אביה
אותה ביום שמעו כל נדריה ואסריה אשר אסרה
על נפשה לוא יקום ויהוה יסלח לה כי הניא
אביה אותה 7 ואים היו תיהיה לאיש
ונדריה עליה או מיבטא ספתיה אשר אסרה על
נפשה 8 ושמע אישה ביום שמעו והחריש לה
וקמו נדריה ואסרה אשר אסרה על נפשה יקומו
9 ואים ביום שמוע אישה יניא אותה והפר
את נידרה אשר עליה ואת מיבטא ספתיה אשר
אסרה על נפשה ויהוה יסלח לה 10 ונדר אלמנה
וגרושה כול אשר אסרה על נפשה יקום עליה
11 ואים בית אישה נדרה או אסרה איסר על
נפשה בישבועה 12 ושמע אישה והחריש לה
לוא הניא אותה וקמו כל נדריה וכל איסר אשר
אסרה על נפשה יקום 13 ואים הפר יפר
אותם אישה ביום שמעו כל מוצא ספתיה
לינדריה ולאיסר נפשה לוא יקום אישה
הפרם ויהוה יסלח לה 14 כל נדר וכל שבועת
איסר לענות נפש אישה יקימנו ואישה
יפרנו 15 ואים החרש יחריש לה אישה
מיום אל יום והקים את כל נדריה או את כל
איסריה אשר עליה הקים אותם כי החריש לה
ביום שמעו 16 ואים הפר יפר אותם אחרי
שמעו ונסא את עונה 17 אלה החוקים אשר ציוה
יהוה את מושה בין איש לאישתו בין אב
לביתו בנעוריה בית אביה

במידבר פרק 31

1 וידבר יהוה אל מושה לאמור 2 נקום ניקמת
בני יסראל מאת המידינים אחר תאסף אל
עמיכה 3 וידבר מושה אל העם לאמור החלצו
מאיתכם אנשים לצבא ויהיו על מידין
לתת ניקמת יהוה במידין 4 אלף למטה אלף
למטה לכול מטות יסראל תשלחו לצבא 5 וימסרו
מאלפי יסראל אלף למטה שנים עסר אלף
חלוצי צבא 6 וישלח אותם מושה אלף למטה
לצבא אותם ואת פינחס בן אלעזר הכוהן לצבא
וכלי הקודש וחצוצרות התרועה בידו 7 ויצבאו על
מידין כאשר ציוה יהוה את מושה ויהרגו כל

[illegible] 8 [illegible]
[illegible]
[illegible]
[illegible] 9
[illegible]
[illegible] 10 [illegible]
[illegible] 11 [illegible]
[illegible] 12 [illegible]
[illegible]
[illegible]
[illegible] 13 [illegible]
[illegible]
[illegible] 14 [illegible]
[illegible]
[illegible] 15 [illegible]
[illegible] 16 [illegible]
[illegible]
[illegible] 17 [illegible]
[illegible]
[illegible] 18
[illegible] 19 [illegible]
[illegible]
[illegible]
[illegible] 20 [illegible]
[illegible] 21 [illegible]
[illegible]
[illegible]
[illegible] 22 [illegible]
[illegible] 23 [illegible]
[illegible]
[illegible]
[illegible] 24 [illegible]
[illegible]
[illegible] 26 [illegible] 25
[illegible]
[illegible] 27 [illegible]
[illegible]
[illegible] 28 [illegible]
[illegible]
[illegible]
[illegible] 29 [illegible]

ונתתה לאלעזר הכוהן תרומת יהוה
30 ומימחצית בני יסראל תיקח אחד אחוז
מין החמישים מין האדם מין הבקר מין
החמורים ומין הצואן מיכל הבהמה ונתתה
אותם ללוים שומרי מישמרת מישכן יהוה
31 ויעס מושה ואלעזר הכוהן כאשר ציוה יהוה
את מושה 32 ויהי המלקוח יתר הבז אשר בזזו
עם הצבא צואן שש מאות אלף ושיבעים אלף
וחמשת אלפים 33 ובקר שניים ושיבעים
אל 34 וחמורים אחד ושישים אל 35 ונפש אדם
מין הנשים אשר לוא ידעו מישכב זכר כל
נפש שניים ושלושים אל 36 ותהי המחצה
חלק היוצאים בצבא מיספר הצואן שלוש
מאות אלף ושלושים אלף ושיבעת אלפים
וחמש מאות 37 ויהי המכס ליהוה מין הצואן
שש מאות חמש ושיבעים 38 והבקר שישה
ושלושים אלף ומיכסם ליהוה שניים
ושיבעים 39 וחמורים שלושים אלף וחמש
מאות ומיכסם ליהוה אחד ושישים 40 ונפש
אדם שישה עסר אלף ומיכסם ליהוה שניים
ושלושים נפש 41 ויתן מושה את מכס תרומת
יהוה לאלעזר הכוהן כאשר ציוה יהוה את
מושה 42 ומימחצית בני יסראל אשר חצה
מושה מין האנשים הצובאים 43 ותהי מחצת
העדה מין הצואן שלוש מאות אלף ושלושים
אלף שיבעת אלפים וחמש מאות 44 ובקר
שישה ושלושים אל 45 וחמורים שלושים
אלף וחמש מאות 46 ונפש אדם שישה עסר אל
47 ויקח מושה מימחצית בני יסראל את
האחוז אחד מין החמישים מין האדם ומין
הבהמה ויתן אותם ללוים שומרי מישמרת
מישכן יהוה כאשר ציוה יהוה את מושה
48 ויקרבו אל מושה הפקודים אשר לאלפי
הצבא סרי האלפים וסרי המאות 49 ויואמרו
אל מושה עבדיכה נסאו את רואש אנשי
המילחמה אשר בידנו ולוא ניפקד מימנו
איש 50 ונקרב את קרבן יהוה איש אשר מצא
כלי זהב אצעדה וצמיד טבעת עגיל וכומז
לכפר על נפשותינו לפני יהוה 51 ויקח
מושה ואלעזר הכוהן את הזהב מאיתם כול כלי
מעסה 52 ויהי כל זהב התרומה אשר הרימו

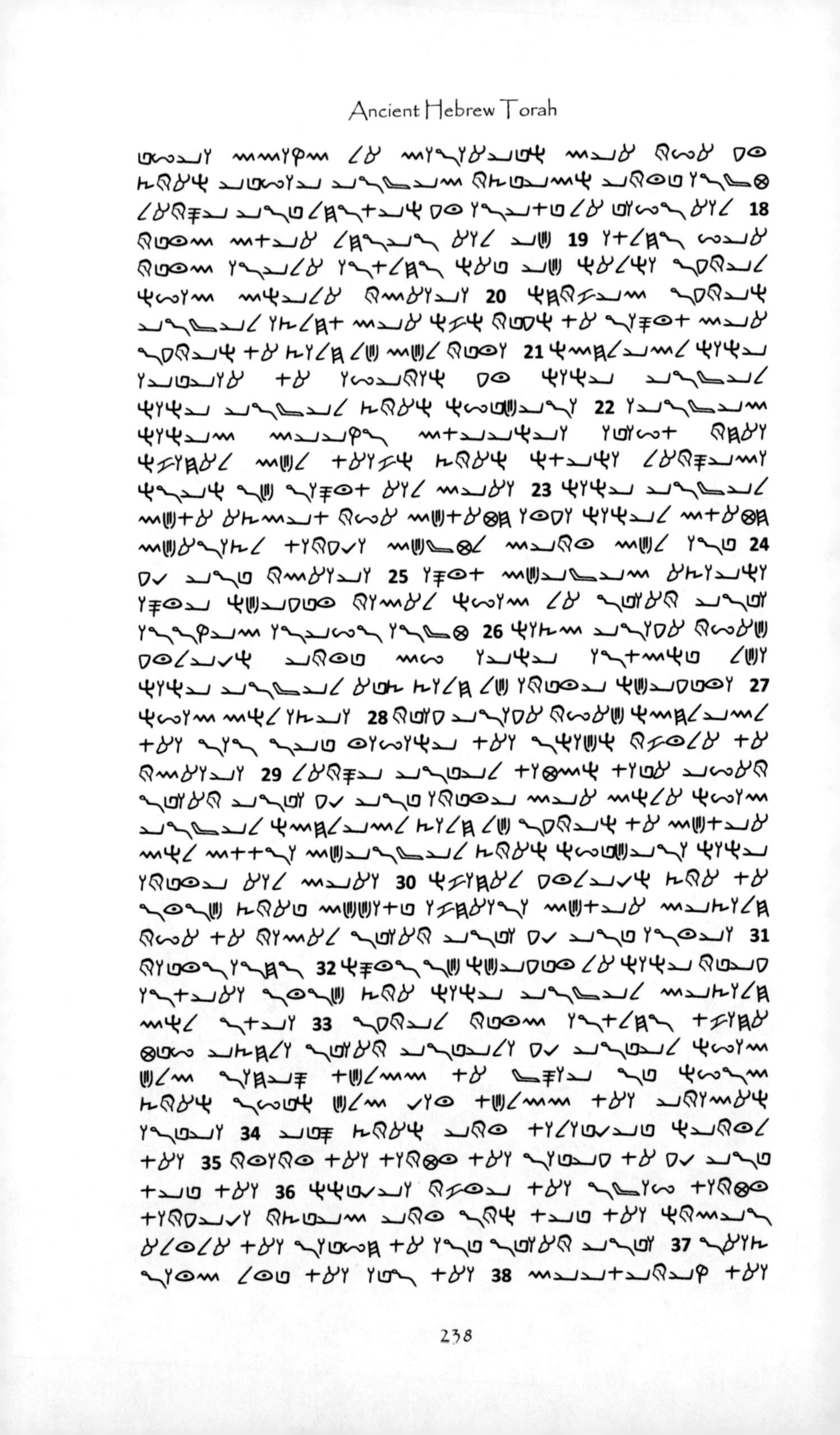

[illegible]
[illegible]
[illegible] 18
[illegible] 19 [illegible]
[illegible]
[illegible] 20 [illegible]
[illegible]
[illegible] 21 [illegible]
[illegible]
[illegible] 22 [illegible]
[illegible]
[illegible]
[illegible] 23 [illegible]
[illegible]
[illegible] 24
[illegible] 25 [illegible]
[illegible]
[illegible] 26 [illegible]
[illegible]
[illegible] 27
[illegible] 28 [illegible]
[illegible]
[illegible] 29 [illegible]
[illegible]
[illegible]
[illegible]
[illegible] 30 [illegible]
[illegible]
[illegible] 31
[illegible] 32 [illegible]
[illegible]
[illegible] 33 [illegible]
[illegible]
[illegible]
[illegible]
[illegible] 34 [illegible]
[illegible] 35 [illegible]
[illegible] 36 [illegible]
[illegible]
[illegible] 37 [illegible]
[illegible] 38 [illegible]

מוסבות שם ואת שיבמה ויקראו בשמות את שמות
הערים אשר בנו 39 וילכו בני מכיר בן
מנשה גילעדה וילכדוה ויורש את האמורי
אשר בה 40 ויתן מושה את הגילעד למכיר בן
מנשה וישב בה 41 ויאיר בן מנשה הלך
וילכוד את חותיהם ויקרא אתהן חות יאיר
42 ונובח הלך וילכוד את קנת ואת בנותיה ויקרא
לה נובח בישמו

במידבר פרק 33

1 אלה מסעי בני ישראל אשר יצאו מארץ
מיצריים לציבאותם ביד מושה ואהרון
2 ויכתוב מושה את מוצאיהם למסעיהם על
פי יהוה ואלה מסעיהם למוצאיהם 3 ויסעו
מרעמסס בחודש הראשון בחמישה עשר יום
לחודש הראשון ממחרת הפסח יצאו בני
ישראל ביד רמה לעיני כל מיצריים
4 ומיצריים מקברים את אשר הכה יהוה
בהם כל בכור ובאלהיהם עשה יהוה שפטים
5 ויסעו בני ישראל מרעמסס ויחנו בסוכות
6 ויסעו מסוכות ויחנו באתם אשר ביקצה
המידבר 7 ויסעו מאתם וישב על פי החירות
אשר על פני בעל צפון ויחנו לפני
מיגדול 8 ויסעו מפני החירות ויעברו בתוך
הים המידברה וילכו דרך שלושת ימים
במידבר אתם ויחנו במרה 9 ויסעו ממרה
ויבואו אילמה ובאילם שתים עשרה
עינות מים ושיבעים תמרים ויחנו שם
10 ויסעו מאילם ויחנו על ים סוף 11 ויסעו
מים סוף ויחנו במידבר סין 12 ויסעו
ממידבר סין ויחנו בדפקה 13 ויסעו
מדפקה ויחנו באלוש 14 ויסעו מאלוש ויחנו
ברפידים ולוא היה שם מים לעם
לשתות 15 ויסעו מרפידים ויחנו במידבר
סיני 16 ויסעו ממידבר סיני ויחנו
בקיברות התאוה 17 ויסעו מקיברות התאוה
ויחנו בחצרות 18 ויסעו מחצרות ויחנו בריתמה
19 ויסעו מריתמה ויחנו ברימון פרץ
20 ויסעו מרימון פרץ ויחנו בלבנה
21 ויסעו מלבנה ויחנו בריסה 22 ויסעו

מריסה ויחנו ביקהלתה 23 ויסעו מיקהלתה
ויחנו בהר שפר 24 ויסעו מהר שפר ויחנו
בחרדה 25 ויסעו מחרדה ויחנו במקהלות 26 ויסעו
מימקהלות ויחנו בתחת 27 ויסעו מיתחת ויחנו
בתרח 28 ויסעו מיתרח ויחנו במיתקה 29 ויסעו
מימיתקה ויחנו בחשמונה 30 ויסעו
מחשמונה ויחנו במוסרות 31 ויסעו מימוסרות
ויחנו ביבני יעקן 32 ויסעו מיבני יעקן
ויחנו בחור הגידגד 33 ויסעו מחור הגידגד
ויחנו ביטבתה 34 ויסעו מיטבתה ויחנו
בעברונה 35 ויסעו מעברונה ויחנו בעציון
גבר 36 ויסעו מעציון גבר ויחנו במידבר
צין היוא קדש 37 ויסעו מיקדש ויחנו בהור
ההר ביקצה ארץ אדום 38 ויעל אהרון הכוהן אל
הור ההר על פי יהוה וימת שם בישנת
הארבעים לצאת בני יסראל מארץ
מיצרים בחודש החמישי באחד לחודש
39 ואהרון בן שלוש ועסרים ומאת שנה במותו
בהור ההר 40 וישמע הכנעני מלך ערד והוא
יושב בנגב בארץ כנען בבוא בני יסראל
41 ויסעו מהור ההר ויחנו בצלמונה 42 ויסעו
מיצלמונה ויחנו בפונן 43 ויסעו מיפונן
ויחנו באובות 44 ויסעו מאובות ויחנו בעיי
העברים ביגבול מוא 45 ויסעו מעיים ויחנו
בדיבון גד 46 ויסעו מידיבון גד ויחנו
בעלמון דיבלתימה 47 ויסעו מעלמון
דיבלתימה ויחנו בהרי העברים ליפני
נבו 48 ויסעו מהרי העברים ויחנו בערבות
מואב על ירדן ירחו 49 ויחנו על הירדן
מיבית הישימות עד אבל השיטים בערבות
מוא 50 וידבר יהוה אל מושה בערבות מואב על
ירדן ירחו לאמור 51 דבר אל בני יסראל ואמרת
אלהם כי אתם עוברים את הירדן אל ארץ
כנען 52 והורשתם את כל יושבי הארץ
מיפניכם ואיבדתם את כל מסכיותם ואת כל
צלמי מסכותם תאבדו ואת כל במותם תשמידו
53 והורשתם את הארץ וישבתם בה כי לכם נתתי
את הארץ לרשת אותה 54 והיתנחלתם את הארץ
בגורל למישפחותיכם לרב תרבו את נחלתו
ולמעט תמעיט את נחלתו אל אשר יצא לו שמה

הגורל לו יהיה למטות אבותיכם תיתנחלו
55 ואים לוא תורישו את יושבי הארץ
מיפיניכם והיה אשר תותירו מהם לסיכים
בעיניכם וליצנינים בצידיכם וצררו
אתכם על הארץ אשר אתם יושבים בה 56 והיה
כאשר דימיתי לעסות להם אעסה לכם

במידבר פרק 34

1 וידבר יהוה אל מושה לאמור 2 צו את בני
יסראל ואמרת אלהם כי אתם באים אל הארץ
כנען זואת הארץ אשר תיפול לכם בנחלה ארץ
כנען ליגבולותיה 3 והיה לכם פאת נגב
מימידבר צין על ידי אדום והיה לכם גבול
נגב מיקצה ים המלח קדמה 4 ונסב לכם הגבול
מינגב למעלה עקרבים ועבר צינה והיה
תוצאותיו מינגב לקדש ברנע ויצא חצר אדר
ועבר עצמונה 5 ונסב הגבול מעצמון נחלה
מיצרים והיו תוצאותיו הימה 6 וגבול ים
והיה לכם הים הגדול וגבול זה יהיה לכם גבול
ים 7 וזה יהיה לכם גבול צפון מין הים
הגדול תתאו לכם הור ההר 8 מהור ההר תתאו לבוא
חמת והיו תוצאות הגבול צדדה 9 ויצא הגבול
זיפרונה והיו תוצאותיו חצר עינן זה
יהיה לכם גבול צפון 10 והיתאויתם לכם
ליגבול קדמה מחצר עינן שפמה 11 וירד
הגבול מישפם הריבלה מיקדם לעיין וירד
הגבול ומחה על כתף ים כינרת קדמה 12 וירד
הגבול הירדנה והיו תוצאותיו ים המלח זואת
תיהיה לכם הארץ ליגבולותיה סביב 13 ויצו
מושה את בני יסראל לאמור זואת הארץ אשר
תיתנחלו אותה בגורל אשר ציוה יהוה לתת
ליתשעת המטות וחצי המטה 14 כי לקחו מטה
בני הראוביני לבית אבותם ומטה בני הגדי
לבית אבותם וחצי מטה מנשה לקחו נחלתם
15 שני המטות וחצי המטה לקחו נחלתם מעבר
לירדן ירחו קדמה מיזרחה 16 וידבר יהוה אל
מושה לאמור 17 אלה שמות האנשים אשר
ינחלו לכם את הארץ אלעזר הכוהן ויהושוע
בין נון 18 ונסיא אחד נסיא אחד מימטה
תיקחו לינחול את הארץ 19 ואלה שמות

האנשים למטה יהודה כלב בן יפנה
20 ולמטה בני שמעון שמואל בן עמיהוד
21 למטה בנימן אלידד בן כסלון
22 ולמטה בני דן נשיא בקי בן יגלי
23 לבני יוסף למטה בני מנשה נשיא
חניאל בן אפד 24 ולמטה בני אפרים
נשיא קמואל בן שפטן 25 ולמטה בני זבולן
נשיא אליצפן בן פרנך 26 ולמטה בני
יששכר נשיא פלטיאל בן עזן 27 ולמטה בני
אשר נשיא אחיהוד בן שלמי 28 ולמטה בני
נפתלי נשיא פדהאל בן עמיהוד 29 אלה אשר
צוה יהוה לנחל את בני ישראל בארץ כנען

במדבר פרק 35

1 וידבר יהוה אל משה בערבת מואב על ירדן
ירחו לאמר 2 צו את בני ישראל ונתנו ללוים
מנחלת אחזתם ערים לשבת ומגרש
לערים סביבתיהם תתנו ללוים 3 והיו
הערים להם לשבת ומגרשיהם יהיו
לבהמתם ולרכשם ולכל חיתם 4 ומגרשי
הערים אשר תתנו ללוים מקיר העיר
וחוצה אלף אמה סביב 5 ומדתם מחוץ לעיר את
פאת קדמה אלפים באמה ואת פאת נגב
אלפים באמה ואת פאת ים אלפים
באמה ואת פאת צפון אלפים באמה והעיר
בתוך זה יהיה להם מגרשי הערים 6 ואת
הערים אשר תתנו ללוים את שש ערי
המקלט אשר תתנו לנס שמה הרצח ועליהם
תתנו ארבעים ושתים עיר 7 כל הערים
אשר תתנו ללוים ארבעים ושמנה עיר
אתהן ואת מגרשיהן 8 והערים אשר תתנו
מאחזת בני ישראל מאת הרב תרבו ומאת המעט
תמעיטו איש כפי נחלתו אשר ינחלו יתן
מעריו ללוים 9 וידבר יהוה אל משה לאמר
10 דבר אל בני ישראל ואמרת אלהם כי אתם
עברים את הירדן ארצה כנען 11 והקריתם
לכם ערים ערי מקלט תהיינה לכם ונס
שמה רצח מכה נפש בשגגה 12 והיו לכם
הערים למקלט מגאל ולא ימות הרצח עד
עמדו לפני העדה למשפט 13 והערים

𐤀𐤔𐤓 𐤕𐤉𐤕𐤍𐤅 𐤔𐤔 𐤏𐤓𐤉 𐤌𐤉𐤒𐤋𐤈 𐤕𐤉𐤄𐤉𐤉𐤍𐤄 𐤋𐤊𐤌
14 𐤀𐤕 𐤔𐤋𐤅𐤔 𐤄𐤏𐤓𐤉𐤌 𐤕𐤉𐤕𐤍𐤅 𐤌𐤏𐤁𐤓 𐤋𐤉𐤓𐤃𐤍 𐤅𐤀𐤕
𐤔𐤋𐤅𐤔 𐤄𐤏𐤓𐤉𐤌 𐤕𐤉𐤕𐤍𐤅 𐤁𐤀𐤓𐤑 𐤊𐤍𐤏𐤍 𐤏𐤓𐤉 𐤌𐤉𐤒𐤋𐤈
𐤕𐤉𐤄𐤉𐤉𐤍𐤄 15 𐤋𐤉𐤁𐤍𐤉 𐤉𐤎𐤓𐤀𐤋 𐤅𐤋𐤂𐤓 𐤅𐤋𐤕𐤅𐤔𐤁
𐤁𐤕𐤅𐤊𐤌 𐤕𐤉𐤄𐤉𐤉𐤍𐤄 𐤔𐤔 𐤄𐤏𐤓𐤉𐤌 𐤄𐤀𐤋𐤄 𐤋𐤌𐤉𐤒𐤋𐤈
𐤋𐤍𐤅𐤎 𐤔𐤌𐤄 𐤊𐤋 𐤌𐤊𐤄 𐤍𐤐𐤔 𐤁𐤉𐤔𐤂𐤂𐤄 16 𐤅𐤀𐤉𐤌
𐤁𐤉𐤊𐤋𐤉 𐤁𐤓𐤆𐤋 𐤄𐤉𐤊𐤄𐤅 𐤅𐤉𐤌𐤅𐤕 𐤓𐤅𐤑𐤇 𐤄𐤅𐤀 𐤌𐤅𐤕 𐤉𐤅𐤌𐤕
𐤄𐤓𐤅𐤑𐤇 17 𐤅𐤀𐤉𐤌 𐤁𐤀𐤁𐤍 𐤉𐤃 𐤀𐤔𐤓 𐤉𐤌𐤅𐤕 𐤁𐤄 𐤄𐤉𐤊𐤄𐤅
𐤅𐤉𐤌𐤅𐤕 𐤓𐤅𐤑𐤇 𐤄𐤅𐤀 𐤌𐤅𐤕 𐤉𐤅𐤌𐤕 𐤄𐤓𐤅𐤑𐤇 18 𐤀𐤅 𐤁𐤉𐤊𐤋𐤉
𐤏𐤑 𐤉𐤃 𐤀𐤔𐤓 𐤉𐤌𐤅𐤕 𐤁𐤅 𐤄𐤉𐤊𐤄𐤅 𐤅𐤉𐤌𐤅𐤕 𐤓𐤅𐤑𐤇 𐤄𐤅𐤀 𐤌𐤅𐤕
𐤉𐤅𐤌𐤕 𐤄𐤓𐤅𐤑𐤇 19 𐤂𐤅𐤀𐤋 𐤄𐤃𐤌 𐤄𐤅𐤀 𐤉𐤌𐤉𐤕 𐤀𐤕 𐤄𐤓𐤅𐤑𐤇
𐤁𐤐𐤉𐤂𐤏𐤅 𐤁𐤅 𐤄𐤅𐤀 𐤉𐤌𐤉𐤕𐤍𐤅 20 𐤅𐤀𐤉𐤌 𐤁𐤎𐤉𐤍𐤀𐤄
𐤉𐤄𐤃𐤐𐤍𐤅 𐤀𐤅 𐤄𐤉𐤔𐤋𐤉𐤊 𐤏𐤋𐤉𐤅 𐤁𐤉𐤑𐤃𐤉𐤄 𐤅𐤉𐤌𐤅𐤕
21 𐤀𐤅 𐤁𐤀𐤉𐤁𐤄 𐤄𐤉𐤊𐤄𐤅 𐤁𐤉𐤃𐤅 𐤅𐤉𐤌𐤅𐤕 𐤌𐤅𐤕 𐤉𐤅𐤌𐤕
𐤄𐤌𐤊𐤄 𐤓𐤅𐤑𐤇 𐤄𐤅𐤀 𐤂𐤅𐤀𐤋 𐤄𐤃𐤌 𐤉𐤌𐤉𐤕 𐤀𐤕 𐤄𐤓𐤅𐤑𐤇
𐤁𐤐𐤉𐤂𐤏𐤅 𐤁𐤅 22 𐤅𐤀𐤉𐤌 𐤁𐤐𐤕𐤏 𐤁𐤋𐤅𐤀 𐤀𐤉𐤁𐤄 𐤄𐤃𐤐𐤅 𐤀𐤅
𐤄𐤉𐤔𐤋𐤉𐤊 𐤏𐤋𐤉𐤅 𐤊𐤋 𐤊𐤋𐤉 𐤁𐤋𐤅𐤀 𐤑𐤃𐤉𐤄 23 𐤀𐤅 𐤁𐤊𐤋 𐤀𐤁𐤍
𐤀𐤔𐤓 𐤉𐤌𐤅𐤕 𐤁𐤄 𐤁𐤋𐤅𐤀 𐤓𐤀𐤅𐤕 𐤅𐤉𐤐𐤋 𐤏𐤋𐤉𐤅 𐤅𐤉𐤌𐤅𐤕 𐤅𐤄𐤅𐤀
𐤋𐤅𐤀 𐤀𐤅𐤉𐤁 𐤋𐤅 𐤅𐤋𐤅𐤀 𐤌𐤁𐤒𐤔 𐤓𐤏𐤕𐤅 24 𐤅𐤔𐤐𐤈𐤅 𐤄𐤏𐤃𐤄
𐤁𐤉𐤍 𐤄𐤌𐤊𐤄 𐤅𐤁𐤉𐤍 𐤂𐤅𐤀𐤋 𐤄𐤃𐤌 𐤏𐤋 𐤄𐤌𐤉𐤔𐤐𐤈𐤉𐤌
𐤄𐤀𐤋𐤄 25 𐤅𐤄𐤉𐤑𐤉𐤋𐤅 𐤄𐤏𐤃𐤄 𐤀𐤕 𐤄𐤓𐤅𐤑𐤇 𐤌𐤉𐤃 𐤂𐤅𐤀𐤋
𐤄𐤃𐤌 𐤅𐤄𐤔𐤉𐤁𐤅 𐤀𐤅𐤕𐤅 𐤄𐤏𐤃𐤄 𐤀𐤋 𐤏𐤉𐤓 𐤌𐤉𐤒𐤋𐤈𐤅 𐤀𐤔𐤓 𐤍𐤎
𐤔𐤌𐤄 𐤅𐤉𐤔𐤁 𐤁𐤄 𐤏𐤃 𐤌𐤅𐤕 𐤄𐤊𐤅𐤄𐤍 𐤄𐤂𐤃𐤅𐤋 𐤀𐤔𐤓 𐤌𐤔𐤇
𐤀𐤅𐤕𐤅 𐤁𐤔𐤌𐤍 𐤄𐤒𐤅𐤃𐤔 26 𐤅𐤀𐤉𐤌 𐤉𐤑𐤅𐤀 𐤉𐤑𐤀 𐤄𐤓𐤅𐤑𐤇 𐤀𐤕
𐤂𐤁𐤅𐤋 𐤏𐤉𐤓 𐤌𐤉𐤒𐤋𐤈𐤅 𐤀𐤔𐤓 𐤉𐤍𐤅𐤎 𐤔𐤌𐤄 27 𐤅𐤌𐤑𐤀 𐤀𐤅𐤕𐤅
𐤂𐤅𐤀𐤋 𐤄𐤃𐤌 𐤌𐤇𐤅𐤑 𐤋𐤉𐤂𐤁𐤅𐤋 𐤏𐤉𐤓 𐤌𐤉𐤒𐤋𐤈𐤅 𐤅𐤓𐤑𐤇
𐤂𐤅𐤀𐤋 𐤄𐤃𐤌 𐤀𐤕 𐤄𐤓𐤅𐤑𐤇 𐤀𐤉𐤍 𐤋𐤅 𐤃𐤌 28 𐤊𐤉 𐤁𐤏𐤉𐤓
𐤌𐤉𐤒𐤋𐤈𐤅 𐤉𐤔𐤁 𐤏𐤃 𐤌𐤅𐤕 𐤄𐤊𐤅𐤄𐤍 𐤄𐤂𐤃𐤅𐤋 𐤅𐤀𐤇𐤓𐤉 𐤌𐤅𐤕
𐤄𐤊𐤅𐤄𐤍 𐤄𐤂𐤃𐤅𐤋 𐤉𐤔𐤅𐤁 𐤄𐤓𐤅𐤑𐤇 𐤀𐤋 𐤀𐤓𐤑 𐤀𐤇𐤅𐤆𐤕𐤅 29 𐤅𐤄𐤉𐤅
𐤀𐤋𐤄 𐤋𐤊𐤌 𐤋𐤇𐤅𐤒𐤕 𐤌𐤉𐤔𐤐𐤈 𐤋𐤃𐤅𐤓𐤅𐤕𐤉𐤊𐤌 𐤁𐤊𐤅𐤋
𐤌𐤅𐤔𐤁𐤅𐤕𐤉𐤊𐤌 30 𐤊𐤋 𐤌𐤊𐤄 𐤍𐤐𐤔 𐤋𐤐𐤉 𐤏𐤃𐤉𐤌
𐤉𐤓𐤑𐤇 𐤀𐤕 𐤄𐤓𐤅𐤑𐤇 𐤅𐤏𐤃 𐤀𐤇𐤃 𐤋𐤅𐤀 𐤉𐤏𐤍𐤄 𐤁𐤍𐤐𐤔 𐤋𐤌𐤅𐤕
31 𐤅𐤋𐤅𐤀 𐤕𐤉𐤒𐤇𐤅 𐤊𐤅𐤐𐤓 𐤋𐤍𐤐𐤔 𐤓𐤅𐤑𐤇 𐤀𐤔𐤓 𐤄𐤅𐤀 𐤓𐤔𐤏
𐤋𐤌𐤅𐤕 𐤊𐤉 𐤌𐤅𐤕 𐤉𐤅𐤌𐤕 32 𐤅𐤋𐤅𐤀 𐤕𐤉𐤒𐤇𐤅 𐤊𐤅𐤐𐤓 𐤋𐤍𐤅𐤎 𐤀𐤋
𐤏𐤉𐤓 𐤌𐤉𐤒𐤋𐤈𐤅 𐤋𐤔𐤅𐤁 𐤋𐤔𐤁𐤕 𐤁𐤀𐤓𐤑 𐤏𐤃 𐤌𐤅𐤕 𐤄𐤊𐤅𐤄𐤍
33 𐤅𐤋𐤅𐤀 𐤕𐤇𐤍𐤉𐤐𐤅 𐤀𐤕 𐤄𐤀𐤓𐤑 𐤀𐤔𐤓 𐤀𐤕𐤌 𐤁𐤄 𐤊𐤉 𐤄𐤃𐤌
𐤄𐤅𐤀 𐤉𐤇𐤍𐤉𐤐 𐤀𐤕 𐤄𐤀𐤓𐤑 𐤅𐤋𐤀𐤓𐤑 𐤋𐤅𐤀 𐤉𐤊𐤅𐤐𐤓 𐤋𐤃𐤌
𐤀𐤔𐤓 𐤔𐤅𐤐𐤊 𐤁𐤄 𐤊𐤉 𐤀𐤉𐤌 𐤁𐤃𐤌 𐤔𐤅𐤐𐤊𐤅 34 𐤅𐤋𐤅𐤀 𐤕𐤈𐤌𐤀
𐤀𐤕 𐤄𐤀𐤓𐤑 𐤀𐤔𐤓 𐤀𐤕𐤌 𐤉𐤅𐤔𐤁𐤉𐤌 𐤁𐤄 𐤀𐤔𐤓 𐤀𐤍𐤉
𐤔𐤅𐤊𐤍 𐤁𐤕𐤅𐤊𐤄 𐤊𐤉 𐤀𐤍𐤉 𐤉𐤄𐤅𐤄 𐤔𐤅𐤊𐤍 𐤁𐤕𐤅𐤊 𐤁𐤍𐤉
𐤉𐤎𐤓𐤀𐤋

36 [illegible]

[illegible] 1
[illegible]
[illegible]
[illegible] 2 [illegible]
[illegible]
[illegible]
[illegible] 3 [illegible]
[illegible]
[illegible]
[illegible]
[illegible] 4 [illegible]
[illegible]
[illegible]
[illegible] 5 [illegible]
[illegible]
[illegible] 6
[illegible]
[illegible]
[illegible] 7
[illegible]
[illegible] 8 [illegible]
[illegible]
[illegible]
[illegible] 9 [illegible]
[illegible]
[illegible] 10
[illegible] 11 [illegible]
[illegible]
[illegible] 12 [illegible]
[illegible]
[illegible] 13 [illegible]
[illegible]
[illegible]

Devariym / Deuteronomy

[illegible]
[illegible]
[illegible] 16 [illegible]
[illegible]
[illegible] 17 [illegible]
[illegible]
[illegible]
[illegible]
[illegible] 18 [illegible]
[illegible] 19 [illegible]
[illegible]
[illegible]
[illegible] 20 [illegible]
[illegible] 21 [illegible]
[illegible]
[illegible]
[illegible] 22 [illegible]
[illegible]
[illegible]
[illegible] 23 [illegible]
[illegible]
[illegible] 24 [illegible]
[illegible] 25 [illegible]
[illegible]
[illegible]
[illegible] 26 [illegible]
[illegible] 27 [illegible]
[illegible]
[illegible]
[illegible] 28 [illegible]
[illegible]
[illegible]
[illegible] 29 [illegible]
[illegible] 30 [illegible]
[illegible]
[illegible] 31 [illegible]
[illegible]
[illegible]
[illegible] 32 [illegible]
[illegible] 33 [illegible]
[illegible]

[illegible]
[illegible] 34
[illegible] 35 [illegible]
[illegible]
[illegible] 36 [illegible]
[illegible]
[illegible] 37 [illegible]
[illegible]
[illegible] 38 [illegible]
[illegible]
[illegible] 39 [illegible]
[illegible]
[illegible]
[illegible] 40
[illegible] 41
[illegible]
[illegible]
[illegible] 42 [illegible]
[illegible]
[illegible]
[illegible] 43
[illegible] 44 [illegible]
[illegible]
[illegible]
[illegible] 45 [illegible]
[illegible]
[illegible] 46
[illegible]

2 [illegible]

[illegible] 1
[illegible]
[illegible] 3 [illegible] 2 [illegible]
[illegible] 4 [illegible]
[illegible]
[illegible]
[illegible] 5 [illegible]
[illegible]
[illegible] 6 [illegible]
[illegible]
[illegible] 7

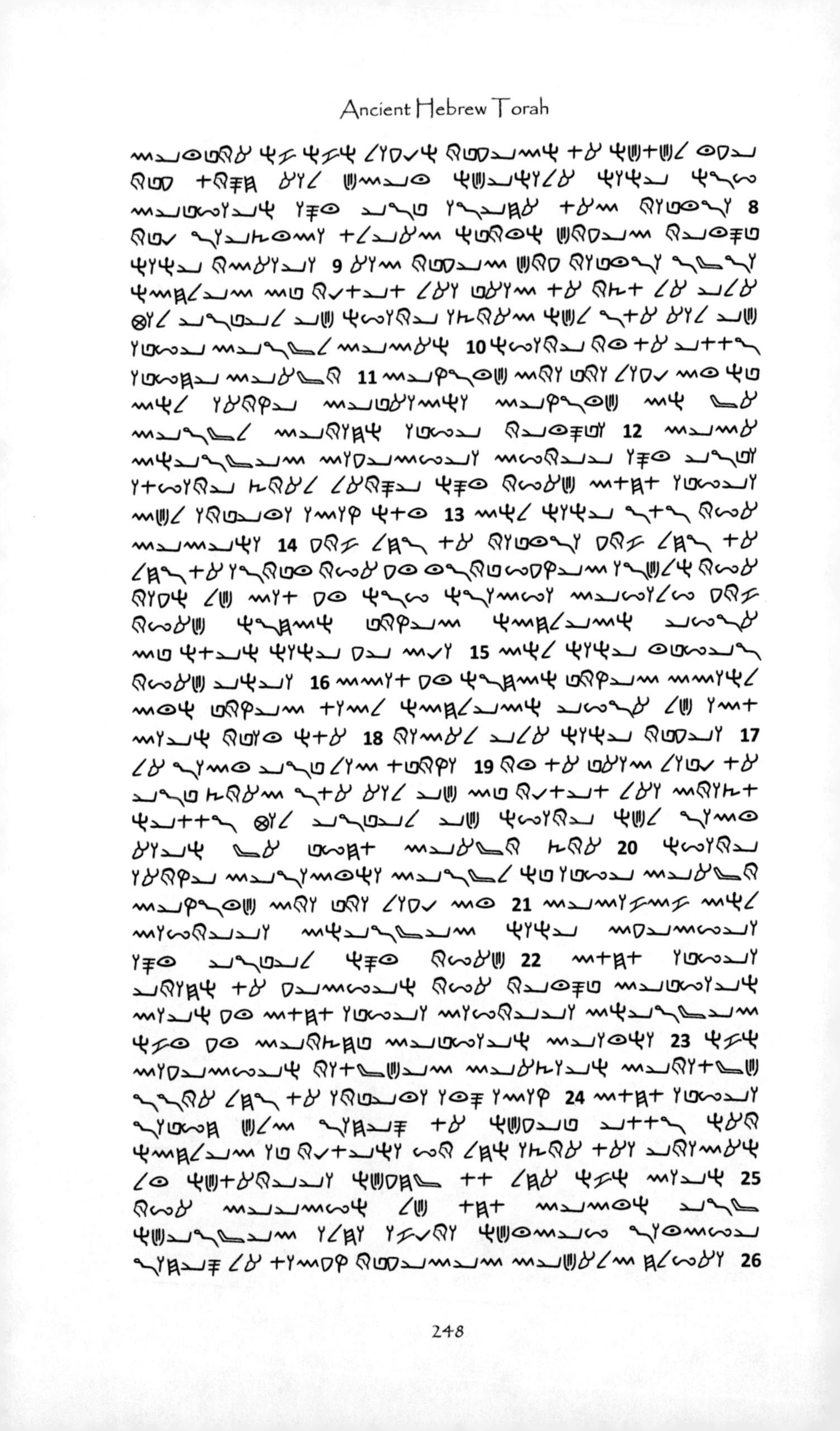

8
9
10
11
12
13
14
15
16
17 18
19
20
21
22
23
24
25
26

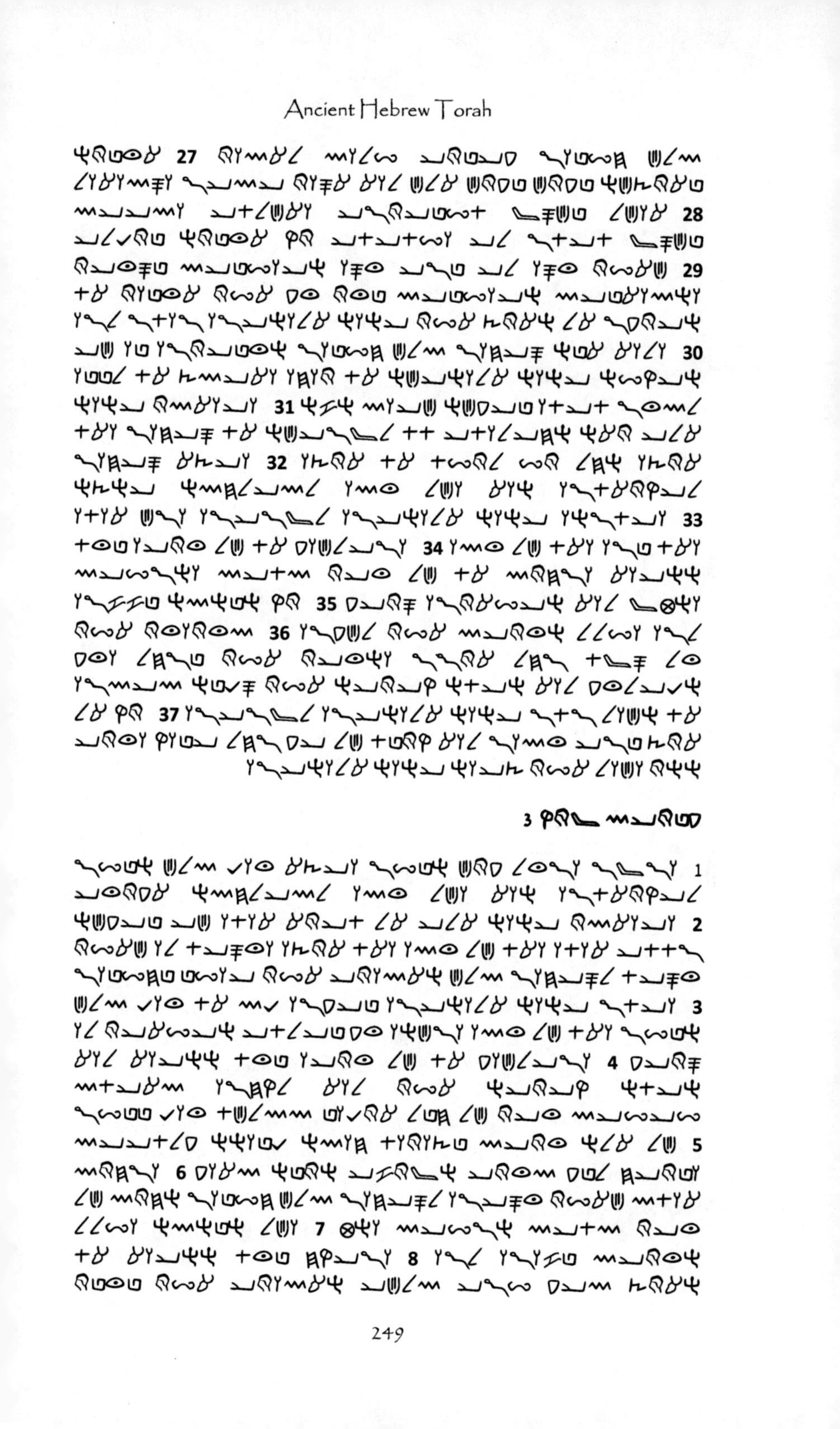

[illegible] 27 [illegible]
[illegible]
[illegible] 28
[illegible]
[illegible] 29
[illegible]
[illegible]
[illegible] 30
[illegible]
[illegible] 31 [illegible]
[illegible]
[illegible] 32 [illegible]
[illegible]
[illegible] 33
[illegible] 34 [illegible]
[illegible]
[illegible] 35 [illegible]
[illegible] 36 [illegible]
[illegible]
[illegible]
[illegible]
[illegible] 37 [illegible]
[illegible]
[illegible]

3 [illegible]

[illegible] 1
[illegible]
[illegible] 2
[illegible]
[illegible]
[illegible] 3
[illegible]
[illegible] 4 [illegible]
[illegible]
[illegible]
[illegible] 5
[illegible] 6 [illegible]
[illegible]
[illegible] 7 [illegible]
[illegible] 8 [illegible]
[illegible]

[illegible]
[illegible] 9
[illegible] 10 [illegible]
[illegible]
[illegible] 11 [illegible]
[illegible]
[illegible]
[illegible] 12 [illegible]
[illegible]
[illegible]
[illegible] 13 [illegible]
[illegible]
[illegible] 14 [illegible]
[illegible]
[illegible]
[illegible] 15 [illegible]
[illegible] 16 [illegible]
[illegible]
[illegible] 17 [illegible]
[illegible]
[illegible] 18 [illegible]
[illegible]
[illegible]
[illegible] 19 [illegible]
[illegible]
[illegible] 20 [illegible]
[illegible]
[illegible]
[illegible]
[illegible] 21
[illegible]
[illegible]
[illegible] 22 [illegible]
[illegible]
[illegible] 23
[illegible] 24
[illegible]
[illegible]
[illegible] 25 [illegible]
[illegible]
[illegible] 26

𐤅𐤉𐤅𐤀𐤌𐤓 𐤉𐤄𐤅𐤄 𐤀𐤋𐤉 𐤓𐤁 𐤋𐤊 𐤀𐤋 𐤕𐤅𐤎𐤐 𐤃𐤁𐤓 𐤀𐤋𐤉 𐤏𐤅𐤃
𐤁𐤃𐤁𐤓 𐤄𐤆𐤄 27 𐤏𐤋𐤄 𐤓𐤅𐤀𐤔 𐤄𐤐𐤉𐤎𐤂𐤄 𐤅𐤎𐤀 𐤏𐤉𐤍𐤉𐤊𐤄
𐤉𐤌𐤄 𐤅𐤑𐤐𐤅𐤍𐤄 𐤅𐤕𐤉𐤌𐤍𐤄 𐤅𐤌𐤉𐤆𐤓𐤇𐤄 𐤅𐤓𐤀𐤄
𐤁𐤏𐤉𐤍𐤉𐤊𐤄 𐤊𐤉 𐤋𐤅𐤀 𐤕𐤏𐤁𐤅𐤓 𐤀𐤕 𐤄𐤉𐤓𐤃𐤍 𐤄𐤆𐤄 28 𐤅𐤑𐤅
𐤀𐤕 𐤉𐤄𐤅𐤔𐤅𐤏 𐤅𐤇𐤆𐤒𐤄𐤅 𐤅𐤀𐤌𐤑𐤄𐤅 𐤊𐤉 𐤄𐤅𐤀 𐤉𐤏𐤁𐤅𐤓
𐤋𐤉𐤐𐤍𐤉 𐤄𐤏𐤌 𐤄𐤆𐤄 𐤅𐤄𐤅𐤀 𐤉𐤍𐤇𐤉𐤋 𐤀𐤅𐤕𐤌 𐤀𐤕 𐤄𐤀𐤓𐤑
𐤀𐤔𐤓 𐤕𐤉𐤓𐤀𐤄 29 𐤅𐤍𐤔𐤁 𐤁𐤂𐤉𐤀 𐤌𐤅𐤋 𐤁𐤉𐤕 𐤐𐤏𐤅𐤓

𐤃𐤁𐤓𐤉𐤌 𐤐𐤓𐤒 4

1 𐤅𐤏𐤕𐤄 𐤉𐤎𐤓𐤀𐤋 𐤔𐤌𐤏 𐤀𐤋 𐤄𐤇𐤅𐤒𐤉𐤌 𐤅𐤀𐤋
𐤄𐤌𐤔𐤐𐤈𐤉𐤌 𐤀𐤔𐤓 𐤀𐤍𐤅𐤊𐤉 𐤌𐤋𐤌𐤃 𐤀𐤕𐤊𐤌 𐤋𐤏𐤎𐤅𐤕
𐤋𐤌𐤏𐤍 𐤕𐤉𐤇𐤉𐤅 𐤅𐤁𐤀𐤕𐤌 𐤅𐤉𐤓𐤉𐤔𐤕𐤌 𐤀𐤕 𐤄𐤀𐤓𐤑 𐤀𐤔𐤓
𐤉𐤄𐤅𐤄 𐤀𐤋𐤅𐤄𐤉 𐤀𐤁𐤅𐤕𐤉𐤊𐤌 𐤍𐤅𐤕𐤍 𐤋𐤊𐤌 2 𐤋𐤅𐤀 𐤕𐤅𐤎𐤉𐤐𐤅
𐤏𐤋 𐤄𐤃𐤁𐤓 𐤀𐤔𐤓 𐤀𐤍𐤅𐤊𐤉 𐤌𐤑𐤅𐤄 𐤀𐤕𐤊𐤌 𐤅𐤋𐤅𐤀 𐤕𐤉𐤂𐤓𐤏𐤅
𐤌𐤉𐤌𐤍𐤅 𐤋𐤉𐤔𐤌𐤅𐤓 𐤀𐤕 𐤌𐤑𐤅𐤕 𐤉𐤄𐤅𐤄 𐤀𐤋𐤅𐤄𐤉𐤊𐤌
𐤀𐤔𐤓 𐤀𐤍𐤅𐤊𐤉 𐤌𐤑𐤅𐤄 𐤀𐤕𐤊𐤌 3 𐤏𐤉𐤍𐤉𐤊𐤌 𐤄𐤓𐤅𐤀𐤅𐤕 𐤀𐤕
𐤀𐤔𐤓 𐤏𐤎𐤄 𐤉𐤄𐤅𐤄 𐤁𐤁𐤏𐤋 𐤐𐤏𐤅𐤓 𐤊𐤉 𐤊𐤋 𐤄𐤀𐤉𐤔 𐤀𐤔𐤓
𐤄𐤋𐤊 𐤀𐤇𐤓𐤉 𐤁𐤏𐤋 𐤐𐤏𐤅𐤓 𐤄𐤉𐤔𐤌𐤉𐤃𐤅 𐤉𐤄𐤅𐤄 𐤀𐤋𐤅𐤄𐤉𐤊𐤄
𐤌𐤒𐤉𐤓𐤁𐤊𐤄 4 𐤅𐤀𐤕𐤌 𐤄𐤃𐤁𐤒𐤉𐤌 𐤁𐤉𐤄𐤅𐤄 𐤀𐤋𐤅𐤄𐤉𐤊𐤌
𐤇𐤉𐤉𐤌 𐤊𐤅𐤋𐤊𐤌 𐤄𐤉𐤅𐤌 5 𐤓𐤀𐤄 𐤋𐤉𐤌𐤃𐤕𐤉 𐤀𐤕𐤊𐤌
𐤇𐤅𐤒𐤉𐤌 𐤅𐤌𐤔𐤐𐤈𐤉𐤌 𐤊𐤀𐤔𐤓 𐤑𐤉𐤅𐤍𐤉 𐤉𐤄𐤅𐤄
𐤀𐤋𐤅𐤄𐤉 𐤋𐤏𐤎𐤅𐤕 𐤊𐤍 𐤁𐤒𐤓𐤁 𐤄𐤀𐤓𐤑 𐤀𐤔𐤓 𐤀𐤕𐤌 𐤁𐤀𐤉𐤌
𐤔𐤌𐤄 𐤋𐤓𐤔𐤕𐤄 6 𐤅𐤔𐤌𐤓𐤕𐤌 𐤅𐤏𐤎𐤉𐤕𐤌 𐤊𐤉 𐤄𐤉𐤅𐤀
𐤇𐤊𐤌𐤕𐤊𐤌 𐤅𐤁𐤉𐤍𐤕𐤊𐤌 𐤋𐤏𐤉𐤍𐤉 𐤄𐤏𐤌𐤉𐤌 𐤀𐤔𐤓
𐤉𐤔𐤌𐤏𐤅𐤍 𐤀𐤕 𐤊𐤋 𐤄𐤇𐤅𐤒𐤉𐤌 𐤄𐤀𐤋𐤄 𐤅𐤀𐤌𐤓𐤅 𐤓𐤒 𐤏𐤌 𐤇𐤊𐤌
𐤅𐤍𐤁𐤅𐤍 𐤄𐤂𐤅𐤉 𐤄𐤂𐤃𐤅𐤋 𐤄𐤆𐤄 7 𐤊𐤉 𐤌𐤉 𐤂𐤅𐤉 𐤂𐤃𐤅𐤋 𐤀𐤔𐤓
𐤋𐤅 𐤀𐤋𐤅𐤄𐤉𐤌 𐤒𐤓𐤁𐤉𐤌 𐤀𐤋𐤉𐤅 𐤊𐤉𐤄𐤅𐤄 𐤀𐤋𐤅𐤄𐤉𐤍𐤅 𐤁𐤊𐤋
𐤒𐤓𐤀𐤍𐤅 𐤀𐤋𐤉𐤅 8 𐤅𐤌𐤉 𐤂𐤅𐤉 𐤂𐤃𐤅𐤋 𐤀𐤔𐤓 𐤋𐤅 𐤇𐤅𐤒𐤉𐤌
𐤅𐤌𐤔𐤐𐤈𐤉𐤌 𐤑𐤃𐤉𐤒𐤉𐤌 𐤊𐤊𐤅𐤋 𐤄𐤕𐤅𐤓𐤄 𐤄𐤆𐤅𐤀𐤕 𐤀𐤔𐤓
𐤀𐤍𐤅𐤊𐤉 𐤍𐤅𐤕𐤍 𐤋𐤉𐤐𐤍𐤉𐤊𐤌 𐤄𐤉𐤅𐤌 9 𐤓𐤒 𐤄𐤉𐤔𐤌𐤓
𐤋𐤊𐤄 𐤅𐤔𐤌𐤅𐤓 𐤍𐤐𐤔𐤊𐤄 𐤌𐤀𐤅𐤃 𐤐𐤍 𐤕𐤉𐤔𐤊𐤇 𐤀𐤕
𐤄𐤃𐤁𐤓𐤉𐤌 𐤀𐤔𐤓 𐤓𐤀𐤅 𐤏𐤉𐤍𐤉𐤊𐤄 𐤅𐤐𐤍 𐤉𐤎𐤅𐤓𐤅
𐤌𐤋𐤁𐤁𐤊𐤄 𐤊𐤅𐤋 𐤉𐤌𐤉 𐤇𐤉𐤉𐤊𐤄 𐤅𐤄𐤅𐤃𐤏𐤕𐤌 𐤋𐤁𐤍𐤉𐤊𐤄
𐤅𐤋𐤁𐤍𐤉 𐤁𐤍𐤉𐤊𐤄 10 𐤉𐤅𐤌 𐤀𐤔𐤓 𐤏𐤌𐤃𐤕 𐤋𐤉𐤐𐤍𐤉
𐤉𐤄𐤅𐤄 𐤀𐤋𐤅𐤄𐤉𐤊𐤄 𐤁𐤇𐤅𐤓𐤁 𐤁𐤀𐤌𐤅𐤓 𐤉𐤄𐤅𐤄 𐤀𐤋𐤉 𐤄𐤒𐤄𐤋 𐤋𐤉
𐤀𐤕 𐤄𐤏𐤌 𐤅𐤀𐤔𐤌𐤉𐤏𐤌 𐤀𐤕 𐤃𐤁𐤓𐤉 𐤀𐤔𐤓 𐤉𐤋𐤌𐤃𐤅𐤍
𐤋𐤉𐤓𐤀𐤄 𐤀𐤅𐤕𐤉 𐤊𐤋 𐤄𐤉𐤌𐤉𐤌 𐤀𐤔𐤓 𐤄𐤌 𐤇𐤉𐤉𐤌 𐤏𐤋
𐤄𐤀𐤃𐤌𐤄 𐤅𐤀𐤕 𐤁𐤍𐤉𐤄𐤌 𐤉𐤋𐤌𐤃𐤅𐤍 11 𐤅𐤕𐤉𐤒𐤓𐤁𐤅𐤍
𐤅𐤕𐤏𐤌𐤃𐤅𐤍 𐤕𐤇𐤕 𐤄𐤄𐤓 𐤅𐤄𐤄𐤓 𐤁𐤅𐤏𐤓 𐤁𐤀𐤔 𐤏𐤃 𐤋𐤁
𐤄𐤔𐤌𐤉𐤉𐤌 𐤇𐤅𐤔𐤊 𐤏𐤍𐤍 𐤅𐤏𐤓𐤐𐤋 12 𐤅𐤉𐤃𐤁𐤓 𐤉𐤄𐤅𐤄
𐤀𐤋𐤉𐤊𐤌 𐤌𐤕𐤅𐤊 𐤄𐤀𐤔 𐤒𐤅𐤋 𐤃𐤁𐤓𐤉𐤌 𐤀𐤕𐤌 𐤔𐤅𐤌𐤏𐤉𐤌

ותמונה אינכם רואים זולתי קול 13 ויגד לכם
אתבריתו אשר ציוה אתכם לעשות עשרת הדברים
ויכתבם על שני לוחות אבנים 14 ואותי ציוה
יהוה בעת ההיוא ללמד אתכם חוקים
ומישפטים לעשותכם אותם בארץ אשר אתם
עוברים שמה לרישתה 15 ונישמרתם מאוד
לנפשותיכם כי לוא ראיתם כל תמונה ביום
דיבר יהוה אליכם בחורב מיתוך האש 16 פן
תשחיתון ועשיתם לכם פסל תמונת כל סמל
תבנית זכר או נקבה 17 תבנית כל בהמה אשר
בארץ תבנית כל ציפור כנף אשר תעוף
בשמיים 18 תבנית כל רומש באדמה תבנית כל
דגה אשר במיים מיתחת לארץ 19 ופן תישא
עיניכה השמיימה וראית את השמש ואת
הירח ואת הכוכבים כול צבא השמיים ונידחת
והישתחוית להם ועבדתם אשר חלק יהוה
אלוהיכה אותם לכול העמים תחת כל השמיים
20 ואתכם לקח יהוה ויוציא אתכם מיכור הברזל
מימיצריים ליהיות לו לעם נחלה כיום
הזה 21 ויהוה היתאנף בי על דיבריכם
וישבע לבילתי עברי את הירדן ולבילתיבוא
אל הארץ הטובה אשר יהוה אלוהיכה נותן לכה
נחלה 22 כי אנוכי מת בארץ הזואת אינני
עובר את הירדן ואתם עוברים וירישתם את
הארץ הטובה הזואת 23 הישמרו לכם פן
תישכחו את ברית יהוה אלוהיכם אשר כרת
עימכם ועשיתם לכם פסל תמונת כול אשר
ציוכה יהוה אלוהיכה 24 כי יהוה אלוהיכה אש
אוכלה הוא אל קנא 25 כי תוליד בנים ובני
בנים ונושנתם בארץ והישחתם ועשיתם פסל
תמונת כול ועשיתם הרע בעיני יהוה
אלוהיכה להכעיסו 26 העידותי בכם היום את
השמיים ואת הארץ כי אבוד תאבדון מהר מעל
הארץ אשר אתם עוברים את הירדן שמה
לרישתה לוא תאריכון ימים עליה כי
הישמד תישמדון 27 והפיץ יהוה אתכם
בעמים ונישארתם מתי מיספר בגויים
אשר ינהג יהוה אתכם שמה 28 ועבדתם שם
אלוהים מעשה ידי אדם עץ ואבן אשר לוא
יראון ולוא ישמעון ולוא יאכלון ולוא
יריחון 29 וביקשתם מישם את יהוה

[illegible]
[illegible] 30 [illegible]
[illegible]
[illegible] 31 [illegible]
[illegible]
[illegible] 32 [illegible]
[illegible]
[illegible]
[illegible]
[illegible]
[illegible] 33
[illegible] 34 [illegible]
[illegible]
[illegible]
[illegible]
[illegible]
[illegible] 35
[illegible] 36 [illegible]
[illegible]
[illegible] 37 [illegible]
[illegible]
[illegible] 38 [illegible]
[illegible]
[illegible]
[illegible] 39 [illegible]
[illegible]
[illegible] 40 [illegible]
[illegible]
[illegible]
[illegible]
[illegible] 41 [illegible]
[illegible] 42 [illegible]
[illegible]
[illegible]
[illegible] 43 [illegible]
[illegible]
[illegible] 44 [illegible]
[illegible] 45 [illegible]
[illegible]
[illegible] 46 [illegible]
[illegible]

אשר יושב בחשבון אשר היכה מושה ובני
יסראל בצאתם מימיצריים 47 ויירשו את
ארצו ואת ארץ עוג מלך הבשן שני מלכי
האמורי אשר בעבר הירדן מיזרח שמש
48 מערוער אשר על ספת נחל ארנן ועד הר
סיאון הוא חרמון 49 וכל הערבה עבר הירדן
מיזרחה ועד ים הערבה תחת אשדות הפיסגה

דברים פרק 5

1 ויקרא מושה אל כל יסראל ויואמר אלהם
שמע יסראל את החוקים ואת המישפטים
אשר אנוכי דובר באזניכם היום ולמדתם
אותם ושמרתם לעסותם 2 יהוה אלוהינו כרת
עימנו ברית בחור 3 לוא את אבותינו כרת יהוה
את הברית הזואת כי איתנו אנחנו אלה פוה
היום כולנו חיים 4 פנים בפנים דיבר
יהוה עימכם בהר מיתוך האש 5 אנוכי עומד
בין יהוה וביניכם בעת ההיוא להגיד לכם
את דבר יהוה כי יראתם מיפני האש ולוא
עליתם בהר לאמור 6 אנוכי יהוה אלוהיכה
אשר הוצאתיכה מארץ מיצריים מיבית
עבדים 7 לוא יהיה לכה אלוהים אחרים על
פני 8 לוא תעסה לכה פסל כל תמונה אשר
בשמיים מימעל ואשר בארץ מיתחת ואשר
במיים מיתחת לארץ 9 לוא תישתחוה להם ולוא
תעבדם כי אנוכי יהוה אלוהיכה אל קנא פוקד
עון אבות על בנים ועל שילשים ועל
רבעים לסונאי 10 ועוסה חסד לאלפים
לאוהבי ולשומרי מיצותו 11 לוא תיסא את שם
יהוה אלוהיכה לשוא כי לוא ינקה יהוה את
אשר יסא את שמו לשוא 12 שמור את יום השבת
לקדשו כאשר ציוכה יהוה אלוהיכה 13 ששת
ימים תעבוד ועסית כל מלאכתכה 14 ויום
השביעי שבת ליהוה אלוהיכה לוא תעסה כל
מלאכה אתה ובינכה וביתכה ועבדכה ואמתכה
ושורכה וחמורכה וכל בהמתכה וגרכה אשר
בישעריכה למען ינוח עבדכה ואמתכה כמוכה
15 וזכרת כי עבד היית בארץ מיצריים
ויוציאכה יהוה אלוהיכה מישם ביד חזקה
וביזרוע נטויה על כן ציוכה יהוה אלוהיכה
לעסות את יום השבת 16 כבד את אביכה ואת

אמך כאשר צוך יהוה אלהיך למען
יאריכן ימיך ולמען ייטב לך על האדמה
אשר יהוה אלהיך נתן לך 17 לא תרצח
18 ולא תנאף 19 ולא תגנב 20 ולא תענה
ברעך עד שוא 21 ולא תחמד אשת רעך ולא
תתאוה בית רעך שדהו ועבדו ואמתו שורו וחמרו
וכל אשר לרעך 22 את הדברים האלה דבר יהוה
אל כל קהלכם בהר מתוך האש הענן והערפל
קול גדול ולא יסף ויכתבם על שני לחת
אבנים ויתנם אלי 23 ויהי כשמעכם את
הקול מתוך החשך וההר בער באש ותקרבון
אלי כל ראשי שבטיכם וזקניכם
24 ותאמרו הן הראנו יהוה אלהינו את כבדו
ואת גדלו ואת קלו שמענו מתוך האש היום הזה
ראינו כי ידבר אלהים את האדם וחי 25 ועתה
למה נמות כי תאכלנו האש הגדלה הזאת אם
יספים אנחנו לשמע את קול יהוה
אלהינו עוד ומתנו 26 כי מי כל בשר אשר שמע
קול אלהים חיים מדבר מתוך האש כמנו
ויחי 27 קרב אתה ושמע את כל אשר יאמר
יהוה אלהינו ואת תדבר אלינו את כל אשר
ידבר יהוה אלהינו אליך ושמענו ועשינו
28 וישמע יהוה את קול דבריכם בדברכם אלי
ויאמר יהוה אלי שמעתי את קול דברי העם
הזה אשר דברו אליך היטיבו כל אשר דברו
29 מי יתן והיה לבבם זה להם ליראה
אתי ולשמר את כל מצותי כל הימים למען
ייטב להם ולבניהם לעלם 30 לך אמר להם
שובו לכם לאהליכם 31 ואתה פה עמד עמדי
ואדברה אליך את כל המצוה והחקים
והמשפטים אשר תלמדם ועשו בארץ אשר
אנכי נתן להם לרשתה 32 ושמרתם לעשות
כאשר צוה יהוה אלהיכם אתכם לא תסרו
ימין ושמאל 33 בכל הדרך אשר צוה יהוה
אלהיכם אתכם תלכו למען תחיון וטוב לכם
והארכתם ימים בארץ אשר תירשון

דברים פרק 6

1 וזאת המצוה החקים והמשפטים אשר
צוה יהוה אלהיכם ללמד אתכם לעשות בארץ
אשר אתם עברים שמה לרשתה 2 למען

תירא את יהוה אלוהיכה לישמור את כל חוקותיו
ומיצותיו אשר אנוכי מצוכה אתה ובינכה ובן
בינכה כול ימי חייכה ולמען יאריכון
ימיכה 3 ושמעת ישראל ושמרת לעשות אשר
ייטב לכה ואשר תירבון מאוד כאשר דיבר יהוה
אלוהי אבותיכה לך ארץ זבת חלב ודבש 4 שמע
ישראל יהוה אלוהינו יהוה אחד 5 ואהבת את
יהוה אלוהיכה בכל לבבכה ובכל נפשכה ובכל
מאודכה 6 והיו הדברים האלה אשר אנוכי
מצוכה היום על לבבכה 7 ושיננתם לבניכה
ודיברת בם בשיבתכה בביתכה ובלכתכה בדרך
ובשכבכה ובקומכה 8 וקשרתם לאות על ידכה והיו
לטוטפות בין עיניכה 9 וכתבתם על מזוזות
ביתכה ובישעריכה 10 והיה כי יביאכה
יהוה אלוהיכה אל הארץ אשר נישבע
לאבותיכה לאברהם לייצחק וליעקוב לתת לך
ערים גדולות וטובות אשר לוא בנית 11 ובתים
מלאים כל טוב אשר לוא מילאת ובורות חצובים
אשר לוא חצבת כרמים וזיתים אשר לוא נטעת
ואכלת ושבעת 12 הישמר לכה פן תישכח את
יהוה אשר הוציאכה מארץ מיצריים
מבית עבדים 13 את יהוה אלוהיכה תירא
ואותו תעבוד ובישמו תישבע 14 לוא תלכון אחרי
אלוהים אחרים מאלוהי העמים אשר
סביבותיכם 15 כי אל קנא יהוה אלוהיכה
בקירבכה פן יחרה אף יהוה אלוהיכה בך
והישמידכה מעל פני האדמה 16 לוא תנסו את
יהוה אלוהיכם כאשר ניסיתם במסה 17 שמור
תישמרון את מיצות יהוה אלוהיכם ועדותיו
וחוקיו אשר ציוך 18 ועשית הישר והטוב
בעיני יהוה למען ייטב לך ובאת וירשת את
הארץ הטובה אשר נישבע יהוה לאבותיכה
19 להדוף את כל אויביכה מיפניכה כאשר
דיבר יהוה 20 כי ישאלכה בינכה מחר לאמור
מה העדות והחוקים והמישפטים אשר ציוה
יהוה אלוהינו אתכם 21 ואמרת לבינכה
עבדים היינו לפרעוה במיצריים
ויוציאנו יהוה מימיצריים ביד חזקה
22 ויתן יהוה אותות ומופתים גדולים
ורעים במיצריים בפרעוה ובכל ביתו
לעינינו 23 ואותנו הוציא מישם למען

𐤄𐤁𐤉𐤀 𐤀𐤅𐤕𐤍𐤅 𐤋𐤕𐤕 𐤋𐤍𐤅 𐤀𐤕 𐤄𐤀𐤓𐤑 𐤀𐤔𐤓 𐤍𐤉𐤔𐤁𐤏
𐤋𐤀𐤁𐤅𐤕𐤉𐤍𐤅 24 𐤅𐤉𐤑𐤅𐤍𐤅 𐤉𐤄𐤅𐤄 𐤋𐤏𐤎𐤅𐤕 𐤀𐤕 𐤊𐤋 𐤄𐤇𐤅𐤒𐤉𐤌
𐤄𐤀𐤋𐤄 𐤋𐤉𐤉𐤓𐤀𐤄 𐤀𐤕 𐤉𐤄𐤅𐤄 𐤀𐤋𐤅𐤄𐤉𐤍𐤅 𐤋𐤈𐤅𐤁 𐤋𐤍𐤅 𐤊𐤋
𐤄𐤉𐤌𐤉𐤌 𐤋𐤇𐤉𐤅𐤕𐤍𐤅 𐤊𐤄𐤉𐤅𐤌 𐤄𐤆𐤄 25 𐤅𐤑𐤃𐤒𐤄 𐤕𐤉𐤄𐤉𐤄
𐤋𐤍𐤅 𐤊𐤉 𐤍𐤉𐤔𐤌𐤅𐤓 𐤋𐤏𐤎𐤅𐤕 𐤀𐤕 𐤊𐤋 𐤄𐤌𐤉𐤑𐤅𐤄 𐤄𐤆𐤅𐤀𐤕
𐤋𐤉𐤐𐤍𐤉 𐤉𐤄𐤅𐤄 𐤀𐤋𐤅𐤄𐤉𐤍𐤅 𐤊𐤀𐤔𐤓 𐤑𐤉𐤅𐤍𐤅

𐤃𐤁𐤓𐤉𐤌 𐤐𐤓𐤒 7

1 𐤊𐤉 𐤉𐤁𐤉𐤀𐤊𐤄 𐤉𐤄𐤅𐤄 𐤀𐤋𐤅𐤄𐤉𐤊𐤄 𐤀𐤋 𐤄𐤀𐤓𐤑 𐤀𐤔𐤓
𐤀𐤕𐤄 𐤁𐤀 𐤔𐤌𐤄 𐤋𐤓𐤉𐤔𐤕𐤄 𐤅𐤍𐤔𐤋 𐤂𐤅𐤉𐤉𐤌 𐤓𐤁𐤉𐤌
𐤌𐤉𐤐𐤍𐤉𐤊𐤄 𐤄𐤇𐤉𐤕𐤉 𐤅𐤄𐤂𐤉𐤓𐤂𐤔𐤉 𐤅𐤄𐤀𐤌𐤅𐤓𐤉
𐤅𐤄𐤊𐤍𐤏𐤍𐤉 𐤅𐤄𐤐𐤓𐤉𐤆𐤉 𐤅𐤄𐤇𐤉𐤅𐤉 𐤅𐤄𐤉𐤁𐤅𐤎𐤉
𐤔𐤉𐤁𐤏𐤄 𐤂𐤅𐤉𐤉𐤌 𐤓𐤁𐤉𐤌 𐤅𐤏𐤑𐤅𐤌𐤉𐤌 𐤌𐤉𐤌𐤊𐤄
2 𐤅𐤍𐤕𐤍𐤌 𐤉𐤄𐤅𐤄 𐤀𐤋𐤅𐤄𐤉𐤊𐤄 𐤋𐤐𐤍𐤉𐤊𐤄 𐤅𐤄𐤉𐤊𐤉𐤕𐤌
𐤄𐤇𐤓𐤌 𐤕𐤇𐤓𐤉𐤌 𐤀𐤅𐤕𐤌 𐤋𐤅𐤀 𐤕𐤉𐤊𐤓𐤅𐤕 𐤋𐤄𐤌 𐤁𐤓𐤉𐤕 𐤅𐤋𐤅𐤀
𐤕𐤇𐤍𐤌 3 𐤅𐤋𐤅𐤀 𐤕𐤉𐤕𐤇𐤕𐤍 𐤁𐤌 𐤁𐤉𐤕𐤊𐤄 𐤋𐤅𐤀 𐤕𐤉𐤕𐤍
𐤋𐤉𐤁𐤍𐤅 𐤅𐤁𐤉𐤕𐤅 𐤋𐤅𐤀 𐤕𐤉𐤒𐤇 𐤋𐤉𐤁𐤍𐤊𐤄 4 𐤊𐤉 𐤉𐤎𐤉𐤓 𐤀𐤕
𐤁𐤉𐤍𐤊𐤄 𐤌𐤀𐤇𐤓𐤉 𐤅𐤏𐤁𐤃𐤅 𐤀𐤋𐤅𐤄𐤉𐤌 𐤀𐤇𐤓𐤉𐤌 𐤅𐤇𐤓𐤄 𐤀𐤐
𐤉𐤄𐤅𐤄 𐤁𐤊𐤌 𐤅𐤄𐤔𐤌𐤉𐤃𐤊𐤄 𐤌𐤄𐤓 5 𐤊𐤉 𐤀𐤉𐤌 𐤊𐤅𐤄
𐤕𐤏𐤎𐤅 𐤋𐤄𐤌 𐤌𐤉𐤆𐤁𐤇𐤅𐤕𐤉𐤄𐤌 𐤕𐤉𐤕𐤅𐤑𐤅 𐤅𐤌𐤑𐤁𐤅𐤕𐤌
𐤕𐤔𐤁𐤓𐤅 𐤅𐤀𐤔𐤉𐤓𐤄𐤌 𐤕𐤂𐤃𐤏𐤅𐤍 𐤅𐤐𐤎𐤉𐤋𐤉𐤄𐤌
𐤕𐤉𐤎𐤓𐤐𐤅𐤍 𐤁𐤀𐤔 6 𐤊𐤉 𐤏𐤌 𐤒𐤃𐤅𐤔 𐤀𐤕𐤄 𐤋𐤉𐤄𐤅𐤄
𐤀𐤋𐤅𐤄𐤉𐤊𐤄 𐤁𐤊𐤄 𐤁𐤇𐤓 𐤉𐤄𐤅𐤄 𐤀𐤋𐤅𐤄𐤉𐤊𐤄 𐤋𐤉𐤄𐤉𐤅𐤕 𐤋𐤅
𐤋𐤏𐤌 𐤎𐤂𐤅𐤋𐤄 𐤌𐤉𐤊𐤅𐤋 𐤄𐤏𐤌𐤉𐤌 𐤀𐤔𐤓 𐤏𐤋 𐤐𐤍𐤉
𐤄𐤀𐤃𐤌𐤄 7 𐤋𐤅𐤀 𐤌𐤓𐤅𐤁𐤊𐤌 𐤌𐤉𐤊𐤋 𐤄𐤏𐤌𐤉𐤌 𐤇𐤔𐤒 𐤉𐤄𐤅𐤄
𐤁𐤊𐤌 𐤅𐤉𐤁𐤇𐤓 𐤁𐤊𐤌 𐤊𐤉 𐤀𐤕𐤌 𐤄𐤌𐤏𐤈 𐤌𐤉𐤊𐤋 𐤄𐤏𐤌𐤉𐤌
8 𐤊𐤉 𐤌𐤀𐤄𐤁𐤕 𐤉𐤄𐤅𐤄 𐤀𐤕𐤊𐤌 𐤅𐤌𐤉𐤔𐤌𐤓𐤅 𐤀𐤕 𐤄𐤔𐤁𐤅𐤏𐤄
𐤀𐤔𐤓 𐤍𐤉𐤔𐤁𐤏 𐤋𐤀𐤁𐤅𐤕𐤉𐤊𐤌 𐤄𐤅𐤑𐤉𐤀 𐤉𐤄𐤅𐤄 𐤀𐤕𐤊𐤌
𐤁𐤉𐤃 𐤇𐤆𐤒𐤄 𐤅𐤉𐤐𐤃𐤊𐤄 𐤌𐤁𐤉𐤕 𐤏𐤁𐤃𐤉𐤌 𐤌𐤉𐤃
𐤐𐤓𐤏𐤅𐤄 𐤌𐤋𐤊 𐤌𐤑𐤓𐤉𐤌 9 𐤅𐤉𐤃𐤏𐤕 𐤊𐤉 𐤉𐤄𐤅𐤄
𐤀𐤋𐤅𐤄𐤉𐤊𐤄 𐤄𐤅𐤀 𐤄𐤀𐤋𐤅𐤄𐤉𐤌 𐤄𐤀𐤋 𐤄𐤍𐤀𐤌𐤍 𐤔𐤅𐤌𐤓
𐤄𐤁𐤓𐤉𐤕 𐤅𐤄𐤇𐤎𐤃 𐤋𐤀𐤅𐤄𐤁𐤉𐤅 𐤅𐤋𐤔𐤅𐤌𐤓𐤉 𐤌𐤉𐤑𐤅𐤕𐤅 𐤋𐤀𐤋𐤐
𐤃𐤅𐤓 10 𐤅𐤌𐤔𐤋𐤌 𐤋𐤎𐤅𐤍𐤀𐤉𐤅 𐤀𐤋 𐤐𐤍𐤉𐤅 𐤋𐤄𐤀𐤁𐤉𐤃𐤅 𐤋𐤅𐤀
𐤉𐤀𐤇𐤓 𐤋𐤎𐤅𐤍𐤀𐤅 𐤀𐤋 𐤐𐤍𐤉𐤅 𐤉𐤔𐤋𐤌 𐤋𐤅 11 𐤅𐤔𐤌𐤓𐤕 𐤀𐤕
𐤄𐤌𐤉𐤑𐤅𐤄 𐤅𐤀𐤕 𐤄𐤇𐤅𐤒𐤉𐤌 𐤅𐤀𐤕 𐤄𐤌𐤔𐤐𐤈𐤉𐤌 𐤀𐤔𐤓
𐤀𐤍𐤅𐤊𐤉 𐤌𐤑𐤅𐤊𐤄 𐤄𐤉𐤅𐤌 𐤋𐤏𐤎𐤅𐤕𐤌 12 𐤅𐤄𐤉𐤄 𐤏𐤒𐤁
𐤕𐤉𐤔𐤌𐤏𐤅𐤍 𐤀𐤕 𐤄𐤌𐤔𐤐𐤈𐤉𐤌 𐤄𐤀𐤋𐤄 𐤅𐤔𐤌𐤓𐤕𐤌
𐤅𐤏𐤎𐤉𐤕𐤌 𐤀𐤅𐤕𐤌 𐤅𐤔𐤌𐤓 𐤉𐤄𐤅𐤄 𐤀𐤋𐤅𐤄𐤉𐤊𐤄 𐤋𐤊𐤄 𐤀𐤕
𐤄𐤁𐤓𐤉𐤕 𐤅𐤀𐤕 𐤄𐤇𐤎𐤃 𐤀𐤔𐤓 𐤍𐤉𐤔𐤁𐤏 𐤋𐤀𐤁𐤅𐤕𐤉𐤊𐤄
13 𐤅𐤀𐤄𐤁𐤊𐤄 𐤅𐤁𐤓𐤊𐤊𐤄 𐤅𐤄𐤉𐤓𐤁𐤊𐤄 𐤅𐤁𐤓𐤊 𐤐𐤓𐤉 𐤁𐤉𐤈𐤍𐤊𐤄
𐤅𐤐𐤓𐤉 𐤀𐤃𐤌𐤕𐤊𐤄 𐤃𐤂𐤍𐤊𐤄 𐤅𐤕𐤉𐤓𐤅𐤔𐤊𐤄 𐤅𐤉𐤑𐤄𐤓𐤊𐤄

𐤔𐤂𐤓 𐤀𐤋𐤐𐤉𐤊𐤄 𐤅𐤏𐤔𐤕𐤓𐤅𐤕 𐤑𐤅𐤀𐤍𐤊𐤄 𐤏𐤋 𐤄𐤀𐤃𐤌𐤄 𐤀𐤔𐤓
𐤍𐤉𐤔𐤁𐤏 𐤋𐤀𐤁𐤅𐤕𐤉𐤊𐤄 𐤋𐤕𐤕 𐤋𐤊 14 𐤁𐤓𐤅𐤊 𐤕𐤉𐤄𐤉𐤄
𐤌𐤉𐤊𐤋 𐤄𐤏𐤌𐤉𐤌 𐤋𐤅𐤀 𐤉𐤄𐤉𐤄 𐤁𐤊𐤄 𐤏𐤒𐤓 𐤅𐤏𐤒𐤓𐤄
𐤅𐤁𐤉𐤁𐤄𐤌𐤕𐤊𐤄 15 𐤅𐤄𐤎𐤉𐤓 𐤉𐤄𐤅𐤄 𐤌𐤉𐤌𐤊𐤄 𐤊𐤋 𐤇𐤅𐤋𐤉 𐤅𐤊𐤋
𐤌𐤃𐤅𐤉 𐤌𐤉𐤑𐤓𐤉𐤉𐤌 𐤄𐤓𐤏𐤉𐤌 𐤀𐤔𐤓 𐤉𐤃𐤏𐤕 𐤋𐤅𐤀
𐤉𐤎𐤉𐤌𐤌 𐤁𐤊 𐤅𐤍𐤕𐤍𐤌 𐤁𐤊𐤋 𐤎𐤅𐤍𐤀𐤉𐤊𐤄 16 𐤅𐤀𐤊𐤋𐤕 𐤀𐤕 𐤊𐤋
𐤄𐤏𐤌𐤉𐤌 𐤀𐤔𐤓 𐤉𐤄𐤅𐤄 𐤀𐤋𐤅𐤄𐤉𐤊𐤄 𐤍𐤅𐤕𐤍 𐤋𐤊 𐤋𐤅𐤀 𐤕𐤇𐤅𐤎
𐤏𐤉𐤍𐤊𐤄 𐤏𐤋𐤉𐤄𐤌 𐤅𐤋𐤅𐤀 𐤕𐤏𐤁𐤅𐤃 𐤀𐤕 𐤀𐤋𐤅𐤄𐤉𐤄𐤌 𐤊𐤉
𐤌𐤅𐤒𐤔 𐤄𐤅𐤀 𐤋𐤊 17 𐤊𐤉 𐤕𐤅𐤀𐤌𐤓 𐤁𐤉𐤋𐤁𐤁𐤊𐤄 𐤓𐤁𐤉𐤉𐤌
𐤄𐤂𐤅𐤉𐤉𐤌 𐤄𐤀𐤋𐤄 𐤌𐤉𐤌𐤍𐤉 𐤀𐤉𐤊𐤄 𐤀𐤅𐤊𐤋 𐤋𐤄𐤅𐤓𐤉𐤔𐤌
18 𐤋𐤅𐤀 𐤕𐤉𐤓𐤀 𐤌𐤄𐤌 𐤆𐤊𐤅𐤓 𐤕𐤉𐤆𐤊𐤅𐤓 𐤀𐤕 𐤀𐤔𐤓 𐤏𐤎𐤄
𐤉𐤄𐤅𐤄 𐤀𐤋𐤅𐤄𐤉𐤊𐤄 𐤋𐤐𐤓𐤏𐤅𐤄 𐤅𐤋𐤊𐤋 𐤌𐤉𐤑𐤓𐤉𐤉𐤌
19 𐤄𐤌𐤎𐤅𐤕 𐤄𐤂𐤃𐤅𐤋𐤅𐤕 𐤀𐤔𐤓 𐤓𐤀𐤅 𐤏𐤉𐤍𐤉𐤊𐤄 𐤅𐤄𐤀𐤅𐤕𐤅𐤕
𐤅𐤄𐤌𐤅𐤐𐤕𐤉𐤌 𐤅𐤄𐤉𐤃 𐤄𐤇𐤆𐤒𐤄 𐤅𐤄𐤆𐤓𐤅𐤏 𐤄𐤍𐤈𐤅𐤉𐤄 𐤀𐤔𐤓
𐤄𐤅𐤑𐤉𐤀𐤊𐤄 𐤉𐤄𐤅𐤄 𐤀𐤋𐤅𐤄𐤉𐤊𐤄 𐤊𐤍 𐤉𐤏𐤎𐤄 𐤉𐤄𐤅𐤄
𐤀𐤋𐤅𐤄𐤉𐤊𐤄 𐤋𐤊𐤋 𐤄𐤏𐤌𐤉𐤌 𐤀𐤔𐤓 𐤀𐤕𐤄 𐤉𐤓𐤀
𐤌𐤉𐤐𐤍𐤉𐤄𐤌 20 𐤅𐤂𐤌 𐤀𐤕 𐤄𐤑𐤉𐤓𐤏𐤄 𐤉𐤔𐤋𐤇 𐤉𐤄𐤅𐤄
𐤀𐤋𐤅𐤄𐤉𐤊𐤄 𐤁𐤌 𐤏𐤃 𐤀𐤁𐤅𐤃 𐤄𐤍𐤉𐤔𐤀𐤓𐤉𐤌
𐤅𐤄𐤍𐤉𐤎𐤕𐤓𐤉𐤌 𐤌𐤉𐤐𐤍𐤉𐤊𐤄 21 𐤋𐤅𐤀 𐤕𐤏𐤓𐤅𐤑
𐤌𐤉𐤐𐤍𐤉𐤄𐤌 𐤊𐤉 𐤉𐤄𐤅𐤄 𐤀𐤋𐤅𐤄𐤉𐤊𐤄 𐤁𐤒𐤉𐤓𐤁𐤊𐤄 𐤀𐤋
𐤂𐤃𐤅𐤋 𐤅𐤍𐤅𐤓𐤀 22 𐤅𐤍𐤔𐤋 𐤉𐤄𐤅𐤄 𐤀𐤋𐤅𐤄𐤉𐤊𐤄 𐤀𐤕 𐤄𐤂𐤅𐤉𐤉𐤌
𐤄𐤀𐤋 𐤌𐤉𐤐𐤍𐤉𐤊𐤄 𐤌𐤏𐤈 𐤌𐤏𐤈 𐤋𐤅𐤀 𐤕𐤅𐤊𐤋 𐤊𐤋𐤅𐤕𐤌 𐤌𐤄𐤓
𐤐𐤍 𐤕𐤉𐤓𐤁𐤄 𐤏𐤋𐤉𐤊𐤄 𐤇𐤉𐤕 𐤄𐤎𐤃𐤄 23 𐤅𐤍𐤕𐤍𐤌 𐤉𐤄𐤅𐤄
𐤀𐤋𐤅𐤄𐤉𐤊𐤄 𐤋𐤐𐤍𐤉𐤊𐤄 𐤅𐤄𐤌𐤌 𐤌𐤄𐤅𐤌𐤄 𐤂𐤃𐤅𐤋𐤄 𐤏𐤃
𐤄𐤉𐤔𐤌𐤃𐤌 24 𐤅𐤍𐤕𐤍 𐤌𐤋𐤊𐤉𐤄𐤌 𐤁𐤉𐤃𐤊𐤄 𐤅𐤄𐤀𐤁𐤃𐤕 𐤀𐤕
𐤔𐤌𐤌 𐤌𐤉𐤕𐤇𐤕 𐤄𐤔𐤌𐤉𐤉𐤌 𐤋𐤅𐤀 𐤉𐤕𐤉𐤉𐤑𐤁 𐤀𐤉𐤔
𐤁𐤐𐤍𐤉𐤊𐤄 𐤏𐤃 𐤄𐤉𐤔𐤌𐤉𐤃𐤊𐤄 𐤀𐤅𐤕𐤌 25 𐤐𐤎𐤉𐤋𐤉
𐤀𐤋𐤅𐤄𐤉𐤄𐤌 𐤕𐤉𐤎𐤓𐤐𐤅𐤍 𐤁𐤀𐤔 𐤋𐤅𐤀 𐤕𐤇𐤌𐤅𐤃 𐤊𐤎𐤐 𐤅𐤆𐤄𐤁
𐤏𐤋𐤉𐤄𐤌 𐤅𐤋𐤒𐤇𐤕 𐤋𐤊 𐤐𐤍 𐤕𐤉𐤅𐤒𐤔 𐤁𐤅 𐤊𐤉 𐤕𐤅𐤏𐤁𐤕 𐤉𐤄𐤅𐤄
𐤀𐤋𐤅𐤄𐤉𐤊𐤄 𐤄𐤅𐤀 26 𐤅𐤋𐤅𐤀 𐤕𐤁𐤉𐤀 𐤕𐤅𐤏𐤁𐤄 𐤀𐤋 𐤁𐤉𐤕𐤊𐤄
𐤅𐤄𐤉𐤉𐤕 𐤇𐤓𐤌 𐤊𐤌𐤅𐤄𐤅 𐤔𐤒𐤑 𐤕𐤔𐤒𐤑𐤍𐤅 𐤅𐤕𐤏𐤁 𐤕𐤕𐤏𐤁𐤍𐤅
𐤊𐤉 𐤇𐤓𐤌 𐤄𐤅𐤀

𐤃𐤁𐤓𐤉𐤌 𐤐𐤓𐤒 8

1 𐤊𐤋 𐤄𐤌𐤉𐤑𐤅𐤄 𐤀𐤔𐤓 𐤀𐤍𐤅𐤊𐤉 𐤌𐤑𐤅𐤊𐤄 𐤄𐤉𐤅𐤌
𐤕𐤉𐤔𐤌𐤓𐤅𐤍 𐤋𐤏𐤎𐤅𐤕 𐤋𐤌𐤏𐤍 𐤕𐤉𐤇𐤉𐤅𐤍 𐤅𐤓𐤁𐤉𐤕𐤌
𐤅𐤁𐤀𐤕𐤌 𐤅𐤉𐤓𐤉𐤔𐤕𐤌 𐤀𐤕 𐤄𐤀𐤓𐤑 𐤀𐤔𐤓 𐤍𐤉𐤔𐤁𐤏 𐤉𐤄𐤅𐤄
𐤋𐤀𐤁𐤅𐤕𐤉𐤊𐤌 2 𐤅𐤆𐤊𐤓𐤕 𐤀𐤕 𐤊𐤋 𐤄𐤃𐤓𐤊 𐤀𐤔𐤓 𐤄𐤅𐤋𐤉𐤊𐤊𐤄
𐤉𐤄𐤅𐤄 𐤀𐤋𐤅𐤄𐤉𐤊𐤄 𐤆𐤄 𐤀𐤓𐤁𐤏𐤉𐤌 𐤔𐤍𐤄 𐤁𐤌𐤉𐤃𐤁𐤓
𐤋𐤌𐤏𐤍 𐤏𐤍𐤅𐤕𐤊𐤄 𐤋𐤍𐤎𐤅𐤕𐤊𐤄 𐤋𐤃𐤏𐤕 𐤀𐤕 𐤀𐤔𐤓 𐤁𐤉𐤋𐤁𐤁𐤊𐤄
𐤄𐤕𐤉𐤔𐤌𐤅𐤓 𐤌𐤉𐤑𐤅𐤕𐤅 𐤀𐤉𐤌 𐤋𐤅𐤀 3 𐤅𐤉𐤏𐤍𐤊𐤄

[illegible]
[illegible]
[illegible]
[illegible] 4 [illegible]
[illegible]
[illegible] 5
[illegible] 6 [illegible]
[illegible]
[illegible] 7 [illegible]
[illegible]
[illegible] 8 [illegible]
[illegible]
[illegible] 9
[illegible]
[illegible] 10 [illegible]
[illegible]
[illegible] 11
[illegible]
[illegible] 12 [illegible]
[illegible] 13 [illegible]
[illegible]
[illegible] 14 [illegible]
[illegible]
[illegible] 15 [illegible]
[illegible]
[illegible]
[illegible] 16
[illegible]
[illegible] 17 [illegible]
[illegible] 18 [illegible]
[illegible]
[illegible]
[illegible] 19 [illegible]
[illegible]
[illegible]
[illegible] 20 [illegible]
[illegible]
[illegible]

דברים פרק 9

1 שמע יסראל אתה עובר היום את הירדן לבוא
לרשת גויים גדולים ועצומים מימכה
ערים גדולות ובצורות בשמיים 2 עם גדול ורם
בני ענקים אשר אתה ידעת ואתה שמעת מי
יתיצב ליפני בני ענק 3 וידעת היום כי
יהוה אלוהיכה הוא העובר לפניכה אש אוכלה
הוא ישמידם והוא יכניעם לפניכה
והורשתם והאבדתם מהר כאשר דיבר יהוה לך
4 אל תואמר בילבבכה בהדוף יהוה אלוהיכה
אותם מילפניכה לאמור בצדקתי הביאני
יהוה לרשת את הארץ הזואת וברישעת הגויים
האלה יהוה מורישם מיפניכה 5 לוא
בצידקתכה וביושר לבבכה אתה בא לרשת את ארצם
כי ברישעת הגויים האלה יהוה אלוהיכה
מורישם מיפניכה ולמען הקים את הדבר
אשר נישבע יהוה לאבותיכה לאברהם ליצחק
וליעקוב 6 וידעת כי לוא בצידקתכה יהוה
אלוהיכה נותן לכה את הארץ הטובה הזואת
לרישתה כי עם קשה עורף אתה 7 זכור אל
תישכח את אשר היקצפת את יהוה אלוהיכה
במידבר למין היום אשר יצאת מארץ
מיצריים עד בואכם עד המקום הזה ממרים
הייתם עים יהוה 8 ובחורב היקצפתם את
יהוה ויתאנף יהוה בכם להשמיד אתכם
9 בעלותי ההרה לקחת לוחות האבנים לוחות
הברית אשר כרת יהוה עימכם ואשב בהר
ארבעים יום וארבעים לילה לחם לוא אכלתי
ומיים לוא שתיתי 10 ויתן יהוה אלי את
שני לוחות האבנים כתובים באצבע אלוהים
ועליהם ככל הדברים אשר דיבר יהוה עימכם
בהר מיתוך האש ביום הקהל 11 ויהי מיקץ
ארבעים יום וארבעים לילה נתן יהוה אלי
את שני לוחות האבנים לוחות הברית
12 ויואמר יהוה אלי קום רד מהר מיזה כי
שיחת עמכה אשר הוצאת מיצריים סרו
מהר מין הדרך אשר ציויתים עסו להם מסכה
13 ויואמר יהוה אלי לאמור ראיתי את העם
הזה והינה עם קשה עורף הוא 14 הרף
מימני ואשמידם ואמחה את שמם מיתחת
השמיים ואעסה אותכה לגוי עצום ורב

[illegible] 15 [illegible]
[illegible] 16 [illegible]
[illegible]
[illegible]
[illegible] 17 [illegible]
[illegible]
[illegible] 18
[illegible]
[illegible]
[illegible] 19 [illegible]
[illegible]
[illegible]
[illegible] 20 [illegible]
[illegible]
[illegible] 21
[illegible]
[illegible]
[illegible] 22 [illegible]
[illegible] 23 [illegible]
[illegible]
[illegible]
[illegible]
[illegible] 24
[illegible] 25 [illegible]
[illegible]
[illegible] 26 [illegible]
[illegible]
[illegible]
[illegible] 27 [illegible]
[illegible]
[illegible] 28 [illegible]
[illegible]
[illegible]
[illegible]
[illegible] 29
[illegible]

10 [illegible]

[illegible] 1
[illegible]
[illegible] 2 [illegible]

[illegible]
[illegible] 22 [illegible]
[illegible]
[illegible]

11 [illegible]

[illegible] 1
[illegible]
[illegible] 2
[illegible]
[illegible] 3 [illegible]
[illegible]
[illegible] 4 [illegible]
[illegible]
[illegible]
[illegible] 5 [illegible]
[illegible] 6 [illegible]
[illegible]
[illegible]
[illegible]
[illegible] 7 [illegible]
[illegible] 8 [illegible]
[illegible]
[illegible]
[illegible] 9 [illegible]
[illegible]
[illegible] 10 [illegible]
[illegible]
[illegible]
[illegible] 11 [illegible]
[illegible]
[illegible] 12 [illegible]
[illegible]
[illegible]
[illegible] 13
[illegible]
[illegible]
[illegible] 14
[illegible] 15 [illegible]
[illegible] 16 [illegible]
[illegible]

17

18

19

20

21

22

23

24

25

26

27

28

29

30

31

32

דברים פרק 12

1 אלה החוקים והמישפטים אשר תישמרון
לעשות בארץ אשר נתן יהוה אלוהי אבותיכה
לכה לרישתה כל הימים אשר אתם חיים על
האדמה 2 אבד תאבדון את כל המקומות אשר עבדו
שם הגויים אשר אתם יורשים אותם את
אלוהיהם על ההרים הרמים ועל הגבעות ותחת
כל עץ רענן 3 וניתצתם את מיזבחותם
ושיברתם את מצבותם ואשריהם תישרפון
באש ופסילי אלוהיהם תגדעון ואיבדתם את
שמם מין המקום ההוא 4 לוא תעשון כן ליהוה
אלוהיכם 5 כי אים אל המקום אשר יבחר יהוה
אלוהיכם מיכל שיבטיכם לשום את שמו שם
לשיכנו תידרשו ובאת שמה 6 והבאתם שמה
עולותיכם וזיבחיכם ואת מעשרותיכם ואת
תרומת ידכם ונידריכם ונידבותיכם ובכורות
בקרכם וצאנכם 7 ואכלתם שם ליפני יהוה
אלוהיכם ושמחתם בכול מישלח ידכם אתם
ובתיכם אשר ברככה יהוה אלוהיכה 8 לוא תעשון
ככול אשר אנחנו עושים פוה היום איש כל
הישר בעיניו 9 כי לוא באתם עד עתה אל
המנוחה ואל הנחלה אשר יהוה אלוהיכה נותן
לך 10 ועברתם את הירדן וישבתם בארץ אשר
יהוה אלוהיכם מנחיל אתכם והניח לכם
מיכל אויביכם מיסביב וישבתם בטח
11 והיה המקום אשר יבחר יהוה אלוהיכם בו
לשכן שמו שם שמה תביאו את כל אשר אנוכי
מצוה אתכם עולותיכם וזיבחיכם מעשרותיכם
ותרומת ידכם וכול מיבחר נידריכם אשר
תידרו ליהוה 12 ושמחתם ליפני יהוה
אלוהיכם אתם ובניכם ובנותיכם ועבדיכם
ואמהותיכם והלוי אשר בשעריכם כי אין לו
חלק ונחלה איתכם 13 השמר לכה פן תעלה
עולותיכה בכל מקום אשר תיראה 14 כי אים
במקום אשר יבחר יהוה באחד שבטיכה שם תעלה
עולותיכה ושם תעשה כול אשר אנוכי מצוכה
15 רק בכל אות נפשכה תיזבח ואכלת בשר כבירכת
יהוה אלוהיכה אשר נתן לכה בכל שעריכה
הטמא והטהור יואכלנו כצבי וכאיל 16 רק הדם
לוא תואכלו על הארץ תישפכנו כמיים 17 לוא
תוכל לאכול בשעריכה מעשר דגנכה ותירושכה

18

19

20

21

22

23

24

25

26

27

28

29

30

31

13

1

ונתן לכה רחמים וריחמכה והירבכה כאשר
נישבע לאבותיכה 19 כי תישמע בקול יהוה
אלוהיכה לישמור את כל מיצותיו אשר אנוכי
מצוכה היום לעסות הישר בעיני יהוה
אלוהיכה

דברים פרק 14

1 בנים אתם ליהוה אלוהיכם לוא תיתגודדו
ולוא תסימו קרחה בין עיניכם למת 2 כי עם
קדוש אתה ליהוה אלוהיכה ובכה בחר יהוה
ליהיות לו לעם סגולה מכול העמים אשר על
פני האדמה 3 לוא תואכל כל תועבה 4 זואת
הבהמה אשר תואכלו שור סה כסבים וסה עיזים
5 איל וצבי ויחמור ואקו ודישון ותאו וזמר
6 וכל בהמה מפרסת פרסה ושוסעת שסע שתי
פרסות מעלת גרה בבהמה אותה תואכלו 7 אך את זה
לוא תואכלו מימעלי הגרה ומימפריסי
הפרסה השסועה את הגמל ואת הארנבת ואת
השפן כי מעלה גרה המה ופרסה לוא
היפריסו טמאים הם לכם 8 ואת החזיר כי
מפריס פרסה הוא ולוא גרה טמא הוא לכם
מיבשרם לוא תואכלו ובניבלתם לוא תיגעו 9 את
זה תואכלו מכול אשר במיים כול אשר לו
סנפיר וקסקסת תואכלו 10 וכול אשר אין לו
סנפיר וקסקסת לוא תואכלו טמא הוא לכם 11 כל
ציפור טהורה תואכלו 12 וזה אשר לוא תואכלו
מהם הנשר והפרס והעזניה 13 והראה ואת
האיה והדיה למינה 14 ואת כל עורב למינו
15 ואת בת היענה ואת התחמס ואת השחף ואת
הנץ למינהו 16 את הכוס ואת הינשוף
והתינשמת 17 והקאת ואת הרחמה ואת השלך
18 והחסידה והאנפה למינה והדוכיפת והעטל
19 וכול שרץ העוף טמא הוא לכם לוא יאכלו 20 כל
עוף טהור תואכלו 21 לוא תואכלו כל נבלה לגר אשר
בישעריכה תיתננה ואכלה או מכור לנכרי
כי עם קדוש אתה ליהוה אלוהיכה לוא תבשל גדי
בחלב אימו 22 עסר תעסר את כל תבואת זרעכה
היוצא הסדה שנה שנה 23 ואכלת לפני יהוה
אלוהיכה במקום אשר יבחר לשכן שמו שם
מעסר דגנכה תירושכה וייצהרכה ובכורות

בקרכה וצואנכה למענ תילמד לייראה את
יהוה אלוהיכה כל הימימ 24 וכי ירבה
מימכה הדרכ כי לוא תוכל סאתו כי ירחק
מימכה המקומ אשר יבחר יהוה אלוהיכה לסומ
שמו שמ כי יברככה יהוה אלוהיכה 25 ונתתה
בכספ וצרת הכספ בידכה והלכת אל המקומ אשר
יבחר יהוה אלוהיכה בו 26 ונתתה הכספ בכול
אשר תאוה נפשכה בבקר ובצואנ וביין ובשכר
ובכול אשר תישאלכה נפשכה ואכלת שמ
ליפני יהוה אלוהיכה וסמחת אתה וביתכה
27 והלוי אשר בישעריכה לוא תעזבנו כי אינ
לו חלק ונחלה עימכ 28 מיקצה שלוש שנימ
תוציא את כל מעסר תבואתכה בשנה ההיוא
והינחת בישעריכה 29 ובא הלוי כי אינ לו
חלק ונחלה עימכ והגר והיתומ והאלמנה אשר
בישעריכה ואכלו וסבעו למענ יברככה יהוה
אלוהיכה בכל מעסה ידכה אשר תעסה

דברים פרק 15

1 מיקצ שבע שנימ תעסה שמיטה 2 וזה דבר
השמיטה שמוט כל בעל משה ידו אשר ישה
ברעהו לוא יגוס את רעהו ואת אחיו כי קרא
שמיטה ליהוה 3 את הנכרי תיגוס ואשר
יהיה לכה את אחיכה תשמט ידכה 4 אפס כי
לוא יהיה בכה אביונ כי ברכ יברככה יהוה
בארצ אשר יהוה אלוהיכה נותנ לכה נחלה
לרישתה 5 רק אימ שמוע תישמע בקול יהוה
אלוהיכה לישמור לעסות את כל המיצוה הזואת
אשר אנוכי מצוכה היומ 6 כי יהוה אלוהיכה
ברככה כאשר דיבר לכ והעבטת גויימ רבימ
ואתה לוא תעבט ומשלת בגויימ רבימ ובכה לוא
ימשולו 7 כי יהיה בכה אביונ מאחד אחיכה
באחד שעריכה בארצכה אשר יהוה אלוהיכה
נותנ לכ לוא תאמצ את לבבכה ולוא תיקפוצ את
ידכה מאחיכה האביונ 8 כי פתוח תיפתח את
ידכה לו והעבט תעביטנו די מחסורו אשר יחסר
לו 9 הישמר לכה פנ יהיה דבר עימ לבבכה
בליעל לאמור קרבה שנת השבע שנת השמיטה
ורעה עינכה באחיכה האביונ ולוא תיתנ לו
וקרא עליכה אל יהוה והיה בכה חטא 10 נתונ
תיתנ לו ולוא ירע לבבכה בתיתכה לו כי ביגלל

הדבר הזה יברככה יהוה אלוהיכה בכל מעסכה
ובכול מישלח ידכה 11 כי לוא יחדל אביון
מיקרב הארץ על כן אנוכי מצוכה לאמור פתוח
תיפתח את ידכה לאחיכה לעניכה ולאביונכה
בארצכה 12 כי ימכר לכה אחיכה העיברי או
העיבריה ועבדכה שש שנים ובשנה
השביעית תשלחנו חפשי מעימך 13 וכי
תשלחנו חפשי מעימך לוא תשלחנו ריקם
14 העניק תעניק לו מיצואנכה ומיגרנכה
ומיקבכה אשר ברככה יהוה אלוהיכה תיתן לו
15 וזכרת כי עבד היית בארץ מיצריים
ויפדכה יהוה אלוהיכה על כן אנוכי מצוכה
את הדבר הזה היום 16 והיה כי יואמר אליכה
לוא אצא מעימך כי אהבכה ואת ביתכה כי טוב לו
עימך 17 ולקחת את המרצע ונתתה באזנו ובדלת
והיה לכה עבד עולם ואף לאמתכה תעסה כן
18 לוא יקשה בעינכה בשלחכה אותו חפשי
מעימך כי מישנה סכר סכיר עבדכה שש
שנים וברככה יהוה אלוהיכה בכול אשר תעסה
19 כל הבכור אשר יולד ביבקרכה ובצואנכה הזכר
תקדיש ליהוה אלוהיכה לוא תעבוד ביבכור
שורכה ולוא תגוז בכור צואנכה 20 ליפני יהוה
אלוהיכה תואכלנו שנה בשנה במקום אשר יבחר
יהוה אתה וביתכה 21 וכי יהיה בו מום פיסח
או עיור כול מום רע לוא תיזבחנו ליהוה
אלוהיכה 22 בישעריכה תואכלנו הטמא והטהור
יחדו כצבי וכאיל 23 רק את דמו לוא תואכל על
הארץ תישפכנו כמיים

דברים פרק 16

1 שמור את חודש האביב ועסית פסח ליהוה
אלוהיכה כי בחודש האביב הוציאכה יהוה
אלוהיכה מימיצריים לילה 2 וזבחת פסח
ליהוה אלוהיכה צואן ובקר במקום אשר יבחר
יהוה לשכן שמו שם 3 לוא תואכל עליו חמץ
שיבעת ימים תואכל עליו מצות לחם עוני
כי בחיפזון יצאת מארץ מיצריים למען
תיזכור את יום צאתכה מארץ מיצריים כול
ימי חייכה 4 ולוא יראה לכה סאור בכל גבולכה
שיבעת ימים ולוא ילין מין הבסר אשר
תיזבח בערב ביום הראשון לבוקר 5 לוא תוכל

6

7

8

9

10

11

12

13

14

15

16

17

18

19

20

21

22

דברים פרק 17

1 לוא תיזבח ליהוה אלוהיכה שור וסה אשר
יהיה בו מום כול דבר רע כי תועבת יהוה
אלוהיכה הוא 2 כי ימצא בקירבכה באחד
שעריכה אשר יהוה אלוהיכה נותן לך איש או
אישה אשר יעסה את הרע בעיני יהוה
אלוהיכה לעבור בריתו 3 וילך ויעבוד אלוהים
אחרים וישתחו להם ולשמש או לירח או לכל צבא
השמיים אשר לוא ציויתי 4 והוגד לכה
ושמעת ודרשת היטב והינה אמת נכון הדבר
נעסתה התועבה הזואת ביישראל 5 והוצאת את
האיש ההוא או את האישה ההוא אשר עסו את
הדבר הרע הזה אל שעריכה את האיש או את
האישה וסקלתם באבנים ומתו 6 על פי
שניים עדים או שלושה עדים יומת המת
לוא יומת על פי עד אחד 7 יד העדים תיהיה
בו בריאשונה להמיתו ויד כל העם באחרונה
וביערת הרע מיקירבכה 8 כי יפלא מימכה
דבר למישפט בין דם לדם בין דין לדין
ובין נגע לנגע דיברי ריבות בישעריכה
וקמת ועלית אל המקום אשר יבחר יהוה
אלוהיכה בו 9 ובאת אל הכוהנים הלוים ואל
השופט אשר יהיה בימים ההם ודרשת
והיגידו לכה את דבר המישפט 10 ועסית על
פי הדבר אשר יגידו לכה מין המקום ההוא
אשר יבחר יהוה ושמרת לעסות ככול אשר יורוכה
11 על פי התורה אשר יורוכה ועל המישפט
אשר יואמרו לכה תעסה לוא תסור מין הדבר אשר
יגידו לכה ימין וסמאל 12 והאיש אשר
יעסה בזדון לבילתי שמוע אל הכוהן העומד
לשרת שם את יהוה אלוהיכה או אל השופט ומת
האיש ההוא וביערת הרע מישראל 13 וכל העם
ישמעו וייראו ולוא יזידון עוד 14 כי תבוא
אל הארץ אשר יהוה אלוהיכה נותן לך
וירשתה וישבתה בה ואמרת אסימה עלי מלך
ככל הגויים אשר סביבותי 15 סום תסים
עליכה מלך אשר יבחר יהוה אלוהיכה בו
מיקרב אחיכה תסים עליכה מלך לוא תוכל לתת
עליכה איש נכרי אשר לוא אחיכה הוא 16 רק
לוא ירבה לו סוסים ולוא ישיב את העם
מיצרימה למען הרבות סוס ויהוה אמר לכם

לוא תוסיפון לשוב בדרך הזה עוד 17 ולוא ירבה לו
נשים ולוא יסור לבבו וכסף וזהב לוא ירבה לו
מאוד 18 והיה כשיבתו על כיסא ממלכתו וכתב לו
את מישנה התורה הזואת על ספר מיליפני
הכוהנים הלוים 19 והיתה עימו וקרא בו כל
ימי חייו למען יילמד לייראה את יהוה
אלוהיו לישמור את כל דיברי התורה הזואת ואת
החוקים האלה לעסותם 20 לבילתי רום לבבו
מאחיו ולבילתי סור מין המיצוה ימין
וסמואול למען יאריך ימים על ממלכתו הוא
ובניו בקרב יסראל

דברים פרק 18

1 לוא יהיה לכוהנים הלוים כל שבט לוי חלק
ונחלה עים יסראל אישי יהוה ונחלתו
יואכלון 2 ונחלה לוא יהיה לו בקרב אחיו יהוה
הוא נחלתו כאשר דיבר לו 3 וזה יהיה מישפט
הכוהנים מאת העם מאת זובחי הזבח אים שור
אים סה ונתן לכוהן הזרוע והלחייים והקבה
4 ראשית דגנכה תירושכה וייצהרכה
וראשית גז צואנכה תיתן לו 5 כי בו בחר יהוה
אלוהיכה מיכל שבטיכה לעמוד לשרת בשם
יהוה הוא ובניו כל הימים 6 וכי יבוא הלוי
מאחד שעריכה מיכל יסראל אשר הוא גר שם
ובא בכל אות נפשו אל המקום אשר יבחר יהוה
7 ושרת בשם יהוה אלוהיו ככל אחיו הלוים
העומדים שם ליפני יהוה 8 חלק כחלק
יואכלו לבד מימכריו על האבות 9 כי אתה בא אל
הארץ אשר יהוה אלוהיכה נותן לך לוא תילמד
לעסות כתועבות הגויים ההם 10 לוא ימצא בכה
מעביר בנו וביתו באש קוסם קסמים מעונן
ומנחש ומכש 11 וחובר חבר ושואל אוב ויידעוני
ודורש אל המתים 12 כי תועבת יהוה כל עוסה
אלה וביגלל התועבות האלה יהוה אלוהיכה
מוריש אותם מיפניכה 13 תמים תהיה
עים יהוה אלוהיכה 14 כי הגויים האלה אשר
אתה יורש אותם אל מעוננים ואל קסמים
ישמעו ואתה לוא כן נתן לכה יהוה
15 נביא מיקירבכה מאחיכה כמוני יקים
לכה יהוה אלוהיכה אליו תישמעון 16 ככול

[illegible]
[illegible]
[illegible]
[illegible] 17 [illegible]
[illegible] 18
[illegible]
[illegible] 19 [illegible]
[illegible]
[illegible] 20
[illegible]
[illegible] 21 [illegible]
[illegible]
[illegible] 22 [illegible]
[illegible]
[illegible]
[illegible]

[illegible] 19

[illegible] 1
[illegible]
[illegible] 2 [illegible]
[illegible]
[illegible] 3 [illegible]
[illegible]
[illegible] 4 [illegible]
[illegible]
[illegible] 5 [illegible]
[illegible]
[illegible]
[illegible]
[illegible] 6 [illegible]
[illegible]
[illegible]
[illegible] 7 [illegible]
[illegible] 8 [illegible]
[illegible]
[illegible]
[illegible] 9 [illegible]
[illegible]
[illegible]
[illegible]

10 ולוא ישפכ דמ נקי בקרב ארצכה אשר יהוה
אלוהיכה נותנ לכה נחלה והיה עליכה דמימ
11 וכי יהיה איש סונא לרעהו וארב לו וקמ
עליו והיכהו נפש ומת ונס אל אחת הערימ
האל 12 ושלחו זקני עירו ולקחו אותו מישמ
ונתנו אותו ביד גואל הדמ ומת 13 לוא תחוס
עינכה עליו וביערת דמ הנקי מיסראל וטוב
לכ 14 לוא תסיג גבול רעכה אשר גבלו
ריאשונימ בנחלתכה אשר תינחל בארצ אשר
יהוה אלוהיכה נותנ לכה לרישתה 15 לוא יקומ
עד אחד באיש לכל עונ ולכל חטאת בכל חטא אשר
יחטא על פי שני עדימ או על פי שלושה
עדימ יקומ דבר 16 כי יקומ עד חמס באיש
לענות בו סרה 17 ועמדו שני האנשימ אשר
להמ הריב ליפני יהוה ליפני הכוהנימ
והשופטימ אשר יהיו בימימ ההמ 18 ודרשו
השופטימ היטב והינה עד שקר העד שקר ענה
באחיו 19 ועסיתמ לו כאשר זממ לעסות לאחיו
וביערת הרע מיקירבכה 20 והנישארימ
ישמעו וייראו ולוא יוסיפו לעסות עוד כדבר
הרע הזה בקירבכה 21 ולוא תחוס עינכה נפש
בנפש עינ בעינ שנ בשנ יד ביד רגל
ברגל

דברימ פרק 20

1 כי תצא למילחמה על אויביכה וראית סוס
ורכב עמ רב מימכה לוא תירא מהמ כי יהוה
אלוהיכה עימכ המעלכה מארצ מיצריימ
והיה 2 כקרבכמ אל המילחמה וניגש הכוהנ
ודיבר אל העמ 3 ואמר אלהמ שמע יסראל אתמ
קרבימ היומ למילחמה על אויביכמ אל ירכ
לבבכמ אל תיראו ואל תחפזו ואל תערצו
מיפניהמ 4 כי יהוה אלוהיכמ ההולכ
עימכמ להילחמ לכמ עימ אויביכמ
להושיע אתכמ 5 ודיברו השוטרימ אל העמ
לאמור מי האיש אשר בנה בית חדש ולוא
חנכו ילכ וישוב לביתו פנ ימות במילחמה
ואיש אחר יחנכנו 6 ומי האיש אשר נטע כרמ
ולוא חיללו ילכ וישוב לביתו פנ ימות
במילחמה ואיש אחר יחללנו 7 ומי האיש
אשר ארס אשה ולוא לקחה ילכ וישוב לביתו

פן ימות במילחמה ואיש אחר יקחנה
8 ויספו השוטרים לדבר אל העם ואמרו מי
האיש הירא ורך הלבב ילך וישוב לביתו ולוא
ימס את לבב אחיו כילבבו 9 והיה ככלות
השוטרים לדבר אל העם ופקדו סרי צבאות ברואש
העם 10 כי תיקרב אל עיר להילחם עליה
וקראת אליה לשלום 11 והיה אים שלום תענכה
ופתחה לך והיה כל העם הנימצא בה יהיו לכה
למס ועבדוכה 12 ואים לוא תשלים עימך ועסתה
עימכה מילחמה וצרת עליה 13 ונתנה יהוה
אלוהיכה בידכה והכית את כל זכורה לפי חר
14 רק הנשים והטף והבהמה וכול אשר יהיה
בעיר כל שללה תבוז לך ואכלת את שלל אויביכה
אשר נתן יהוה אלוהיכה לך 15 כן תעסה לכל
הערים הרחוקות מימכה מאוד אשר לוא מערי
הגויים האלה הנה 16 רק מערי העמים האלה
אשר יהוה אלוהיכה נותן לכה נחלה לוא תחיה
כל נשמה 17 כי החרם תחרימם החיתי
והאמורי הכנעני והפריזי החיוי
והיבוסי כאשר ציוכה יהוה אלוהיכה 18 למען
אשר לוא ילמדו אתכם לעסות ככול תועבותם אשר
עסו לאלוהיהם וחטאתם ליהוה אלוהיכם 19 כי
תצור אל עיר ימים רבים להילחם עליה
לתפסה לוא תשחית את עצה לינדוח עליו גרזן
כי מימנו תואכל ואותו לוא תיכרות כי האדם
עץ הסדה לבוא מיפניכה במצור 20 רק עץ אשר
תדע כי לוא עץ מאכל הוא אותו תשחית וכרת
ובנית מצור על העיר אשר היוא עוסה עימכה
מילחמה עד רידתה

דברים פרק 21

1 כי ימצא חלל באדמה אשר יהוה אלוהיכה
נותן לכה לרישתה נופל בסדה לוא נודע מי
היכהו 2 ויצאו זקניכה ושופטיכה ומדדו אל
הערים אשר סביבות החלל 3 והיה העיר הקרובה
אל החלל ולקחו זיקני העיר ההיוא עגלת בקר
אשר לוא עובד בה אשר לוא משכה בעול 4 והורידו
זיקני העיר ההיוא את העגלה אל נחל איתן
אשר לוא יעבד בו ולוא יזרע וערפו שם את
העגלה בנחל 5 וניגשו הכהנים בני לוי כי
בם בחר יהוה אלוהיכה לשרתו ולברך בשם יהוה

ועל פיהם יהיה כל ריב וכל נגע 6 וכול
זיקני העיר ההיוא הקרובים אל החלל ירחצו
את ידיהם על העגלה הערופה בנחל 7 וענו
ואמרו ידינו לוא שפכה את הדם הזה
ועינינו לוא ראו 8 כפר לעמכה ישׂראל אשר
פדית יהוה ואל תיתן דם נקי בקרב עמכה
ישׂראל וניכפר להם הדם 9 ואתה תבער הדם
הנקי מיקירבכה כי תעשׂה הישר בעיני
יהוה 10 כי תצא למילחמה על אויביכה ונתנו
יהוה אלוהיכה בידכה ושבית שיביו 11 וראית
בשיביה אשת יפת תואר וחשקת בה ולקחת לכה
לאישה 12 והבאתה אל תוך ביתכה וגילחה את
רואשה ועשׂתה את ציפרניה 13 והסירה את
סימלת שיביה מעליה וישבה בביתכה ובכתה
את אביה ואת אימה ירח ימים ואחר כן תבוא
אליה ובעלתה והיתה לכה לאישה 14 והיה אים
לוא חפצת בה ושילחתה לנפשה ומכור לוא
תימכרנה בכסף לוא תיתעמר בה תחת אשר
עיניתה 15 כי תיהיין לאיש שתי
נשים האחת אהובה והאחת שׂנואה וילדו לו
בנים האהובה והשׂנואה והיה הבן הבכור
לשׂניאה 16 והיה ביום הנחילו את בניו את
אשר יהיה לו לוא יוכל לבכר את בן האהובה על
פני בן השׂנואה הבכור 17 כי את הבכור בן
השׂנואה יכיר לתת לו פי שניים בכול אשר
ימצא לו כי הוא ראשית אונו לו מישפט
הבכורה 18 כי יהיה לאיש בן סורר ומורה
איננו שומע בקול אביו ובקול אימו וייסרו
אותו ולוא ישמע אליהם 19 ותפסו בו אביו
ואימו והוציאו אותו אל זיקני עירו ואל שער
מקומו 20 ואמרו אל זיקני עירו בננו זה סורר
ומורה איננו שומע בקולנו זולל וסובא
21 ורגמוהו כל אנשי עירו באבנים ומת
וביערת הרע מיקירבכה וכל ישׂראל ישמעו
וייראו 22 וכי יהיה באיש חטא מישפט מות
והומת ותלית אותו על עץ 23 לוא תלין ניבלתו
על העץ כי קבור תיקברנו ביום ההוא כי קיללת
אלוהים תלוי ולוא תטמא את אדמתכה אשר יהוה
אלוהיכה נותן לכה נחלה

22 [illegible]

[illegible] 1
[illegible] 2 [illegible]
[illegible]
[illegible]
[illegible] 3 [illegible]
[illegible]
[illegible] 4 [illegible]
[illegible]
[illegible] 5 [illegible]
[illegible]
[illegible]
[illegible] 6
[illegible]
[illegible]
[illegible] 7 [illegible]
[illegible] 8 [illegible]
[illegible]
[illegible] 9 [illegible]
[illegible]
[illegible] 10 [illegible]
[illegible] 11 [illegible]
[illegible] 12 [illegible]
[illegible] 13 [illegible]
[illegible] 14 [illegible]
[illegible]
[illegible]
[illegible] 15 [illegible]
[illegible] 16 [illegible]
[illegible]
[illegible] 17 [illegible]
[illegible]
[illegible]
[illegible] 18 [illegible]
[illegible] 19 [illegible]
[illegible]
[illegible]
[illegible] 20 [illegible]
[illegible] 21 [illegible]
[illegible]

22

23

24

25

26

27

28

29

23

1

2

3

4

5

6

7

8

9

10

11

𐤌𐤉𐤒𐤓𐤄 𐤋𐤉𐤋𐤄 𐤅𐤉𐤑𐤀 𐤀𐤋 𐤌𐤉𐤇𐤅𐤑 𐤋𐤌𐤇𐤍𐤄 𐤋𐤅𐤀 𐤉𐤁𐤅𐤀
𐤀𐤋 𐤕𐤅𐤊 𐤄𐤌𐤇𐤍𐤄 12 𐤅𐤄𐤉𐤄 𐤋𐤉𐤐𐤍𐤅𐤕 𐤏𐤓𐤁 𐤉𐤓𐤇𐤑
𐤁𐤌𐤉𐤉𐤌 𐤅𐤊𐤁𐤅𐤀 𐤄𐤔𐤌𐤔 𐤉𐤁𐤅𐤀 𐤀𐤋 𐤕𐤅𐤊 𐤄𐤌𐤇𐤍𐤄
13 𐤅𐤉𐤃 𐤕𐤉𐤄𐤉𐤄 𐤋𐤊𐤄 𐤌𐤉𐤇𐤅𐤑 𐤋𐤌𐤇𐤍𐤄 𐤅𐤉𐤑𐤀𐤕 𐤔𐤌𐤄
𐤇𐤅𐤑 14 𐤅𐤉𐤕𐤃 𐤕𐤉𐤄𐤉𐤄 𐤋𐤊𐤄 𐤏𐤋 𐤀𐤆𐤍𐤊𐤄 𐤅𐤄𐤉𐤄
𐤁𐤔𐤉𐤁𐤕𐤊𐤄 𐤇𐤅𐤑 𐤅𐤇𐤐𐤓𐤕𐤄 𐤁𐤄 𐤅𐤔𐤁𐤕 𐤅𐤊𐤉𐤎𐤉𐤕 𐤀𐤕
𐤑𐤀𐤕𐤊𐤄 15 𐤊𐤉 𐤉𐤄𐤅𐤄 𐤀𐤋𐤅𐤄𐤉𐤊𐤄 𐤌𐤉𐤕𐤄𐤋𐤊 𐤁𐤒𐤓𐤁
𐤌𐤇𐤍𐤊𐤄 𐤋𐤄𐤑𐤉𐤋𐤊𐤄 𐤅𐤋𐤕𐤕 𐤀𐤅𐤉𐤁𐤉𐤊𐤄 𐤋𐤐𐤍𐤉𐤊𐤄
𐤅𐤄𐤉𐤄 𐤌𐤇𐤍𐤉𐤊𐤄 𐤒𐤃𐤅𐤔 𐤅𐤋𐤅𐤀 𐤉𐤓𐤀𐤄 𐤁𐤊𐤄 𐤏𐤓𐤅𐤕 𐤃𐤁𐤓
𐤅𐤔𐤁 𐤌𐤀𐤇𐤓𐤉𐤊𐤄 16 𐤋𐤅𐤀 𐤕𐤎𐤂𐤉𐤓 𐤏𐤁𐤃 𐤀𐤋 𐤀𐤃𐤅𐤍𐤉𐤅
𐤀𐤔𐤓 𐤉𐤍𐤑𐤋 𐤀𐤋𐤉𐤊𐤄 𐤌𐤏𐤉𐤌 𐤀𐤃𐤅𐤍𐤉𐤅 17 𐤏𐤉𐤌𐤊𐤄
𐤉𐤔𐤁 𐤁𐤒𐤉𐤓𐤁𐤊𐤄 𐤁𐤌𐤒𐤅𐤌 𐤀𐤔𐤓 𐤉𐤁𐤇𐤓 𐤁𐤀𐤇𐤃 𐤔𐤏𐤓𐤉𐤊𐤄
𐤁𐤈𐤅𐤁 𐤋𐤅 𐤋𐤅𐤀 𐤕𐤅𐤍𐤍𐤅 18 𐤋𐤅𐤀 𐤕𐤉𐤄𐤉𐤄 𐤒𐤃𐤔𐤄 𐤌𐤉𐤁𐤍𐤅𐤕
𐤉𐤎𐤓𐤀𐤋 𐤅𐤋𐤅𐤀 𐤉𐤄𐤉𐤄 𐤒𐤃𐤔 𐤌𐤉𐤁𐤍𐤉 𐤉𐤎𐤓𐤀𐤋 19 𐤋𐤅𐤀
𐤕𐤁𐤉𐤀 𐤀𐤕𐤍𐤍 𐤆𐤅𐤍𐤄 𐤅𐤌𐤇𐤉𐤓 𐤊𐤋𐤁 𐤁𐤉𐤕 𐤉𐤄𐤅𐤄
𐤀𐤋𐤅𐤄𐤉𐤊𐤄 𐤋𐤊𐤋 𐤍𐤃𐤓 𐤊𐤉 𐤕𐤅𐤏𐤁𐤕 𐤉𐤄𐤅𐤄 𐤀𐤋𐤅𐤄𐤉𐤊𐤄 𐤂𐤌
𐤔𐤍𐤉𐤄𐤌 20 𐤋𐤅𐤀 𐤕𐤔𐤉𐤊 𐤋𐤀𐤇𐤉𐤊𐤄 𐤍𐤔𐤊 𐤊𐤎𐤐 𐤍𐤔𐤊
𐤀𐤅𐤊𐤋 𐤍𐤔𐤊 𐤊𐤋 𐤃𐤁𐤓 𐤀𐤔𐤓 𐤉𐤔𐤊 21 𐤋𐤍𐤊𐤓𐤉 𐤕𐤔𐤉𐤊
𐤅𐤋𐤀𐤇𐤉𐤊𐤄 𐤋𐤅𐤀 𐤕𐤔𐤉𐤊 𐤋𐤌𐤏𐤍 𐤉𐤁𐤓𐤊𐤊𐤄 𐤉𐤄𐤅𐤄
𐤀𐤋𐤅𐤄𐤉𐤊𐤄 𐤁𐤊𐤅𐤋 𐤌𐤉𐤔𐤋𐤇 𐤉𐤃𐤊𐤄 𐤏𐤋 𐤄𐤀𐤓𐤑 𐤀𐤔𐤓 𐤀𐤕𐤄
𐤁𐤀 𐤔𐤌𐤄 𐤋𐤓𐤉𐤔𐤕𐤄 22 𐤊𐤉 𐤕𐤉𐤃𐤅𐤓 𐤍𐤃𐤓 𐤋𐤉𐤄𐤅𐤄
𐤀𐤋𐤅𐤄𐤉𐤊𐤄 𐤋𐤅𐤀 𐤕𐤀𐤇𐤓 𐤋𐤔𐤋𐤌𐤅 𐤊𐤉 𐤃𐤓𐤅𐤔 𐤉𐤃𐤓𐤔𐤍𐤅
𐤉𐤄𐤅𐤄 𐤀𐤋𐤅𐤄𐤉𐤊𐤄 𐤌𐤏𐤉𐤌𐤊 𐤅𐤄𐤉𐤄 𐤁𐤊𐤄 𐤇𐤈𐤀 23 𐤅𐤊𐤉
𐤕𐤇𐤃𐤋 𐤋𐤉𐤍𐤃𐤅𐤓 𐤋𐤅𐤀 𐤉𐤄𐤉𐤄 𐤁𐤊𐤄 𐤇𐤈𐤀 24 𐤌𐤅𐤑𐤀
𐤎𐤐𐤕𐤉𐤊𐤄 𐤕𐤉𐤔𐤌𐤅𐤓 𐤅𐤏𐤎𐤉𐤕 𐤊𐤀𐤔𐤓 𐤍𐤃𐤓𐤕 𐤋𐤉𐤄𐤅𐤄
𐤀𐤋𐤅𐤄𐤉𐤊𐤄 𐤍𐤃𐤁𐤄 𐤀𐤔𐤓 𐤃𐤉𐤁𐤓𐤕 𐤁𐤐𐤉𐤊𐤄 25 𐤊𐤉 𐤕𐤁𐤅𐤀
𐤁𐤊𐤓𐤌 𐤓𐤏𐤊𐤄 𐤅𐤀𐤊𐤋𐤕 𐤏𐤍𐤁𐤉𐤌 𐤊𐤍𐤐𐤔𐤊𐤄 𐤎𐤁𐤏𐤊𐤄 𐤅𐤀𐤋
𐤊𐤋𐤉𐤊𐤄 𐤋𐤅𐤀 𐤕𐤉𐤕𐤍 26 𐤊𐤉 𐤕𐤁𐤅𐤀 𐤁𐤒𐤌𐤕 𐤓𐤏𐤊𐤄 𐤅𐤒𐤈𐤐𐤕
𐤌𐤋𐤉𐤋𐤅𐤕 𐤁𐤉𐤃𐤊𐤄 𐤅𐤇𐤓𐤌𐤔 𐤋𐤅𐤀 𐤕𐤍𐤉𐤐 𐤏𐤋 𐤒𐤌𐤕 𐤓𐤏𐤊𐤄

𐤃𐤁𐤓𐤉𐤌 𐤐𐤓𐤒 24

1 𐤊𐤉 𐤉𐤒𐤇 𐤀𐤉𐤔 𐤀𐤉𐤔𐤄 𐤅𐤁𐤏𐤋𐤄 𐤅𐤄𐤉𐤄 𐤀𐤉𐤌 𐤋𐤅𐤀
𐤕𐤉𐤌𐤑𐤀 𐤇𐤍 𐤁𐤏𐤉𐤍𐤉𐤅 𐤊𐤉 𐤌𐤑𐤀 𐤁𐤄 𐤏𐤓𐤅𐤕 𐤃𐤁𐤓 𐤅𐤊𐤕𐤁
𐤋𐤄 𐤎𐤐𐤓 𐤊𐤓𐤉𐤕𐤅𐤕 𐤅𐤍𐤕𐤍 𐤁𐤉𐤃𐤄 𐤅𐤔𐤉𐤋𐤇𐤄 𐤌𐤉𐤁𐤉𐤕𐤅
2 𐤅𐤉𐤑𐤀𐤄 𐤌𐤉𐤁𐤉𐤕𐤅 𐤅𐤄𐤋𐤊𐤄 𐤅𐤄𐤉𐤕𐤄 𐤋𐤀𐤉𐤔 𐤀𐤇𐤓
3 𐤅𐤎𐤍𐤀𐤄 𐤄𐤀𐤉𐤔 𐤄𐤀𐤇𐤓𐤅𐤍 𐤅𐤊𐤕𐤁 𐤋𐤄 𐤎𐤐𐤓 𐤊𐤓𐤉𐤕𐤅𐤕
𐤅𐤍𐤕𐤍 𐤁𐤉𐤃𐤄 𐤅𐤔𐤉𐤋𐤇𐤄 𐤌𐤉𐤁𐤉𐤕𐤅 𐤀𐤅 𐤊𐤉 𐤉𐤌𐤅𐤕
𐤄𐤀𐤉𐤔 𐤄𐤀𐤇𐤓𐤅𐤍 𐤀𐤔𐤓 𐤋𐤒𐤇𐤄 𐤋𐤅 𐤋𐤀𐤉𐤔𐤄 4 𐤋𐤅𐤀 𐤉𐤅𐤊𐤋
𐤁𐤏𐤋𐤄 𐤄𐤓𐤉𐤀𐤔𐤅𐤍 𐤀𐤔𐤓 𐤔𐤉𐤋𐤇𐤄 𐤋𐤔𐤅𐤁 𐤋𐤒𐤇𐤕𐤄
𐤋𐤉𐤄𐤉𐤅𐤕 𐤋𐤅 𐤋𐤀𐤉𐤔𐤄 𐤀𐤇𐤓𐤉 𐤀𐤔𐤓 𐤄𐤅𐤈𐤌𐤀𐤄 𐤊𐤉
𐤕𐤅𐤏𐤁𐤄 𐤄𐤉𐤅𐤀 𐤋𐤉𐤐𐤍𐤉 𐤉𐤄𐤅𐤄 𐤅𐤋𐤅𐤀 𐤕𐤇𐤈𐤉𐤀 𐤀𐤕

הארץ אשר יהוה אלוהיכה נותן לכה נחלה 5 כי
יקח איש אישה חדשה לוא יצא בצבא ולוא
יעבור עליו לכל דבר נקי יהיה לביתו שנה
אחת וסמח את אישתו אשר לקח 6 לוא יחבול
רחיים ורכב כי נפש הוא חובל 7 כי ימצא
איש גונב נפש מאחיו מבני יסראל
והתעמר בו ומכרו ומת הגנב ההוא ובערת הרע
מקרבכה 8 השמר בנגע הצרעת לשמור
מאוד ולעסות ככול אשר יורו אתכם הכוהנים
הלוים כאשר צויתם תשמרו לעסות 9 זכור
את אשר עסה יהוה אלוהיכה למרים בדרך
בצאתכם ממצרים 10 כי תשה ברעכה
משאת מאומה לוא תבוא אל ביתו לעבוט עבוטו
11 בחוץ תעמוד והאיש אשר אתה נושה בו יוציא
אליכה את העבוט החוצה 12 ואם איש עני הוא
לוא תשכב בעבוטו 13 השב תשיב לו את העבוט
כבוא השמש ושכב בסלמתו וברככה ולכה תהיה
צדקה לפני יהוה אלוהיכה 14 לוא תעשוק
סכיר עני ואביון מאחיכה או מגרכה אשר
בארצכה בשעריכה 15 ביומו תתן סכרו ולוא
תבוא עליו השמש כי עני הוא ואליו הוא נוסא
את נפשו ולוא יקרא עליכה אל יהוה והיה בכה
חטא 16 לוא יומתו אבות על בנים ובנים לוא
יומתו על אבות איש בחטאו יומתו 17 לוא תטה
משפט גר יתום ולוא תחבול בגד אלמנה
18 וזכרת כי עבד היית במצרים ויפדכה
יהוה אלוהיכה משם על כן אנוכי מצוכה
לעסות את הדבר הזה 19 כי תקצור קצירכה בסדכה
ושכחת עומר בסדה לוא תשוב לקחתו לגר ליתום
ולאלמנה יהיה למען יברככה יהוה אלוהיכה
בכול מעסה ידיכה 20 כי תחבוט זיתכה לוא
תפאר אחריכה לגר ליתום ולאלמנה יהיה
21 כי תבצור כרמכה לוא תעולל אחריכה לגר
ליתום ולאלמנה יהיה 22 וזכרת כי עבד
היית בארץ מצרים על כן אנוכי מצוכה
לעסות את הדבר הזה

דברים פרק 25

1 כי יהיה ריב בין אנשים ונגשו אל
המשפט ושפטום והצדיקו את הצדיק

והירשיעו את הרשע 2 והיה אים בין הכות
הרשע והיפילו השופט והיכהו לפניו כדי
רישעתו במיספר 3 ארבעים יכנו לוא
יוסיף פן יוסיף להכותו על אלה מכה רבה
וניקלה אחיכה לעיניכה 4 לוא תחסום שור
בדישו 5 כי ישבו אחים יחדו ומת אחד מהם
ובן אין לו לוא תיהיה אשת המת החוצה לאיש
זר יבמה יבוא עליה ולקחה לו לאישה ויבמה
6 והיה הבכור אשר תלד יקום על שם אחיו המת
ולוא ימחה שמו מיסראל 7 ואים לוא יחפוץ
האיש לקחת את יבימתו ועלתה יבימתו
השערה אל הזקנים ואמרה מאין יבמי
להקים לאחיו שם ביסראל לוא אבה יבמי
8 וקראו לו זיקני עירו ודיברו אליו ועמד
ואמר לוא חפצתי לקחתה 9 וניגשה יבימתו
אליו לעיני הזקנים וחלצה נעלו מעל רגלו
וירקה בפניו וענתה ואמרה ככה יעסה לאיש
אשר לוא יבנה את בית אחיו 10 וניקרא שמו
ביסראל בית חלוץ הנעל 11 כי ינצו אנשים
יחדו איש ואחיו וקרבה אשת האחד להציל את
אישה מיד מכהו ושלחה ידה והחזיקה
בימבושיו 12 וקצותה את כפה לוא תחוס עינכה
13 לוא יהיה לכה בכיסכה אבן ואבן גדולה
וקטנה 14 לוא יהיה לכה בביתכה איפה
ואיפה גדולה וקטנה 15 אבן שלמה וצדק יהיה
לך איפה שלמה וצדק יהיה לך למען יאריכו
ימיכה על האדמה אשר יהוה אלוהיכה נותן
לך 16 כי תועבת יהוה אלוהיכה כל עוסה אלה כול
עוסה עול 17 זכור את אשר עסה לכה עמלק בדרך
בצאתכם מימיצריים 18 אשר קרכה בדרך
ויזנב בכה כל הנחשלים אחריכה ואתה עיף
ויגע ולוא ירא אלוהים 19 והיה בהניח יהוה
אלוהיכה לכה מיכל אויביכה מיסביב בארץ
אשר יהוה אלוהיכה נותן לכה נחלה לרישתה
תימחה את זכר עמלק מיתחת השמיים לוא
תישכח

דברים פרק 26

1 והיה כי תבוא אל הארץ אשר יהוה אלוהיכה
נותן לכה נחלה וירישתה וישבת בה 2 ולקחת

𐤌𐤓𐤀𐤔𐤉𐤕 𐤊𐤋 𐤐𐤓𐤉 𐤄𐤀𐤃𐤌𐤄 𐤀𐤔𐤓 𐤕𐤁𐤉𐤀 𐤌𐤀𐤓𐤑𐤊𐤄
𐤀𐤔𐤓 𐤉𐤄𐤅𐤄 𐤀𐤋𐤅𐤄𐤉𐤊𐤄 𐤍𐤅𐤕𐤍 𐤋𐤊 𐤅𐤎𐤌𐤕 𐤁𐤈𐤍𐤀 𐤅𐤄𐤋𐤊𐤕
𐤀𐤋 𐤄𐤌𐤒𐤅𐤌 𐤀𐤔𐤓 𐤉𐤁𐤇𐤓 𐤉𐤄𐤅𐤄 𐤀𐤋𐤅𐤄𐤉𐤊𐤄 𐤋𐤔𐤊𐤍 𐤔𐤌𐤅
𐤔𐤌 3 𐤅𐤁𐤀𐤕 𐤀𐤋 𐤄𐤊𐤅𐤄𐤍 𐤀𐤔𐤓 𐤉𐤄𐤉𐤄 𐤁𐤉𐤌𐤉𐤌 𐤄𐤄𐤌
𐤅𐤀𐤌𐤓𐤕 𐤀𐤋𐤉𐤅 𐤄𐤉𐤂𐤃𐤕𐤉 𐤄𐤉𐤅𐤌 𐤋𐤉𐤄𐤅𐤄 𐤀𐤋𐤅𐤄𐤉𐤊𐤄
𐤊𐤉 𐤁𐤀𐤕𐤉 𐤀𐤋 𐤄𐤀𐤓𐤑 𐤀𐤔𐤓 𐤍𐤉𐤔𐤁𐤏 𐤉𐤄𐤅𐤄
𐤋𐤀𐤁𐤅𐤕𐤉𐤍𐤅 𐤋𐤕𐤕 𐤋𐤍𐤅 4 𐤅𐤋𐤒𐤇 𐤄𐤊𐤅𐤄𐤍 𐤄𐤈𐤍𐤀 𐤌𐤉𐤃𐤊𐤄
𐤅𐤄𐤉𐤍𐤉𐤇𐤅 𐤋𐤉𐤐𐤍𐤉 𐤌𐤉𐤆𐤁𐤇 𐤉𐤄𐤅𐤄 𐤀𐤋𐤅𐤄𐤉𐤊𐤄
5 𐤅𐤏𐤍𐤉𐤕 𐤅𐤀𐤌𐤓𐤕 𐤋𐤉𐤐𐤍𐤉 𐤉𐤄𐤅𐤄 𐤀𐤋𐤅𐤄𐤉𐤊𐤄
𐤀𐤓𐤌𐤉 𐤀𐤅𐤁𐤃 𐤀𐤁𐤉 𐤅𐤉𐤓𐤃 𐤌𐤉𐤑𐤓𐤉𐤌𐤄 𐤅𐤉𐤂𐤓 𐤔𐤌
𐤁𐤉𐤌𐤕𐤉 𐤌𐤏𐤈 𐤅𐤉𐤄𐤉 𐤔𐤌 𐤋𐤂𐤅𐤉 𐤂𐤃𐤅𐤋 𐤏𐤑𐤅𐤌 𐤅𐤓
6 𐤅𐤉𐤓𐤏𐤅 𐤀𐤅𐤕𐤍𐤅 𐤄𐤌𐤉𐤑𐤓𐤉𐤌 𐤅𐤉𐤏𐤍𐤅𐤍𐤅 𐤅𐤉𐤕𐤍𐤅
𐤏𐤋𐤉𐤍𐤅 𐤏𐤁𐤅𐤃𐤄 𐤒𐤔𐤄 7 𐤅𐤍𐤉𐤑𐤏𐤒 𐤀𐤋 𐤉𐤄𐤅𐤄 𐤀𐤋𐤅𐤄𐤉
𐤀𐤁𐤅𐤕𐤉𐤍𐤅 𐤅𐤉𐤔𐤌𐤏 𐤉𐤄𐤅𐤄 𐤀𐤕 𐤒𐤅𐤋𐤍𐤅 𐤅𐤉𐤓𐤀 𐤀𐤕
𐤏𐤍𐤉𐤍𐤅 𐤅𐤀𐤕 𐤏𐤌𐤋𐤍𐤅 𐤅𐤀𐤕 𐤋𐤇𐤑𐤍𐤅 8 𐤅𐤉𐤅𐤑𐤉𐤀𐤍𐤅
𐤉𐤄𐤅𐤄 𐤌𐤉𐤌𐤉𐤑𐤓𐤉𐤉𐤌 𐤁𐤉𐤃 𐤇𐤆𐤒𐤄 𐤅𐤁𐤉𐤆𐤓𐤅𐤏
𐤍𐤈𐤅𐤉𐤄 𐤅𐤁𐤌𐤅𐤓𐤀 𐤂𐤃𐤅𐤋 𐤅𐤁𐤀𐤅𐤕𐤅𐤕 𐤅𐤁𐤌𐤅𐤐𐤕𐤉𐤌
9 𐤅𐤉𐤁𐤉𐤀𐤍𐤅 𐤀𐤋 𐤄𐤌𐤒𐤅𐤌 𐤄𐤆𐤄 𐤅𐤉𐤕𐤍 𐤋𐤍𐤅 𐤀𐤕 𐤄𐤀𐤓𐤑
𐤄𐤆𐤅𐤀𐤕 𐤀𐤓𐤑 𐤆𐤁𐤕 𐤇𐤋𐤁 𐤅𐤃𐤁𐤔 10 𐤅𐤏𐤕𐤄 𐤄𐤉𐤍𐤄 𐤄𐤁𐤀𐤕𐤉
𐤀𐤕 𐤓𐤀𐤔𐤉𐤕 𐤐𐤓𐤉 𐤄𐤀𐤃𐤌𐤄 𐤀𐤔𐤓 𐤍𐤕𐤕𐤄 𐤋𐤉 𐤉𐤄𐤅𐤄
𐤅𐤄𐤉𐤍𐤇𐤕𐤅 𐤋𐤉𐤐𐤍𐤉 𐤉𐤄𐤅𐤄 𐤀𐤋𐤅𐤄𐤉𐤊𐤄 𐤅𐤄𐤉𐤔𐤕𐤇𐤅𐤉𐤕
𐤋𐤉𐤐𐤍𐤉 𐤉𐤄𐤅𐤄 𐤀𐤋𐤅𐤄𐤉𐤊𐤄 11 𐤅𐤎𐤌𐤇𐤕 𐤁𐤊𐤋 𐤄𐤈𐤅𐤁 𐤀𐤔𐤓
𐤍𐤕𐤍 𐤋𐤊𐤄 𐤉𐤄𐤅𐤄 𐤀𐤋𐤅𐤄𐤉𐤊𐤄 𐤅𐤋𐤁𐤉𐤕𐤊𐤄 𐤀𐤕𐤄 𐤅𐤄𐤋𐤅𐤉
𐤅𐤄𐤂𐤓 𐤀𐤔𐤓 𐤁𐤒𐤓𐤁𐤊𐤄 12 𐤊𐤉 𐤕𐤊𐤋𐤄 𐤋𐤏𐤎𐤓 𐤀𐤕 𐤊𐤋
𐤌𐤏𐤎𐤓 𐤕𐤁𐤅𐤀𐤕𐤊𐤄 𐤁𐤔𐤍𐤄 𐤄𐤔𐤋𐤉𐤔𐤉𐤕 𐤔𐤍𐤕 𐤄𐤌𐤏𐤎𐤓
𐤅𐤍𐤕𐤕𐤄 𐤋𐤋𐤅𐤉 𐤋𐤂𐤓 𐤋𐤉𐤕𐤅𐤌 𐤅𐤋𐤀𐤋𐤌𐤍𐤄 𐤅𐤀𐤊𐤋𐤅
𐤁𐤉𐤔𐤏𐤓𐤉𐤊𐤄 𐤅𐤎𐤁𐤏𐤅 13 𐤅𐤀𐤌𐤓𐤕 𐤋𐤉𐤐𐤍𐤉 𐤉𐤄𐤅𐤄
𐤀𐤋𐤅𐤄𐤉𐤊𐤄 𐤁𐤉𐤏𐤓𐤕𐤉 𐤄𐤒𐤅𐤃𐤔 𐤌𐤉𐤍 𐤄𐤁𐤉𐤉𐤕 𐤅𐤂𐤌
𐤍𐤕𐤕𐤉𐤅 𐤋𐤋𐤅𐤉 𐤅𐤋𐤂𐤓 𐤋𐤉𐤕𐤅𐤌 𐤅𐤋𐤀𐤋𐤌𐤍𐤄 𐤊𐤊𐤋
𐤌𐤑𐤅𐤕𐤊𐤄 𐤀𐤔𐤓 𐤑𐤉𐤅𐤉𐤕𐤍𐤉 𐤋𐤅𐤀 𐤏𐤁𐤓𐤕𐤉
𐤌𐤉𐤌𐤉𐤑𐤅𐤕𐤉𐤊𐤄 𐤅𐤋𐤅𐤀 𐤔𐤊𐤇𐤕𐤉 14 𐤋𐤅𐤀 𐤀𐤊𐤋𐤕𐤉
𐤁𐤀𐤅𐤍𐤉 𐤌𐤉𐤌𐤍𐤅 𐤅𐤋𐤅𐤀 𐤁𐤉𐤏𐤓𐤕𐤉 𐤌𐤉𐤌𐤍𐤅 𐤁𐤈𐤌𐤀
𐤅𐤋𐤅𐤀 𐤍𐤕𐤕𐤉 𐤌𐤉𐤌𐤍𐤅 𐤋𐤌𐤕 𐤔𐤌𐤏𐤕𐤉 𐤁𐤒𐤅𐤋 𐤉𐤄𐤅𐤄
𐤀𐤋𐤅𐤄𐤉 𐤏𐤎𐤉𐤕𐤉 𐤊𐤊𐤅𐤋 𐤀𐤔𐤓 𐤑𐤉𐤅𐤉𐤕𐤍𐤉
15 𐤄𐤔𐤒𐤉𐤐𐤄 𐤌𐤉𐤌𐤏𐤅𐤍 𐤒𐤃𐤔𐤊𐤄 𐤌𐤉𐤍 𐤄𐤔𐤌𐤉𐤉𐤌
𐤅𐤁𐤓𐤊 𐤀𐤕 𐤏𐤌𐤊𐤄 𐤀𐤕 𐤉𐤎𐤓𐤀𐤋 𐤅𐤀𐤕 𐤄𐤀𐤃𐤌𐤄 𐤀𐤔𐤓 𐤍𐤕𐤕𐤄
𐤋𐤍𐤅 𐤊𐤀𐤔𐤓 𐤍𐤉𐤔𐤁𐤏𐤕 𐤋𐤀𐤁𐤅𐤕𐤉𐤍𐤅 𐤀𐤓𐤑 𐤆𐤁𐤕 𐤇𐤋𐤁
𐤅𐤃𐤁𐤔 16 𐤄𐤉𐤅𐤌 𐤄𐤆𐤄 𐤉𐤄𐤅𐤄 𐤀𐤋𐤅𐤄𐤉𐤊𐤄 𐤌𐤑𐤅𐤊𐤄 𐤋𐤏𐤎𐤅𐤕
𐤀𐤕 𐤄𐤇𐤅𐤒𐤉𐤌 𐤄𐤀𐤋𐤄 𐤅𐤀𐤕 𐤄𐤌𐤉𐤔𐤐𐤈𐤉𐤌 𐤅𐤔𐤌𐤓𐤕
𐤅𐤏𐤎𐤉𐤕 𐤀𐤅𐤕𐤌 𐤁𐤊𐤋 𐤋𐤁𐤁𐤊𐤄 𐤅𐤁𐤊𐤋 𐤍𐤐𐤔𐤊𐤄 17 𐤀𐤕 𐤉𐤄𐤅𐤄
𐤄𐤀𐤌𐤓𐤕 𐤄𐤉𐤅𐤌 𐤋𐤉𐤄𐤉𐤅𐤕 𐤋𐤊𐤄 𐤋𐤀𐤋𐤅𐤄𐤉𐤌 𐤅𐤋𐤋𐤊𐤕
𐤁𐤉𐤃𐤓𐤊𐤉𐤅 𐤅𐤋𐤉𐤔𐤌𐤅𐤓 𐤇𐤅𐤒𐤉𐤅 𐤅𐤌𐤉𐤑𐤅𐤕𐤉𐤅

ומישפטיו ולישמוע בקולו 18 ויהוה
האמירכה היום ליהיות לו לעם סגולה כאשר
דיבר לכ ולישמור כל מיצותיו 19 ולתיתכה
עליונ על כל הגוים אשר עסה ליתהילה
ולשם ולתיפארת וליהיותכה עם קדוש ליהוה
אלוהיכה כאשר דיבר

דברים פרק 27

1 ויצו מושה וזיקני יסראל את העם לאמור
שמור את כל המיצוה אשר אנוכי מצוה אתכם
היום 2 והיה ביום אשר תעברו את הירדנ אל
הארצ אשר יהוה אלוהיכה נותנ לכ והקמות לכה
אבנים גדולות וסדת אותם בסיד 3 וכתבת עליהנ
את כל דיברי התורה הזואת בעברכה למענ אשר
תבוא אל הארצ אשר יהוה אלוהיכה נותנ לכה
ארצ זבת חלב ודבש כאשר דיבר יהוה אלוהי
אבותיכה לכ 4 והיה בעברכם את הירדנ תקימו
את האבנים האלה אשר אנוכי מצוה אתכם
היום בהר עיבל וסדת אותם בסיד 5 ובנית שם
מיזבח ליהוה אלוהיכה מיזבח אבנים לוא
תניפ עליהם ברזל 6 אבנים שלמות תיבנה
את מיזבח יהוה אלוהיכה והעלית עליו עולות
ליהוה אלוהיכה 7 וזבחת שלמים ואכלת שם
וסמחת לפני יהוה אלוהיכה 8 וכתבת על
האבנים את כל דיברי התורה הזואת באר היט
9 וידבר מושה והכוהנים הלוים אל כל יסראל
לאמור הסכת ושמע יסראל היום הזה ניהיית
לעם ליהוה אלוהיכה 10 ושמעת בקול יהוה
אלוהיכה ועסית את מיצותו ואת חוקיו אשר
אנוכי מצוכה היום 11 ויצו מושה את העם
ביום ההוא לאמור 12 אלה יעמדו לברכ את העם
על הר גריזים בעברכם את הירדנ שימעונ
ולוי ויהודה ויסשכר ויוספ ובינימינ
13 ואלה יעמדו על הקללה בהר עיבל ראובנ גד
ואשר וזבולונ דנ ונפתלי 14 וענו הלוים
ואמרו אל כל איש יסראל קול רמ 15 ארור האיש
אשר יעסה פסל ומסכה תועבת יהוה מעסה ידי
חרש וסמ בסתר וענו כל העם ואמרו אמנ 16 ארור
מקלה אביו ואימו ואמר כל העם אמנ 17 ארור
מסיג גבול רעהו ואמר כל העם אמנ 18 ארור

משגה עור בדרך ואמר כל העם אמן 19 ארור
מטה משפט גר יתום ואלמנה ואמר כל העם
אמן 20 ארור שכב עם אשת אביו כי גלה
כנף אביו ואמר כל העם אמן 21 ארור שכב
עם כל בהמה ואמר כל העם אמן 22 ארור שכב
עם אחתו בת אביו או בת אמו ואמר כל העם
אמן 23 ארור שכב עם חתנתו ואמר כל העם
אמן 24 ארור מכה רעהו בסתר ואמר כל העם אמן
25 ארור לקח שחד להכות נפש דם נקי ואמר כל
העם אמן 26 ארור אשר לא יקים את דברי
התורה הזאת לעשות אותם ואמר כל העם אמן

דברים פרק 28

1 והיה אם שמוע תשמע בקול יהוה
אלהיך לשמר לעשות את כל מצותיו אשר
אנכי מצוך היום ונתנך יהוה אלהיך
עליון על כל גויי הארץ 2 ובאו עליך כל
הברכות האלה והשיגך כי תשמע בקול יהוה
אלהיך 3 ברוך אתה בעיר וברוך אתה בשדה 4 ברוך
פרי בטנך ופרי אדמתך ופרי בהמתך
שגר אלפיך ועשתרות צאנך 5 ברוך טנאך
ומשארתך 6 ברוך אתה בבאך וברוך אתה
בצאתך 7 יתן יהוה את איביך הקמים
עליך נגפים לפניך בדרך אחד יצאו
אליך ובשבעה דרכים ינוסו לפניך
8 יצו יהוה אתך את הברכה באסמיך ובכל
משלח ידך וברכך בארץ אשר יהוה אלהיך
נתן לך 9 יקימך יהוה לו לעם קדוש כאשר
נשבע לך כי תשמר את מצות יהוה
אלהיך והלכת בדרכיו 10 וראו כל עמי הארץ
כי שם יהוה נקרא עליך ויראו ממך
11 והותרך יהוה לטובה בפרי בטנך
ובפרי בהמתך ובפרי אדמתך על האדמה
אשר נשבע יהוה לאבתיך לתת לך 12 יפתח
יהוה לך את אוצרו הטוב את השמים לתת מטר
ארצך בעתו ולברך את כל מעשה ידך והלוית
גוים רבים ואתה לא תלוה 13 ונתנך יהוה
לראש ולא לזנב והיית רק למעלה ולא
תהיה למטה כי תשמע אל מצות יהוה
אלהיך אשר אנכי מצוך היום לשמר

ולעסות 14 ולוא תסור מיכל הדברים אשר אנוכי
מצוה אתכם היום ימין וסמואול ללכת אחרי
אלוהים אחרים לעבדם 15 והיה אים לוא
תישמע בקול יהוה אלוהיכה לישמור לעסות את
כל מיצותיו וחוקותיו אשר אנוכי מצוכה היום
ובאו עליכה כל הקללות האלה והיסיגוכה 16 ארור
אתה בעיר וארור אתה בסדה 17 ארור טנאכה
ומישארתכה 18 ארור פרי ביטנכה ופרי
אדמתכה שגר אלפיכה ועשתרות צואנכה
19 ארור אתה בבואכה וארור אתה בצאתכה 20 ישלח
יהוה בכה את המארה את המהומה ואת המיגערת
בכל מישלח ידכה אשר תעסה עד הישמדכה ועד
אבדכה מהר מיפני רוע מעלליכה אשר
עזבתני 21 ידבק יהוה בכה את הדבר עד כלותו
אותכה מעל האדמה אשר אתה בא שמה לרישתה
22 יככה יהוה בשחפת ובקדחת ובדלקת ובחרחור
ובחרב ובשידפון ובירקון ורדפוכה עד אבדכה
23 והיו שמיכה אשר על ראשכה נחושת והארץ
אשר תחתיכה ברזל 24 יתן יהוה את מטר ארצכה
אבק ועפר מין השמיים ירד עליכה עד
הישמדך 25 יתנכה יהוה ניגף ליפני
אויביכה בדרך אחד תצא אליו ובשיבעה דרכים
תנוס לפניו והיית לזעוה לכול ממלכות הארץ
26 והיתה נבלתכה למאכל לכל עוף השמיים
ולבהמת הארץ ואין מחריד 27 יככה יהוה
בשחין מצרים ובעפלים ובגרב ובחרס
אשר לוא תוכל להרפא 28 יככה יהוה בשיגעון
ובעיורון ובתימהון ל 29 והיית ממשש
בצהריים כאשר ימשש העיור באפלה ולוא
תצליח את דרכיכה והיית אך עשוק וגזול כל
הימים ואין מושיע 30 אישה תארס ואיש
אחר ישגלנה ביית תיבנה ולוא תשב בו כרם
תיטע ולוא תחללנו 31 שורכה טבוח לעיניכה
ולוא תואכל מימנו חמורכה גזול מילפניכה
ולוא ישוב לך צואנכה נתונות לאויביכה ואין
לכה מושיע 32 בניכה ובנותיכה נתונים
לעם אחר ועיניכה רואות וכלות אליהם כל
היום ואין לאל ידכה 33 פרי אדמתכה וכל
יגיעכה יואכל עם אשר לוא ידעת והיית רק
עשוק ורצוץ כל הימים 34 והיית משוגע
מימראה עיניכה אשר תיראה 35 יככה יהוה

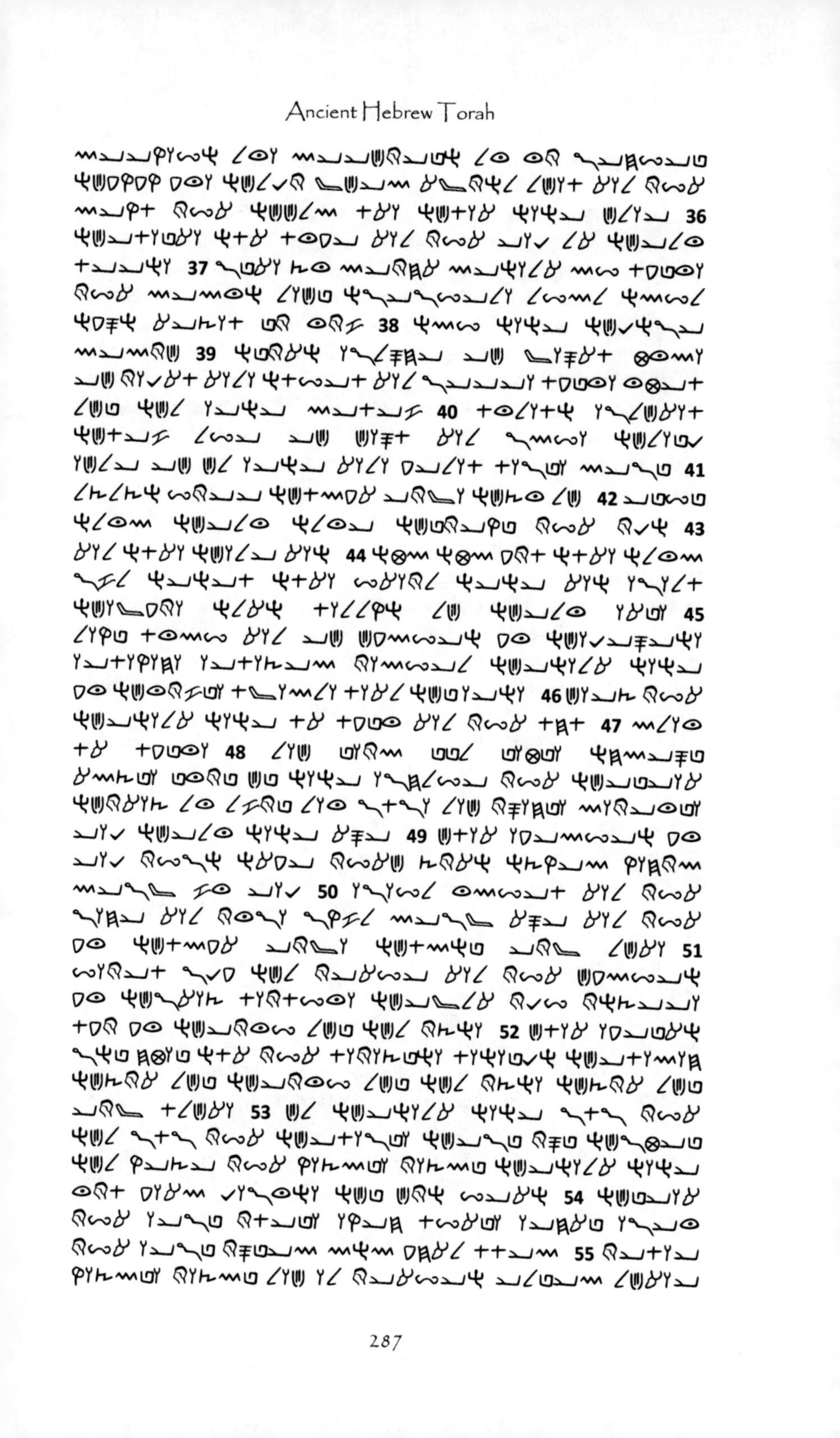

36

37

38

39

40

41

42

43

44

45

46

47

48

49

50

51

52

53

54

55

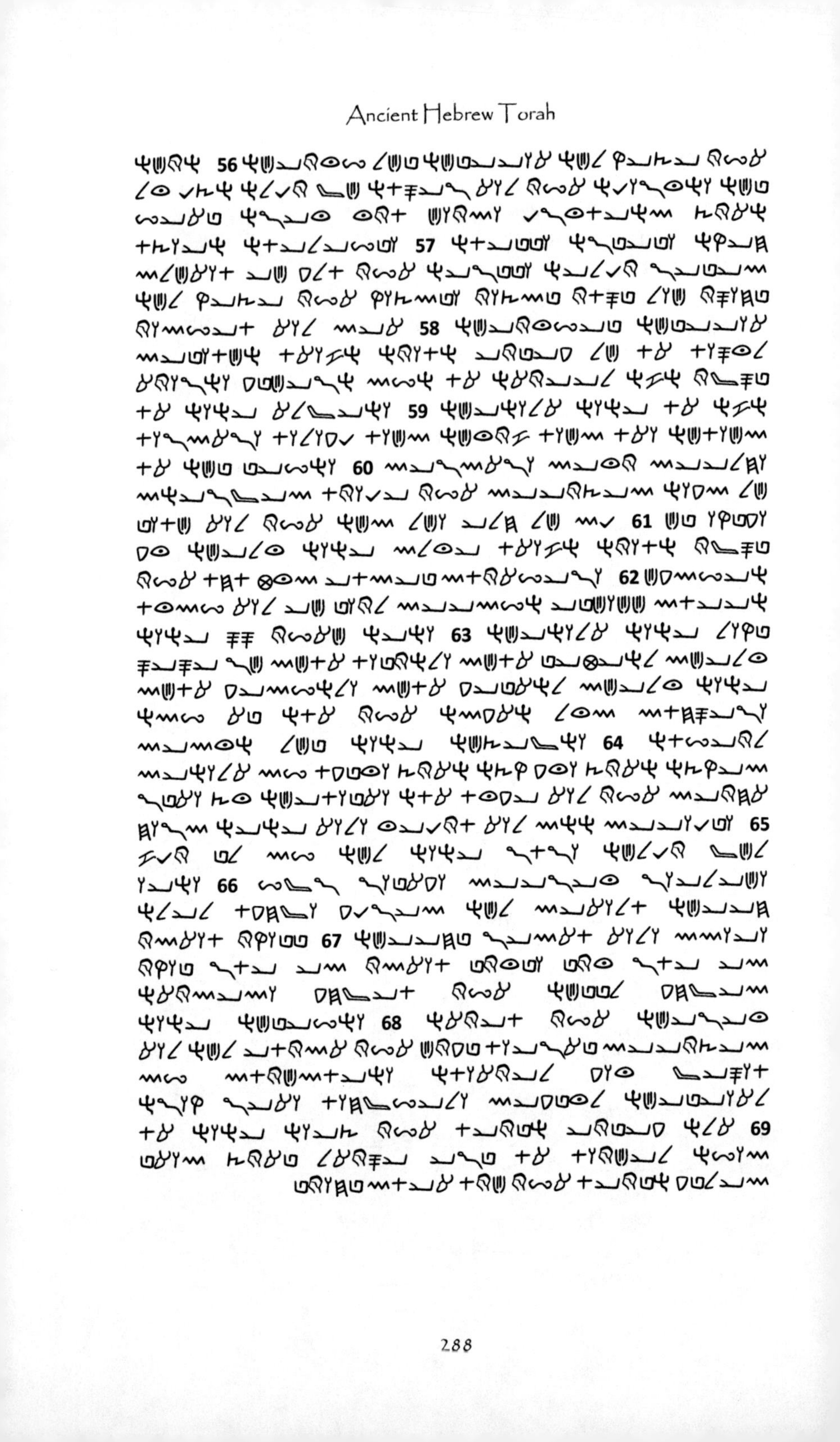

56

57

58

59

60

61

62

63

64

65

66

67

68

69

דברים פרק 29

1 ויקרא מושה אל כל ישראל ויואמר אלהם אתם
ראיתם את כל אשר עשה יהוה לעיניכם בארץ
מצרים לפרעוה ולכל עבדיו ולכל ארצו
2 המסות הגדולות אשר ראו עיניכה האותות
והמופתים הגדולים ההם 3 ולוא נתן יהוה
לכם לב לדעת ועינים לראות ואוזנים
לשמוע עד היום הזה 4 ואולך אתכם ארבעים
שנה במדבר לוא בלו שלמתיכם מעליכם
ונעלכה לוא בלתה מעל רגלכה 5 לחם לוא אכלתם
ויין ושכר לוא שתיתם למען תדעו כי אני
יהוה אלהיכם 6 ותבאו אל המקום הזה ויצא
סיחון מלך חשבון ועוג מלך הבשן לקראתנו
למלחמה ונכם 7 ונקח את ארצם ונתנה
לנחלה לראובני ולגדי ולחצי שבט המנשי
8 ושמרתם את דברי הברית הזאת ועשיתם
אותם למען תשכילו את כל אשר תעשון 9 אתם
נצבים היום כולכם לפני יהוה
אלהיכם ראשיכם שבטיכם זקניכם
ושטריכם כול איש ישראל 10 טפכם נשיכם
וגרכה אשר בקרב מחניכה מחטב עציכה עד
שואב מימיכה 11 לעברכה בברית יהוה
אלהיכה ובאלתו אשר יהוה אלהיכה כורת
עמכה היום 12 למען הקים אותכה היום לו
לעם והוא יהיה לכה לאלהים כאשר דבר לך
וכאשר נשבע לאבותיכה לאברהם ליצחק
וליעקוב 13 ולוא אתכם לבדכם אנוכי כורת את
הברית הזאת ואת האלה הזאת 14 כי את אשר
ישנו פה עמנו עומד היום לפני יהוה
אלהינו ואת אשר איננו פה עמנו היום
15 כי אתם ידעתם את אשר ישבנו בארץ
מצרים ואת אשר עברנו בקרב הגוים
אשר עברתם 16 ותראו את שקוציהם ואת
גלוליהם עץ ואבן כסף וזהב אשר עמהם
17 פן יש בכם איש או אשה או משפחה או
שבט אשר לבבו פונה היום מעם יהוה
אלהינו ללכת לעבוד את אלהי הגוים ההם
פן יש בכם שורש פורה ראש ולענה 18 והיה
בשמעו את דברי האלה הזאת והתברך בלבבו
לאמור שלום יהיה לי כי בשרירות לבי

אלך למען ספות הרוה את הצמאה 19 לוא יואבה
יהוה סלוח לו כי אז יעשן אף יהוה וקינאתו
באיש ההוא ורבצה בו כל האלה הכתובה בספר הזה
ומחה יהוה את שמו מיתחת השמיים
20 והיבדילו יהוה לרעה מיכול שיבטי
יסראל ככול אלות הברית הכתובה בספר התורה
הזה 21 ואמר הדור האחרון בניכם אשר יקומו
מאחריכם והנכרי אשר יבוא מארץ רחוקה וראו
את מכות הארץ ההוא ואת תחלואיה אשר חילה
יהוה בה 22 גפרית ומלח סרפה כל ארצה לוא
תיזרע ולוא תצמיח ולוא יעלה בה כל עסב
כמהפכת סדום ועמורה אדמה וצבויים אשר
הפך יהוה באפו ובחמתו 23 ואמרו כל הגויים
על מה עסה יהוה ככה לארץ הזואת מה חרי האף
הגדול הזה 24 ואמרו על אשר עזבו את ברית יהוה
אלוהי אבותם אשר כרת עימם בהוציאו אותם
מארץ מיצריים 25 וילכו ויעבדו אלוהים
אחרים וישתחוו להם אלוהים אשר לוא ידעום
ולוא חלק להם 26 ויחר אף יהוה בארץ ההיוא
להביא עליה את כל הקללה הכתובה בספר הזה
27 ויתשם יהוה מעל אדמתם באף ובחמה
ובקצף גדול וישליכם אל ארץ אחרת כיום הזה
28 הניסתרות ליהוה אלוהינו והנגלות לנו
ולבנינו עד עולם לעסות את כל דיברי התורה
הזואת

דברים פרק 30

1 והיה כי יבואו עליכה כל הדברים האלה
הברכה והקללה אשר נתתי לפניכה והשבות אל
לבבכה בכל הגויים אשר הידיחכה יהוה
אלוהיכה שמה 2 ושבת עד יהוה אלוהיכה
ושמעת בקולו ככול אשר אנוכי מצוכה היום אתה
ובניכה בכל לבבכה ובכל נפשכה 3 ושב יהוה
אלוהיכה את שבותכה וריחמכה ושב וקיבצכה
מכל העמים אשר הפיצכה יהוה אלוהיכה
שמה 4 אים יהיה נידחכה ביקצה השמיים
מישם יקבצכה יהוה אלוהיכה ומישם יקחכה
5 והביאכה יהוה אלוהיכה אל הארץ אשר ירשו
אבותיכה וירשתה והיטיבכה והירבכה
מאבותיכה 6 ומל יהוה אלוהיכה את לבבכה ואת
לבב זרעכה לאהבה את יהוה אלוהיכה בכל לבבכה

ובכל נפשכה למען חייכה 7 ונתן יהוה
אלוהיכה את כל האלות האלה על אויביכה ועל
סונאיכה אשר רדפוכה 8 ואתה תשוב ושמעת בקול
יהוה ועסית את כל מיצותיו אשר אנוכי
מצוכה היום 9 והותירכה יהוה אלוהיכה בכול
מעסה ידכה ביפרי ביטנכה וביפרי
בהמתכה וביפרי אדמתכה לטובה כי ישוב
יהוה לסוס עליכה לטוב כאשר סס על אבותיכה
10 כי תישמע בקול יהוה אלוהיכה לישמור
מיצותיו וחוקותיו הכתובה בספר התורה הזה כי
תשוב אל יהוה אלוהיכה בכל לבבכה ובכל נפשכה
11 כי המיצוה הזואת אשר אנוכי מצוכה היום
לוא ניפלאת היוא מימכה ולוא רחוקה היוא
12 לוא בשמיים היוא לאמור מי יעלה לנו
השמימה ויקחה לנו וישמיענו אותה
ונעסנה 13 ולוא מעבר לים היוא לאמור מי
יעבר לנו אל עבר הים ויקחה לנו
וישמיענו אותה ונעסנה 14 כי קרוב אליכה
הדבר מאוד בפיכה ובילבבכה לעסותו 15 ראה
נתתי לפניכה היום את החיים ואת הטוב ואת
המות ואת הרע 16 אשר אנוכי מצוכה היום
לאהבה את יהוה אלוהיכה ללכת בידרכיו
ולישמור מיצותיו וחוקותיו ומישפטיו
וחיית ורבית וברככה יהוה אלוהיכה בארץ אשר
אתה בא שמה לרישתה 17 ואם יפנה לבבכה
ולוא תישמע ונידחת והישתחוית לאלוהים
אחרים ועבדתם 18 היגדתי לכם היום כי אבוד
תואבדון לוא תאריכון ימים על האדמה אשר
אתה עובר את הירדן לבוא שמה לרישתה
19 העידותי בכם היום את השמיים ואת
הארץ החיים והמות נתתי לפניכה הברכה
והקללה ובחרת בחיים למען תיחיה אתה
וזרעכה 20 לאהבה את יהוה אלוהיכה לישמוע
בקולו ולדבקה בו כי הוא חייכה ואורך ימיכה
לשבת על האדמה אשר נישבע יהוה לאבותיכה
לאברהם לייצחק וליעקוב לתת להם

דברים פרק 31

1 וילך מושה וידבר את הדברים האלה אל כל
יסראל 2 ויאמר אליהם בן מאה ועסרים שנה
אנוכי היום לוא אוכל עוד לצאת ולבוא ויהוה

אמר אלי לוא תעבור את הירדן הזה 3 יהוה
אלוהיכה הוא עובר לפניכה הוא ישמיד את
הגויים האלה מילפניכה וירישתם
יהושוע הוא עובר לפניכה כאשר דיבר יהוה
4 ועסה יהוה להם כאשר עסה לסיחון ולעוג
מלכי האמורי ולארצם אשר הישמיד אותם
5 ונתנם יהוה ליפניכם ועסיתם להם ככל
המיצוה אשר ציויתי אתכם 6 חיזקו ואימצו
אל תיראו ואל תערצו מיפניהם כי יהוה
אלוהיכה הוא ההולך עימך לוא ירפכה ולוא
יעזבכה 7 ויקרא מושה ליהושוע ויואמר
אליו לעיני כל יסראל חזק ואמץ כי אתה תבוא
את העם הזה אל הארץ אשר נישבע יהוה
לאבותם לתת להם ואתה תנחילנה אותם 8 ויהוה
הוא ההולך לפניכה הוא יהיה עימך לוא
ירפכה ולוא יעזבכה לוא תירא ולוא תחת
9 ויכתוב מושה את התורה הזואת ויתנה אל
הכהנים בני לוי הנוסאים את ארון ברית
יהוה ואל כל זיקני יסראל 10 ויצו מושה
אותם לאמור מיקץ שבע שנים במועד שנת
השמיטה בחג הסוכות 11 בבוא כל יסראל לראות את
פני יהוה אלוהיכה במקום אשר יבחר תיקרא
את התורה הזואת נגד כל יסראל באזניהם
12 הקהל את העם האנשים והנשים והטף
וגרכה אשר בישעריכה למען ישמעו ולמען
ילמדו ויראו את יהוה אלוהיכם ושמרו לעסות
את כל דיברי התורה הזואת 13 ובניהם אשר לוא
ידעו ישמעו ולמדו לייראה את יהוה
אלוהיכם כל הימים אשר אתם חיים על
האדמה אשר אתם עוברים את הירדן שמה
לרישתה 14 ויואמר יהוה אל מושה הן קרבו
ימיכה למות קרא את יהושוע והיתיצבו באוהל
מועד ואצונו וילך מושה ויהושוע ויתיצבו
באוהל מועד 15 וירא יהוה באוהל בעמוד ענן
ויעמוד עמוד הענן על פתח האוהל 16 ויואמר
יהוה אל מושה הינכה שוכב עים אבותיכה וקם
העם הזה וזנה אחרי אלוהי נכר הארץ אשר הוא
בא שמה בקירבו ועזבני והפר את בריתי אשר
כרתי אתו 17 וחרה אפי בו ביום ההוא
ועזבתים והיסתרתי פני מהם והיה לאכול
ומצאוהו רעות רבות וצרות ואמר ביום ההוא הלוא
על כי אין אלוהי בקירבי מצאוני הרעות

[illegible] 18 [illegible]
[illegible]
[illegible] 19 [illegible]
[illegible]
[illegible]
[illegible] 20
[illegible]
[illegible]
[illegible] 21 [illegible]
[illegible]
[illegible]
[illegible]
[illegible] 22 [illegible]
[illegible] 23 [illegible]
[illegible]
[illegible]
[illegible] 24 [illegible]
[illegible]
[illegible] 25 [illegible]
[illegible] 26 [illegible]
[illegible]
[illegible] 27 [illegible]
[illegible]
[illegible]
[illegible] 28 [illegible]
[illegible]
[illegible]
[illegible] 29 [illegible]
[illegible]
[illegible]
[illegible]
[illegible] 30 [illegible]
[illegible]
[illegible]

32 [illegible]

[illegible] 1
[illegible] 2 [illegible]
[illegible]
[illegible] 3 [illegible]
[illegible] 4 [illegible]

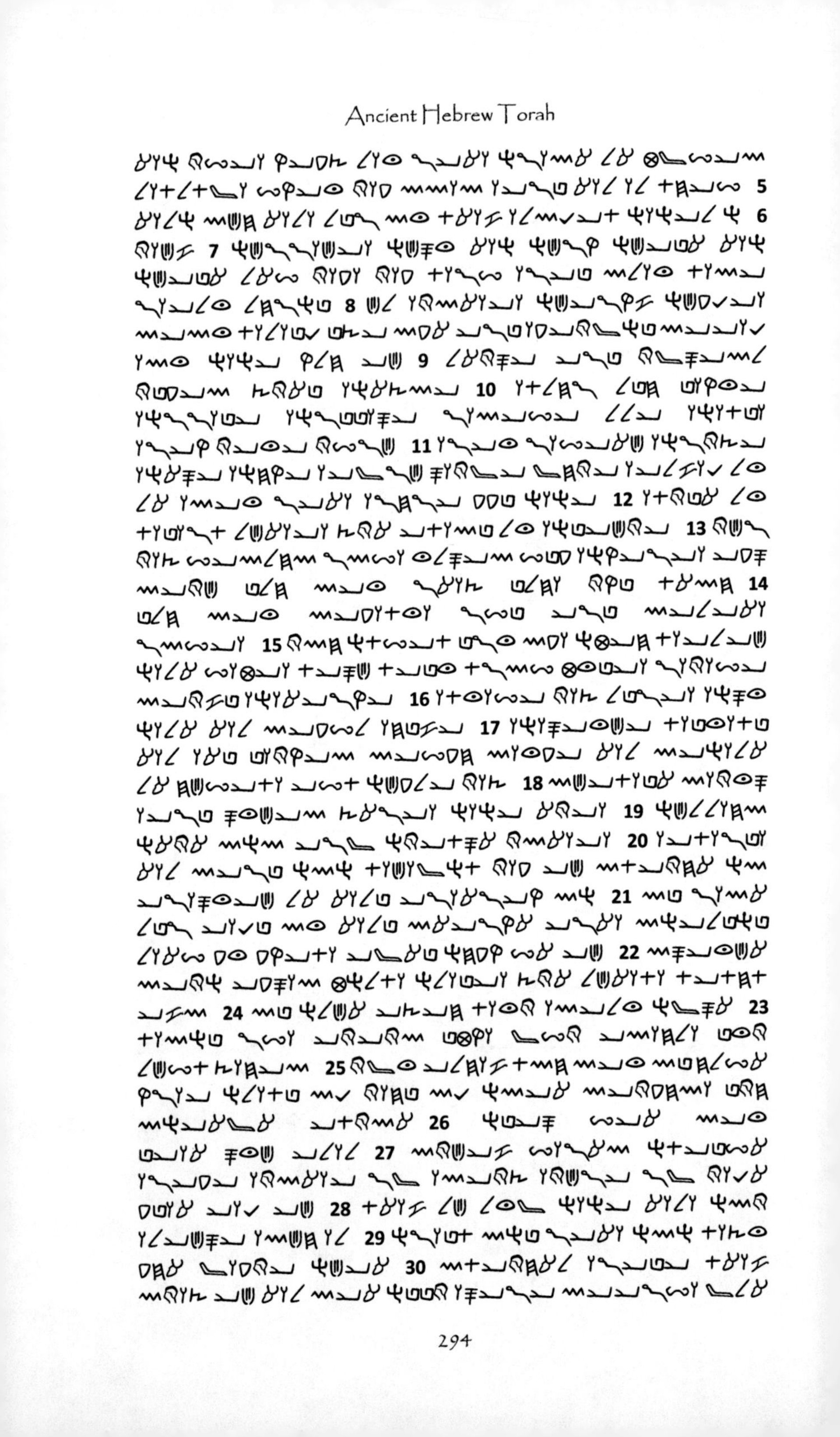

[illegible]
5 [illegible]
6 [illegible]
[illegible] 7 [illegible]
[illegible]
[illegible] 8 [illegible]
[illegible]
[illegible] 9 [illegible]
[illegible] 10 [illegible]
[illegible]
[illegible] 11 [illegible]
[illegible]
[illegible] 12 [illegible]
[illegible] 13 [illegible]
[illegible]
14 [illegible]
[illegible]
[illegible] 15 [illegible]
[illegible]
[illegible] 16 [illegible]
[illegible] 17 [illegible]
[illegible]
[illegible] 18 [illegible]
[illegible] 19 [illegible]
[illegible] 20 [illegible]
[illegible]
[illegible] 21 [illegible]
[illegible]
[illegible] 22 [illegible]
[illegible]
23 [illegible] 24 [illegible]
[illegible]
[illegible] 25 [illegible]
[illegible]
[illegible] 26 [illegible]
[illegible] 27 [illegible]
[illegible]
[illegible] 28 [illegible]
[illegible] 29 [illegible]
[illegible] 30 [illegible]
[illegible]

31
32
33
34
35
36
37
38
39
40
41
42
43
44
45
46
47
48
49
50
51
52

דברים פרק 33

1 וזואת הברכה אשר ברך מושה איש האלוהים
את בני יסראל ליפני מותו 2 ויואמר יהוה
מסיני בא וזרח מסעיר למו הופיע מהר
פארן ואתה מרבבות קודש מימינו אשדת למו
3 אף חובב עמים כל קדושיו בידכה והם תוכו
לרגלכה יסא מידברותיכה 4 תורה ציוה לנו
מושה מורשה קהילת יעקוב 5 ויהי בישורון
מלך בהיתאסף ראשי עם יחד שיבטי יסראל
6 יחי ראובן ואל ימות ויהי מתיו מיספר
7 וזואת ליהודה ויואמר שמע יהוה קול יהודה
ואל עמו תביאנו ידיו רב לו ועזר מצריו
תיהיה 8 וללוי אמר תומיכה ואוריכה לאיש
חסידכה אשר ניסיתו במסה תריבהו על מי
מריבה 9 האומר לאביו ולאמו לוא ראיתיו
ואת אחיו לוא היכיר ואת בניו לוא ידע כי שמרו
אמרתכה ובריתכה ינצורו 10 יורו
מישפטיכה ליעקוב ותורתכה ליסראל יסימו
קטורה באפכה וכליל על מיזבחכה 11 ברך יהוה
חילו ופועל ידיו תירצה מחץ מתנים
קמיו ומסנאיו מן יקומון 12 לבנימין
אמר ידיד יהוה ישכון לבטח עליו חופף
עליו כל היום ובין כתיפיו שכן 13 וליוסף
אמר מבורכת יהוה ארצו ממגד שמים
מטל ומתהום רובצת תחת 14 וממגד תבואות
שמש וממגד גרש ירחים 15 ומרואש הררי
קדם וממגד גבעות עולם 16 וממגד ארץ
ומלאה ורצון שכני סנה תבואתה לרואש יוסף
ולקדקוד נזיר אחיו 17 בכור שורו הדר לו וקרני
ראם קרניו בהם עמים ינגח יחדו אפסי ארץ
והם רבבות אפרים והם אלפי מנשה
18 ולזבולון אמר סמח זבולון בצאתכה
ויסשכר באוהליכה 19 עמים הר יקראו שם
יזבחו זבחי צדק כי שפע ימים יינקו
וספוני טמוני חול 20 ולגד אמר ברוך מרחיב גד
כלביא שכן וטרף זרוע אף קדקוד 21 וירא
ראשית לו כי שם חלקת מחוקק ספון ויתא
ראשי עם צדקת יהוה עסה ומשפטיו עם
יסראל 22 ולדן אמר דן גור אריה יזנק מן
הבשן 23 ולנפתלי אמר נפתלי סבע רצון

ומלא בירכת יהוה ים ודרום ירשה 24 ולאשר
אמר ברוך מיבנים אשר יהי רצוי אחיו וטובל
בשמן רגלו 25 ברזל ונחושת מינעליכה
וכימיכה דבאכה 26 אין כאל ישורון רוכב
שמיים בעזרכה ובגאותו שחקים 27 מעונה
אלוהי קדם ומיתחת זרועות עולם ויגרש
מיפניכה אויב ויואמר השמד 28 וישכון
יסראל בטח בדד עין יעקוב אל ארץ דגן ותירוש
אף שמיו יערפו טל 29 אשריכה יסראל מי
כמוכה עם נושע ביהוה מגן עזרכה ואשר חרב
גאותכה וייכחשו אויביכה לך ואתה על
במותימו תידרוך

דברים פרק 34

1 ויעל מושה מערבות מואב אל הר נבו רואש
הפיסגה אשר על פני ירחו ויראהו יהוה את
כל הארץ את הגילעד עד דן 2 ואת כל נפתלי ואת
ארץ אפריים ומנשה ואת כל ארץ יהודה עד
הים האחרון 3 ואת הנגב ואת הכיכר ביקעת
ירחו עיר התמרים עד צוער 4 ויואמר יהוה
אליו זואת הארץ אשר נישבעתי לאברהם
לייצחק וליעקוב לאמור לזרעכה אתננה
הראיתיכה בעיניכה ושמה לוא תעבור
5 וימת שם מושה עבד יהוה בארץ מואב על פי
יהוה 6 ויקבור אותו בגי בארץ מואב מול בית
פעור ולוא ידע איש את קבורתו עד היום הזה
7 ומושה בן מאה ועסרים שנה במותו לוא כהתה
עינו ולוא נס לוחה 8 ויבכו בני יסראל את
מושה בערבות מואב שלושים יום ויתמו ימי
בכי אבל מושה 9 ויהושוע בין נון מלא רוח
חכמה כי סמך מושה את ידיו עליו וישמעו
אליו בני יסראל ויעסו כאשר ציוה יהוה את
מושה 10 ולוא קם נביא עוד ביסראל כמושה אשר
ידעו יהוה פנים אל פנים 11 לכל האותות
והמופתים אשר שלחו יהוה לעסות בארץ
מיצריים לפרעוה ולכל עבדיו ולכל ארצו
12 ולכול היד החזקה ולכול המורא הגדול אשר עסה
מושה לעיני כל יסראל

LaVergne, TN USA
24 November 2010
206187LV00002B/7/P